Praise for *Longing for Darkness*

"Exhilarating . . . *Longing for Darkness* joins a venerable tradition of adventure stories that take place in the outer and inner landscapes simultaneously."
—*San Francisco Chronicle*

"Galland can write beautifully. . . . Iluminating and moving, travel writing at its best."
—*New Statesman & Society*
(London)

"Ambitious . . . *Longing for Darkness* is an impressive, moving document of the spirit."
—*Booklist*

"This is no ordinary pilgrimage book. . . . There is no prettying up of the dark side, no romanticizing, just a straightforward and gracefully composed account of an urgent search. This is a work I certainly commend."
—Harvey Cox, professor,
Harvard Divinity School, and
author of *Many Mansions* and *The Secular City*

"A major contribution to the re-emergence of the feminine in traditional religious experience."
—Elinor W. Gadon, author of
The Once and Future Goddess

"*Longing for Darkness* is a moving tale of a woman's spiritual quest. It draws on the best of feminine insights in recognizing real power at the junction of spirituality and politics."
—Karen McCarthy Brown,
professor, Drew University, and
author of *Mama Lola: A Voudou Priestess in Brooklyn*

"Written clearly and vividly, *Longing for Darkness* is a fascinating study of comparative religion, one that brings closer together the yearnings for God experienced by all mankind."
—*The Anniston Star*

PENGUIN
COMPASS

LONGING FOR DARKNESS

China Galland was born in Texas and has been a university lecturer, wilderness guide, journalist, and long-time student of Buddhism and comparative religion. Her works of nonfiction include *Women in the Wilderness*. She is currently a research associate at the Center for Women and Religion and was a visiting scholar at the Office for programs in Comparative Religion at the Graduate Theological Union in Berkeley, California. She is married, has three grown children, and lives in California. Her fiction has won awards from the California Arts Council. She is currently at work on a novel.

LONGING FOR DARKNESS

Tara and the Black Madonna
A Ten-Year Journey

CHINA GALLAND

PENGUIN / COMPASS

COMPASS

Published by the Penguin Group
Penguin Putnam Inc.,
375 Hudson Street, New York, New York 10014, U.S.A.
Penguin Books Ltd, 27 Wrights Lane,
London W8 5TZ, England
Penguin Books Australia Ltd, Ringwood,
Victoria, Australia
Penguin Books Canada Ltd, 10 Alcorn Avenue,
Toronto, Ontario, Canada M4V 3B2
Penguin Books (N.Z.) Ltd, 182–190 Wairau Road,
Auckland 10, New Zealand

Penguin Books Ltd, Registered Offices:
Harmondsworth, Middlesex, England

First published in the United States of America by
Viking Penguin, a division of Penguin Books USA Inc., 1990
Published in Penguin Books 1991

11 13 15 16 14 12 10

THE LIBRARY OF CONGRESS HAS CATALOGUED THE HARDCOVER AS FOLLOWS:
Galland, China.
Longing for darkness: Tara and the Black Madonna / China Galland.
p. cm.
Includes bibliographical references.
ISBN 0-670-82818-1 (hc.)
ISBN 0 14 01.2184 6 (pbk.)
1. Galland, China. 2. Religious biography—United States.
3. Tara (Goddess). 4. Black Virgins. 5. Goddesses. 6. Women and Religion.
7. Pilgrims and pilgrimages. 8. Voyages and travels.
I. Title. II. Title: Darkness.
BL73-G35A3 1990
291.2'114—dc20 89–40694

Printed in the United States of America
Set in Perpetua and Gill Sans Bold
Designed by Amy Hill

*For my teachers, East and West, but especially
for my daughter, Madelon, and
my mother, Ruth
And in memory of my beloved grandfather,
Walter Verhalen*

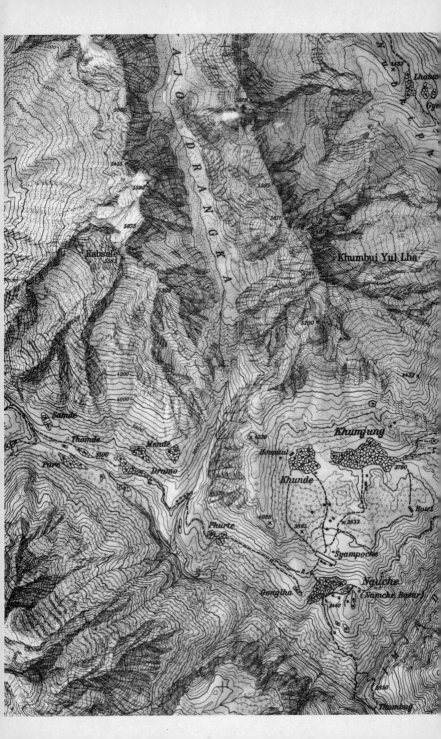

Within the light there is darkness, but do not be attached to this darkness. Within the darkness there is light, but do not look for that light.

——The *Sandokai*
(Buddhist poem by Sekito Kisen,
the eighth Chinese ancestor of Soto Zen,
translated by R. H. Blyth)

Acknowledgments

I am grateful to many. The help of some is openly acknowledged within this story, more are mentioned in the notes. There remain many to whom my acknowledgment here can only suggest a gratitude that stretches beyond these pages. I could not have accomplished this work without the help of many individuals, organizations, and institutions.

My work overseas was made possible in part by consecutive awards from the California State Arts Council Fellowship in Literature and the Marin Arts Council Individual Grants Program. Travel and research grants through the Melia Foundation provided substantial help as well. I am especially grateful to Gale Lipsyte of the Melia Foundation for her help in overseeing this project. Josh Mailman and the Skaggs Foundation also helped to support my travel and research.

Ella Langdon's generous friendship was essential to this work, her support unfailing. Neltje's understanding of the commitment required by this book, her encouragement and backing, was crucial in bringing this story into being. Jola Jurzykowski deserves my thanks as well.

I am grateful to Dr. Robert Thurman, who holds the Jey Tsong

Khapa Chair of Indo-Tibetan Buddhist Studies at Columbia University in New York City, for having taken the time to read the manuscript in its entirety as it drew nearer to completion. His encouragement, comments, and criticism over the last two years of writing were helpful, the time he took to explain key Buddhist concepts invaluable. His unique ability to accurately translate the complexity of Buddhist thought into lively, accessible English provided a bridge for me into material and texts that I might otherwise have missed. Yvonne Rand of San Francisco Zen Center's Green Gulch Farm and Tsering Everest, under the aegis of the Venerable Chagdud Tulku Rinpoche at Rigdzin Ling Tibetan Buddhist Center in Junction City, California, read the manuscript in its entirety as well, in the hopes of ensuring that my limited understanding of the Soto Zen and Tibetan traditions touched upon in these pages will prove reliable.

Special thanks goes to Bhiksuni Karma Lekshe Tsomo of Dharamsala, India, and Carol Savvas and the Venerable Geshe Champa Lodro Rinpoche of Switzerland for the care and precision with which they reviewed certain portions of the manuscript. Wendy Johnson and Norman Fischer of San Francisco Zen Center's Green Gulch Farm, Judith Skinner of the Ewam Choden Tibetan Buddhist Center in Berkeley, the Private Office of His Holiness the Dalai Lama in Dharamsala and in New York must be acknowledged for having reviewed portions of the manuscript as well, though not all of it, where it relates to Buddhism.

Dean Judith Berling of the Graduate Theological Union, Berkeley, California, gave me a joint appointment as a research associate at the Office for Programs in Comparative Religion and the Center for Women and Religion at the G.T.U. (1988–1990) for which I am grateful. The University of California and the Graduate Theological Union especially were generous in extending library privileges. Through the Office for Programs in Comparative Religion I was given research assistance by Yvonne Vowels, a doctoral candidate at the Graduate Theological Union, to whom I am also grateful.

I would like to thank Joel Garreau of the Washington Post, Joanne

Edgar at *Ms.* magazine, Janet Vitt from her days at *Westward,* and Janet Fullwood of the *Sacramento Bee* for their interest and assignments while I was at work on various parts of this manuscript and the ideas that underscore it. Mountain Travel, Overseas Adventure Travel, Above the Clouds Trekking, Air India, the Indian Government Tourist Board, the Orient Express Private, Ltd., of Delhi, India, the Polish National Tourist Office of Chicago, Lot Airlines, and Orbis are to be thanked for having provided support for this project as well.

Dr. Marilyn Rhie, Professor of Art and East Asian Studies at Smith College, guided me to some of the outstanding examples of Tibetan art in the various museums and collections around the country. Ugyen Chudon and Alan Schaaf provided translation of Tibetan material at a pivotal moment in the manuscript.

The Rev. Dean James Parks Morton of the Cathedral of St. John the Divine in New York has had a special interest in this work because of the Cathedral's leadership in bridging cultures and communities. The Cathedral houses an important copy of Our Lady of Czestochowa, the Black Madonna of Poland.

Father Matthew Meyer, archivist and historian of the Benedictine Monastery at Einsiedeln generously provided me with whatever assistance I needed on my several visits to the monastery. His devotion to the Madonna of Einsiedeln exerted a strong and quiet influence on this work.

Dr. Pauline Napier, of Pittsburgh, Pennsylvania, diplomate of the Jung Institute in Küsnacht-Zurich, shared her original material on the Black Madonna at Tindari, Sicily. Peter Hopkirk, author of *Trespassers on the Roof the World* and other books on the East, introduced me to materials on Tibet to be found only in the India Office Secret Files of the India Office Library in London. John Snelling, the editor of the Buddhist journal in London, *The Middle Way,* provided an important perspective on Buddhism as it takes root in the West. Discussions with Martin Willson, author of *In Praise of Tara,* of his work on Tara and our subsequent correspondence was valuable. Carin Simon provided me with important photographic support in London, before and after the pilgrimage in Poland. I am grateful to Oliver Caldecott, my initial editor at Century Hutchinson, for the confidence he had in this book. I am sorry that he did not live to see it published. My thanks to Maggie Noach, my British agent, for giving him this book. I am grateful to Mark Booth, my editor at Century, for his confidence. Lorna St. Aubyn's help upon my return to London meant getting essential medical supplies to Poland.

Father Marian Zalecki at the Shrine of Our Lady of Czestochowa in Doyleston, Pennsylvania, gave me essential information that enabled me to make the pilgrimage in Poland. The Pauline fathers in Warsaw, Krakow, and Czestochowa extended their hospitality to me graciously and often. The generosity of the people I met in Poland knew no bounds, especially that of Jadwiga and Josef Zalecki, Father Dominik Luszczek, and Jola Hellich's family. Jola Hellich and Joanna Zawalska generously provided translation whenever necessary.

Ewa Osiantinski's help in setting up meetings with various scholars on my second trip to Warsaw was invaluable. Wiktor Osiantinski's help was also important. Professor Aleksander Gieysztor of the University of Warsaw provided me with information on pre-Christian Poland as did Elzbieta Choinska-Bochdan, archeologist and curator of the Archeological Museum in Gdansk.

Sara Nelson and William Davis, S.J., of the Christic Institute provided me with information and contacts with the religious community in Texas. My experience with the Catholic nuns, priests, brothers, and lay community of the Rio Grande Valley transformed this book. Robert Rubin of the San Francisco Lawyer's Committee for Urban Affairs deserves special thanks for his help.

Conversations with Sister Pascaline Coff at Osage Monastery, Forest of Peace Retreat Center in Oklahoma, Dan O'Hanlin, S.J., Brother David Steidhl-Rast, and the Rev. Charles Murphy on Buddhist-Christian dialogue were essential to the growth of this work. Each at critical moments provided encouragement to move forward onto unknown ground. John Pavlicek's letters from the Christ in the Desert

Monastery in Abiquiu, New Mexico, marked a turning point for me.

The inspiration of the painter Meinrad Craighead is not visible on these pages but runs throughout this book. The bold, contemporary paintings of her "Mothergod" in *The Mother's Songs, Images of God the Mother,* and our correspondence about her own encounters with the Black Madonna were a frequent support to this work.

I am especially grateful for the work of Robert Lentz, the icon painter, whose Madonna appears in these pages, and to Bridge Building Icons for making his work available. Its powerful impact is evident in the narrative.

Vietnamese Buddhist monk and Zen master Thich Nhat Hanh's influence was increasingly felt as this book drew to a close. The Buddhist Peace Fellowship and the young people of the Peace Project, especially Otis Kriegel, and Erica Sward, continually renewed my spirits.

Patricia Hopkins was an ongoing source of support with stories from her work-in-progress with Sherry Anderson, *The Feminine Face of God.* Hera's long-standing friendship provided a base of support for me over the years of this project. My Tuesday night meditation and prayer group was a wellspring of love and common sense that sustained me through the roughest part of this work. I am grateful to the women of this circle. Diana Rowan provided healing respites at critical moments during the length of this work.

Marion Woodman's work, *The Pregnant Virgin,* and our subsequent conversations were important in crystallizing one of the main premises of this book—from Carl Jung—"it takes spirit to cure spirit." I want to thank Fred Gustafson, author of *The Black Madonna,* not only for sharing his research, but for pointing out the large 1939 granite sculpture by Beniamino Bufano of the Black Madonna entitled "Peace" that stands at the entry to San Francisco International Airport. Professor Anne Klein of Rice University's Department of Religious Studies, author of commentaries on Buddhist texts, provided assistance on the subject of Buddhism and feminism. Elaine Pagels of Princeton University's Department of Religion and author of *The Gnostic Gospels,* helped me begin to understand "What Happened to God the Mother."

Theresa Koke provided valuable support not only in preparing the manuscript, but in holding the rest of my life together while I worked. Her assistance was critical. I am grateful to Bill Keener for his reading of the manuscript and helpful comments. Both Bill and Dana Marks Keener's review of the legal issues involved in the Central American refugees' plight benefited my understanding significantly. I appreciate the help of John Glover, Marjorie Mitchell, and Betty Simmons. Jane Hirshfield, Johnnie Chace, Richard West, and Nancy Bardacke extended themselves with generosity.

Sandra Lopez's friendship and discerning comments encouraged me always to go deeper. Helen Stoltzfus, Albert Greenberg, and Marita Gunther helped me bring out the voice, both figuratively and literally, that wanted to be heard.

Certain friendships have had little direct relationship with the specific subject matter with which I have been so caught up these last few years, yet they have been just as instrumental in supporting this work as others whose roles are more obvious. In this regard I would like to thank Barry Lopez and Sherry Anderson for the special grace their friendships lend to my life.

I am grateful to my agent, Molly Friedrich. Her reading of the manuscript at different stages was vital to its development. Perhaps most important of all has been my editor Dawn Seferian, who believed in this book so strongly from the start. Her calm assurance and ready support helped sustain me through the long process of bringing the work to fruition. I will remain grateful to her always. The staff of Viking Penguin, especially Beena Kamlani, have my abiding gratitude as well. I am also grateful to Amy Hill, Design Director.

I am grateful for the sustaining love and confidence of my very large family, and especially my children, Matthew, Madelon, and Benjamin Galland.

The experience of my husband, Corey Fischer, with his own

creative process and the fearlessness with which he approaches his own craft, has inspired and sustained me through the several years that my life has centered around this work. His help and support gird this entire book.

I am grateful to these people and many others who remain unnamed. The hospitality I was provided with both in this country and others was remarkable.

Any errors found herein I claim solely as my own. No one else can be held accountable. I have attempted always to provide the reader with information that is reliable, but many of the matters touched upon herein are subject to interpretation and various opinions. Many have spent whole lifetimes devoted to a single aspect of any one of the several subjects touched upon in this book. My intent is to provide a first-hand account of a long and complicated journey, and the vision that has grown from that experience.

Contents

LONGING FOR
DARKNESS

*Tara and
the Black Madonna*

CHAPTER I

The Unremembered Gate

♦

Kathmandu, Nepal

"Male and female He created them."
From here we learn:
Any image that does not embrace male and female
is not a high and true image.
                                        —The Zohar[1]

Kathmandu, Nepal
October 1980

Villagers come up behind me now, walking this narrow, cloudy string of a trail that climbs a thousand feet above a crashing river gorge. My legs are shaky. There is nothing to do but keep walking, no place to stop. I am trekking with a group in the foothills of the Himalayas, in the tiny kingdom of Nepal.

My head is light and pounding from the altitude, now over eight thousand feet. My body refuses to adjust. Despite the two layover days in Kathmandu at nearly five thousand feet, I am slow to acclimatize. I live at sea level. This is our third day of walking and already we have gained another three thousand feet of altitude. The trails are steep, going up and down, up and down; the going down even harder on my knees. It is late afternoon and I have yet to get a good night's sleep. The air is cool on my face. Monsoon season has just ended, leaving the rice terraces we walk through brilliant green and mirrored with gray clouds. Monsoons compound the deforestation of the Himalayas, creating one of the world's worst soil-erosion problems, affecting the entire Indian subcontinent as the mountains wash down to the sea. Our trail is pocked with washouts.

As I walk, I see on my left a deep blue flower like an enormous morning glory, so large that inside it a spider sits spinning its web. I walk more slowly, turning to watch the spider, not wanting to hold up the villagers, Sherpas, and porters carrying hundred-pound loads who are coming up behind me.

My attention is drawn into the flower and the spider's web; my legs are unsteady and my head light. In the spinning, in the push to keep moving up this green mountain, I fail to see a washout on the trail. In the next step I am catapulted into a world that slides out of control. Plummeting down the mountainside, dirt and scree flying, I catch myself within seconds, arresting a fall to the frothing Sun Kosi River at what seems to be a thousand feet below. For a moment I am breathless. I have fallen fifteen feet at the most, but something is wrong and I know it the moment I come to a stop. The pain is searing and quickly takes me over. By the time I drag myself back to the lip of the trail with the help of others reaching down, hand over hand, it is clear that I have either broken my ankle or sprained it badly. It is swelling rapidly. I sit on the edge of the trail in shock, alternately laughing and crying.

"Can you move it at all?" "Unlace your shoes," "Don't put any pressure on it," people say in a steady stream of directives that I can barely hear. The trek doctor arrives, rotating and palpating the rapidly swelling foot until I finally let out a howl.

"Hurts, does it," he says matter-of-factly. "You'll make it. Might be a break, might just be a bad sprain. Hard to say. Come on," he urges, "I'll put a temporary splint on it, then you can get up and try walking."

He gives me two pain pills, splints the ankle, and suggests that I stand up. My leg crumples under me. I cannot walk and I can't believe that he's suggesting that I do so. Dawa, a young Sherpa, comes up with a smile and puts me on his back as if I weigh no more than a three-year-old child. We continue walking uphill, in a hurry now to make our camp before nightfall.

My legs through his arms, my arms over his shoulders, I hang on, bouncing and periodically quietly crying out of pain, the effect of the drugs, embarrassment, and gratitude for the astonishing generosity of this man's back. Dawa carries me for miles, talking with the other Sherpas and porters, laughing, stopping occasionally to deposit me on the hillside to give himself a rest and then, putting me back on his back, walks on. With his limited English he manages to assure me that my weight is no problem for him. He is young and strong. The Sherpa people are Tibetan Buddhists whose homeland is the Solu Kumbhu at the base of Mount Everest.

I had hoped to reach the Solu Kumbhu in time for Mani Rimdu, the semi-annual full-moon ceremony at Thyangboche Monastery, at nearly fifteen thousand feet. Dawa had a kind of indefatigable merriment and cheer that I was soon to learn is characteristic of many Tibetans, despite the brutal occupation of their homeland by the Chinese government. Though I had only recently begun to study Tibetan Buddhism, the primacy of compassion and loving kindness were clearly values that many of its adherents lived out, whether they were Tibetan or Nepali.

That night with the help of our sirdar, the lead Sherpa in charge of the various porters and cooks that accompany us, and our American trekking guide, we come up with an evacuation plan and map out a route. Pasang, one of the Sherpas, and one trek member will go with me to Charikot, a village a day away where there is a bus stop and a Swiss doctor. The doctor will examine the leg again, have proper materials for a cast if necessary, and can make the final decision as to whether or not it is truly fractured or just sprained. In the morning, we will get a pony for me to ride to the village. Such an animal is hard to come by in these mountains. I am assured that this is great luck. We will have to separate from the group; the trail they take is too narrow for a horse and rider, but we will meet up with them at a campground two days from now in Charikot.

"The leg is broken, just above the ankle. Absolutely. And perhaps in two places," the Swiss doctor in Charikot tells me. "I can put a temporary cast on now, but you must go back to Kathmandu on the next bus. There's one in the morning. Once you get back, you must have an X-ray and that leg properly cast. What I can do for you is only temporary. There is an orthopedist at the Mission Hospital. You're in luck. There are only two in Nepal."

Meeting up with the group again that night at our campsite is a blur of shock, disbelief, and pain medication. Disappointment hangs in the air. It took nearly a year to organize this trek. Friends have joined me from across the United States. This is not just a group of strangers.

Though I must leave, the group is in good hands. We have a good Nepali sirdar and our trekking guide is a competent American woman who is familiar with the route as well as fluent in Hindi and Urdu.

Dogs bark continuously as an Australian expedition camped nearby tries to organize itself in the dark by flashlights and curses. It is a fitful night and I get little sleep.

The next morning I say goodbye to the group. A beautiful young Nepali girl, about eight years old, slips a bright pink rhododendron into my pocket with a smile, as if to say, "Get well soon!" Pasang Sherpa and I board the bus, waving out the window as it roars off down the dusty road. The bus is spilling over with villagers inside and out, people hanging on the top, sitting in spare tires and between boxes, chickens squawking, a baby goat sleeping through the commotion on a villager's lap across from me, and a drunken old man throwing up out of the back. It is a fifteen-hour ride back to Kathmandu on this hairpin, bone-jarring road.

The Nepali and Sherpa people are friendly, and though I can speak little more than perfunctory greetings, they point at my leg in the cast, nod their heads in understanding, and make long faces of sympathy, followed by bursts of shy laughter.

On the bus ride back I conclude that since I had been able to ride a pony with my leg broken and temporarily splinted, surely I can resume the trek as soon as I have my leg cast more securely in Kathmandu. I should be able to get a flight out to the airstrip at Lukla, eleven thousand feet, where the group will be in a matter of a few days. There I will rent another pony, or perhaps a yak, and continue on with the group.

The madness of such an idea was not yet apparent to me. I needed to believe that a broken leg was only a temporary setback, a complication. It never occurred to me that I might not complete the trek.

Late that night Pasang Sherpa carried me on his back into the hotel lobby, exhausted. I was given a room overlooking the garden. The next day, still groggy and now running a fever, I was carted off to the hospital, X-rayed under an antique radiating device from high overhead. The leg was properly certified as "broken." The doctor gave me a new, heavy plaster cast, a pair of crutches, and sent me limping on my way through the noisy, crowded, narrow hallway of Mission Hospital.

The following day I ignored the pain, fever, and shock, and took a taxi to the trekking company's office. Raising my willpower like a piece of dry wall, I nailed it into place. Pain medication helped to finish it off.

I informed the office manager of my desire to rejoin the group and carried on as though breaking a leg amounted to a toe stub. Certainly he could help me, I thought. After all, he was British. That represented some kind of perverse but admirable arrogance in the face of great odds. Nor did he bat an eye when I told him my plans. He politely agreed to try to get me on a flight into the Solu Kumbhu as though this was a perfectly reasonable request. That gave me another three days to catch up with the group and a better chance of finding a yak or a pony to ride. He suggested that I come back in two days. We had plenty of time, he assured me, to pull the logistics together.

But when I went back two days later, he cautioned me, "You must understand, madam, that even if we could get you on a flight, our contacts have been unable to find any villager willing to give up a pony or yak for any length of time. Ponies are hard to come by in these mountains, you were fortunate. As for yaks, though more common, they can also be very disagreeable. Some are simply mean and unpredictable. They're not like riding a horse.

"Still, we will keep trying to arrange it so that you can meet up with your group. Please come back again the day after tomorrow. Perhaps we will know something then."

He was either too polite or felt too uncomfortable to ask if I really believed that I could complete this trek. It was evident that the possibility that I might not go on had not yet occurred to me. I stood there on crutches, in a cast from my left foot up to my thigh, and thanked him for his efforts, agreeing to return whatever day he suggested.

By the time I got back to the hotel from the trekking company office, my leg was throbbing. I ran into a mountaineer whom I had recently met and joined him in the bar for a drink. He was an old hand at life in Nepal, having spent years there off and on. I rested my broken leg up on a chair and began to order brandies. Though he was too gruff a man to call it that, he'd come to make a pilgrimage of sorts, to visit the grave of a friend who had died in a mountaineering accident years before.

"We were on Everest, at about nineteen thousand feet in the Kumbhu ice fall at about noon, going between ice towers, winding our way along in a maze of crevasses, when a huge wall of ice the size of a house came down and fell on the first three climbers. It was like an explosion. Everything went blinding white. When the ice dust settled there was an eerie silence with blocks of ice everywhere and no people. I was just behind them. I fell fifty feet, but was relatively unhurt. When I climbed back up to the first rope I found two of them very confused and badly injured—one man was dangling upside down in a crevass—and the third one had a concussion but wasn't as badly injured. From where I found them, the rope they were tied to went back and disappeared under an ice block the size of a railroad car. We had one more climber, a very close friend of mine, in there.

"He was as good as dead if he wasn't already. There was no way to know. I called to him for what seemed like hours, until I was hoarse. No answer. Only this eerie silence. Daylight wouldn't last much longer. I was shivering and starting to get frostbite.

"I had two injured people on my hands who were going to die if we didn't get down quickly. I was the only one in a position to make a decision at that point. Then it hit me like thunder. I was going to have to cut the rope. There was nothing left to do.

"I called out to him one last time. I called out so loud that I thought I'd bring the snows down. But there was only silence and ice. Nothing. The moment had come. I pulled out my knife and began to cut the rope as fast as I could. Done.

"Just after we began to make our way down I heard a strange sound and my heart stopped. Oh my God, had I made the wrong decision? Could he still be alive? Impossible.

"There, I heard it again. It was a muffled, strangled cry that came up out of the ice and cut right through me. Then I saw it. It was a *gorak,* raven, flying right up out of the crevass where our friend was. It was the first time I'd seen ravens that high up in the mountains, but there he was, all shiny and black. I never got over that.

"Ten years later, his body came out of the glacier. Another expedition found it. A couple of years ago he was finally buried at Thyangboche Monastery, where you were going. That's where I'm headed."

The next morning in Kathmandu I wakened early. The day was cool, overcast, and gray. Even the birds' songs seemed muffled by the clouds. How strange it was to find myself sitting in the garden of a hotel with my leg in a cast instead of walking in the Himalayas. After the months of preparation for the trek, to have it snatched away in an instant was more than I could absorb.

I sat outside on a lawn chair with a table set up for me in the garden to read and write. Small white butterflies fluttered low on the lawn. A small stupa, a shrine, sat on a mound in the center of the garden, a pair of the Buddha's eyes painted on each of the four sides, seeing everything. I thought back to the path I had set out upon years ago that brought me here.

The seeds of this trip to Nepal had been planted in Big Bend National Park in Texas along the Mexican border, six years earlier, on a river trip. Big Bend was a place most people forgot, full of creosote bushes (of limited use to man and beast except as food for the camels that lived here briefly with the U.S. Army in the 1850s), javelina, mule deer, cougar, ring-tailed cats, fox, coyote, pronghorn antelope, all manner of snakes, giant dagger yucca plants, lechuguilla, cactus of over forty varieties, candelilla wax plants, and quicksilver. For the most part, Big Bend was an inhospitable place. Some came to the nearby Davis Mountains to hunt deer, as did my grandfather over fifty years ago.

Big Bend was named for the bend in the Rio Grande River. The Spanish explorer Álvar Núñez Cabeza de Vaca passed through this area in the early part of the sixteenth century after his expedition from Spain had been shipwrecked and lost.

It was de Vaca who left us the first description of the land that he found there during his years as a captive, trader, and medicine man. He traveled through the Davis Mountains, at eight thousand feet, full of game and water, and then further south, nearer the river, into the Chisos Mountains at five thousand feet. He would have seen the spectacular river canyons from twelve hundred to seventeen hundred feet deep made by the sawing water as the mountain ranges grew.

In the early 1970s Big Bend was still pretty desolate and deserted, with so few roads to cut across it that you were considered rude if you didn't wave to every car that passed. Flash floods from a rainstorm twenty miles away could send down a tongue of water within minutes to swallow up your camp in a box canyon on a starry night. Dry arroyos became swollen torrents that could sweep your car off the road. The desert was wild, barren, and ruthless; life along the border sometimes dangerous, with a mix of smugglers, banditos, lawmen, refugees, and outcasts. Lajitas, a trading post—filling station and put-in point for river trips, was an old Comanche trail crossing. Pancho Villa controlled much of this area in days that seemed not that far past.

I was on a river trip on the Rio Grande in 1972. Late one afternoon we took off up a side canyon for a hike and short climb, led by a woman guide. It was the first time I'd climbed with another woman. I expected a man to be able to lead a climb, but to see a woman do this taught me something new and put me right up against my own preconceptions about men and women.

We climbed late in the day, moving slowly, carefully, at her direction up the rocks: *breathe,* when I was not defeated by the fear that naturally arises, *breathe,* keep going, one foot at a time, *breathe,* get your balance, be sure that the rock where you step can hold you, *breathe,* fear makes you hold your breath, let go, *breathe,* it's energy, breathe through it, excitement, *breathe,* you're alive, be in your feet, *breathe,* and when we made it, in the nearly dark, to the summit, I threw both arms up in the air and let out a loud "Whoopee!" that echoed off the canyons now far below. We were on top.

I wakened in the morning at first light to watch the sun move down the canyon walls, a pinky-gold wash that overtook the dark. Then came the call of the canyon wren with its plaintive long series of descending notes. By the time he reached the seventh one, some wildness was drawn out in me.

Then I recalled the river itself and an all-women's white-water rafting trip in 1974. Santa Elena is one of the most stunning canyons cut by the Rio Grande, narrowing down to thirty feet wide in some places, with walls reaching up to fifteen hundred feet. We had pulled ashore to sight a rapid we were about to run at a point where the river swept wide into a broad curve and ricocheted off steep canyon walls before it narrowed and shot through the Rock Slide.

The Rock Slide is part of the canyon wall that has broken off and fallen into a nearly 250-foot-high pile in the river, partially damming it. This dangerous, rock-choked section generally has to be portaged for at least a quarter mile. Many boats have been broken up on these rocks or wrapped around a boulder by strength of the current as the river narrows. A number of people are known to have been pinned underwater against the rocks, life jackets on or not, and drowned.

We watched the woman who'd been captain of our raft trace the sweep of the river's current into the sand. With a stick she etched out our strategy for running this stretch above the Slide. We would have to pull out just above it and make the portage.

"You be captain," she said, turning to me when she had finished. I thought she was kidding. I was not that experienced. She was getting back at me for the mud fight, or was it the water fight? Maybe it was the dead tarantula I found. I had been known to revert to age five when on the river. Some people found this behavior hilarious, "spirited." Others did not.

"I can't do it," I replied. "I ran this rapid two weeks ago and had a man overboard. Almost lost him. We barely got him and the boat to shore before the Rock Slide."

"Do it," she replied calmly, giving me a smile and staring down my "can't" with her blue eyes. "You can. I've been watching."

My heart was pounding, my knees felt watery. I heard myself say "Okay," then it was time to go. My palms were sweaty as I took the longer captain's paddle and signalled everyone to tighten up their life jackets and get in.

By the time we pushed off, I was on fire with the excitement and fear. The bottom of the rubber raft made a familiar *whoosh* as it was pushed off the sand and was taken by the water. "Stroke, together now," I said loud, and called for a left turn and then a fast right. Everyone paddled together, was responsive, knew the commands. It was a good crew; without them, there was little I could do.

Now we had to pull into the main current and cut across to avoid being swept into the canyon wall as the river made its bend.

"Right turn, dig in, and don't let up!"

We got our paddle boat through the upper part of the rapid and around the bend fine. But the other raft with us had flipped and was now traveling downriver, upside down, with all its crew members in the water. Was there someone missing, I thought to myself, trying to read the water, call the turns, paddle, and count six heads all at once. I could only see five.

"Paddle! Harder! Harder!"

We paddled like crazy to them, now luckily caught in an eddy on the left, the Texas side. But there's no place to land, only sheer canyon wall straight up hundreds of feet to the sky. Five women, damn! Oh, another head's popped up. It's Pete—she's the sixth. As soon as her head popped up she started yelling at us. After she fell out of the boat, she came up under it and didn't think she'd ever get out. She was terrified and angry, "I thought I'd die!"

"Get in the boat. This isn't over yet," I yelled back. Too many people scrambled to one side to pull the others in and we started to tip, so half the women threw themselves back against the pontoon on the other side.

We got everybody in or on one of the two boats, but we still had to get to the other side. The only landing spot was on the Mexican side. We pulled out hard across the drag of the eddy fence, where opposing currents meet, the noses of our rafts at a sharp angle, pointed almost directly into the current to buy a few seconds of time.

"Paddle! Paddle! Pull! Harder! Right turn! Dig in! Harder! *Harder!*" I yelled at the top of my lungs, over and over. Even as we pulled across at a diagonal we were rapidly being swept downstream. The roar of the Rock Slide below us grew louder, my heart was pounding. "Harder! Harder!" I shouted. We were just above the Rock Slide. The water sounded like continuous thunder when we pulled up onto the sandy, cane-filled banks, safe, all together, on the Mexican side.

Water became my teacher, reading it an essential skill. The obstacle
was the path. The main current would take you right up to a rock
and around, you had to head straight for the obstacle. To avoid it
meant getting sucked into an eddy and circling back and in on oneself,
stuck, unable to move downstream. To stay in the main current
required a great deal of skill. I learned by metaphor. Women became
my teachers, giving me a part of myself that no man could find. I
began to learn to be a river guide.

From Texas, I moved to California in 1975. I met other women
who loved the wilderness. We hiked together, climbed, skiied, rafted,
and kayaked. Like a confluence of streams, our gatherings grew into
a nonprofit organization called Women in the Wilderness. Many trips
were open to men. Our only stipulation was that leadership had to
be provided by women. We had a dual purpose: to support and
protect our kinship with the natural world and to develop women's
leadership. Our motto was "Grow Wild."

We found that in 1694 there had been a group called the Order
of the Woman in the Wilderness. The Order was comprised of
German Pietist men who fled the religious persecutions of the day
in Europe. Followers of the great Christian mystic, Jakob Boehme,[2]
they settled in the Wissahickon Woods outside of Philadelphia.

Led by Johann Kelpius, the Order took its name from their
central belief in the coming of the Apocalypse. The appearance of
the Woman Clothed in the Sun with the moon under her feet as
described in the Book of the Apocalypse would signal the Second
Coming, calculated at that time to occur at the end of the seventeenth
century. Their task was to keep a vigil for her and wait. Some members
taught, many lived as hermits in the woods. According to their
predictions, she would soon appear.

Ten years passed. The world did not end and the Order of the
Woman in the Wilderness faded out, now referred to in history as
an early American Utopian society.

The wilderness gave me solace, taught me, and filled up the empty places. Native American practices like the sweat lodge, the history of the Order of the Woman in the Wilderness, my own experiences and those of other women all confirmed the spiritual value to be found in the natural world, pointed to a sacred landscape.

Yet I did not live in the wilderness. As a single mother of three children (ages six, ten, and eleven) with sporadic child support, family life was often chaotic and painful. Dogged by a gnawing sense of failure, unable to get work, child care, and income to balance, I thought of packing up my children and retreating to a remote forest. But I was always stopped by considerations of how I would shelter, feed, clothe, and educate three children. I hardly knew how to grow a tomato, much less farm, fish, forage, or hunt.

Underneath the surface I was lost in the wilderness of the single-parent family. Raised a strict Roman Catholic, I married at nineteen. No one in my family had ever been divorced. But in less than two years, a Catholic priest had suggested that for my own safety and that of my children, I should file for a divorce and an annulment concurrently. Divorce would take place in civil court, but an annulment had to be granted by the Church. I had one child and was pregnant with my second when I left the marriage at twenty-one.

Annulments in the Catholic Church were decided upon in Rome at that time. You could remain in the Church as a divorced person but you could never remarry without an annulment. I elected to wait for the annulment to go through; I had a strong case, and did not go out socially with men. After a year, it was suggested that I send a canon lawyer to Rome to expedite my case. Going through the normal channels meant that I might have to wait as long as seven years.

I made my first adult decision and left the Church. I was unwilling to let a group of celibate men who had never had families have this kind of power over my life. With no money of my own and no enforceable order for child support, the suggestion that I fly a priest to Rome, however well intended and practical, was a cruel joke.

I buried my spiritual life with that decision. I began to date, to have a social life, go to parties, drink. I worked, went to school, and cared for my children in a state of walking numbness and unspoken shock. Four years later I remarried and had my third child. After seven years that marriage ended.

Then I longed for the woods with a vengeance. I was driven. At home I took my sleeping bag and slept outside for a long time after the breakup. Though I remained physically present, my children virtually lost their mother. Only the trees could hide me, the rivers soothe me.

Whatever time I spent in the wilderness made the need for a spiritual life obvious and apparent. When the second marriage failed, I could no longer deny that part of myself. Something was terribly wrong. I tried to go back to the Catholic Church.

In January 1977, I went to the Christ in the Desert Monastery, in Abiquiu, New Mexico. I remember it clearly, even as I sit here thousands of miles away in the hotel garden in Nepal, three years after the fact:

The sound of fresh snow crunches under my boots. I am walking to the chapel at three in the morning. The sky is black and clear over the desert, strewn with hot stars. I haven't been inside a church for years.

Morning matins last half an hour, then back to sleep and up again at five-thirty for a 6:00 a.m. mass. The temperature outside is twelve degrees. Inside, we huddle in a clear plastic-sheeted area partitioned off for warmth. Now they are saying the words again, "And God gave man dominion," "Our Father," "His Body," "His Blood," "Glory be to the Father." Each time I hear "God the Father," "His," "man," I feel smaller and smaller, as though something in the room is suffocating me. Communion comes and I receive it in good faith, having made my first confession in seven years. My legs are trembling as the priest puts the host on my tongue. My heart is racing, I can hardly breathe. As soon as mass is over, I go to a side chapel where there's a statue of the Blessed Mother and kneel. Air. Then the tears come, pouring out the frustration and sorrow, the welter of feelings brought up by having come home again, such a long way, only to find that I am a stranger.

I am consoled by the presence of the Virgin, the idea of the Blessed Mother, but she is so remote! Impossibly good, inhumanly pure, I cannot reach her. There is a glass curtain, an invisible barrier between us. I don't know why I'm crying, only that I can't stop. I am shaking when Father Peter leans over and touches my shoulder and asks what's wrong. I ache for the comfort of the Blessed Mother, but her perfection and purity leave me in despair. I am filled with faults. I have built my life outside the Church. There is no way back. I shake my head, not knowing what to say, how to tell him that the very language of the mass fills me with grief. It says that I have no place here, keeps me outside, makes me the other.

It is early the next morning in Kathmandu, after another day of reading and sitting in the hotel garden. Lakshmi and Bhawaghita, two young Nepali women, will soon come to clean the room and bring fresh flowers for the makeshift altar I keep on the desk across from my bed.

Each morning while one changed the linens, the other helped me bathe and dress, taking turns brushing and fixing my hair Nepali style into a braid made longer by weaving in bright red tassels that finished off the plait, making it hang down to the waist. They spoiled me. Though between us we had very little language to make ourselves understood, they taught me basic Nepali phrases and explained that Lakshmi's name was also that of Lakshmi the great Hindu goddess of good fortune and wealth, Vishnu's model wife.

Lakshmi and Bhawaghita explained why some Nepalis looked at me so strangely when I told them my name. In Nepali, the sound of the syllables *Chi-na* means roughly "I don't have any," so people thought that I was saying I didn't have a name. Lakshmi and Bhawaghita doubled over giggling as a look of understanding began to come over my face.

"No wonder," I said, embarrassed and trying to smile too now that I finally understood. "No wonder!" I was both discomforted and oddly pleased by this fact.

I would spend most of today in the garden, too. No word was expected from the trekking company about the Lukla flight until tomorrow. I wasn't up to hobbling in and out of rickshaws by myself; I tired easily. The hotel garden was quiet and protected. I was still puzzling over how I ended up in this predicament. Something didn't fit. I couldn't sort it out. I had to put together a chronology in my own mind. I remembered becoming interested in Buddhism not long after the retreat at Abiquiu's Christ in the Desert Monastery.

San Francisco Zen Center's Green Gulch Farm was within a mile of our house. I began to go there on Sunday mornings after my failed attempt to return to the Catholic Church. They provided child care, poetic lectures, included women as priests, and did not talk about God. The answer was in my own backyard.

Green Gulch had been a working cattle ranch nestled in a widening valley on the Pacific Ocean just north of San Francisco. The large tin-roofed hay barn had been converted into a zendo, the meditation hall. The old horse stalls were left intact below. Sparsely furnished and spotless, with a highly polished wooden floor, the zendo soon became a refuge for me. I began to go to meditation, zazen, at 5:00 a.m. before my children were up, arriving back home in time to make breakfast. The one blue-enameled wood-burning stove in the zendo could never heat the room. The wooden floor was hard and cold on bare feet. Still, I loved the quiet, simple practice, the sitting in silence and just breathing with a community of other people.

Sitting on the zafu, the round black meditation cushion, looked easy enough, but the wild monkey of the mind climbed all over me inside, swinging from future to past, past to future, rarely ever settling into this present moment. If there was any point or goal that I could understand, it was to be found in the present moment. Without this intention, I found myself often drifting into the past or worrying over the future, all the while awash in a wide spectrum of feelings that might come up about either.

"Focus on the breath, count to ten, and then start over again," the meditation teacher said. "Don't think about anything. Empty your mind. If a thought arises, let it go. Don't resist it, but don't entertain it either. Return to your breathing. Always go back to the breath."

"Don't judge," I was told, "don't give up. Keep going back to the breath. This is why it is called spiritual *practice*. We have to keep going back to the breath again and again before we can tame the mind. If you give up, you will never progress. The breath, go back to the breath. Have some humility. It took the Buddha himself years to accomplish this."

I was attracted by the Buddha's insistence that he was in no way divine. He was completely and utterly human. He maintained that his enlightenment was the end result of being fully and completely human. Enlightenment, he held, is possible for everyone.

Siddhārtha Gautama, Sakyamuni Buddha, the historical Buddha, was born in the sixth century B.C. in northern India in Lumbini in what is now Rummindei, Nepal. Born into the aristocratic Sakya clan, he was referred to as Prince Siddhārtha or Gautama, before his enlightenment underneath the bodhi tree at Bodh Gayā, India, which the Buddhists consider the greatest event in human history. Historians estimate that this event took place in 560 B.C., when Siddhārtha Gautama was in his mid-thirties. After this, he was called the Buddha, "The Enlightened One."

Rather than remain a solitary recluse, Gautama Buddha chose to return to the world and teach the understanding he had reached. He lived until the age of eighty, traveling on foot and teaching to all, whether men, women, Brahmins, kings, robbers, outcasts, or beggars.

He refused to recognize the distinctions of the caste system, a very radical position for that day. His teachings were for anyone who wished to listen.

The Buddha's decision to teach is an example of the bodhisattva's path, surely one of the most heartening concepts in world religions. A bodhisattva is one who has reached enlightenment but who voluntarily postpones entering nirvana, a state in which all suffering has ceased. The bodhisattva remains in the world to help others achieve the "supreme liberation" of enlightenment.

The Buddha's childhood was spent behind palace walls, protected from the outside world where he was afforded all the luxuries of his father Suddhodana's wealth. He was married early to the beautiful Yasodhara, who bore him his only child, a son, Rahula.

One day, against his father's wishes, Siddhārtha left the palace and for the first time he saw that there was suffering in the world, old age, disease, and death. He became obsessed by the thought of finding an end to suffering. Abandoning his family, he fled the palace, gave away his robes of luxury and retreated to the forests where he became a wandering seeker.

For six years he practiced severe physical austerities, nearly starving himself to death. Finally he realized that there must be a middle way and abandoned the harsh practices to which he had subjected himself. Without his body, he concluded, there was no hope for enlightenment, no release. This fragile vessel, the physical body, was the very means by which he would achieve the awakening he so wholeheartedly sought. With this realization, he accepted a bowl of milk and rice offered by a woman from a nearby village. When his strength returned, he began to forge his own path.

He went immediately to a nearby bodhi tree and sat down, vowing to remain there until he became enlightened. He would not stir! He wanted to understand the cause of suffering and the way by which beings—all beings—could be released.

Day and night Gautama sat. Mara, the king of the demons and his retinue appeared to tempt him, bombarding him with distractions, storms, temptations, and visions, but Gautama's concentration was imperturbable. Despite the onslaught by Mara, Gautama achieved enlightenment, calling upon the Earth itself in the form of the goddess Pravirti, to witness his attainment. At the moment his fingers touched the earth, Mara and his host of demons disappeared, defeated.

Wisdom arose and just before dawn, it is said, at the sight of the morning star, Gautama achieved the supreme release of full enlightenment.

What the Buddha understood was that suffering exists, that it has a discernible cause, and that one can be released from it entirely, within this life, by practicing the spiritual principles of the path. These insights are called the Four Noble Truths and are the foundation of the teachings that he gave for the next forty-five years. His special emphasis was on developing compassion, loving kindness, and an understanding of the complete, inextricable interdependence of all phenomena.

The Buddha is more than an historical personage; he represents the possibility of enlightenment within all beings. There have been Buddhas before him and there are Buddhas yet to come.

Roughly paraphrased, Sakyamuni Buddha counseled his followers to be like goldsmiths testing gold before accepting his teachings. The teachings are like a nugget a goldsmith examines by sight, then hammers, bites, and even subjects to fire before deciding whether it is genuine and worth buying. The teachings are not to be accepted until they are known to be true through direct personal experience. The Buddha was a pragmatist. He called his teachings a raft, a boat for crossing over, not something to be carried around once one has reached the other shore. One of his most quoted aphorisms is "Look within, thou art the Buddha."[3]

Drawn by the Buddha's words to his followers, I became a student of Zen. The Buddha's comments were the perfect antidote for my Roman Catholic upbringing, in which everything—the Virgin birth, original sin, the Immaculate Conception, no meat on Friday, the loss of my father's soul because he was a Methodist, Limbo, the Assumption, Purgatory, and papal infallibility, came from above and had to be taken on faith.

San Francisco Zen Center was part of the Soto Zen School, a Japanese variant of Mahayana Buddhism, the "Great Vehicle," one of the two main forms of Buddhism known in the world today. Theravada, "the School of the Elders," is the other main form, regarded as "original orthodox Buddhism."[4]

In Mahayana Buddhism, the focus is on the great altruistic thought of the Buddha—"May I become enlightened for the sake of all beings!" One cultivates enlightenment in order to benefit all beings, not just oneself. One of the main focuses in Buddhism is on breaking up the dualistic notion that we are separate. In the process of becoming enlightened for everyone, we become enlightened ourselves; but that is a by-product, not an aim. There is no separate, independent self, only the great interconnectedness of all being, rising and falling like a great swell of water, no more separate than a wave is from the ocean.

Within the year, I became a Zen student, formally entering the practice and study of Buddhism. Green Gulch was a great gift. Here was an entire community of people who, like myself, came from traditional religious backgrounds (or the lack thereof), and felt that there must be another way. But they had gone further. They had actively dedicated themselves to the study and development of a spiritual way of life grounded in the Buddha's way. Waking at 4:30 a.m. to sit *zazen* at Green Gulch became part of everyday life.

I kept sitting, sitting, sitting. I wanted to sit through my black cushion, down through the wood of the *zendo* floor, down into the horse stalls below, into the dirt, down into the earth. If I could just sit in meditation, I would sit all the way through the world and come out the other side. How long would that take? Was there enough time? If I could just be still and sit, count my breath, not move.

There was a woman who led the chanting after *zazen* on Wednesday mornings. It was dark when she began. Leah Asher had a deep, low voice that filled up every corner of the room. It was more penetrating than the sound of the rain falling on the tin roof. It fanned the fire and made it pop in the stove at the end of the room. Her voice poured over me like fresh, warm water, bathing me. Underneath the words, by its tone it said, sit, be still, don't give up, you can do this, breathe, chant with me, you are not alone. She chanted the sun up. She chanted from a place I remembered but hadn't been to before. I drew her voice around me like a heavy shawl and it kept me warm.

Then one day at Green Gulch someone told me about a female Buddha in the Tibetan Buddhist tradition. Her name was Tara. Despite the traditional Buddhist belief that a person could only reach enlightenment in a man's body, thousands and thousands of aeons ago, in a time before time, this Tara had taken a vow to be enlightened only in a woman's body, and she had kept her vow.

Hearing this fragment of Tara's story was electrifying. I was jolted out of the ongoing background frustration of being a woman trying to practice in traditional, organized religions. Women could not become priests in the Catholic Church. And though the notion was rejected at Zen Center, there was the discomforting tradition within Buddhism in general that women could not reach enlightenment. This tradition was downplayed as Buddhism came to the West, yet the belief had had its effect, no matter what was said now. There were only a handful of women teachers in the entire country at the time.

Standing on the deck at Green Gulch hearing about the Buddha Tara that morning after a lecture galvanized me. The idea that a woman so long ago had rejected this notion, had vowed that she would become enlightened in a female body, and had done so, inspired me to begin a search for her that would set me off halfway around the world.

A woman had said, "Enough!" Having a woman's body is good

enough. A woman's body can carry one across the river of suffering; it can transform the world of suffering, samsara, into the world of peace, nirvana. It can show that there is nothing to cross, no other side.

I could find little that had been translated about Tara beyond Stephan Beyer's book, *The Cult of Tara*.[5] His work supported my sense that the Buddha Tara was a major figure we needed to know much more about. Now after two years of studying and practicing *zazen* I wanted to know more about Tibetan Buddhism. The Japanese Zen School which I studied, though elegant, was severely limited for me by the emphasis on the monks' practice. Though Kannon is the Japanese equivalent of Tara (she is Kuan Yin in China), I found few images of the feminine in Japanese Zen Buddhism.

I continued my Zen practice, but now began readings in Tibetan Buddhism to find out what I could about Tara. Within a year I decided to organize a trek to Nepal. I had read that the Tara was especially revered by the Sherpas, devout Tibetan Buddhists whose home was the Solu Kumbhu area of the Himalayas at the base of Chomolungma, the Great Mother, known to us in the West as Mount Everest. My dream had been to walk in the Himalayas, the highest mountains on earth. There I would learn about the Buddha Tara where she is known and loved, among people who revere her.

Now I am in Nepal, but not the mountains. The gray sky covering Kathmandu Valley makes the garden flowers stand out sharply against the dark green foliage. Full of fall roses blooming in pinks, reds, salmons, yellows and oranges and white, the turquoise and orange stalks of the Bird of Paradise flower, the garden at the hotel is cut off from the street, enclosed by towering, thick shrubs and pine trees.

This morning I was late in calling room service. Ram, the head-waiter in the dining room upstairs, was worried when I hadn't telephoned for the tray by 8:30 a.m. "Something wrong, madam?" he asked when he brought the tray of hot oatmeal, milk, and Sanka,

White Tara, Nepal, eighteenth century.

the only kind of coffee one could get in Nepal, to my room at ten o'clock. I didn't want to answer, but assured him that I was all right.

While I sit in meditation this morning, old feelings emerge: sorrow, guilt, anger, bitterness. My children, at home in the States, are often on my mind. Though my brother had come to live with us to help take care of them, being a single parent is hard and the quiet of meditation sometimes surfaces my feelings about that. The anger I feel this morning bewilders me, it is so volatile. Buddhists say not to entertain it for a moment, psychologists say you dare not ignore it. How to acknowledge such a strong emotion without losing my temper is difficult, yet I know better than to try to disregard it. It will simply take another form.

Sitting *zazen,* focusing on the breath, is all I know how to do at this point. Take no action, do no harm. I don't have to "do" anything. If I can allow these feelings to surface, the quiet time of meditation can help them change. How seldom I can count to ten without distraction. My mind is a wild horse, racing from one thought to another. Will I get a flight into the Kumbhu, a pony, a yak? I am still easily exhausted, the leg hurts, swelling and throbbing quickly if I use it too much.

The makeshift altar that sits on the table across from my bed reminds me of what to do. After dressing, I prop myself up on two pillows, stretch out my broken leg, and sit in meditation.

I had brought pictures of Padmasambhava to Nepal with me, to give away when I reached the Solu Kumbhu. The beloved saint of Tibetan Buddhists, also known as Guru Rinpoche, he is widely venerated for bringing Buddhism to Tibet from India in the eighth century. Some call him another Buddha.

Now I've set one of the pictures of him up against the wall. On each side are glasses of bright flowers, yellow dahlias, gold dandelions, pink dahlias, and a deep red flower I do not know. The silk *khata,* a ceremonial scarf, that I had bought to present to Tulshig Rinpoche, the abbot of Thyangboche Monastery, lies folded in front of the picture. Two thick white candles sit in small clay pots shaped like peacocks, the bird who eats poison and turns it into beauty. I have no incense to offer, so in its place this morning I copy a verse of Tulshig Rinpoche's to place on the altar:

> Arriving now in the wilderness,
>   in an uncertain place of solitude,
> accompanied by unbiased spiritual friends,
> I have drawn forth this song of separation
>   for the fulfillment of myself and all others.[6]

Kathmandu was in the midst of celebrating the Festival of Durga, the Hindu goddess and warrior queen. Later, I took a rickshaw from the hotel out into the festival crowds to observe.

Animal sacrifice went on in many parts of the city. Durga's festival was bloody. It seemed that there were pools of blood and flowers everywhere, roses and bright yellow marigolds, their petals scattered in the already filthy streets. The heavy odor of feces and flowers hung in the air, while on the road ahead a water buffalo bellowed loudly, as if sensing that he was on the way to slaughter. I forced myself to watch a goat have her throat slit, the blood caught in a small copper bowl and carried into a temple. Tiny rivulets of blood ran in the street like veins. I made my way back to the hotel, past fruit vendors, past open-air butcher shops with fly-covered meats laid out on wooden boxes, past jewelry shops, flower stalls, and a Buddhist stupa where the monks circumambulated, walking around the shrine in prayer, at each third step stopping to make a full prostration bow as if they could atone for the slaughter. Buddhists do not believe in animal sacrifice, it is forbidden. Nor do all Hindus believe in it or practice it; many do not, but in Nepal those who did held sway during this festival.

The story of Durga that was being celebrated in this festival warmed me. It's the story of her victory over Mahisa or Mahisasura, the great buffalo demon. This cosmic battle with the buffalo demon was being re-enacted here in Kathmandu as well as all over India, as it is every fall, a major holiday. It was from this battle between Durga and Mahisa that the Hindu goddess Kali came into being. Included in the battle account was the story of Durga's creation.[7] It bears retelling.

Mahisa and his company of demons were rapidly defeating the gods in battle. Chaos would shortly prevail. Soon not only would the gods themselves be destroyed, but the order of the world as well. The gods prayed to the Daughter of the Himalayas. They knew that their only hope was a woman, for Mahisa had been granted a boon making him invincible to all opponents but a female. Together the gods combined their energies into streams of fire, generating the towering form of the goddess Durga, "whose splendor spread throughout the universe."[8] Her very name meant "Beyond Reach."

Durga was so powerful that she could generate her own female battalions just by sighing. A soft sound from her lips and armed battalions sprang forth, with no effort on her part. Furious and bloody battles were waged, Mahisa and his demons were defeated again and again. Mahisa and Durga changed forms throughout. Mahisa was finally decapitated when he took the form of the buffalo demon. Still his demons, *asuras*, came at Durga.

Withdrawn from battle, seated on her lion on a mountain peak, smiling at the buffalo demon's defeat, Durga became furious when she saw two *asuras* approach. Her face darkened like ink with rage.[9]

From her forehead sprang Kali, full-blown, a terrible black hag with a sword in one hand and noose in the other. Kali's wild laughter filled the skies as she charged into battle, swooping up armies of demons, throwing whole elephants and riders into her maw, devouring them in a bite, crushing chariots and horses with every step of her feet. Kali was victorious.

But Durga was to fight one last battle in this tale. Challenged by the demon Sumbha to fight alone as herself, he chided her for calling up Kali and her armies to help. Durga took Kali and all her many forms back into herself.

Durga and Sumbha fought alone in what rose from the earth to become a cosmic battle in the sky. After what seemed an eternity of battle, with one last blow, Durga pierced Sumbha's heart with her dart and he fell defeated, out of the sky.

Durga, the warrior queen, called upon by the male gods when the cosmic balance was about to be lost, was the only one who could restore harmony and set the world at peace. Skies cleared, rivers returned to their course, singing and dancing were restored.

Durga promised to return in time of need, nourishing the world with food grown from her own body. She would vanquish enemies and give her devotees her blessings. The gods sang her praises, called her the "Queen of the Universe," the "lamp of understanding," the one "who removes the suffering of all." Then she simply vanished, to return again only when she was needed.

Durga's story gladdened me. Here was a fearless being, a brilliant tactician, full of independence, valor, *and* care. Her strength was towering, her fierceness used only when necessary to protect and restore the world's order. At the same time, it was she who would grow food from her own body to sustain the world in time of need.

I had come to find the Buddha Tara, but instead I found the goddesses Durga and Kali. Kali, sprung from Durga, Kali the death-dealer and life-giver, the end and beginning of time. She was a deity of such proportions as I had heard only God the Father in Christianity described. The fact that Kali is dark and female turned my Catholic upbringing inside out. She is naked, "sky-clad," because she has stripped away illusion; some say, to her nothing is hidden. Some say she is black because black is the color in which all distinctions are dissolved, others say she is black because she is eternal night.[10] The *Tantra of Great Liberation*[11] tells us that she is Creator, Protector, and Destroyer, all in one. Unless one comes to know Kali, it is said that the desire for liberation is futile.

Kali is the darkness before time and the formless dark that will

come again. *Kala* means time, and she devours it. Terrible black Kali
with her long red tongue lolling out of her mouth, a necklace of
skulls, earrings of children's corpses, her four arms with weapons,
hair flying, upright, naked, in the midst of a great ecstatic dance on
Shiva, her consort's sleeping body or was it his corpse, I didn't know,
I didn't understand, I was shocked, most of all because I recognized
these images, they were familiar, though I didn't know from where.
Seeing them was like the experience of finding words for feelings
that I had long held but had never been able to express. In Kathmandu
they seemed to be all around me, painted on the sides of buildings,
in temples, statues, books, paintings, postcards, the hotel lobby sou-
venir shop. They broke through and knocked down the false images
I had had of myself. They stripped me of the veneer of nicety. I saw
Kali, frenzied, embattled, destroying everything in sight, and Durga,
regal in her finery, demure, serene, calm, and deadly, I saw them
both in me. Kali and Durga were like mirrors, reflecting back anything
I had been afraid of in myself.

I was relieved to be a student of Buddhism and not Hinduism.
I found Kali and Durga energizing but overwhelming. Finding Tara,
no matter how circuitous the path, was still the object of my search.

I fell asleep that night exhausted.

Time to get a flight to Lukla was running out. Soon I had to go back
to the trekking company's office, but not today. I had been invited
to tour some outlying temples in the valley and to picnic with some
Westerners I'd met, Keith Dowman, his wife Meryl White, and
others. They had been living in Kathmandu for years. That night we
would have a Nepali dinner.

We set out in the morning on old motorcycles, rolling back in
time into ancient villages, taking roads that were long and tortuous
at some points, dusty, crisscrossed with sidepaths, blurred, nearly
indistinct, and at other times breezing down modern pavement or
blacktop, my braids flying. I held my crutches tight over the bumps,

under my arm. Every stop was a lesson in Tibetan Buddhism and Hinduism, and how they overlapped. Kathmandu Valley had its own indigenous Newari culture that added more complexity to this unique cultural mix. There are thousands of Hindu deities and perhaps as many in Tibetan Buddhism. The multiplicity of deities began to soften and blur, running together like watercolors on still-wet paper.

The day was broken up with a visit to a Hindu shrine where a family *puja,* a devotional ceremony to a deity, was taking place. Money, blood, flowers, bells, and water were all offered to Shiva, one of the main Hindu deities and Kali's consort. Lunch was hard to swallow. The bread was heavy, the peanut butter thick and oily. We washed it down with tea and Nepali whiskey. That took the edge off everything.

Keith was writing his book on Yeshe Tsogyel,[12] the famous eighth-century Tibetan woman master, consort, and leading disciple of Guru Padmasambhava. It was Yeshe Tsogyel who received all the *termas,* the hidden teachings, from him. Tsogyel, the "Sky Dancer," then preserved and transmitted Padmasambhava's teachings, the basis of the Nyingmapa School, one of the four main sects of Buddhism in Tibet. Yeshe Tsogyel is also considered to be a manifestation of Tara.

Both Keith and Meryl had been students of Tibetan Buddhism for some time. They patiently tried to explain something of what we had seen that day, including the representations of deities in union, which are found in many places. I had heard of tantric practices that conceived of sexuality as a means of liberation and union with the Divine.

Tara is one of the main tantric deities. Both Hinduism and the Buddhism of Tibet include tantric practices, but I am told that they cannot be equated, that they are not the same. I am not clear about how they differ, but I understand that the images of deities in union are symbolic and to be interpreted metaphorically. Union indicates harmony or nonduality in the tantric tradition and dissolves the concept of a separate self, the primary root of delusion.

Whether symbolic or literal, Tibetan or Hindu, the depiction of sexual union as sacred was refreshing to me. At first I was startled to see images of male and female deities making love, but the effect was life-affirming. This was sacred art.

There is a beautiful bronze statue in Nepal that depicts a female deity with a phallus. She is both male and female.[13] The statue shows the antiquity of the understanding of a biological truth that science has only in this century grasped. Both men and women have male and female chromosomes within them. As embryos, we all go through a stage embryologists have labeled the "indifferent period"—a period of development which is indistinguishable as either male or female.[14] We take on the attributes of one sex or another by virtue of only a chromosome or two. Wholeness is a composite or union of what we know as male and female; it is not a contemporary psychological insight, but a biological fact.

At dinner that night I heard of Ugratara, a dark, fierce form of Tara. I was assured that Tara can be quite fierce, though this aspect of her is less well known.[15] She has many aspects, twenty-one in some texts, one hundred and eight in others. She is also well known as Green Tara. (In Tibetan, the word for "green" can also mean "dark" or "swarthy.") She is most commonly seen in her green and white forms, both of which are peaceful and lovely.

An old Tibetan man sat in the corner of the room, saying his *mala,* a Tibetan rosary. I wondered how I would ever come to understand all the complexities that arose as I tried to find Tara. I imagined myself in an ancient maze that twisted and turned back into itself, connecting everything but never clearly revealing the way. There was no simple answer, no single source of Tara.

Tibetans I have spoken with deny any relationship between Kali and Tara, yet there are Hindu texts that address Kali as Tara. "She who is Kali, the supreme Vidya, is Tara also."[16] The great eighteenth-century Bengali devotional poet Ramprasad used the names of Kali and Tara almost interchangeably. He describes Kali's skin as "a dark that lights the world," her name was a sword to him, Tara's a shield.[17] He chanted Durga's name until he brought the sun up. He seeded his heart with Kali's name, knotted Tara's into his hair. They were all Mother to him.[18]

The darkness of these female gods comforted me. It felt like a balm on the wound of the unending white maleness that we had deified in the West. They were the other side of everything I had ever known about God. A dark female God. Yes.

Kali seemed familiar, more lifelike to me in that moment than the Blessed Mother, her image more fraught and complicated than the Virgin's, containing a larger truth. Yet I was not drawn to Kali, only to the Buddha Tara.

I held on to the fragment of Tara's story that I knew like the rosary I had slept with as a child to ward off bad dreams. Her vow to be enlightened in a woman's body promised that, somehow, I could find my way back, that this human, childbearing body I found so difficult could be redeemed.

The dinner party went on into the night, my head was reeling by the time I got a ride back to the hotel. The crisp, cold October air on my face was bracing as I clung to the back of a motorcycle, my leg throbbing from the long day, the crutches close to my side.

I slept fitfully with the cast, often waking in the middle of the night, only to fall back asleep over a book, then wake again with a start. I slipped into a time warp.

The cast had been changed again the day before. I had sat in a warm tub for an hour, softening the plaster, until Lakshmi and Bhawaghita arrived with a pair of garden shears. We cut, unwrapped, cut, tore, and unwound the gauze and plaster until finally the leg was visible again, still swollen and very bruised. No wonder it hurt. Dr. Banskota arrived, wrapped the leg in a shorter, lighter cast, prescribed more medication to take the edge off the pain, and then everyone left. I was alone again.

I felt restless, disoriented, at odds with myself. This situation was much harder than I wanted to admit, and I could feel something inside coming apart. A subtle kind of disintegration between consciousness and unconsciousness had begun to occur. Lack of sleep, physical pain, the effect of seeing no one I had known longer than two weeks gradually had begun to wear on me.

There was no electricity that night in Kathmandu. Power failure was a common occurrence. I sat alone in my room by candlelight, writing.

The heel of my broken leg was on fire. The birds had stopped singing, it was dark outside. A chorus of dogs started up, car horns blared. I had stayed in bed all morning, slipping between dreaming and waking. I was talking to people, only to waken startled and find them not there. I had an image of monks in black robes with red bands around the bottom hem. Something had happened, had someone died? I kept seeing the monks walking and chanting. I could barely distinguish between dreaming and waking.

I wrote in my journal that when I returned to the States, I needed to sell everything and move into a spiritual community. Was there such a place for mothers and children? Trying to care for three children, bear the brunt of financial support, get over a bitter divorce—I felt I could no longer manage.

The contrast between the exotic place I found myself in now, the hunger I had for female deities, and the harsh practicalities I faced at home twisted me inside like a corkscrew. I didn't know how to talk about these things. I was deeply ashamed of being divorced. I wanted desperately to be a good mother, but felt doomed to failure. I was convinced that children had to have at least two parents. There was no father around. I couldn't be a man for my two sons. No matter how much I wanted it to be otherwise, I had found marriage a disaster, being a wife to the men I had picked impossible. How could I help my daughter?

A man walked by my window, still open to the garden, and spat loudly with a long, hard hack. Though I had spent most of the day in or on my bed with the leg elevated, by 4:00 p.m. the pain was intense. I considered the new codeine the doctor had ordered. My head was swimming. I'd tried to avoid taking it whenever possible. I knew that I must have a clear sense of the injury that had to be accommodated if I was to go on with this trek. Yet there came a point when it seemed self-defeating not to take it and I gave in. Combined with alcohol, the codeine would provide a sure reprieve. I swallowed the pills, called room service, and had a beer sent down. I drank it fast, grabbed my crutches, and went outside to find a rickshaw in front of the hotel.

Within half an hour I no longer had to feel the restlessness; the beer and the codeine had taken effect. The city was beautiful in the dark with no electricity, only candles burning and flickering in windows everywhere. I paid the driver extra to go for a long time, and let myself be lost.

The next day I went out to look for a temple that held the complete *Prajnaparamita,* the Heart sutra, written in gold on lapis lazuli. The Heart sutra is a quintessential Buddhist text. I had tried to find the small temple several times but there are hundreds.

Finally I found it, just around the corner from my hotel, but it was all locked up. The barred gate jarred me, awoke me from the illusion in which I had been living. Suddenly I knew that I would not get to the Solu Kumbhu, I would not complete the trek, I would not see Thyangboche Monastery, and I despaired. Though I banged and rattled and banged again at the entry, no one came. The courtyard inside was deserted. The gate was firmly locked. I had been living in a dream and it was over. No entry.

Then night again, the fitful sleeping. I woke up the next morning badly frightened by a nightmare that seemed an ominous warning. A man in the dream was going to shoot everyone inside my house, including my children.

Fortunately, I was no longer alone in Kathmandu. Two friends from the trek had just arrived. They had left the trek early and flown back from Lukla. I met them for breakfast. When I told them about the nightmare, my friend Ann tried to reassure me. She reminded me that my eldest son had just left home for the first time to go away to school. Children leaving is a small death, she assured me. Hers were older and she'd been through it. We agreed to spend the day together sightseeing.

At the river there were ghats, steps down into the water, with women doing laundry, children bathing, and bodies being cremated on wooden funeral pyres alongside one another. Swaddled in white cloth on a furiously burning pyre, the body I watched could hardly be distinguished from the flames, yet to know that it was a body going up in smoke was startling. Monkeys climbed along the bridge railing screeching.

Later we went to visit the Great Stupa at Boudhanath with its mysterious eyes on top. A stupa is a physical symbol of the Buddha's mind, originally built to contain relics. The four pairs of eyes, one on each side of the square that juts out above the great round of the stupa, are the eyes of the four Buddhas who have already appeared. This stupa is said to contain relics of the Buddha Mahakashyapa, the Buddha of the previous age.[19]

We made our round, the circumambulation, circling the stupa clockwise. We turned prayer wheels suspended on cylinders in the circular wall, sending out prayers on the wind as we walked along. A handful of older Tibetans were circumambulating too, telling their beads, saying their mantras under their breath.

Halfway around the stupa we came to the carving of a ferocious deity whose image riveted me to the stones under my feet. Devouring her own entrails, she pulled them out of her stomach and stuffed them into her mouth. She seemed to have been there for centuries. I shook my head in unwelcome recognition. "Spare me that fate!" I thought, as I spun round a prayer wheel and, under my breath, begged for even a seed of enlightenment. We walked on.

By early afternoon I was overwhelmed by all the sights we'd seen at the river and the smells. Bodies burning, the sick, the lame, beggars, lepers, the poor, wide-eyed children, holy men in bright orange robes or merely a loin cloth, their bodies bright with ashes and vermilion stripes across the forehead; and now at Boudhanath, the red-robed monks, the shopkeepers, and at the entry, a legless beggar on a wooden cart.

I waited in the hotel tour bus, unable to purchase the smallest item from any of the shops, there was so much poverty in front of me. Though the driver could protect me from the beggars for a moment, he could never fend off what I had seen today. Nothing of life was hidden. It seemed that humanity in all the misshapen forms of suffering had paraded before me. An old smiling monk with his shaved head hobbled down the street past the bus and disappeared into a tea stall.

I felt nauseated. Once we got back to the hotel, I knew something strange was happening. I was suddenly very hot. As I stood inside my room by one of the beds, my friends Ann and Maggie walked in, but before I could even say anything, a kind of paralysis began to come over me. It started with a searing pain in my neck. I recognized it.

Yes, it is coming back, I have had this pain before, but this time I am also beginning to burn up with fever. Within the next three steps, I am going to be sick to my stomach. I rush past them into the bathroom and vomit hard. Then begins the diarrhea. I am dizzy. The diarrhea, the vomiting are all projectile, propelled out of my body by an enormous force. A few minutes later, I am emptied, weakened and feverish. I walk back into the hallway. They keep saying, "Are you all right?"

The paralysis is moving down my neck into my back, soon I will not be able to move at all. I recognize the sensations. Ann and Maggie stand there surprised and helpless. One moment we are talking about sightseeing and their departure from Kathmandu tomorrow and the next moment I am violently ill. Being good friends, how can they leave me alone like this and just take off tomorrow, they ask.

It is the height of the fall trekking season and airline ticketing seems completely arbitrary, close to impossible. It has taken several days for them to finally get tickets out, and now I am sick. But I know that they can leave and that they must. I was paralyzed nine months ago and now the paralysis has returned. There is nothing they can do. It rushes down my body even as I stand here in the hallway talking, moving down from the neck, through, down the back, I can describe it as it's happening. It's a very strange sensation and yet I am completely calm. "My left arm is going," I tell them as I walk toward the bed, "and now the right.

"Go. This has happened before. I will be all right. I will lie down. Lucy is coming. I won't be left alone. She was coming to get me for dinner. She will help. Keep your tickets, leave, now that you can.

"What you can do is find Dr. Banskota, the orthopedist who took care of my leg. I trust him. Get Dr. Banskota, A. K. Banskota, at the Mission Hospital. Tell him to come. Do not medicate me, do not take me to the hospital under any circumstances. You must promise me that.

"This happened to me before, nine months ago, this same paralysis. Listen to me. I was taken to the hospital, shot full of valium, and it didn't work. That's why it's back. I told everyone then, the doctors, my brother who was there, that this wasn't a medical problem, that it was something else, this is not about the pain in my neck, this is not about muscle spasms. I begged them not to take me to the hospital, but no one listened. The doctors, the nurses, my brother, they all said, 'We know best, here, we're going to give you this medicine, it will make your muscles relax, the pain will go away.' We were in the emergency room by then, they had taken me there by ambulance, and they began an IV valium drip.

"It didn't work. See? Whatever happens, *don't* medicate me, *don't* take me to a hospital. Here it is again. Whatever this is I have to go through with it this time. There is no other way. Go. Find Dr. Banskota."

Soon the paralysis is complete. I can move nothing—arms, legs, head, nothing. I lie on my back on my bed in the hotel room. The fever is strong, the pain consuming, like in childbirth. I slip into an altered state of consciousness. I cannot tell if I'm hallucinating or if what I'm seeing is real, it is so vivid.

I see a mountain outside my window in the garden. But unlike Mount Everest, Chomolungma, Mother Goddess of the Earth to the Nepalese, which I had hoped to see from a climb above Thyangboche, this mountain I view has no snow. It is a mountain of darkness. There is a mountain in darkness. I go into the darkness of the mountain. My children are inside the mountain, I can see inside the mountain. I am seeing into the heart of the world. Is Tara inside the mountain? Is the mountain Tara coming to me?

It is my children coming to me now, somehow I have never had them before. Now Dr. Banskota is here. I can hear him on my right. He is speaking softly. He is telling me to move my hand, my right hand. It doesn't matter if I can only move it the tiniest bit, he says, he wants me to know that I can do it, that I can do this, that I can move, even the slightest bit. He wants me to know that what he is telling me is true, that I will not be paralyzed like this forever. I will be able to move again someday, see, even as he is telling me now to move my hand, with the greatest effort and concentration I am moving my fingers ever so slightly. My hand is extended, my fingers, extended with this seizure, this complete paralysis of my body.

I have lost my body. I can't find my body. It is a terrifying experience to suddenly become completely paralyzed, and yet the terror passes quickly now, like a cloud-shadow moving fast overhead on a sunny, windswept day, it is gone, and I see into the heart of this mountain. There is a huge, nameless Himalayan mountain outside my window. I am seeing it from a distance, for I can see all of it, but it has completely taken up the window and there is no more garden. My fever shoots past 102. I cannot move. How can I see this mountain? Dr. Banskota is on my right, holding my hand. "Yes, try again," he says, "you can do this. It will be all right, you will be able to walk again, yes, this will pass. I have seen this before, you will be all right."

And now he is gone. Who is here, I don't know, I only know that a woman always stays, from the beginning to the end. For three days, she is with me. Lucy. From the beginning I knew she would be with me, that the others could leave, that Lucy would stay, that the paralysis was coming back, that I could not run away, that something was happening inside my body that would not let me go, was not done with me, that by treating it with drugs intravenously in the hospital nine months ago, it had not gone away, it was still inside of me. Now it would have its way with me. Now, as then, I sensed that hospitals and medication were fruitless, that what was happening, though it had taken over my body, was something in my soul.

I am lying on the bed. The doctor is back with me again. Night has come and still I cannot move. The mountain is in the garden. I cannot turn my head, how can I see this mountain, but yet I see it. I must be out of my head, but I have never felt clearer.

I hear a voice from inside the mountain. The voice tells me that there is nothing to fear. I know that Dr. Banskota will think that I am crazy but I do not care. The voice says not to fear. I try to tell Dr. Banskota what I am hearing as he holds my hand, but the words that come out cannot match the clarity of what I hear. I speak in nonsense. I tell Dr. Banskota as he is holding my hand that I am seeing into the heart of the world, that in the heart of the world there are no accidents. The heart of the world broke my leg, stopped me, is holding me down, makes me lie still like this because I couldn't stop myself. I know that this is good. I begin to sing.

Perspiring, fevered, imprisoned by my own body, then the pains begin, deep down in my abdomen. They are ripping me apart. Pain pushes me inside the mountain; it is moving, the mountain is walking inside my body, the mountain is heavy. It is excruciating to be walked on by a mountain, to have this mountain moving inside of me, and I push back, I begin pushing against this mountain inside of me, pushing, working with the pain, as I did in childbirth. I take a breath when the pain comes, breathe out, breathe in, hold my breath and then push, it is coming, and I am in the hospital room again where I had my first son. They have me bound with cuffs around my legs and wrists chained down to a steel delivery table. I don't know what is happening, only that I see a clock, that I am restrained against my will, can't get up, that I thought that I was having a baby, but where is the baby, the baby isn't coming, why isn't the baby coming? Something's gone wrong. He's breech, he is fighting for his life, the cord is twisted, is it wrapped around his neck? How could he be caught inside, why can't I get him out, save him, give him his life? But I am tied down, like a machine that produces boxes, not a person with a mind and heart, not a mother giving birth to a child.

The doctor thinks he knows what to do. He thinks that I don't know how to deliver a baby, that I don't know what to do. He says that he is going to give me a special medication so that I won't remember how bad this delivery is going to be, because if I did, he told me, *You'd never want to have a baby again. Don't worry, I'm going to give you scopolamine. It's an amnesiac,* he tells me. *You won't remember a thing. There, there.* But I know, I know that I need to get up, get off my back, get my feet on the ground, stand up, then gravity can work with me.

I know what to do, I have been doing this for thousands of years, I have delivered millions of babies, for aeons and aeons of time, I know how to give birth, to give life to a child, only I am chained to this table, I cannot help this child whose foot instead of his head has emerged, I cannot get up, there is so little time that he can last struggling like this, he will die if we do not get him out, the sack is broken, he must have air. I am screaming at them, "Let go!", howling like a beast, wild and chained, feet and hands. The doctor reaches over, then the nurse. She puts a gas mask over my face and says,

"Breathe! Breathe this!" I hear the doctor, farther and farther away.

"Scissors." He cuts open the vagina quickly now, gives a yank, and pulls Matthew out. I lose consciousness from the gas. I am twenty years old.

Thirteen months later, I am on a delivery table again. Again I am waking up from the medication, again I see the clock behind the doctor's head. This time I do not even understand that I am giving birth. I only know that I am strapped down, arms and legs. *We can't have you touch yourself, you're not sterile,* someone explains. The doctor is trying to talk to me, but his words are underwater and so far away. All voices are distorted and muffled. I cannot make out the words. I am trying very hard. What is he trying to say? Something about "Push," something about a baby. "Now push," he says again, "don't stop, keep pushing, you have to keep pushing. *Push!*"

Pushing, I am in Nepal and I am pushing, pushing this mountain outside of me, still I cannot move, but now it is my entire body that is held down by some invisible force. There are no chains or straps, but I am held just as surely by whatever paralyzes me and I am thrown back into the experience on the delivery table in the hospital in Texas, where I screamed for them to let me go. Now I am twenty-one, it is my second child, and this time I cannot understand that I am having a baby, all I know is that they won't let me go. There is something black that someone is holding over my face. I turn away, terrified, they are trying to put it over my nose and mouth. Are they trying to kill me? Are they trying to suffocate me, is it a man trying to suffocate me with a pillow, holding it over my face? I am fighting and twisting, pregnant, it is not only my life I fight for but my child's. I am screaming, kicking, finally I manage to scratch his face—does he have a scar?—and he lets me go, but on the delivery table they are still trying to get this black form over my face, and the smell, I cannot tell the difference between then and now, and I fight and scream still, being held down only makes me frenzied. I am sure they are trying to kill me, I am coming out of my skin, I don't understand what people are saying. Finally someone from behind grabs my head, holds it, they put a black gas mask over my face, someone says, "Breathe!" and I go unconscious, am knocked out. Madelon is born. I am twenty-one years old.

Now I am thirty-six and I am in Nepal and I am finally remembering what I was told I would forget.

The voice inside the mountain speaks to me, tells me again not to be afraid, tells me that there is only love in this world. Our choice is to be in love or to be in fear. But to choose to be in love means to have a mountain inside of you, means to have the heart of the world inside you, means you will feel another's suffering inside your own body and you will weep. You will have no protection from the world's pain because you will know it as your own. You will understand that this pain is your own because you are not separate, from life, or from anyone or anything else. But you will fall into a forgetting. You may die before you remember. You will forget that you know this, again and again. Do not be afraid. The body remembers, it never forgets. It is your own knowing that you hide from and do not know.

Now I can feel the labor pains and the doctor is here and I am pushing and I know this is good. I tell Dr. Banskota that I am finally giving birth, I am delivering my son, I am having Matthew, and he says "Good," and holds my hand while I push. I am lying in my own feces and urine and now it is Madelon, and I am pushing, pushing, and again, feces come out, not babies, but I am having the labors I never had, the experience of the muscles contracting and pushing the baby down the birth canal. It is the second stage of labor and this time I can hear the doctor, I can listen, I can understand, I can speak, even if I can't move, and I breathe, hold my breath, then push, and then I am done; then a third labor begins and I am so tired, how can this go on?

No, it is not my third child, Benjamin. No, I didn't have scopolamine when I delivered him.[20] I had finally educated myself, I had learned. I had him without anesthetics. I knew what to do, how to breathe, I was present. His father was with me. I was in my body.

No, this is not Benjamin I am delivering, I don't know who this is. One last push, wet with perspiration, still running a fever, hot, there, is it the afterbirth? I am unable to move, spent. Done.

◆

The body remembers, it never forgets. The voice stopped. I fell asleep. Over eighteen hours had passed. The paralysis was gone, but still I ran a fever and could not eat. Hardly anything would stay down. A culture had been taken to the Peace Corps lab. The diagnosis was severe amoebic dysentery. I was given Furamide, codeine, valium. I could hold down sips of Coca-Cola, suck on a napkin of crushed ice. I was still very sick, but I was no longer paralyzed.

No matter how sick I still was with dysentery, it was clear that something that had always been with me was gone. Some particular kind of fear, fear that I didn't know I had, fear that had weighed me down, been a heavy wooden yoke across the back of my neck, was no longer there. I had the physical sensation of being emptied and lightened. I was like a diver who doesn't feel the weights she uses to stay submerged in water, but on land finds herself burdened. I didn't know that I was held down until the weight was removed and then I shot to the surface.

The words of the Prajnaparamita mantra from the Heart sutra, the Buddhist text, run through my mind: "Gone, gone, gone beyond, and into, Awakening Mind! *Gate, gate, gate, parasamgate! Bodhi! Svaha!*" The gold Sanskrit letters cut into lapis lazuli, treasure of the little temple I had tried to find, engraved on my mind, forever.

Someone put me in a wheelchair, poured me onto a plane, where I was given three seats to stretch out across and fell asleep. I was met in Hong Kong by someone with a wheelchair, taken to a hotel, wheeled to a room, chicken soup was sent up. I tried to eat and could only vomit. I laid down and fell asleep—or did I pass out? The next morning someone came for me with another wheelchair.

There was another ride to the airport, who took me through this? Another airplane, again the seats, again lying down and falling asleep, then over the ocean and San Francisco. Home. Who met me? Another wheelchair, my home, my own home, my children, all three of them, all in one piece unlike me, my own bed, then falling asleep. Then my mother, trying to feed me, undone, so upset because I would not eat, could not. She came to take care of me, but I could not eat. It was too late for my mother to feed me, I was beyond that. Days had passed and still I couldn't keep anything down, not even water.

The nightmare that I had in Nepal of dying began to come true. The slightest noise became unbearable, my senses were completely distorted. When a child closed the window, the sound caused pain. Madelon made a card for me out of cardboard covered with tinfoil. There was a heart drawn in the tinfoil with a streak of lightning through the middle that broke the heart in two. She knew the grief that I held over the dissolution of our family. I had lost 25 pounds in three weeks.

Now I am alone in a hospital room and they are trying to find the vein for an IV. I have been dehydrating badly. The nurse who is trying to find the vein is having trouble. She sticks the needle in, over and over, but each vein she finds collapses. Finally another nurse takes over, finds a good one, gets the drip going, and I tell her, "I am dying, I can feel it, I am so close, all I have to do is say *yes* and I will be gone. I don't know what to do."

She says, "Wait, don't decide now. Put off your decision. It's not time yet," and I fall asleep.

CHAPTER 2

Underneath
◆
California

*whatever you have to say, leave
the roots on, let them
dangle*

And the dirt

*Just to make clear
where they come from.*

—Charles Olson[1]

*California
February 1981*

There is a story underneath this story, behind it, next to it, everywhere
around it but on the page.

I was an alcoholic. I was also addicted to prescription drugs at
one point. Nothing in my life was to make sense until I acknowledged
this fact and began a recovery. I began that process within four
months after my return from Nepal, in February 1981.

It was six o'clock at night and I thought it was morning. I had
fallen asleep on the couch after drinking myself into a blackout while
talking, calling people on the phone, screaming at my daughter, none
of which I could remember until she reminded me of the episode.
Then it came back in fragments, floating like a dream I could barely

remember, only knew that I had had, but could not describe. I knew something was wrong when I woke up.

I asked Madelon to pour me another glass of wine. She refused. She refused to pour the wine and she refused to accept the apologies that I instinctively knew I owed her. I had made them so many times.

She had had enough. She was thirteen years old and she was not fooled. I knew that was the end. I was finished. She had seen through me and called my bluff. She would no longer cooperate and play her part in the alcoholic family. I reached for the phone and called for help.

No alcohol or drugs—absolute abstinence—was the foundation of getting sober, but being able to stay that way, to recover, was another story. It wasn't about not drinking or using, it was about turning my psyche inside out, shaking loose all the broken parts, and throwing out what had gone bad or didn't work. Addiction steals souls. Mine had almost been lost.

There is a direct relationship between addiction and spirituality. Some now describe addiction as a spiritual emergency.[2] I would have to replace my dependence on a substance, something material, with something insubstantial, immaterial. I would have to give up control, I would have to rely on something larger than my mistaken ideas about an individual self.

I would have to find a way of conceiving of a power greater than myself and a way to improve whatever contact I might have with it. I couldn't go back to the God I had grown up with and meditation by itself was not enough. I had to listen to what other recovering alcoholics told me. My ability to stay sober would depend on my spiritual condition. I had a daily reprieve, that was all. I did not want to drink again. I was willing to go to any lengths not to do so. The search for Tara took on a new dimension. It became more than a passionate interest and a longing, finding her became a matter of life and death.

I had gone through five years of "controlled" drinking after it first occurred to me that I *might* have a problem with alcohol. Years of giving myself strict limits, not drinking for months at a time, not drinking at lunch, never drinking in the morning, running, becoming a Zen student, organizing wilderness trips, giving up vodka, gin, bourbon, any hard liquor, not keeping alcohol in the house, only drinking white wine or beer "a little," "only with dinner," only taking a drink after a run in the evening *if* I had sat *zazen* at Green Gulch that morning at 5:00 a.m. and run three miles to the Muir Woods and back in the evening. If I did that it meant that I could have two beers or two glasses of wine at the Pelican Inn before going home to fix dinner for my children. I had an elaborate system of checks and balances worked out mentally. Sometimes it worked and sometimes it did not. What became apparent was that I could not rely on my ability to stop at the limit I had given myself. This inability to rely upon myself was inexplicable, self-defeating in my continued attempts to do so, and utterly degrading and humiliating whenever I failed again.

No matter how much I did to feel good about myself, how many periods of *zazen* I sat at Green Gulch, how many miles I ran, how pristine the wilderness I hiked into, how far, how exciting the rafting trip was, how successful the climbing seminar, how many books I read, how a relationship was going, how many pounds I lost, it would all be obliterated by alcohol. One evening I could stop at the Inn, have a glass of wine, visit with friends and neighbors, and go home. No problem. Another time I would stop for a drink at five-thirty and have several before finding myself on the phone at eight-thirty or nine at night, calling my children, telling them that I was coming home "soon," to go ahead and have a bite to eat and begin their homework. They had done that hours ago and were getting ready for bed.

That experience, repeated again and again, against all my best intentions, against all my willpower, against reason, against everything I knew about being a good mother, against my upbringing, against all my promises to myself and to my children, that experience repeated, with no *predictability*, beat me into the ground. The times I was able to stop were mere seduction. They gave me false hope, fed the illusion that I really could control my drinking, shored up my crumbling self-esteem. I would always walk into the inn full of good intentions. But when I walked out again was no longer in my control.

Now being able to stay sober depended upon making a radical change. Staying alive meant staying sober. I had gone through suicidal depressions and blackouts. I had been completely and hopelessly demoralized. To drink again meant risking suicide. The fact that I almost died after dreaming that my life and my children's were in danger underscored the gravity of the situation. The message was clear. I had to start all over, in earnest, at a deeper level than I had ever known before. I had to put my life on a spiritual basis or die.

Jung gave us the alchemical formula for healing alcoholism and addiction many years ago—"Spiritus contra spiritum," it takes spirit to cure spirit.[3] In the early 1930s he treated a man for alcoholism whom all had given up being able to help maintain sobriety. Jung's prescription was for nothing less than a spiritual transformation.[4] He wrote later that he thought it no accident that in Latin, "we use the same word for the highest religious experience as well as the most depraving poison." Spiritus. That was the answer.[5]

CHAPTER 3

*Fallen Down
Out of the Sky*

♦

Cambridge, Massachusetts

The Great Mother *remains true to her essential and eternal and mysterious darkness, in which she is the center of the mystery of existence.*

—Erich Neumann[1]

Cambridge, Massachusetts
October 1983

I arrived late, well after dark. Someone opened the door and from the end of the hallway I could make out a screen with slides being shown of Nepal. I had never been to my friend Johnnie's house before. She was out of town, but the woman who lived downstairs assured me that there was plenty of room. "Come over, stay here, it's fine," she had said to me over the phone when I called.

"There's plenty of room. No one here but me. I'm Tara, Tara Doyle. I'm showing slides tonight of Nepal. Perhaps you'd like to see them too?"

The slide changed as I was walking into the darkened room. Now on the screen was a picture of Thyangboche Monastery in the Solu Kumbhu. Just over the courtyard, along the balcony watching the monks dancing in their elaborately carved masks, were at least three members of the trek that I had been on and had to leave in 1980.

I burst out in surprise, "How did you get these pictures? Those are my friends, they're from the group I was with, that's my neighbor on the left. Were you there too?"

"Yes, I was with a friend, but I met those people at the lama dances," she said. "Where were you?"

On the screen the sky over Thyangboche Monastery was an azure blue, clean and brilliant. High in the Himalayas the air is washed and purified, dry and sharp.

I did not know how to tell her what it would take me years to put down on paper. So I told her only that I had broken my leg and that I had been in Kathmandu. I told her that I wanted to go back, that I was very interested in the Buddha Tara. Clearly she knew something about her or she would not have taken that name.

"True," she began.

Tara Doyle was a graduate student at Harvard Divinity School and co-founder of the Buddhist Studies Program in Bodh Gayā, India, for Antioch College. She spent several months out of the year in India and Nepal.

"Have you heard about the image of Tara growing out of the rock in Pharping, Nepal?" she asked. Pharping is a little village in the Kathmandu Valley.

"Let me show you a picture of her. I saw her first in 1976 and then again last year. It seems that she's growing, at least that's what the Tibetans and Nepalis believe. When the image first appeared in the rock it was only about two inches tall. Now it's at least eight inches high. It's all happened within the last ten years."

That night, before going to sleep, I thumbed through Tara Doyle's copy of *Mother Worship,* a collection of anthropological studies and field research on Mother Goddess worship around the world. There was a photograph of the Black Madonna in Switzerland, Our Lady of the Dark Forest at Einsiedeln. A black Madonna in Switzerland struck me as a strange and remarkable occurrence. I didn't recall that there were any dark female divinities in Christianity. I thought they were unique to religions such as Hinduism and Buddhism. I could remember virtually nothing about a dark or black Madonna despite my years of Catholic upbringing.

Was the blackness of the Virgin a thread of connection to Tara, Kali, or Durga, or was it mere coincidence? A black Virgin in Africa would be self-explanatory, but a Virgin painted coal black in Switzerland, what did it mean? The features seemed caucasian. The essay "Why the Virgin Is Black"[2] mentioned several such Virgins in Europe. I read the piece with great curiosity, then fell asleep.

Before the stay in Cambridge was over, Tara and I had begun to plan a trip to Nepal. She would lead a Buddhist Studies trek for Women in the Wilderness to Thyangboche Monastery in the spring of 1985. I would try to join them and complete the trek that ended for me with the broken leg in 1980. But whether I made it in time or not, she would take me to see the Buddha Tara in the rock at the village of Pharping.

Some months later a brief entry in *Newsweek* magazine caught my eye. The Virgin Mary was reported to be appearing in the barks of trees in at least three villages in Poland.[3] I was intrigued, not that I believed it was actually happening, but that it seemed to be such a similar phenomenon to what had been reported about the Tara in Pharping. I wondered what was going on in the *spiritus mundi,* the spirit of the world, that reports of female deities literally emerging out of rocks and trees were surfacing in both East and West. The simultaneity was symbolically important. My growing interest in Poland was heightened by the fact that the patron of Poland is one of the most famous Black Madonnas of Europe, Our Lady of Czestochowa, the treasure of the Monastery of Jasna Gora.

Coincidences began to multiply. Gilles Quispel, Historian of Religion at Utrecht University and a protégé of Jung, came to lecture at the Jung Institute in San Francisco on the Black Madonna. Quispel played an important role in the acquisition, translation, and publication of Christian Gnostic Gospels such as the Gospel of Thomas. Elaine Pagels' book, *The Gnostic Gospels,* notes Quispel's early role in the international effort of scholars to retrieve and translate these early texts, originals of which may contain Christian traditions older than the New Testament.[4] The leather-bound papyrus manuscripts were found preserved in an earthenware jar at Nag Hammadi in Upper Egypt in 1945. For Quispel, the Black Madonna plays a crucial psychic role which he described in Jungian terms as symbolizing the earth, matter, the feminine in man, and the self in woman. He had written earlier that unless men and women alike become conscious of this primeval image of the Black Madonna and integrate it within themselves, humankind would be unable to resolve the problems of materialism, racism, women's liberation, and all that they imply.[5] I was eager to hear him. The Unitarian Church was crowded to overflow capacity for his talk.

Hearing Quispel added another dimension. For him, the Black Madonna is the only living symbol left in Christianity. He related her to the early Christian Gnostic tradition in which the Mother was also called "Wisdom," the "Holy Spirit," "Earth," "Jerusalem," even "Lord."[6] To the early Jewish Christians, the Holy Spirit was personified as the Mother and prayed to because She was God as well.[7] Jesus called the Holy Spirit his Mother in the *Gospel According to the Hebrews*.

Among the early Christian texts found at Nag Hammadi is a poem uttered by a feminine power that sounds closer to Kali than to the Blessed Mother.

Thunder, Perfect Mind

> For I am the first and the last.
> I am the honored one and the scorned one.
> I am the whore and the holy one.
> I am the wife and the virgin. . . .
> I am the barren one,
>   and many are her sons. . . .
> I am the silence that is incomprehensible . . .
> I am the utterance of my name.[8]

It was a powerful voice, lost to the desert silence where it lay buried for over two thousand years. In the meantime, the liturgy developed ouside of the traditions in which the Holy Spirit was feminine. By the time Rome took control of the Church, the Holy Spirit was defined in Latin as *spiritus sanctus,* undisputedly masculine.[9]

The Black Madonna has had a widespread effect on Western culture, whether we have known about her or not. She is the symbol of the Polish nation. She was Goethe's inspiration for the eternal feminine in *Faust.* St. Ignatius gave his sword to the Black Madonna of Montserrat in Spain, became a priest, and founded the Jesuit Order.

Ephesus, the ancient center for the worship of the Great Goddess Artemis/Diana, was the same place that Mary was declared *Theotokos,* the Mother of God, by the early Christians on June 22, A.D. 431, at the Third Ecumenical Council amidst all manner of controversy and celebrations,[10] torchlight processions through the streets, cheering and shouting of "Praise to the *Theotokos.*"

Ephesus, capital of the Roman province of Asia, was home to the Temple of Diana, one of the seven wonders of the world. Diana was the Roman form of the Greek Artemis. According to Quispel, the archaic Greek wooden statue in the temple was black like the meteorite that had preceded it, the *Diopetes,* which means "fallen down out of the sky." Artemis at Ephesus, now western Turkey, had been worshipped before the Greeks arrived in 1200 B.C. It was on this temple site of Artemis/Diana, or near it some say, that later a shrine to Mary was built. Quispel traces the tradition of the Black Madonna back to the iconography of this black Artemis/Diana at Ephesus.[11] The great pre-Christian center of worship of the Great Mother became the center of worship for Mary the Mother of God, the *Theotokos.*

Then Quispel showed slides. One was of a medieval fresco showing the Black Madonna with a woman's face and torso with huge wings, all in black. When he connected this fresco with the biblical Woman in the Wilderness of Revelation, I was startled.

Is it possible to trace out connections through such obscure fragments? The mind is always trying to make the world fit, to assure itself that there is order, reason, and explanation. Perhaps the only place these deities are contiguous is inside my mind. I spoke directly with Quispel after the lecture.

"Yes, the Black Madonna and the Woman in the Wilderness are the same," he assured me. I left not knowing what this meant, though my heart was pounding.

I turned back to the seventeenth-century Order of the Woman in the Wilderness in Pennsylvania. The Book of Revelations (especially the apocryphal gospels) had broad impact on the European migrations to the colonies,[12] often overlooked in mainstream historical accounts. The Order of the Woman in the Wilderness was one of the spiritual communities important to the founding days. Mystical feminism runs through the American grain. This Order was part of the phenomenon of "mystic communitarians" that formed in the colonies.[13] The Shakers and the Ephrata followed in the early eighteenth century. Quakers came in the name of the "Holy Experiment" as well.

Following the thread of the Woman in the Wilderness led back to the Christian mystical tradition. Jakob Boehme, the Christian mystic that the founder Johann Kelpius followed, was in turn influenced by the great medieval mystic Meister Eckhart, who wrote of God as Mother.

Eckhart taught that one had to become a womb in order to receive God's spirit. Meister Eckhart, the abbess Hildegarde of Bingen, Mechtild of Magdeburg, and Julian of Norwich all spoke of the Motherhood of God.

Julian, the medieval English anchoress, wrote that "this fair lovely word 'mother' is so sweet and so kind in itself that it cannot truly be said of anyone or to anyone except of him who is the true Mother of life and all things. To the property of motherhood belong nature, love, wisdom and knowledge, and this is God."[14] She described God as Mother and God as Father and Mother. Jesus was Mother to her. Early Gnostic Christians spoke of a Divine Mother as well as Divine

Father. The sixteenth-century Christian nun and mystic Maria Mad-
dalena De'Pazzi used the image of lovemaking in her meditations.
She was found stripping the ornaments from an image of the child
Jesus, saying, "I want you naked, O my Jesus, for I could not bear
you in the infinity of your virtues and perfections; I want your naked,
naked humanity."[15] Hebrew tradition contains the Shekinah, God's
Bride, or the Indwelling of God.

I was not alone in the desire for another kind of God. Longing
for darkness was also a longing for the womb of God. The Buddhists
call it *emptiness*. It is the female principle. One could also say this
womb, this emptiness, is the Buddha Tara in her many forms.

The time had come for me to leave again for India and Nepal.

CHAPTER 4

Where Tara Emerges

♦

*The Way to Pharping Village,
Kathmandu, Nepal*

*I went to a sister
I thought I could trust.
She taught me the dharma,
the elements that make me,
the nature of perception,
and earth, water, fire and wind.*

*I heard what she said
and sat cross-legged
seven days full
of joy.*

*When on the eighth
I stretched my feet out,
the great dark was torn apart.*

—The *Therigata*[1]

*Khajuraho, India
March 1985*

The village of Khajuraho, on the way to Varanasi. The evening air
was balmy and soft at the thousand-year-old temples of the Chandela
clan, stunning sandstone fragments of medieval Hindu sacred art and
architecture. All the temples stand empty now but for Shiva's, Kali's
consort.

That spring night in front of the temples, dancers in brilliant colors flashed like flames, the soles of their feet hot pink, the palms of their hands dyed red, whirling deeper, boring a hole into night.

Varanasi, the ancient pilgrimage site, is sacred to both Hindu and Buddhist alike. At Sarnath, Deer Park, Buddha gave his first sermon. I circumambulated the stupa that marks the site of his first public teaching.

The great Mother Ganga rolls down out of the Himalayas, pouring out of blue ice at the mouth, the sacred waters to which all return. Down at the ghats before dawn, I bought candles in tiny boats of stitched-together leaves to float like prayers on the water. The boat rocked as I stepped in. We pushed off in the dark, just before dawn, rowing out into the river to watch the sunrise. Leaning down over the side of the boat I set my tiny candle adrift in the darkness now dotted with tiny flames.

The sun rose like a giant drum beating, the great God Shiva, Hindus believe. The light pulsed and revealed a day of people bathing in the river, old men praying on the steps above, and adepts in yogic postures. Smoke rose from the funeral pyres, where bodies burned. Sacred to Shiva, Varanasi is the most auspicious place for a devout Hindu to die.

On shore, I made my way back to a taxi through the thin, winding, crowded streets—holy men in prayer seated in tiny alcoves, cows lumbering slow and dusty, smells of food cooking, hot pink flowers for sale, the bustle of shops opening, monkeys chattering on a temple roof, and the beggars.

I went into a large Shiva temple. Shiva is well known for his fierce side. He is frequently depicted with a necklace of skulls, like his consort, Kali. Walking down the long main hallway barefooted, I was drawn off to a small room on the right with only one statue in it. It was an unusual statue, a goddess, seated and peaceful, coal black but for the whites of her eyes and a dark yellow necklace of fresh marigolds around her neck.

It was Kali. I could hardly believe our guide, despite the fact that he was very knowledgeable. How could this be, I asked. He assured me that despite the preponderance of her image as ferocious, Kali has many manifestations; this is only another one. Yes, even Kali has a peaceful side.

I had never seen her depicted in this way before. No necklace of skulls, no red tongue protruding, this was not the embattled, gaunt hag sprung from Durga's brow. This was a lovely, peaceful being seated in the cross-legged posture of meditation, her hands gracefully folded, wearing a beneficent smile much like the Buddha Tara or the Madonna.

I was relieved to see this side of Kali. I wondered if being sober allowed me to see her peaceful aspect. Caught in the downward spiral of addiction, I had seen her only as a wrathful destroyer. Finding this statue felt like a small benediction. The blackness of her form seemed almost luminous to me, affirming my sense of a beneficent and redeeming dark. This was a darkness I longed for. My mind leaped to the Black Madonna at Einsiedeln in Switzerland. Intuition told me that these two deities were connected.

There was a quality of peacefulness that the two statues shared that was striking and curious to me. Both were painted coal black. I needed to know more about the relationship I sensed was there. I had my camera with me, but no flash. Putting my camera bag on the floor, I stood off to one side, set the aperture as wide open as I could to get a reading in the dim light. Despite the poor conditions, I took several photographs. I needed to know more about this Kali. I wanted her image with me.

Kathmandu, Nepal
March 1985

From Varanasi I fly to Kathmandu. Now it's late March. I wait for spring, but the rains won't come. The clouds settle and gather around the foothills of the Himalayas, blocking the view, but no rain falls. Dust hangs in the air, whipped up by the wind each afternoon. It catches in my throat, already dry with the unfamiliar altitude of nearly five thousand feet. It seems too dry to be spring. But in Nepal it won't rain until summer, then the monsoons come. Familiar seasons are reversed.

The morning cloud cover meant that the flights are canceled to Lukla, day after day. Lukla, the tiny, planewreck-laden airstrip at eleven thousand feet that I had wanted to fly into so long ago. I wanted to go to Thyangboche Monastery and see what I had missed before, but now I'm unwilling to risk the uncertainty of the flights and the chance of being stranded for days at Lukla waiting for a flight back to the valley.

Here in Kathmandu I have work to do. I've missed the trek with Tara Doyle, but I will at least see the image of the Goddess Tara that's growing in the rock at Pharping. Trekking will have to be put off again to another year. I will stay in the valley, dry as it is.

Tara Doyle and I plan to meet at the Vajra Hotel, where the group stayed before the trek. The day before they were due back from the mountains, I wandered up to the top floor of the hotel to the library. While I was studying the titles, an old man came around from a corner of the room. He had long white hair, a full white beard, and wore the orange robes of a *sanyasin,* a holy man. His appearance startled me.

"What book are you looking for?" he asked in English.

"I'm interested in Tara, and especially the Tara in the rock at Pharping," I told him.

He began to take down books that he said I should become familiar with. "Here," he said, handing me one after another, "you must know that Tara is also Kali and Parvati and Durga." I stood there as he loaded my arms down with books.

"She has a thousand names," he assured me. "Here, sit down, child," he said, motioning to a table underneath the open window. "Let me sing something for you."

The morning was bright and sunny. I could hardly believe my

luck at coming across this *sanyasin*. It felt like a sign that I was on the right path.

When he had finished, he handed me a thin, blue-lined notebook with the song handwritten both in Sanskrit and in English.

"It's a Hymn to the Divine Mother Craving Forgiveness," he explained. "You can copy down what it means if you like it." Then he turned and walked out of the room, humming to himself.

Alone in the library, sitting by the open window with a fresh soft morning breeze, I quickly copied down the translation:

Alas, I do not know either the mystical word or the mystical diagram, nor do I know the songs of praise to thee, nor how to welcome thee, nor how to meditate on thee, . . . nor how to inform thee of my distress. But this much I know, O Mother, that to take refuge in thee is to destroy all my miseries.

It was the first day of spring.

Tara Doyle arrived the next day and soon made arrangements for us to get to the village of Pharping. She found a translator, a Swiss woman who had also taken the name of Tara. Taras surrounded me. We took off in a cloud of dust one afternoon in a Nepalese taxi for the half-hour drive to the village of Pharping. Noisy, windy, dusty, and bumpy on the road to Pharping, I tried to tape-record and take notes in the back of the taxi on everything our translator was telling us about the Goddess Tara.

"Kali corresponds to the Tibetan goddess Palden Lhamo, a wrathful form of Tara that is indeed a fierce protector. She's known as the goddess Sri Devi in Sanskrit. Yet Kali and Tara cannot be looked at in the same way. Debate continues as to whether or not the goddess Tara came from Hinduism or is a completely Tibetan creation that was later incorporated into Hinduism and then became immensely popular. There is more agreement about the idea that Palden Lhamo is Tibetan in origin."

I gave up note taking; the road was full of potholes now and I could hardly keep my hand to the page. It was a warm day and we had to keep the windows rolled down, despite the dust, so Swiss Tara was shouting this information to me across the back seat of the taxi. In between the translator's shouts, Tara Doyle tried to dissuade me from worrying too much about the connection between Tara and Kali.

"To try to sort this out would be very frustrating. Imagining that there might be a single source is itself a Western idea. Give it up, dear. This is a very different world," she assured me, with the emphasis on the *very*, "it's multivalent, enormously complicated and ancient."

The road ended in the village. We walked the rest of the way on footpaths, past village homes with prayer flags flying, rice fields, and wide-eyed children playing. Tara Doyle stopped us just below the shrine, to visit the shrine keeper's house and have a cup of tea.

Tara's rock was only recently enclosed in the small cement shrine. Until the Tara began to emerge from it a few years ago, the large rock sat out in the open air. It has a carving of the Hindu elephant god Ganesh on one side, making this a Hindu shrine as well.

A monk in claret robes looks down on us from the doorway. His expression is skeptical—What do we want with his shrine? The shrine is small, a room perhaps ten feet by fourteen. As we enter, bowing, the two Taras begin talking in Tibetan and Nepali.

Our translator starts to explain the purpose of our visit to the little nun, the *ani,* who has been sitting and chanting to this emerging Tara for the past eleven years.

She wears the red robes of a nun, has a shaved head, and bright eyes that greet us warmly, despite her crooked smile. Her jaw is misshapen, her face distorted. At first she doesn't understand what we are asking about. Then I show her a color Xerox made from the photograph of the Tara in the rock taken by Tara Doyle when she

Tara in the rock at Pharping, Nepal. (Author)

last visited Pharping. The *ani* bursts out laughing, begins waving the Xerox in the air to show the monk and the shrine keeper's wife, then touches the bottom edge to the top of her head, a gesture of reverence to the deity. The exchange comes alive when she realizes that we are interested in her goddess Tara. I want to secure her permission to photograph, to measure the height of the Tara as well as make a traditional offering.

This little Tara is delicate, small, and somewhat indistinct. Covered with *tika,* bright vermilion powder, the *ani* explains that Tara is growing into a taller, fuller image than when she first appeared.

Tara is also counted as the mother of the Tibetan people, their progenitor. Their father was Avalokitesvara, the Great Bodhisattva of Compassion. There are many different versions of this story, but as I see this Tara in the rock, I am reminded of an ancient pre-Buddhist version of the legend in which a divine rock ogress united with a divine red monkey to produce the stock of the Tibetan people.[2] Buddhists later determined that the rock ogress was an incarnation of Tara, the red monkey an incarnation of Avalokitesvara. A rock ogress. I liked that.

The monk offers one of the cushions stacked against the wall. I bow to thank him for his offer and sit down. I want to sit in front of this image of Tara in the rock, just sit, like in the *zendo* at Green Gulch in the morning. It is a new day. The sky is clear and windswept. It has been a long way to Pharping. Now I am sitting on the other side of the world surrounded by Taras. There could be no more auspicious sign.

Could this image really be growing out of the rock? It was an appealing notion. The *ani* swore to it, but I had been inoculated with Western skepticism. It was too much to ask that I believe this. Faith. I didn't think that faith was required in Buddhism. I wanted someone to prove or disprove that Tara is emerging to me. I had had enough of belief.

The Tibetan nun had no such problem. Her belief and devotion were clear. When I offered her my Xerox of this image of Tara in the rock as a gift, she laughed. Our translator explained to me that while she was grateful for the gesture, the *ani* thought that I would need the picture of the Goddess Tara more than she would. After all, she assured us through our translator with her crooked, knowing grin, she has the real Tara.

I returned to Pharping twice more. I wanted scientists, not believers, to see the rock. Three days later, the senior geologist of His Majesty's Royal Department of Geology and Mines, Mr. G. S. Thapa, accompanied me.

It is very dry and windy, dusty, as we walk along the road to the shrine. As we near the hillside, we pass a small, ochre-colored, thatched-roof house on our left. Three small children are laughing and calling to one another, while an old man, his face lined with crevasses like the mountains, squats near them in the yard and stares at me. He steadies himself with a bamboo pole. He wears dirty white pants and a white shirt. He has a shock of white hair, and though his body is bent with age, his face has the air of a three-year-old child. His look is arresting. I am startled by the sense that he is not looking at me, but through me.

I had seen him the other day when I was out to visit the shrine. I wanted to stop and take his photograph, his look was so striking, but he was bent over, just buttoning up his pants having relieved himself by the side of the road, and I felt uncomfortable, as though I shouldn't have noticed him in this awkward stance. I had not turned back.

Today I pass him again. Still the same intense look in his eyes. No smile, no particular expression, just the looking. Mr. Thapa and I reach the shrine and make our offerings to the deities. Since he is Hindu, we also make offerings today to Ganesh, the elephant-headed god carved out of the rock near where the shape of Tara has emerged. Then we step aside to examine the figure of Tara more closely. With the ani's permission, we make a precise measurement of Tara's height, and afterwards we take a bit of red vermilion powder from the rock with our fingers and smudge it on our foreheads, symbolizing the opening of the mythical third eye of wisdom, between and just above the brows.

"The rock is primarily limestone with a lot of silica in it, like this rock here," Mr. Thapa tells me once we are outside the shrine, knocking a chip off the rocky surface we stand next to on the hillside. "Limestone leaches water. That would explain the stories of milk coming from her breasts. Water leaching through limestone is cloudy and can look milky.

"It must have been carved. Yes, I think so," he says. "I agree that much of the shape looks as though it is 'growing' out of the rock, but that would be impossible. Impossible. Whoever carved it was very, very good. Yes, perhaps he saw something like the shape of Tara in the rock, the way it was already eroding. Yes, that is possible, and then he simply brought out that form of Tara and added to it. But 'growing,' I don't think it's possible. No."

Just after midnight I am wakened in my hotel room by the sound of dogs barking nearby. Their sound throbs on the night air. The old man's face that I had seen again today floats up amidst the jumble of the day's color. His eyes hold me and I begin to see.

The following day Tara Doyle and I go to Boudhanath to meet the Venerable Tulku Chos Kyi Nyima Rinpoche, who has also seen the image of Tara in the rock at Pharping. Tara Doyle has known him for some time. He's one of the younger lamas, in his thirties, and he teaches in the Buddhist Studies Program at Bodh Gayā, India.[3] He speaks English and has been to the West. She suggested him as an authority to consult amongst the Tibetans who are familiar with this phenomenon.

Rinpoche means "precious jewel" and is a term of respect for a recognized teacher. But Chos Kyi Nyima is also a Tulku, a recognized reincarnation of an enlightened being, one might even say an actual form of the Buddha.[4] In the Tibetan tradition, a Tulku is a reincarnated lama who has voluntarily come back to be helpful to others, an act of supreme generosity and selflessness.

We stop to buy oranges and a *khata,* the long white ceremonial scarf traditionally offered to a lama as a sign of respect. Chos Kyi Nyima's monastery sits just behind the giant stupa at Boudha. Circumambulating the stupa, turning prayer wheels as I had done five years ago, I feel a rush of delight at being back in Nepal, whether I get to Thyangboche or not.

"I have seen such things, yes, of course it is happening," the Venerable Tulku Chos Kyi Nyima Rinpoche smiles and tells me when I ask if he believes that Tara is growing out of the rock at Pharping.

"Yes, I have seen it myself. At first it was only this high," he moves his hands apart to show a height of four inches or so, "and now it is this big, yes?" he says, indicating a height of ten to twelve inches.

"Yes, Rinpoche," I reply. Tara Doyle sits next to me on a thick, rose-colored Tibetan carpet covering the floor of Chos Kyi Nyima's receiving room. Erik Hein Schmidt, his translator, is to my left. Over Rinpoche's head is an elaborate yellow silk canopy embroidered with gold threads. A pot full of purple and white orchids blooms on the red-lacquered chest in front of Rinpoche. Next to the orchids is a vase of large, open roses, pale pinks and brilliant reds. The chest itself is elaborately carved with figures of lions, painted in bright hues of blue, yellow, and green. Chos Kyi Nyima sits cross-legged in his red robes and sleeveless yellow silk top on his couch behind the red-lacquered chest, laughing.

"Is it so strange to imagine that the mind when concentrated could do this?" he asks. "The power of devotion calls Tara out of the rock, yes?"

I show him the magazine clipping on the reported appearance of the Madonna in the bark of trees in Poland.

"If no one is making this image, then it is very similar to what we are talking about here. We have many occurrences like this in Tibetan Buddhism. We call it *rangjung,* it means 'self-arising.' I have seen a skull with the imprint of the deity that that person had visualized every day in his meditation.

"Some people came here from Russia not too long ago and told me that the words *Om Mani Padme Om* were growing in a rock on a special mountain. Twenty years ago, the letters began to appear. They wanted to know what that means. I told them that *Om Mani Padme Om* is a very important mantra, it means 'the jewel in the lotus.' They should say it themselves, over and over, then they will know what it means.

" 'Why does it appear?' they asked.

"So I asked them: 'Do you have some people who are interested in Buddhism?'

" 'Oh, yes,' they said. 'Then that is why,' I explained. These things appear because of the power and blessings of enlightened beings. Such beings work through the power of mental substance and the power of concentration. We already know about the power of material substance.

"Western science has been working with the power of material substance for some time, but the power of mental substance and the power of concentration can accomplish incredible things as well. Under the right circumstances, the enlightened mind concentrated in a certain direction can even bring an image of the deity out of solid rock.

"Do you believe these things?" he asks me with his warmest smile.

I don't know what to think. Not so long ago, we scoffed at people who said we would fly. Now we have reached the moon and the planets, peered into the outer galaxies, gone far beyond. Why could it not be possible? Do we say something is "impossible" because we have no explanation? My mind is open. Believe? I'm not sure that I know what that means any more. I only know that I am happy here.

But I have one more question. Just above the rock with Tara in the village of Pharping is the famous Asura Cave where Padmasambhava, Guru Rinpoche, spent a great deal of time meditating before he went to Tibet to teach. I had begun to puzzle with the question of whether or not a site becomes sacred because, for example, Guru Rinpoche went there, or if the ground was already holy and that's why he was drawn to that specific place. I ask Chos Kyi Nyima what he thinks, "Why this one? Why Asura Cave and not another one nearby?"

"The location itself was already special, it's believed that that's why Guru Rinpoche went there," he says. "That's most likely why the image of Tara is appearing there too," Erik adds.

It had been pointed out to me that uranium was often found on land that traditional peoples, both in the United States and around the world, had designated as sacred ground. A North American Indian friend once assured me that there was a rationale to what had been designated sacred. Not all sacred lands hold uranium. But the designation of a site as sacred to native peoples may be informed by a wisdom that we disregard at our peril.

How could people thousands of years ago know about uranium? A professor of botany explained that it was simple—the meticulous observation of plants. Ever since then I had wanted to know what was underneath or around a sacred site.

Chos Kyi Nyima's reply confirmed my sense that there might be a unique feature of natural history to be found at the site as well. Stories can also be maps, guides to a sacred landscape.

Tara Doyle and I met for morning meditations in her quiet corner room over the garden. It had been a long time since I sat in meditation with anyone else. I had been sitting *zazen* alone for the most part the past three years; the abbot of San Francisco Zen Center had been asked to leave amid a series of both sexual and financial scandals that disrupted and threatened the community.

Some left. Others stayed to rebuild the gifted but now fragmented community. I withdrew more and more. The result was that I lost both a teacher and a *sangha,* the spiritual community. I couldn't talk about Buddhist practice to the recovery community and I couldn't talk about the struggle to recover from alcoholism to the Buddhist community. I was too uncomfortable with it myself. But whether I sat alone or with others was not an issue. I knew that spiritual practice was critical to my ability to continue to stay sober.

Over time something in my meditation practice changed. At first I had continued the simple form of *zazen* that I had begun with, counting the breath up to ten and beginning again. This is an elementary, basic practice. Yet as I continued to sit, Christ began to appear in my meditation, then Mary. I didn't like this. I didn't like this at all. I wanted them to go away. I was done with them, I thought, I had left the Church. I tried to ignore them, to let them go, tried to go back to my breath, but the very effort to resist fed them, the resistance gave them energy and they got stronger. I had to find a way to face them.

In Zen Buddhism there is a *koan,* a wisdom riddle, which advocates radical acceptance: "The Way is easy, only avoid picking or choosing." Buddhism teaches that we create suffering, in part, by having desires and aversions. Practice meant working with what is so, whether I liked it or not. I began to let myself see Christ, to visualize him behind me. I accepted him into my practice. As I continued the daily meditations, Mary gradually took a place on my left, the Buddha on my right (from time to time they changed sides). Mary and Jesus were my witnesses at first; then over time, beloved friends. The Buddha Tara was always in front of me.

It was not easy for me to talk about this, especially to another Buddhist. I thought I would be chided for doing something wrong. But I spoke up, and to my surprise, Tara Doyle pointed out that the form of meditation that had evolved was very Tibetan, similar to a mandala, a concentric pattern or "blueprint" used to focus certain meditation practices. She encouraged me to talk about this with Chos Kyi Nyima Rinpoche when we went back to see him.

"You can ask for teachings about Tara too if you want. You can take Refuge with him. I'll do it with you. I've taken them before but it's good to renew the vows.

"Taking Refuge is a ceremony that marks the Buddhist path. It separates Buddhists from non-Buddhists. The next step is to take the bodhisattva vows. In the bodhisattva vows you promise that you will seek enlightenment for the benefit of all beings, not just for yourself, but for everyone, even beyond that, for all beings. We could ask him for those too if you like," she said.

"Taking Refuge" is basic to all Buddhist practice, despite the tremendous diversity among the different schools. It is sometimes described as a ceremony akin to baptism, the formal entrance to the path. It remains central to all the traditions within Buddhism. In it one takes refuge in the Buddha, the Dharma, and the Sangha, the Three Jewels, and vows to refrain from harming all beings. The Buddha is simply the Buddha or the principle of enlightenment; the Dharma means the teachings; the Sangha, the community of fellow seekers who have embarked upon this path, the spiritual community.

Two days later, midmorning, we took Refuge with Chos Kyi Nyima in a brief version of this important ceremony. Sitting in the corner of a large shrine room upstairs in his monastery, surrounded by statues and tangkha paintings of the Buddhas and bodhisattvas, we sat on the floor in front of Rinpoche. He read texts in Tibetan which we repeated phrase by phrase after him. I was told to imagine the Buddha appearing above his head, but not only Gautama Buddha, all the Buddhas of the past and future who are yet to come. They would be the witnesses to our vows.

The ceremony felt ancient. I sat cross-legged, with one of Rinpoche's dogs curled up quietly at my feet. In the middle of the ceremony, an old monk came in to ask for a blessing. Unperturbed by the interruption, Rinpoche received him, blessed him, and sent the monk on his way. Then turning his attention back to Tara Doyle and me, Chos Kyi Nyima cut a lock of hair from the tops of our heads, symbolizing the departure from old ways onto this path. I was to leave behind the past and now place my trust in the Three Jewels of the Buddha, Dharma, and the Sangha. Then he snapped his fingers to indicate the precise moment that we embarked anew upon this path.

Afterwards, in his receiving room again, I spoke to him about my meditation practice. He nodded and smiled. I pressed him about the relationship of student and teacher. How is one to know? He said that the appropriate relationship becomes obvious. Sometimes it takes one minute, sometimes three years.

I had begun thinking about asking him to be my teacher and I told him so. I knew that I needed guidance. I wanted him to be thinking about it too. How could this work? I didn't know how we could have a relationship ten thousand miles apart, but he was not concerned. He grinned and simply said to come back the day after tomorrow.

Two days later we return to Chos Kyi Nyima's monastery. Tara Doyle guides me through this experience a step at a time, explaining patiently what to do, what's appropriate to ask, the correct protocol. Today we will take the bodhisattva vows together, promising to work for enlightenment for the sake of all beings, for all times, not just this lifetime. A new kind of bond is formed between Tara Doyle and me in this ceremony. We become dharma sisters and our relationship takes on a new depth. We begin more openly to share our spiritual path.

Next, I request a Tara initiation from Rinpoche. An initiation or empowerment ceremony constitutes permission to do a particular meditation practice. An initiation is the entrance to Vajrayana or tantric practice, in which one visualizes oneself as the meditational deity. Chos Kyi Nyima agrees, then tells me precisely how to visualize Tara and instructs me to see the deity merge into myself, to become Tara.

"Green Tara or White Tara, you can work with either one. See who comes to you," he says.

I purposely leave out many details as it is inappropriate to reveal much of what is taught at an initiation. There are aspects of the Tibetan teachings that can in no way be conveyed in a book. They must be received orally, by direct transmission, from a fully qualified teacher. A good deal of harm can and has been done by not being aware of this method of transmitting the teachings. The teaching can only be transmitted through experience and actual practice.[5]

These ancient ceremonial teachings give detailed maps of the human psyche or mind. Printed texts of rituals are like the rutters or portolan charts kept by ship's pilots in the days before there were reliable maps of the world: they can only be used by someone who has already been there him- or herself, at least once.

After I received the Tara initiation, I knew that I wanted Chos Kyi Nyima to be my teacher.

"Yes," he said. "You will write to me. Here, take this medicine with you. If you are having great difficulty and need me, take a little of this." He rolled a handful of tiny Tibetan medicine balls onto a small sheet of brown paper neatly folded. He tucked the ends in so that nothing could fall out. "You only need a little of this," he said. Then he gave me a small gold-painted statue of the Buddha, two inches high, to take with me.

Next, he took a piece of paper with the letterhead of the monastery on it, wrote out a new name for me in Tibetan, "Karma Choying Sangmo, Noble Lady of Dharmadatu," and stamped it with his seal. He tied a knot in a thin red silk cord, drew it through his lips, then blew on it, charging it with his blessings. I was to tie it around my neck. Protection.

I thought that I had come to Nepal to study the image of Tara in the rock at Pharping, but instead I discovered Tara taking root in me. Tara Doyle and I left Rinpoche's receiving room and sat down on a couch by the balcony doors in the larger shrine room. Erik joined us and pulled up a chair in front of the couch. Sunlight streamed in, warming us in the late morning light.

I burst into tears the moment we sat down. The ceremony had been deeply moving to me. I felt released, freed, and immensely grateful, both to Tara Doyle and to Rinpoche. Over the last few days, Erik had spent hours with us as well, answering questions, explaining. So much was being given freely. The contrast between my last visit to Nepal, with a broken leg, drinking, getting dysentery and nearly dying, and where I was sitting today was staggering. My heart exploded. I had received a great blessing and I felt it fully.

It is hard to fall asleep tonight in my hotel room. It is the night before the full moon—the sky is clear and starry. A fly buzzes. I start to kill him, but remember the vow I took this morning not to do harm. Instead, I turn off the lights, open the window and screen to the night air, and hope that he will fly out.

Tara Doyle moved into her tiny room at Swayambhunath today to begin a meditation retreat. Swayambhunath is a famous stupa, like Boudhanath, that we can see from the roof of the Vajra Hotel. According to Buddhist legend, the Buddha traveled here from India and gave teachings at what is now Swayambhunath.

At 1:30 a.m. I still can't sleep. Someone plays a guitar nearby. Dogs bark in the distance and are rarely quiet until three in the morning when I finally fell asleep.

By 6:00 a.m. I am awake again. Someone is drumming. It has been a fitful night. The dogs are finally quiet, though the air is full of the sounds of birds and Nepali voices. I lean outside my window, overlooking the mountains and the little Nepali house next door to the hotel. A tiny boy clad only in a bright turquoise top jabbers gaily to his sister. He has no cares in the world. She is perhaps five. She sits on the front stoop searching a green satchel. Three roosters strut around their yard, alongside the small ochre-brick house. The tin roof is held down with an assortment of bricks and upside-down clay pots. The children's mother comes out of the house and begins her morning house sweeping, then clears the dusty yard with a clump of dried twigs. Someone begins to play a flute down the street.

A large black crow swoops down. Doves flicker pearly gray above the rooftops. The sweet pea vines are bright green against the dull orange of the brick wall that separates the hotel garden from the neighbors. A little brown and gray wren with a white cap and a white stripe on each wing sits on the bamboo beneath me considering the day.

The haze is so thick that the foothills that surround us are completely obscured. But the sun is bright and blue patches can be seen through the gauze that drifts across the sky. The high brick wall that separates the hotel garden below from the neighbors has broken glass cemented across the top at a 45-degree angle, a harsh division.

Later, I go into town. We bump along in a creaking pink, green, and blue, gaudy auto-rickshaw, with cracked black leather seats, brass armrests, and beads dangling from the cover. A Basque friend tells me a story of his countryman, Juglio, who decided one day to walk home to Spain from Kathmandu. Juglio began walking with no money, only a toothbrush, a diary, and a pen. He made it.

I like the story of walking home, just walking. The bareness of the road, the simplicity of the way I forget. I imagine that I need so much, must have so many things first, before I can set out. The story of Juglio cuts through that, reminds me that I need very little outwardly; but inwardly, I need a ferocity of intention.

CHAPTER 5

This Nameless Path

◆

California

There is no way, the way is made by walking.

—Antonio Machado[1]

California
October 1985

For months after I came home to California from Nepal and the initiation with Chos Kyi Nyima, I was happy just to sit practicing the meditation form as he had instructed, alone in my room. I was glad to have Chos Kyi Nyima in Nepal. He was correct—he could be my teacher even though we were thousands of miles apart. In my morning meditation I visualized the room in his monastery at Boudha where I took Refuge and the bodhisattva vows. I would see him giving me the Tara initiation again and then I would do the meditation on Tara as he had instructed. The daily effort required to remember Chos Kyi Nyima, the claret red and saffron yellow of his robes, the color of the roses and orchids on his table, my friend Tara Doyle at my side, Chos Kyi Nyima's smile, his laugh, the sunlit window behind him, the Refuge and bodhisattva vows, taught me a great deal. It helped develop concentration and gratitude.

The visualization changed over time. I began to see Tara whispering in the ear of someone far away, a mountain hermit. She in turn told another solitary practitioner in the mountains about Tara, and then Tara appeared over his head, pouring love and compassion over him from a small pitcher. This practitioner in turn would tell another solitary seeker over whom Tara poured her love and compassion, and this one would tell another and another, so that the presence of Tara became known until at last it was Chos Kyi Nyima Rinpoche who received the vision of Tara during a retreat and from whom I received it. My love for the Buddha Tara grew.

In fact I needed the distance between myself and Chos Kyi Nyima. The Tibetan emphasis on devotion to a teacher made me uncomfortable. I did not seek out the local communities of Tibetan Buddhists. It would have been foolish not to be wary of the student-teacher relationship, having seen its potential for harm at Zen Center. There had been problems with the student-teacher relationship at other centers around the country, too. The issue of power was not well understood in America, either by students who gave themselves without appropriate discrimination or by the teachers who abused their trust. Despite the idealism with which we Westerners can approach it, Buddhism is not immune to the ills to which other organized religions have fallen prey.

I had embarked on a course that would require years of study and practice. Tibetan Buddhism came from a radically different culture and Buddhism itself is older than Christianity by at least five hundred years. There are numerous sects, thousands of scriptures, and well over a dozen teachers in the Bay Area alone. I wanted someone geographically closer as well as Chos Kyi Nyima but I did not know where to begin. I needed guidance, but I was not confident of my powers of discernment between the many Tibetan teachers available. Being in Nepal with a knowledgeable Western friend to whom I could turn was one thing, but now I was home alone—on my own. I stayed with what I knew could be relied upon: my meditation cushion, the natural world, and continued sobriety. Without being sober I had no path.

I was removed from the kind of security that many people seemed to have within spiritual communities. Meditation practice had been a deterrent and helped me control my drinking—a pounding headache for two forty-minute periods of meditation starting at 5:00 a.m. was to be avoided—but it hadn't kept me sober. Being sober was not something I could accomplish by meditation or by myself, despite the years of trying. When I was initially sober, I needed two spiritual communities: Green Gulch and my friends in recovery. The recovery community became a floating *sangha,* fellow seekers, though they would never have called themselves that. I began to think of sobriety as something one cultivates, like mindfulness in Buddhist practice. The shared emphasis on the present moment provided common ground on which to stand. Perhaps staying sober, the practice of sobriety, was American Zen without the Buddhist vocabulary. Still, there were limits to both situations.

Religion was not a topic of discussion in recovery groups, though spirituality certainly was. A crucial and clear distinction was made between the two. I couldn't talk about Buddhism or find any guidance along that path in my floating *sangha,* nor had the understanding of recovery penetrated the isolation of Green Gulch. Between the turmoil from which I had withdrawn and the fact that Green Gulch was a community based in Japanese Zen Buddhism, not Tibetan, there was less and less for me to contribute to or draw from at Green Gulch. A scattering of acquaintances and a handful of friendships remained.

I was further isolated because I wanted a woman teacher. Women teachers were rare and I knew of none close at hand[2] in either the Zen or Tibetan tradition. I had no illusion about women teachers being incorruptible, but I did know that I could learn from another woman what I couldn't learn from a man. It was as simple as that. The success of my recovery from alcoholism came from the experience of one alcoholic helping another. My life rested on that fact.

I turned to what resources I had: tapes of the visits with Chos Kyi Nyima Rinpoche and a handful of books to read. There was still some untranslated Tibetan on the tapes of my visit with Chos Kyi

Nyima, primarily his mother's comments. She had joined us during one of our talks. Erik had translated some of what she said about women teachers, but there was a good deal that remained encoded in Tibetan. She herself was a teacher, but she was in Nepal and I didn't even know her name. I knew her only as "Mother." I resolved to find a translator, put the tape in a growing stack of overseas interviews, and forgot about it.

Through Green Gulch I found *Kahawai, a Journal of Women and Zen,* published by the Diamond Sangha, Robert Aitken Roshi's group in Hawaii, a lifeline. Over time, at Robert Aitken's urging, translations of ancient koans with women masters done by Thomas Cleary would appear. These became known as the *Kahawai* koans.

Susan Murcott, one of the founding editors of *Kahawai,* came to visit Zen Center and our women's group. Tall, brown-haired, thin, intense, and funny, Susan was an inspiration to me. She too had found Buddhism after spending time in the wilderness. She had walked the length of the Appalachian Trail, over two thousand miles, in a long homemade skirt to see what life had been like for early American women settlers. She walked in lace-up buckskin moccasins to be in more direct contact with the earth than boots allowed. This was the detail she always remembered, the feel of the earth under her moccasins, the rough shape of the ground. Susan too was hungry for stories of women masters. Her solution had been to learn Pali and work on retranslating the *Therigata,* the anthology of poems by Indian Buddhist nuns of the Buddha's time, before going on to help found *Kahawai* and to lecture on the topic.

I tried to plow through Stephan Beyer's *Cult of Tara* but became lost in descriptions of esoteric rituals. Reading it demanded a level of familiarity with Tibetan Buddhism that I didn't yet have. In Nepal, Chos Kyi Nyima had suggested reading *Women of Wisdom* by Tsultrim Allione, a collection of biographies of historical Tibetan women teachers which he had on his bookshelf.[3] It had just been published.

The work of Murcott, the *Kahawai* collective, Allione, and Beyer provided much encouragement and affirmation. Yet much of what was affirmed was precisely the lack that I felt—women teachers were scarce, historical models few, and the situation of a householder practicing not well documented or particularly valued. Having women and men practice together was in itself revolutionary for Buddhism.

Allione's introductory comments proved more interesting to me than the six Tibetan women masters' spiritual biographies that made up the book. Her remarks about the possibility of regarding motherhood as a "sacred and powerful spiritual path" begged for further development.

The stories she included gave a double message: yes, there were accomplished women masters in the Tibetan tradition, but nearly all of them had either lost their children, left them, or never had them in the first place. Was there no image of raising a family as spiritual practice?

The same childlessness was true of the women in Susan Murcott's moving work on the *Therigata*. There were mothers included in the *Therigata*, but they had written poems of grief describing their madness at having lost or left their children behind. Only meeting the Buddha provided them with relief.

Kahawai published a handful of little-known Zen koans that featured a wise woman who always confounded the monks. Yes, of course there had been women of wisdom. Now we had begun to have fragments of their stories, both Chinese and Tibetan, sometimes without names, sometimes with, but still I found no stories of women with families who were exemplars of spiritual practice.

I refused to believe that motherhood was second-rate or not a spiritual path in itself. My children were not holes in me but openings, unwitting teachers on this nameless path. I found great comfort in rereading the prayer that the *sanyasin* had given me that morning in Nepal. I typed it up and carried it everywhere, taped it up in my office, put it on my altar, in my wallet:

Alas, I do not know either the mystical word . . . , nor do I know the songs of praise to thee, nor how to welcome thee, nor how to meditate on thee, . . . nor how to inform thee of my distress. But this much I know, O Mother, that to take refuge in thee is to destroy all my miseries.

Yet Allione's comments were helpful to me in an unexpected way. She mentioned the Tibetan *delog,* a person who unwittingly gets catapulted onto the spiritual path. They begin by accident, "involuntarily," usually because of a serious illness. Hearing of *delog* stories gave me a new way to understand both the paralyzing illness I had experienced in 1980 in Nepal and alcoholism. It provided a context or way of viewing both those experiences.

Initiates in various ceremonies throughout the world are often plunged into darkness, but they have chosen to enter this state. It is voluntary. By contrast, the *delog* can unwittingly be plunged onto the path. The journey to the underworld is preceded in most cases by a grave illness.[4] The illness begins the *delog* on their spiritual path.

Beset by fears, visions, and hallucinations, imagining oneself at the mercy of terrible storms, tossed this way and that, the everyday world disappears from view and one is surrounded by death. The *delog* has reached the underworld or "the hereafter." Some stories record the actual physical death of the *delog* who returns to life bearing information known only to the dead or messages from them. The return from the underworld, as well as the knowledge of the descent, was used to help the living, a motif akin to shamanistic experience, as well as recovery from addiction. Thence the value of both the experience and the *delog* for the community.

I could only assume that some *delogs* must have been taken over by the illness and the descent. They never made the journey back, like so many alcoholics and addicts. I was ashamed to have been an alcoholic mother. The mention of *delog* stories helped create a healthier perspective on the illness. Like a diabetic, I might not be responsible for having it, but I am responsible for treating it. It put my experience into an older framework, into

a communal context, and helped make it part of the spiritual
search. I was immensely grateful for that.

One day it occurred to me to go back to India to see the Dalai Lama.
The idea seemed both preposterous and exciting. I wanted to go to
the source. In Tibetan Buddhism that meant His Holiness, Tenzin
Gyatso, the Fourteenth Dalai Lama. I knew him to be someone I
could trust completely. Why this occurred to me I do not recall. I
only know that the idea of going to India to see him made me happy.
Yes, such an undertaking was perhaps impossible, but nonetheless I
would ask.

Walking out the door of my house to the sage-covered hills at
sunset, overlooking the ocean, the purple fog bank on the horizon
darkens and blocks out the last rays of the setting sun. The edge of
Mount Tamalpais and the hills below have the thinnest band of pink
between themselves and the blue-dark sky. A few small birds twitter
in the brush. No black-tailed deer or owl this twilight. The muddied
fire road I walk across the ridge toward the ocean is without trees
but for giant weathered-white eucalyptus stumps, the salted wind
too harsh and steady for growing here. Puddles mirror falling light
in a low spot as I slosh and slip downhill, hands in my pockets, lost
in thought. Twilight falls and the moon rises. I walk home in the
dark, a clear crisp night overhead surrounded by a softening haze
that says by morning, the fog will roll in.

Months pass, letters go back and forth to India. Finally I receive
a reply to my question. Yes, the Dalai Lama will see me. In India.
A private audience. Before I go to see him in Dharamsala, I will go
walking in the Garwhal region. Back to the foothills of the Himalayas,
this time the Indian side. My daily walks take on more purpose.

Then, setting out in the dark, hiking to the top of the hill in
blowing fog, protected until the summit, leaning into the cold, wet

wind, bundled up, no longer hot or sorry that I wore so much, now in the gale, just right.

Breaking new boots in, walking day after day, walking up and down hills, across ridges, trees swirled in fog, the sky lost, no difference in the sky's shades of blue-grays and the sea's watery shadows and the fog bank above. Where one stops and the other begins becomes indiscernible and lost. The sound of waves breaks over me when I stop still a mile from shore and above the ocean on a ridge. The small beach at the valley's outlet is swept clean, empty but for the waves that come in at a slight curve and sweep across.

The mountain and hills darken, giving over the green shape of day, steamed and blurred by fog swirling in and out like breath frosted in the distant hillside's trees. I walk until the fire road dwindles to a small trail. Just before it drops down off the ridge onto the hillside grazed by horses to the valley below, I can see the lower fields of Green Gulch Farm. From this place I see the shape of the winding valley from Muir Woods, dark at one end, to the light green of winter pastures at the other end just above the beach. How many times would I have to make this walk to cover the same amount of distance as I would if I walked to India, I wondered. To the south, the headlands fade, turning a light gray, and pale in the distance. The darker shapes grow closer.

Walking. Walking to India, walking up and down the hills, around the flanks of Mount Tamalpais, I tell myself that I'm getting in shape, though we can never know for what we are readied.

Tides tug and sweep, stars wheel overhead, again I am leaving home. I pull some sage off a bush and make a small bow of thanks. My hands are strong with its smell; by the time I reach home, my pockets are reeking.

Who Is Leaving, Who Will Return?

♦

*Meeting with the Dalai Lama,
Dharamsala, India*

*Thinking that all the living beings extensive as space are my mothers,
and remembering their kindness again and again,
bestow your blessings so that I may proceed on the stages of the
path,
training in love, compassion and Bodhicitta.*[1]

—The Prayer of Request to the Lady Tara

*On the Way to Dharamsala, India
September 1986*

I had been granted permission for a private meeting and interview
with His Holiness the Dalai Lama, Tenzin Gyatso, after months of
complicated correspondence. Such a trip began long before departure.
Now it was September 1986. The tempo picked up with last-minute
changes. A friend called from Delhi, shouting over our bad connection.

"You must change your program. His Holiness won't be in Dharamsala. You will see him in Delhi. You mustn't bring gifts, but if
you do, bring teas," his voice faded. "Tea?" I said in disbelief. "No,
c-h-e-e-s-e!" he said, our voices sounding as though they were bub-
bling underwater. "Oh, cheese!" "Yes, and chocolates."

My youngest son, Ben, was going to accompany me on the trip for school credit. But the week before we were to leave, he came down with a burning fever. Infection caused a swelling that was rapidly closing his throat. He was unable to breathe through his nose and antibiotics didn't work. I was distraught as he continued to worsen. Finally we got a proper diagnosis and medication. He had severe mononucleosis.

I had already put off our departure for over a week to nurse him, missing the trek he and I had planned in the Garwhal. He was better but the doctors still advised against his going. He was in a greatly weakened condition and might easily relapse. We had nearly seven weeks of travel left ahead of us in India, Nepal, and Europe. I was terribly conflicted about going. With proper treatment Ben had improved rapidly. He was young, fifteen, and strong. Perhaps we should take the risk—when might we ever have such an opportunity again? Should I go on alone or should I give up the whole trip to stay home with him?

I knew Ben to be a wise person. I left the decision in his hands. If he wanted strongly to come I would take him, but he said, "You go on by yourself, Mom. I'll be all right. Go on. Don't miss the Dalai Lama. I mean it. Go."

When the morning came for me to leave, my back went into spasms as I put my pack on over my shoulders. There was a stabbing pain everytime I took a breath. Finally, it subsided.

I went to wake Ben and tell him goodbye. But it was more than to Ben that I had to say goodbye. I had to let go of the dream of our traveling together and, most of all, I had to give up what it symbolized, a passage from our life together as mother and child as he became a young adult. He was my last one.

I stood in his room in the dark at 5:00 a.m. in the morning with years compressed into this brief goodbye. Now I could hardly breathe. I felt a physical weight that was almost overpowering. There was an invisible eddy-fence, the barrier created by river currents moving in opposite directions, that I had to cross but I could barely move. It was only the momentum of a year's planning that propelled me across. Finally I was able to lean down to kiss him, half asleep. "Goodbye, Ben, I love you."

To my surprise he was wide awake. "Love you too, Mom, you're the best mom I could have had. If I never see you again, you should know that," he said. Throwing his arms around my neck, he gave me a big hug and a kiss on both cheeks. Then I was out the door walking to the car as if in a dream. How much my children had forgiven me. How little I had forgiven myself. On the bus ride to the airport in the dark I felt uprooted, cried, and longed to turn back. Who is leaving? Who will return? The same person never comes back.

New York. The afternoon I was due to fly to Delhi there was an assassination attempt on Rajiv Gandhi. "Delhi's a madhouse," the cabbie told me just before leaving for the airport. "Just heard it over the radio. Won't be in the papers till tomorrow. You're not going there, are you?"

Maybe I should change my flight, maybe I'm not supposed to go on this trip at all. Maybe I need to remember that there were always obstacles for pilgrims. "Go," said one friend.

"Don't go. I've been in India when there're riots. You don't want to be there. The world gets turned inside out," another said.

My friend Sunil Roy's voice boomed over the phone from Delhi. "Oh, it's nothing, they've caught the fellow, just a crazy man. It's got nothing to do with the Sikhs. We're a bit unhappy about the attempt, but Gandhi's fine, the city is calm. It's perfectly safe, come ahead." Two hours later I took off from New York on Air India. I decided that if the national carrier wasn't worried, I wouldn't be.

By the time I arrived in Delhi the next day, it was apparent that the would-be assassin was a Sikh. The violence between Sikhs and Hindus, compounded by the overtones of a holy war, has troubled India more and more, threatening the fabric of its then nearly forty-year-old independence. I went for a tour of Old Delhi and found myself ringed in by troops. My guide took me by the hand and we slipped into a house. We climbed up three flights of stairs onto the roof and watched the growing crowd while tea was being served.

By evening the headlines told of riots a block from where I had been. Tension was growing. I was relieved to get a phone call from the Office of Tibet informing me that plans had changed again. Now I would have to get to Dharamsala to see the Dalai Lama. "Security reasons, you see. Delhi isn't safe just now. There's a private group who have a charter bus leaving in the morning. You can ride up with them, they have plenty of room. Be at the hotel at four a.m."

The air was humid and cool as I rode in an auto-rickshaw to the hotel at three-thirty in the morning to meet the bus for Dharamsala. In three days I had gotten a total of six hours of sleep. I entered an altered state of consciousness from sheer exhaustion.

The bus did not leave until well after eight o'clock in the morning and by then the air was muggy and thick. On the outskirts of the city, we saw a corpse being carried down the street by mourners. The body was wrapped in a spotless white cloth and draped with bright flowers strung back and forth across the litter. The mourners sang and walked along with everyone else—people on their way to work or market, school—not separate from everyday life. A sense of relief washed over me. What goes on in life, even death, is obvious in India, not hidden.

The bus picked up speed once we left the city, setting off a streak of colors—hot pink, turquoise, emerald, rose, and the saffron of saris worn by women digging along the road, against the grays and browns of the landscape. A truck laid overturned on the roadside, top heavy with hay. All our windows were opened to the day's heat, the bus full of noise and dust. It was difficult to talk. The roads were bumpy, the bus had little in the way of springs. I tried to stretch out across three seats but that proved even more precarious than sitting upright and intermittently being tossed into the air. I had to hold on to the seat or get wedged between baggage not to go bouncing to the floor at the next unexpected stop.

Sikhs with their bright-colored turbans stood out amidst the stream of traffic that whizzed by on motor scooters. Decorated with red and gold silk tassles hanging from the sides, Hindu deities on the dashboard, the big Tata trucks roared by, growling in clouds of dust. Ambassadors, India's domestic car, wove in and out of the narrow roads choked with buses, trucks, tractors, bicycles, bullock carts, scooters, and cows, blaring their horns all the way as though they were permanently switched on.

Dharamsala, in the lower Himalayas in the state of Himachal Pradesh, is the center of the Tibetan Diaspora and the seat of the Tibetan government-in-exile. The word *dharamsala* itself means a shelter for pilgrims. In order to reach Dharamsala, normally fifteen hours away by bus, we had to drive through the Punjab, the Sikh homeland.

By afternoon we had reached the Punjab, northwest of Delhi. Tension over the assassination attempt was high, the Sikhs were afraid of a Hindu backlash of violence. Roadblocks and checkpoints had been thrown up on the main roads. Many of us on the bus, myself included, did not have papers stamped by the Indian Home Office authorizing us to be in the Punjab where the presence of Westerners had been strictly forbidden. Not to have the papers meant being liable for arrest.

Left to the back roads, we were often stuck behind farmers taking water buffaloes to market in carts pulled by ancient tractors. The day wore on, hot, dusty, and slow. By the time we neared Chandigarh, the capital, we could no longer avoid the roadblocks and finally we were stopped. Oblivious to the conflict that was building, I sat in the back talking, unaware that the police had ordered everyone off the bus. Our Tibetan guide refused to obey the policeman's orders. A crowd was gathering. Just as I began to be aware that something was wrong, we were suddenly allowed to pass and drove off.

The late afternoon light washed pink and golden over green fields, broken up by the sharp lines of rectangular fields of freshly plowed dark soil. Pink and purple bougainvillea bloomed in great clusters along the road for miles. The tall, pale stalks of pampas grass caught fire in the sunset and lit up like flames. It was hard to absorb the stories I had read of the violence in the Punjab when surrounded by the peacefulness of its countryside.

We stopped later for dinner in a small village. The Punjabis themselves were friendly in contrast to the authorities in Chandigarh. The problems were strictly between Sikhs and Hindus. As Westerners we were a curiosity, but of no particular interest. The food was so highly spiced I couldn't eat, and had to settle for a dinner of tea. Later we stopped across the road from one of the main Sikh temples, pale white in the starlight, and listened to the chanting of evening prayers across the open field.

At three in the morning, we were finally deposited at the foot of a rocky hillside trail, nineteen hours after leaving Delhi. The bus could go no further. The road was too steep, curved, and narrow. We had to walk with our bags, stopping every few feet to rest, up to Kashmiri Cottage, one of the guesthouses of the Tibetan government, where we spent the night. The next morning we were taken by Jeep to McLeod Ganj, also known as Upper Dharamsala, still twenty minutes away, and another three thousand feet higher.

The next morning, the sun sparkled on the snow-capped peaks of the Dhauladar Range behind the pine-covered ridge on which McLeod Ganj sat at 6,500 feet. Ravens swooped and cried through the trees as we drove into the village. Once a popular British hillside station, India's partition and independence in 1947 left McLeod Ganj almost deserted until the arrival of the Dalai Lama and the Tibetan government-in-exile in 1960. Now McLeod Ganj, "Little Lhasa," its streets bustling with Tibetans and Tibetan shops everywhere, has a population of nearly four thousand people.

When the Chinese invaded in 1949, Tibet was catapulted into the twentieth century.[2] Isolated for centuries, called the "Roof of the World" at an average altitude of twelve thousand to thirteen thousand feet, Tibet lies strategically between India and China. Its story is one of the least understood international tragedies of our time.

Tibet, independent for two thousand years of recorded history, was the only country in the world that contained the entire corpus of the Buddha's teaching, both the oral teachings passed on one-to-one from teacher to disciple, and the written texts, some of which are now housed in the Library of Tibetan Works and Archives in Dharamsala.

But in 1959, soon after the Tibetan National Uprising, the Chinese clamped down with ruthless force targeted at destroying the Buddhist religion, culture, and people of Tibet. Tibet lost over 1.2 million people, roughly one sixth of its population, to massacres, executions, and starvation by the Chinese. Most of Tibet's 6,254 monasteries were destroyed by the Chinese, 80 percent of them *before* the Cultural Revolution. The remaining 20 percent were attacked during the Cultural Revolution. Fourteen monasteries remained.

Scholars estimate that perhaps 7,000 monks survived out of the 600,000 that there were when the Chinese came, and only a few hundred of the estimated 6,500 recognized reincarnated lamas escaped.

Men, women, and children were forced to beat the monks and urinate on them during the "struggle sessions." Monks were forced to break their vows. Children were forced to beat their own parents, students to beat their teachers, servants to beat their employers.

Tibetan children were not allowed to study Tibetan, only Chinese. Priceless religious art was either destroyed or stolen to be sold in antique shops or on the black market. Centuries-old hand-carved woodblocks of Buddhist teachings were chopped up for use in road-building or ground up for pulp to make toilet paper.

In 1949, Tibet's fate had been thrust into the hands of the Fourteenth Dalai Lama, Tenzin Gyatso, then sixteen years old. Ten years later, the Chinese authorities occupying Tibet invited the Dalai Lama to a show at military headquarters near the capital of Lhasa. Apparently the Chinese were planning to kidnap the Dalai Lama and the Tibetan people uncovered the plot.

On March 10, 1959, with the women of Lhasa leading the throng, thousands of Tibetans poured into the streets and massed themselves around the Potala, the Dalai Lama's palace, to protect him. The people refused to let him go alone to meet the Chinese. Chinese troops were called in, cannons fired on the palace. The situation worsened and soon became a national uprising. Under cover of the revolt, the Dalai Lama and his family were able to escape to safety in India. Thousands followed.

Tibet has been ruled by the Dalai Lamas since the seventeenth century, when the Fifth Dalai Lama reunited the three provinces of Tibet. The Dalai Lama is both the spiritual head of Tibetan Buddhism and the temporal head of the government of Tibet. The Fourteenth Dalai Lama, Tenzin Gyatso, is considered by many to be the greatest Dalai Lama of them all. The devotion and loyalty accorded to Tenzin Gyatso, now in his mid-fifties, by the Tibetans is legendary.

There are over 6 million Tibetans still inside Tibet today, and over 120,000 refugees living in communities mainly in India, Nepal, and Switzerland. The rest are scattered in thirty countries around the world, including the United States and Canada.

Tenzin Gyatso, the Dalai Lama, is a gifted world leader, whose advocacy of nonviolence is an ongoing demonstration of his teachings of love and compassion toward all. To the Tibetans, he is a symbol of their continuing political struggle for the recovery of a free Tibet, their greatest hope, as well as being an incarnation of Chenrisig or Avalokitesvara, the Great Bodhisattva of Compassion. He himself has little use for his many elevated and poetic titles and describes himself as a simple Buddhist monk.

I stayed at the Hotel Tibet, in one of the two rooms on the roof. It was a large, private room, right over the street, an extravagance at $8 a night. The private bath occasionally had hot running water, making this room the best in the house. The view of the mountains from the rooftop was worth the inconvenience of periodically flicking

a long cockroach from my bed at night before I climbed in. Morning
came early, when the shopkeepers started hacking and spitting, and
rolled up their screeching metal blinds to the world on the street
below my room.

The night before my interview with the Dalai Lama, I spoke with
a young Tibetan woman, Dolma Gyari, then a law student from Delhi,
over dinner at the Hotel Tibet. Dolma told me more about the
Chinese takeover.

"My great-grandfather was the chief of Kham, one of the three
provinces of Tibet. We are Khampas. The Khampas are known for
being great warriors. My father was a chief and a leader whom the
Chinese put under house arrest in another town from ours.

"My mother wouldn't stand for it. She was a great warrior herself.
She led the revolt against the Chinese in eastern Tibet, fighting from
horseback with her rifle. She and her followers killed many, many
Chinese. After a day of fighting she would sit by the river with her
prayer wheel, chanting and praying for the souls of the Chinese she
had killed. But in the end the whole family had to flee, leaving our
home, our possessions, almost everything. They left with only their
horses, rifles, fifty or so of the best servants and the clothes on their
backs. They had no money, nothing else. My grandmother was in
another part of Tibet, and finally in 1981, when the Chinese allowed
more information to get out, we found out that she had starved to
death years before."

We talked late into the night after dinner. Rain began to fall,
punctuated by thunder that cracked so loud it stopped the conversation.

"Inside Tibet, it's like the problem of the South African people:
first and foremost, in their own country Tibetans are treated like
slaves, they are second-class citizens. In South Africa, the problem
is black and white, you can see it clearly. But with Tibet, it's not
black and white, everyone just looks Asian to the rest of the world,
so they can't see what has happened to us," Dolma said as her eyes
moistened and her face flushed.

"That thunder is so loud that it's like the outside world. It's in such a state of confusion, so noisy, how can they hear us when we talk about Tibet?"

October 9, 1986.

"Testing, testing," I said into the tape recorder. It was one-thirty in the afternoon, only an hour and a half until I was to see His Holiness the Dalai Lama at three o'clock.

The voice in the tape recorder was calmer now. I had been up since five o'clock, close to tears off and on all morning. No sorrow, no identifiable feeling, nothing special, just waves of emotion washing over me. I was very moved to be here in Dharamsala getting ready to see the Dalai Lama. I had been dreaming of going to see him when the alarm went off. Even my unconscious was aware of this meeting. I got up, piled the three bed pillows on top of one another, straightened the sheets and blankets, then climbed back into the top of the bed still in my long underwear and nightgown, crossed my legs, pulled a shawl around me, and sat up in bed in prayer and meditation for an hour.

Now that the moment has arrived, I feel calmer. I had written out a prayer asking that "I" be removed from the interview, that something larger be asked through me. Whether or not this happens is completely out of my hands now. All I can do is walk down to the monastery as prepared as I know how to be. I run through a mental checklist: equipment working, fresh batteries inserted, extra blank tapes, film in camera, light meter set for indoors, correspondence reviewed, questions listed, gifts in hand.

I consider wearing a blue *chuba,* the traditional Tibetan woman's dress, but finally decide to dress as I am, a Westerner, and pull on a khaki green jumper dress. At the last moment I tie a light blue bandana around my neck from a friend's ranch in Texas. The act of tying it on grounds me, reminds me of where I'm from, connects me to the length of string I've laid down so that I don't get lost, no matter how far I stray from home. It reminds me: the way back is the way through, is the way home, is the way on. Bonded to the landscape of Texas, for better or for worse, the scarf has become a tiny talisman of protection and good luck.

Kalsang Ngodup Shaklho arrived to help me buy a suitable *khata,* the ceremonial scarf, to present to the Dalai Lama. Kalsang was a monk from the Dalai Lama's Private Office who had been assigned to help me. He had lived in the West and was fluent in English. We found an appropriate scarf in a Tibetan shop just below the hotel.

"This one, I think," he said, holding up a long narrow scarf of white silk, "this is a nice one. See the difference?" he said, holding it next to several others of rougher quality on a pile. Then he showed me how to fold the scarf properly so that it would open out when I offered it to the Dalai Lama.

A door bangs shut, I hear voices outside growing louder, coming toward the waiting room where I am sitting with the monk who will serve as our translator, Thupten Jinpa. The people from the preceding interview are done. Now it is our turn and we are walking outside under the vine-covered breezeway, through the green opened double screen door into the Dalai Lama's receiving room. His secretary, Tenzin Geyche Tethong, stands to the left.

"Greetings," the Dalai Lama said warmly in English, coming toward me from the other side of the room as I walked toward him. Though I started to bow, he preempted me and reached out to shake my hand Western-style. I was flustered. I tried to just take in the large comfortable room, filled with broad, plump chairs and couches, multicolored bouquets of fresh flowers, statues of the Buddhas and bodhisattvas, tangkha paintings covering the walls, altars, and His Holiness the Dalai Lama standing there in front of me, beaming.

"Please sit down," he said, motioning me to the couch next to his chair. "Would you like some tea?"

"Just a moment, please, let me put these things down." Self-conscious that I have so much with me, I take off the equipment bag and put down the gift I'm carrying. Standing unencumbered in front of him at last, I offer the *khata*. He takes it from me and drapes it over the back of my neck as I bow. Then I offer the small gift I've brought. He opens it, smiles, says simply, "Thank you," and sits down, motioning for me to do likewise. The translator sits in a chair nearby.

"Now," he said, indicating that he was ready for me to start. I pulled out the tape recorder, set up the mike on the table in front of us, and checked sound levels. Was the pause button off, the red light flashing, the counter at zero? There, I push the record button. We're on.

"Thank you for taking the time to see me," I began. "I need your good counsel, blessings, and guidance in this effort."

Did he even know why I was here? I didn't have the presence of mind to ask him. The pages of background material, book summary, and the list of questions to be asked that I had submitted to his Private Office were nowhere in sight. After a few more preliminary remarks and the sense that he was waiting for me, I pulled out a paper summarizing my topic and sat there reading to him.

Did it make sense to link Tara and Mary? Was the Madonna growing out of trees in Poland a phenomenon similar to Tara growing out of the rock at Pharping? What were his thoughts about women teachers, did he know of any himself, were there examples in Tibetan Buddhism of outstanding lay practitioners with families, what could he say about the importance of female deities for men? These were some of the questions I asked.

"Yes, Tara and Mary create a good bridge. This is a good direction to go in," he commented first.

Then I got lost in my own explication and floundered momentarily, starting out with a question about lay practice though that had not been my intention.

"According to Tibetan history, the highest lama after the Dalai Lama is the Sakya Lama. He is regarded as the number-two lama and he is a layman. Dilgo Khyentse Rinpoche is a layman with a wife and one daughter. He is a layman and a great lama, a guru. Just last month I received more than five days of teachings from him. So you see, these are highly qualified lamas and they are all lay people.

"There is one nun in Lumbini, Nepal, who is qualified to teach. She must be nearly seventy now. She is the sister of Chogyey Trichen Rinpoche, but I can't remember her name. Chogyey Trichen is a very good lama, a Sakya lama, from whom I've received many teachings.

"Then among the younger nuns there are some very bright women. Here in the nunnery I advise them to engage in debate. No doubt that in ten years, fifteen years, there will be qualified women teachers. No doubt.

"There have been women lamas in the past. There was also a category of lama called *rangjung* in which women teachers were sometimes found too.

"*Rangjung* lama was that type of master we call self-created, or self-arisen, or self-realized lamas or yoginis," he explained. "There was a famous woman hermit, said to be over one hundred years old, who was a *rangjung* lama when I was a boy in Lhasa."

"But I thought that this phenomenon of a deity growing out of a rock was called *rangjung?*"

"Yes, that's right," the Dalai Lama assured me, "self-arisen. Both are self-created. Yes, you see, same thing."

"Do you believe this Tara is growing out of the rock at Pharping?" I asked.

"Oh yes. These things depend on many factors, many," the Dalai Lama begins to explain. "There's a great sort of interrelationship between the appropriateness of the time, the place, and also a person intimately related to it. All these factors must be taken into account. When suitable people remain there, the image remains. When there are no more suitable people there, the image also disappears.

"I myself have one very little pebble, white quartz. There is one Tara in that pebble, very clear, very clear," he repeats for emphasis.

"I found it somewhere in the Potala in Lhasa, before I left Tibet. It's very small, but the figure is clear.

"When I was very young I loved that small stone with the Tara image, so I put the stone next to a statue of the Buddha that I also very much loved. The pebble with Tara on it was off to one side. Eventually that Tara turned toward the Buddha all by itself. Strange, beautiful," he says with his warm laugh, "beautiful."

When I tell him about the reports of the Blessed Mother appearing in the bark of trees in Poland, he concurs with my initial impression. "Yes, this would be *rangjung*, the same thing as we have been talking about, of course, the same thing."

"Your Holiness, please tell me about this belief in Buddhism that one must have a man's body to be enlightened."

"There is no distinction between the sexes in the highest Buddhist tantra. The idea that one can only be enlightened in a man's body comes from other traditions. In the highest school of Mahayana tradition, though being a monk is praised, there are many stories of bodhisattvas who are lay persons. In the highest class of tantra it mentions that a person can achieve enlightenment within this lifetime and that such a person could also be a female.

"Tara could actually be taken as a very strong feminist. According to the legend, she knew that there were hardly any Buddhas who had been enlightened in the form of a woman. So she was determined to retain her female form and to become enlightened only in this female form. That story has some meaning in it, doesn't it?" he says with an infectious smile.

"For Buddhist practitioners there is no difference between men and women. After all, we are the same, human beings. In Buddhist practice there is some feeling of discrimination, but this is imaginary, superficial."

Tenzin Geyche Tethong, his secretary, walked over to us pointing to his watch, indicating that time was nearly up. I nodded, quickly scanning my list. I had wanted to talk with the Dalai Lama about alcoholism and addiction, but I could not think of a way to broach the subject on the spot. I was writing about Tara. Instead, I told him that I hoped whatever I write might help to show what a treasure Tibetan Buddhism is for all of us. He invited me to attend three days of teachings that he was going to give in Delhi for a small group. I thanked him and asked him for his blessing.

He got up out of his chair, came over to me as I stood up, and took me firmly by the arms with a laugh. The Dalai Lama, Tenzin Gyatso, is irrepressibly cheerful. His touch surprised me. It was strong and energetic, like a black belt in aikido. The physical power in his hands belied the softness of his appearance. He put his forehead to mine, then pulled away smiling and stood there looking at me, his hands holding my shoulders. His look cut through all the words exchanged and warmed me. I sensed that I was learning the most about him and that I was being given the most by him, right then, though what it was could not be put into words. This was the real blessing.

Then he let go of me with a chuckle, put his arm under mine, and walked me to the door where Tenzin Tethong stood with a book for me. His Holiness signed it in Tibetan and handed it to me as a gift. It was his own book, *Kindness, Clarity and Compassion.*[3] I bowed once more, put the book under my arm, and walked out the door.

The meeting with the Dalai Lama had come and gone quietly. I was grateful to have met him. I looked forward to attending the private teachings he had invited me to in Delhi. His presence alone cheered me. His insistence that there was no distinction between men and women in practice, his encouragement of the nuns now studying in Dharamsala was heartening, yet not even his enlightened attitude could erase the discouragement I had felt for three days preceding the audience. I had been taken from scholar to scholar, meeting with learned and respected lamas and rinpoches to ask my questions about

Tenzin Gyatso, His Holiness the Fourteenth Dalai Lama at Dharamsala, India. (Angela Gennino)

Tara and women teachers. I had learned a great deal more about Tara but little about women teachers, past or present.

"There must have been some, yes, I heard of one woman teacher, but the name, I don't remember. No one wrote her teachings down . . ."

"Many women had great knowledge but they kept it a secret, or they were never known . . ."

"Perhaps women didn't have enough courage to do the practices so they didn't become teachers . . ."

"Many women were eminent in the fifteenth and sixteenth centuries, but their names have been lost . . ."

As I walked down the road from the monastery, I passed a beggar and suddenly realized that that's how I had been feeling, like a beggar, for stories of women masters. My tape recorder was the cup that I held out.

I gave the man more than enough for one meal. He said, "Thank you, madam," in a clipped British accent with such genuine warmth that I was taken aback. His eyes were bright and clear, his smile broad.

Over the next few days whenever I passed, I gave him rupees and stopped to chat. His limbs were so afflicted with leprosy that he couldn't walk. He asked me to bring him medicines for his sores from the village and I was happy to do as he asked. I wasn't worried about being foolish or taken advantage of, nor did I judge him for his choice to leave the lepers' colony where he and his wife had lived. He spoke enough English to tell me that life in the lepers' colony had been like a prison; he wanted his freedom. Every day he took a bus to this roadside spot to beg. This was how he chose to live. It was better than the lepers' colony. He had a daughter who had finished the eighth form of whom he was very proud. He would go to visit her at Christmas.

It was a life I couldn't imagine. He taught me something important about dignity. He had not a trace of self-pity. Some beggars were angry, some were aggressive, some were shy, some were ashamed, some were impassive. He was different. He had made peace with himself. What had I to complain about? Like the sun burning off the morning mists of these mountains, our brief daily exchanges dispelled my discouragement and increased my gratitude a hundred-fold. I could walk!

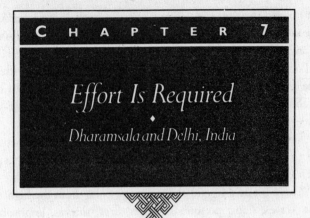

CHAPTER 7

Effort Is Required

Dharamsala and Delhi, India

*Once a monk on a pilgrimage met a woman living in a hut. The
monk asked, "Do you have any disciples?"*

The woman said, "Yes."

The monk said, "Where are they?"

*She said, "The mountains, rivers and earth, the plants and trees, are
all my disciples."*

The monk said, "Are you a nun?"

She said, "What do you see me as?"

He said, "A layperson."

The woman in the hut said, "You can't be a monk!"

The monk said, "You shouldn't mix up Buddhism."

She said, "I'm not mixing up Buddhism."

The monk said, "Aren't you mixing up Buddhism this way?"

*She said, "You're a man, I'm a woman—where has there ever been
any mixup?"*

—A *Kahawai* Koan[1]
T'ang period, ca. A.D 618–922.

Namgyal Monastery, Upper Dharamsala
October 1986

Ravens cawed loudly and swooped through the pine trees outside as
Dupchok Gyaltsen, the translator, and I sat in Lochö Rinpoche's small
two-room apartment in the monastery complex. The late morning

light poured through the window over Rinpoche's open smiling face as he sat, lotus-style, on an ornate handwoven Tibetan rug, his simple red and yellow robes folded around him.

Lochö Rinpoche is the abbot of Namgyal Monastery, the Dalai Lama's own monastery in McLeod Ganj. I had been sent to him to ask about Tara. He begins by telling me about her better-known form—Green Tara.

"Green Tara is renowned for coming quickly to help a petitioner, even to one who has not believed in her in the past.[2] Very speedy! Green is related to action. She is faster than the others.

"There is also a legend about Tara rescuing from the Eight Fears: ocean waves, lions, poisonous snakes, fires, thieves, imprisonment, and other dangers.[3] But most importantly, she rescues us from what these dangers symbolize—our internal enemies—the fires of anger, the lion of pride, the snake of envy, the chains of avarice, and so forth."

I was curious about the belief in reincarnation as well. Lochö Rinpoche seemed such a kindly man that I did not think he would be offended if I asked him more about it.

"Since he is a reincarnated lama and it is possible to know past lives, is it possible that Rinpoche has ever been reincarnated as a woman?" I asked.

Dupchok grimaced slightly, but good-humoredly inquired. A young monk in his twenties, he has endured a great deal of teasing for spending so much time with a Westerner. Dupchok Gyaltsen has been generously translating for me for three days now and has gotten used to my questions about Tara and women masters. He had asked me to wear my *chuba,* the traditional Tibetan dress, today so that he would not be made fun of by his fellow monks. When I arrived at his room in the monastery before going to Lochö Rinpoche's room, he pointed out that the *chuba* was tied incorrectly and to my surprise reached around my waist and retied it for me as though I were simply another monk. Then he proudly showed me the English Bible

Green Tara, ready to step into the world to help.
(Line drawing by Andy Weber)

he's been studying, reading aloud verses from Paul's Epistle to the Corinthians, his favorite passage in the New Testament.

"There is one deity who always comes in the form of a woman, Samdhang Dorje Phagmo,"[4] Lochö Rinpoche explained, "but such a thing is very rare. Most of the reincarnated lamas are born only in the form of a man. Although I cannot say for certain what will happen in the future, I am eighty percent certain that I will not be born in a woman's body."

"I wanted to ask him about my own practice and I don't know where to start, Dupchok. Shall I describe my meditation to him?" Yes, he nodded.

"After sitting for five years, some of my Christian roots began to crop up in my meditation. What has evolved is a kind of mandala in which I visualize Tara, the Virgin Mary, Buddha, and Jesus Christ."

Dupchok turned and began to translate this in Tibetan to Lochö Rinpoche. He listened thoughtfully, nodding when he understood, repeating a word here and there when he didn't. Dupchok turned back. "In front Tara; in back, Jesus Christ, yes?"

"Yes."

"Go on," Dupchok says.

"Then I imagine Tara coming closer, emerging out of the seed syllable, as Chos Kyi Nyima Rinpoche told me to do, radiating light in all the ten directions, coming closer and closer until she merges into me. Then sometimes I have visualized Tara and Jesus Christ as consorts and the Blessed Mother and Lord Buddha as consorts."

Dupchok paled slightly. I laughed to cover my own awkwardness. Now the problem is his. How strange this all is, sitting in the foothills of the Himalayas on this bright morning, telling this venerable Rinpoche and a young monk this visualization of deities in sacred union. In Tibetan Buddhism, the symbolic union of male and female deities is completely bound up with the highest spiritual experience of enlightenment. This is not the world of God the Father or even God the Mother. This is the world of ecstatic union, of father and mother, male and female, the Great Bliss, the union of Wisdom (female) and

Compassion (male), in which Emptiness is the great primordial fact.[5]

Dupchok began translating, Lochö Rinpoche just listened with a smile, no change of expression on his face, no comment. Had Dupchok understood me correctly? I had no way of knowing. In an effort to dispel my own discomfort, I found myself going on the moment Dupchok stopped speaking in Tibetan. I was afraid of being scolded or told I was a heretic, a thoroughly Christian reaction.

I was crossing cultures, mixing deities. It had been a momentous interior event even to let myself have such a vision. To reveal it to a traditional teacher was unnerving. Yet I was unwilling to spare myself whatever discomfort my enthusiasm, need, and lack of knowledge might cost me. I was on unknown ground. By conferring with recognized, traditional teachers, both Buddhist and Christian, I hoped that I would not deceive myself.

I immediately began to tell the abbot about the next part of the meditation. Here I was more comfortable, I knew that I was on safer ground. Was it only because of my Catholic background that I imagined he might not approve? I was the foreigner here, not only geographically but symbolically. I do not know this landscape, the boundaries, the signs or markers whereby people take direction. I am thrown back completely on myself. It is an unnerving experience. This could be the worst kind of delusion or a source of fresh insight, "beginner's mind," as it's called in Zen. Time would tell which.

"But most often," I continued, "I imagine Tara taking a pitcher of compassion and pouring it over the heads of all the people I love— my family, my friends, everyone, as well as all the people I don't love—that I find difficult or hard.

"My teacher, Chos Kyi Nyima Rinpoche, is in Nepal. I don't really have anyone in the States to work with, though I am looking. In the meantime, would he make some suggestions about practice?"

The two red-robed monks leaned their close-cropped heads together and conversed in Tibetan. Lochö Rinpoche's voice was lower and huskier than Dupchok's. The varied sounds of their conversation with its inflections was melodic.

"If you have greater faith in Tara among them, maybe it is better to meditate in the form of Tara. The external form may be Tara, but internally, all these beings are forms of compassion, love, affection, and so forth. You should realize that all these deities are born in this world to benefit the sentient beings. Just take the one you have the most faith in, understand?"

"Yes," I understand. "Tara."

"Do you have time to come back tomorrow?" Rinpoche asks through Dupchok.

"Yes, of course. If Rinpoche has time, that would be wonderful."

"He makes appointment at ten a.m. tomorrow. Your questions are very interesting," Dupchok tells me with a wide smile.

I don't know if this is Dupchok's comment or Lochö Rinpoche's. I am deeply grateful for the time they are giving me. Dupchok has examinations approaching and has taken time out from his studies to serve as a translator. As the abbot, Lochö Rinpoche has many responsibilities besides meeting with a beginning student like myself. After the microphone was unplugged, the earphones removed, the tape recorder bundled up and placed in my already too full equipment bag, I stood up, made a low bow to Rinpoche, and left.

I began the walk back to the Hotel Tibet, about a mile away from the monastery. The equipment bag was heavy, weighed down with notebooks, camera, lens, tape recorder, batteries, and tapes. I get possessed by the fear of missing something while I'm traveling—a word, a phrase, an explanation, a story—after having come such a long way. The opportunities for misunderstanding abound while working through translators. The distance of ten thousand miles was a formidable obstacle. Anything that I could not check against an original would be lost altogether, so I taped all my talks with the various lamas and certain other conversations besides. Like the childhood fears I had of missing something or being left out, this grasping weighed me down. But I am stubborn. I give in to this part of myself, shoulder the load, and walk on.

The air was sharp as I labored uphill, the sky clear. I took a secondary path, off the main road, past the tiny nunnery where Karma Lekshe Tsomo lives, a Western woman who has been here studying for ten years. I stop at the door of her tiny room to knock, but the locks are in place. No one there.

In the middle of town I am accosted by a beggar child with a huge eye popping out of her head. She is hard to look at. I know that giving to her in the front of the other beggars has now made me a mark for the rest. Many I give nothing to, to others plenty. I cannot resolve myself in these matters.

Back at the hotel, I sit downstairs in the dining room having tea and write out my notes from breakfast. I had eaten breakfast this morning with a woman from Denmark, a photographer who had been on the bus ride with me from Delhi to Dharamsala.

It was early, before seven o'clock, when we talked. She sat with her back to the window that overlooked the silvery slate rooftops of the village. The morning light rose and grew behind her, giving the edge of her face and her blond hair a soft fire.

"The eyes, the road," she said, "it is the way to God. It took me such a long time to realize that this is why I am always paying attention to eyes when I photograph portraits. I pay attention to roads when I do landscapes in the same way.

"There was a road lined with chestnuts where I grew up in Denmark. I always loved that road and I never knew why. I was always taking pictures of that road, pictures and pictures. Why so many pictures? The road. Then I realized. In all my photographs, what I am looking for is the way to God."

I returned to see Lochö Rinpoche the next day promptly at ten o'clock. Though I had only met with him the one time the day before,

I felt as though I was seeing an old friend when I arrived at his apartment.

The mountain air felt clear and rinsed as I stood in the doorway taking off my shoes, jays squawking in the trees, a child calling in the distance. I had brought a *khata* with me this morning to show my respect and appreciation for Rinpoche's generosity.

Dupchok, who was with me, walked in first. "Good morning, Rinpoche," I said, stopping just in front of him to make a bow and offer him the scarf. He placed it around my neck and waved me to be seated.

"Tara's mantra is *Om Tare Tutare Ture Soha,*" Rinpoche began, patiently waiting while Dupchok looked over my shoulder to be sure that I had written it down correctly. "This is a very important mantra," he assured me.

"*Om* is the beginning syllable. *Tare* means that she can rescue us from the ceaseless round of cyclic existence and *Tutare* means that she can rescue us from the Eight Great Fears. *Ture* means that she has the power to heal us from chronic diseases. *Soha* is the last syllable of the mantra as *Om* is the beginning. Repeating this mantra can extend our life."

"Is there a particular mantra for removing fear? I seem to have a lot of it and I would certainly like to be rid of it," I told Rinpoche.

"Oh, this mantra is very good for rescuing from fear. Just recite it over and over and Tara will remove your fears," Rinpoche assured me.

"Now, when you visualize yourself as Tara, you must imagine that your cushion is a full moon being held up by a beautiful flowering lotus. Behind you there is another full moon. On your forehead is the syllable *Om* and its color is white. On the throat is the syllable *Tare* in the color red. *Hum* syllable is in the heart, its color is blue. After that you must visualize many rays radiating from your heart in the ten directions and you should invite White Tara from her abode. See her coming from down your head into your heart, she dissolves into your body from the head.

"Then you must have the image of all the destitute beings around you and you must pray to Tara to save them from suffering. Compassion is the main method in Buddhism that we need in order to attain enlightenment. Compassion and kindness are called for in all religions, but compassion is particularly important in Buddhism. The altruistic mind that we speak of attaining means that we intend to become enlightened for the sake of all beings, bodhicitta. This is the great thought and it can only arise out of deep compassion.

"I will tell you a story about Tara," Rinpoche said, "perhaps you have heard it.

"When Avalokitesvara, the Lord of Compassion, first took his vows to liberate all beings from suffering, it was a very bad age, an incalculable number of ages of time ago.

"The world was filled with suffering. People behaved very badly toward each other, toward animals, toward the earth, everything! They were completely caught up in the world of delusion. Just as Avalokitesvara would liberate one being from suffering, another would be struck down. It seemed as though he had taken on a hopeless task, made an impossible vow, and he grew discouraged. He became so discouraged that he began to hit his head on the wall. When he did this, eight different heads appeared because of the blessings of the Buddhas.

"Two eyes opened at the back of his head at the same time and from those eyes, tear began to fall. Out of these tears, two Taras appeared, White Tara and Green Tara.

"White Tara spoke to the Lord Avalokitesvara and said, 'Don't worry, I will help you. I will work to help sentient beings increase their fortunes and prolong their lives.'

"Then Green Tara spoke to him and comforted him as well, saying, 'I will work to remove all obstacles for beings and clear their path.'

"Though Avalokitesvara is the god of Compassion, still it is easier for sentient beings to receive the blessings of Tara. If one calls on her, she removes any obstacle very quickly.

"You must go to the Tushita Meditation Center on the road above the village and find the poster of the Twenty-one Taras. Some of the colors are not so accurate, but still it would be helpful for you to have the poster. On the poster you will also find Red Tara, Yellow Tara, and Dark Blue or Black Tara. Green is considered a mix of the four main colors: white, red, yellow, and black."

"When you get the poster of the Twenty-one Taras, would you like to meet with Rinpoche again?" Dupchok inquired.

"Oh, very much! I will go to Tushita this afternoon. When should I come back?"

"Ten o'clock in the morning, Rinpoche says. If he's busy and not able to be here, that means that something important came up. But if he's not busy, then he is happy to meet you again and explain the Twenty-one Taras."

"Thank you, Rinpoche. Please tell him that I am very grateful to him for this time and please ask him if he will give me his blessing," I said to Dupchok as I leaned down to put the tape recorder in my bag. Then I stood up and made a bow to Lochö Rinpoche. He placed his hands on my head and said a prayer softly in Tibetan.

◆

The visualization practices presented in the Tibetan Buddhist tradition have been especially helpful to me, I realized, in thinking about the visit with Lochö Rinpoche. But beyond the visualization, the actual merging of the deity into myself helped make honorable what I had rejected and sought to escape, a woman's body.

The Tibetans are very clear on this matter of visualization. Envisioning a deity outside yourself, either in the space in front of you or at the crown of your head, is a practice that can be done by anyone. But to visualize yourself merging with the deity, becoming the deity, which is the Vajrayana or tantric path, one must have an initiation. This means receiving a qualified teacher's permission to do the meditation and detailed instructions on precisely what to visualize.

I found John Blofeld's explanation of visualization in *The Tantric Mysticism of Tibet*[6] helpful. The final aim of the practice is to arrive at a point where one can actually feel, not just believe in, the nondual nature of reality. Through conception, one goes beyond conception. The purpose of visualization practice is to gain control of the mind. One works on developing skill in creating the elaborate images of deities and their palatial abodes, as well as the multitude of other deities that surround them, and the sea of beings in the six different realms of existence. It is a fantastic cosmos that one enters in Tibetan practice, the description of it forming a kind of literary astronomy.

Visualization not only helps us gain control of the mind, but the very act of doing it serves to purify the mind of defilements and obscurations as well, "the water of the mind runs through the cleansing filter of the image."[7]

"We actually do become the deity," Blofeld says. "The subject is identified with the object of faith. 'The worship, the worshipper and the worshipped, those three are not separate.' "[8] But the deity is not a deity in the ordinary sense of the word, not like an external god or goddess as we might think of in the West. These deities are personifications of what Blofeld calls "mind-force," the object of worship not the historical Buddha Gautama or the Buddha Tara, or the Bodhisattva Avalokitesvara, for example, but the principle of enlightenment itself, within everyone.

◆

I walked back uphill to McLeod Ganj by myself and dropped off my notebooks in my room at the Hotel Tibet. I had just enough time to get up to the Tushita Center, another mile or so uphill on the way to Triund, the Forest Lodge, at ten thousand feet. Beyond Triund floats Indrahar Pass at eighteen thousand feet, full of rolling meadows and huge boulders, ringed in on all sides by snow-capped peaks.

Below the pass, a summer grazing spot for sheep, lies Chamba Valley, which means the land of milk and honey, the other side.

At first the trail is blacktopped, wide enough for a small car to pass the usual foot traffic of monks, villagers, and foreigners who walk this way. A piece of the road has recently fallen off, down the hillside. A road crew labors, digging and cursing, making rudimentary repairs. Around a curve is the Mountaineering Center, an old British compound that was the first home of the Dalai Lama when he arrived in Upper McLeod Ganj in 1960. Beyond are the old English summer houses left from the days of the British hill stations. Their walls are darkened by the mildew that pervades northern India. Lichen adds a sheen of vibrant green and has its way with the slow rot that eats the houses here.

Distracted from my walk to the Tushita Center by a sign that says YETI TREKKING, I open the gate into a garden where roses and tall purple and white cosmos bloom. No one seems to be around as I wander across the lawn. Finally a young Nepali appears, a "refugee" from Kathmandu, already overrun with trekking companies. I want to take off for three days, just walking in these mountains. I spend so much time sitting, talking, so often through someone else. I am torn. The opportunities to talk to different scholars and lamas about Tara are not to be taken lightly. The monastery here, access to the library and scholars, translators and guidance from the Dalai Lama's Private Office, all provide me with an incomparable treasure. But the weather today is so beautiful, the air like crystal, making my head snap. How long can I keep up this talking? I long to bolt and run, keep going up this trail, beyond Tushita, up to the Forest Lodge, up to the bear's cave at the pass, and up and out into the high meadow in the center of the ring rising high and silent in these mountains.

The mountains here are known mostly to shepherds, but with a trekking company just established, this will not last indefinitely. I can make a short trek, the proprietor assures me, but the way back will take another day and an eight-hour Indian bus ride. I would miss the possibility of meeting with Lochö Rinpoche again and the possibility of attending private teachings with the Dalai Lama in Delhi.

I continue walking up to Tushita. Nearby, a Tibetan woman puts her laundry out on her roof to dry. Two young children leap out at me in play on this path, laughing when I throw up my hands in mock surprise. I stop to take their picture, the younger one coming closer and closer, curious, peering as if she could jump inside the lens itself and turn the world upside down.

Soon I am past the houses. The forest hillside steepens and drops away into the valley below. After stopping at the trekking company, I've lost time. I hurry now, for it is late afternoon and I don't quite know where I'm going. The path is wooded, increasingly beautiful and less civilized. A troop of gray monkeys walk along the edge, single file and bold, chattering amongst themselves. I see a tiny hut above me in the trees and a fork in the wide trail. I turn and cut back up the hillside until I come to a low, whitewashed wooden house and a sign: TUSHITA. A small white stupa with a solitary meditation room enclosed sits just below the lodge.

The door to the lodge is open though there is no one around. I step inside, calling out "Hello? Hello?" No one answers. On the right is the meditation hall. The door is open, the floor covered by rows of red, brown, or black *zabutons,* meditation mats. Entering, I wander around looking at the tangkha paintings and statues that fill the empty room. Finally I pull up a cushion in front of the windows that overlook the garden and the mountains and sit down to collect myself.

I can go trekking over the next few days, living in the out-of-doors, walking in the mountains, or I can stay in Dharamsala. Staying in Dharamsala, going on to Delhi for the teachings, means that I have to give up my plans to go to Nepal and trek up to Thyangboche Monastery on this trip. Lochö Rinpoche may or may not be able to make our scheduled meeting, I may or may not be able to get into the teachings once I'm back in Delhi. The complexities of travel in India, ticket refunds, and the telex messages I will have to send loom large in contrast to taking off walking in these mountains. My mind is full of chatter like the monkeys I saw on the trail. It won't stop.

I tell myself to go back to my breath, to be quiet. Coming back to my breath, returning, I remember what lies under the surface of my life. I need to be willing to go to any lengths to find a spiritual experience. I want to stay sober. Breathe. My ankle hurts in this position and I adjust my posture. Back to the breath, then the memory, I have put my life on a spiritual path. Breathe. I have only a daily reprieve from addiction, I am not cured. Breathe. One should not be surprised nor complain about the work required to develop spiritually. It isn't easy! Effort is required, difficulties to be expected and tolerated. Breathe. Being discouraged is not useful. How fortunate I am to have come this far! It is a great gift to even hear of the Buddha's teachings, much less to have the possibility of hearing them directly from the Dalai Lama, I remind myself. Breathe, pay attention to what's in front of you, what's being offered. "Breathe, return to the breath, empty your mind." "Sit as though you could sit this way forever." Sit through to the other side of the world.

The decision becomes clear. I will go for the teachings, whether Lochö Rinpoche meets me again or not, whether I am turned away at the door in Delhi. I will make the effort. I will show up. It is the trail of delusion inside myself that I must climb; the wild bear I want to see, the one who lives in the cave of the heart. I will stay. I will take refuge in the Buddha, the Dharma, and the Sangha. I know too well how to go off alone.

I have been sitting now for close to an hour. My right leg has fallen asleep. I stretch it out in front of me, shake it, rise, and bow to the cushion. Back in the hallway, I follow the corridor to the back and by the kitchen. There, a fellow stirs a big pot of soup, cooking for an invisible crowd. He turns the fire down and agrees to open up the store for me.

"I think we're out of the Twenty-one Tara poster," he says as we walk down the hall. He opens the door into a small, well-stocked store. Pulling out a wide, shallow drawer, he says, "No, I'm wrong, you're in luck. We have one left. It's yours."

When I got back to the Hotel Tibet, there was a message from Bhiksuni Karma Lekshe Tsomo with a meeting time at last. (The title "Bhiksuni" means that she's a fully ordained nun.) Though it involved traipsing back down the hill a mile or more to Jamyang Chöling, a small monastery for Westerners, with my camera bag, tape recorder, and notebooks, I was nonetheless relieved to be able to sit down and meet with Lekshe. She's an American woman in her forties who became a nun in the Tibetan tradition in 1977. She has lived and studied here in Dharamsala for the last ten years.

Lekshe greeted me with a warm smile at the door. Her head was shaved, her dress the simple red robes of a nun. She invited me into her home, a single room with a bed, a typewriter, a stove, two chairs, a small table, and a large altar. There was no running water or indoor plumbing at Jamyang Chöling, only simple, bare, whitewashed rooms with a wooden platform for a bed and a shelf or two. Secluded from the main path to the Dalai Lama's monastery, set back amongst pine trees, the view overlooking the plains below was spectacular. It made a good place for a retreat. While water boiled for tea on her kerosene stove, she told me a little of the circuitous route that had brought her to Dharamsala.

Lekshe had grown up in California, surfing. At nineteen she dropped out of college to attend the first international surfing championship in Japan. She was the only young woman in the contest. "But in winter it got too cold to surf, so I went to a monastery and began to do zazen. From there I went to Vietnam, Singapore, Malaysia, Cambodia, Sri Lanka, India, Nepal, mostly by myself. Everywhere I was drawn to Buddhism, just naturally."

After two years of traveling in Asia, she returned to the States, studying Chinese and Japanese at Berkeley and doing graduate work in Asian studies in Hawaii. From there she returned to India, to Dharamsala, the center of the Tibetan diaspora.

"The very first day I walked into class at the library here in Dharamsala, all the questions that I had had as a child about dying and what happens after death were finally being explained. No one had ever been able to answer them fully before. That was 1972."

Lekshe was the only Westerner and the only woman studying at the Institute of Buddhist School of Dialectics when I visited. In addition to the demanding studies, she was in the midst of organizing the first International Conference on Buddhist nuns that would take place in Bodh Gayā, India, the following February 1987. The Dalai Lama would address the conference. It promised to be an historic event.[9] It was exciting to hear of her plans. But what moved me particularly was hearing of Lekshe's work on behalf of Tibetan nuns.

In the past, Tibetan nuns have not become *bhiksunis* (fully ordained nuns) because the *bhiksuni* lineage was not transmitted to Tibet. Consequently they can only practice as novices. "Lineage" refers to a direct transmission of the Buddha's teachings from one person to another, thus assuring continuity, authenticity, and accuracy. Why the *bhiksuni* lineage for nuns in Tibetan Buddhism was not instituted is not clear. Some lamas maintain that it was established but lost during a wave of persecution in the ninth century in Tibet when monks and nuns were forced underground. Most hold that the lineage for nuns never reached Tibet from India, only the lineage for monks.[10] Since the entire monastic community is responsible for authentic ordination, without support from both monks and nuns ordination could not take place.

Formal rules hold that certain procedures explained in ancient texts must be followed during an ordination; a set number of monks and nuns who have maintained their monastic practice for a minimum of ten or twelve years must be present. If any one of the required elements is missing, such as the requisite number of monks and nuns, the ordination is not considered authentic and the lineage discontinues.

This is not an esoteric matter, but a practical procedure of monastic discipline. Still, the social consequences of not being fully ordained have been severely limiting for many of the Tibetan nuns and have served to create obstacles to the development of women as teachers. Due to their status as novices, nuns generally received a poorer quality of education and training. Over the last thousand years, some Tibetan nunneries became places to put unmarriageable women, widows, or women who didn't fit into traditional society. Today, many find themselves living a marginal existence, often in poor health, impoverished and illiterate.

Most Tibetan nuns, however, were women sincerely seeking to study and practice the Buddhist teachings because of a deep spiritual motivation. Moreover, the nunnery was often the only place a single woman could find a decent, protected life for herself, as was true in the West until quite recently.

Whether fully valued or not, the nunneries represented an important Tibetan institution. Before the Chinese takeover there were over six hundred nunneries with more than eighteen thousand nuns inside Tibet. Now there are only an estimated nine hundred nuns in the entire Tibetan tradition in Nepal and India.[11]

The Tibetan nuns' own efforts to rectify and improve their situation have been augmented radically by the influx of Western thought. The issue of restoring full ordination for nuns in the Tibetan tradition has come to the fore during the past twenty years as Western women have entered monastic life and found themselves limited to novice status. The personal support of His Holiness the Dalai Lama and the late Gyalwa Karmapa, the head of the Kargyu sect, are also key elements in the changes taking place today around the issue of ordination.

The first nun was the Buddha's aunt, Mahaprajapati, a noblewoman. She had raised the young Gautama as her own child because his mother, her sister Queen Maya, died shortly after his birth. At first, Gautama Buddha refused to accept her into his community of monks and novices, but she would not be dissuaded. She continued to press for ordination.

It gave me great pleasure to listen to Lekshe telling this story and to think of Mahaprajapati, who was an older woman when this encounter took place. She had raised this man they now called the Buddha, cleaned him, nursed him. No wonder she would not be turned away.

"For the Buddha to allow her into his community would provide encouragement for women to leave home, a radical move in Indian society twenty-five hundred years ago," Lekshe went on to say. "The Buddha was on the spot, wasn't he? It was a threat to the social order of the day. More tea?" she asked, getting up to turn the kettle on again.

Mahaprajapati's request had enormous ramifications. She was not traveling alone. A large group of women who also wanted to be ordained were traveling with her. Still he said no.

When the Buddha left for another town, Vaisali, the women followed. Mahaprajapati cut off her hair, put on saffron robes, and walked the one hundred twenty miles barefoot with her followers.[12] Her determination deepened. By the time she arrived at the door of the monks' hall, she was disheveled and weeping, but adamant. Covered with dust, her feet swollen, she would not leave even after the Buddha refused her request three more times. Finally his main disciple, Ananda, intervened. He convinced the Buddha that since he taught that women could become enlightened, it only followed that they should be able to be ordained too. At this the Buddha gave in. Mahaprajapati and her followers were ordained. Reason had won over crippling social custom and the Buddhist order of nuns, the Bhiksuni *sangha* was born that day.

Lekshe received her ordination through a Korean lineage transmitted from China and has taken up the issue of establishing Tibetan *bhiksuni* lineage on behalf of her Tibetan sisters. I was astonished by the depth of her commitment. She lived with no plumbing, no hot water, the cold of mountain winters, periodic flareups of hepatitis from bad water, and rats. To support herself and her work, she periodically disrupted her life by returning to the West to renew her visa and earn enough money to continue her studies. She had taken on formidable obstacles and was quietly, slowly, wearing them down with no complaint.

She was supported by her complete conviction in the value of the Buddha's teachings. As Buddhism comes to the West, the role of the first generation of Western nuns and monks is crucial. Lekshe has taken her role to heart. Having studied Buddhism for twenty-five years, she was now concerned with properly translating texts and maintaining the purity of the teachings. She has worked both with Tibetan and Chinese sources, encouraging other women to take up this task as well.

"Women do have to work harder than men, it's true. We have the handicap of centuries of baggage that we carry along, both inside and out," Lekshe said matter-of-factly. Yet she was convinced that there is so much value in these texts for everyone that the discrepancies between what the Buddha taught and the way different cultures had adapted the teachings could be resolved. These discrepancies seemed to fuel her efforts rather than become a source of frustration. Lekshe knew that there is no time to waste.

"There have been problems with some of the teachers in the States and their women students in particular," I told Lekshe, "though perhaps it's no different than the priest or minister who sleeps with his parishioners. Issues of sexuality, power, and money have all reared their heads. Perhaps we have been too idealistic as Buddhism comes to the West.[13]

"And yet part of what drew me to Tibetan Buddhism was what seemed to be a radically different way of viewing the body and sexuality. The image of deities in union reaffirmed the dimension of the sacred in sexuality," I told her, "and yet from the little I've learned, tantric practice in Buddhism has little or nothing to do with ordinary sexuality.

"There seem to be great misunderstandings about sexuality and tantric practice. I'm not sure what people are making of 'tantric' practices in the States. From the little time I've spent in Asia, my sense is that it's something altogether different from what gets bandied about in the West under the rubric of 'improving your sex life'."

Nodding her head, Lekshe said:

"Misunderstandings abound over sexuality and teachers. Tantric practice is *not* about ordinary sex. The tantric teachings have often been interpreted in a very dangerous and distorted way in the West. Tantric symbolism is actually used to illustrate the importance of uniting wisdom with skillful, compassionate deeds. People see the form of a deity in union and they misunderstand the male/female symbolism. Buddhist tantric teachings explain profound methods of meditation for visualizing oneself as an enlightened being in order to develop enlightened qualities. This is what is known as 'deity yoga.'

"People need to study Buddhism before they start making commitments and taking vows. Know what you are getting into. Spiritual evolution is something that continues lifetime after lifetime. Bodhisattva vows are something a person takes until the time of your final enlightenment, which may be aeons and aeons away. We commit ourselves to work eternally for the welfare of beings. If we are not ready to do that, we should give ourselves time to develop. We need to ask ourselves some hard questions before we take on a teacher, no matter which tradition we're in," she added. "It's our responsibility to examine the teacher from the beginning.

"Ask yourself if this is a person to whom you want to entrust your spiritual development. Women especially need to be very clear about this. There are a lot of people who are saying they are teachers, calling themselves 'enlightened.' Watch out. The people who know the most are usually the ones that are the most humble and reserved and would never brag about their development. Sometimes we have to search a long time for these people, but that's our responsibility. Even if it takes years of watching that person before we ask them to be our teacher, do it. We need to make sure the teacher's behavior is in accordance with the teachings."

"Haven't you wanted or tried to find a woman teacher?" I asked.

"Out of my twenty-one teachers, three are women. One has passed away," she replied. "There are great women teaching meditation in many traditions, in Sri Lanka, Nepal, India, Korea, Japan, Taiwan, some very fine teachers. But one has to seek them out.

"If we concentrate on the practice and do it well, then perhaps we can become teachers ten or twenty years from now. Women teachers will arise naturally. In the meantime we practice the Dharma. It's more important for us to think of evolving ourselves spiritually than to have a set goal of developing as women teachers.

"Since men and women both have male and female elements, the most important thing is to find a qualified teacher. If it happens to be a woman, fine. If it happens to be a man, fine. The main thing is to study and practice and to learn from each other. We don't have to have reached Buddhahood in order to encourage each other on the path.

"We are all teachers. Ultimately, the Buddha is our teacher. In the Buddhist tradition, we can always go to Buddha's teachings and we can find the answers there. He gave teachings for forty-five years and he gave them for a reason. We have volumes of teachings and volumes of the commentaries to explain them. We just need to take the time to look at them. It's inspiring to see people who are living the teachings and people who can answer our personal questions, but the Dharma teachings themselves are the ultimate refuge. The teachings are our truest guide. The Dharma will never lose its value."

There are other women beside Lekshe who have taken up these issues and made great contributions to women on this path,[14] but circumstances were such that it was Lekshe that I found. Her comments on Tibetan Buddhism fed me, spurred me deeper in my own commitment to practice. Her life was pared down, lived simply.

Pay attention, I told myself. I continued to meet women who were guides for me, further along on this path, who held out their hands, helped me along. Not formally recognized as teachers, they were teachers for me. I was finding women teachers, though not in the form I had sought. Valuing them was crucial. I could dismiss them because they weren't formally acclaimed, or I could recognize the teachings in what they had given me. The Dharma is everywhere. I am the one who makes the assumption that it must come from a male authority figure, a holdover from my upbringing. No one is telling me that this is the case. It is my own thinking—habitual, unconscious, and unexamined—that is my worst enemy. There are women teachers everywhere. It is for me to recognize and acknowledge this fact.

At the Library of Tibetan Works and Archives in Dharamsala I met Tashi Tsering, a Tibetan scholar who took me into a room of Tibetan looseleaf texts all wrapped and tied in yellow and orange cloth from floor to ceiling, and was able to find a passage on a Black Tara for me. Many female deities that are painted blue-black are actually described as black in the texts, he explained. Most of the fierce deities are dark blue-black. Some are red, most are blue-black.

"She is the eleventh Tara. Yes, she is black. She has the ability to call all beings to her side. She removes poverty. It doesn't say much more than that about her."

Tashi Tsering suggested that I see Thupten Sangye, now an old man, who had served the Thirteenth Dalai Lama. His office was on the top floor of the library. We sat over tea as he told me, through Dupchok, about *rangjung*.

"*Rangjung* is a very precious thing. The veil drops, another reality penetrates, and all the blessings of that deity are concentrated. To us it is natural, not amazing."

The next morning I went back to Lochö Rinpoche's apartment with Dupchok and the Twenty-one Tara poster, but the abbot wasn't in. There would be no time to try to see him again. I had to leave for Delhi the next day in order to arrive in time for His Holiness's teachings. I still hadn't been able to get a train ticket or a ride to the station, some hours away, in Pathankot, back in the Punjab. But I had the good fortune to have met an American woman, Prema Dasara, who was staying at Jamyang Chöling, in the room next to Lekshe Tsomo's, who had offered to travel with me.

Striking, auburn-haired, and graceful from years of dancing, Prema had lived in southern India for years and now spent four or five months of the year in India studying the classical temple dance of Odissi. The rest of the year she lived in Hawaii, where she was involved with the Maui Tibetan Buddhist Center and taught sacred dance. She was in Dharamsala to attend some of the Dalai Lama's teachings. From here she had to go to Delhi as well, on her way to Orissa.

Prema and I left Dharamsala the next day, mid-afternoon. We had hired a Jeep with a Tibetan driver to get us to Pathankot in the Punjab in time for the fourteen-hour night train to Delhi. I was nervous about going back into the Punjab since we had been able to make no arrangements before we had to leave. Prema didn't have the proper papers for travel in the Punjab either, so we were both illegal. Tickets would have to be bought at the station; whether or not they were available, and what class, remained unknown. This was not a situation in which one could just pick up a telephone. Someone, preferably a Tibetan, had to go to the station for you, a five-hour drive each way, buy tickets, and deliver them to Dharamsala. We had been unable to arrange this. Now there was nothing to do but go ourselves.

"Buy first-class tickets, or second-class A.C., they're all right. But if you end up on regular second-class, chain your bags to yourself before you go to sleep if you want to see them when you wake up," said one friend..

I was very relieved that Prema had elected to travel with me to Delhi. Her Tibetan name, Kelzang Drolkar, meant "White Tara of Good Fortune." Having crisscrossed India for years she was much more relaxed about our travel arrangements, or the lack thereof.

We took off with our driver and a surly young Tibetan man, neither of whom spoke English. The young Tibetan had a badly cut finger that I was able to treat with an antibiotic ointment and to bandage. He was friendlier after that. Our Tibetan friends in Dharamsala had given them instructions to take us to the one Tibetan hotel in Pathankot, the only place where we could wait safely until time for the eight o'clock train without being noticed. The hotel was only a block or two from the station and we could easily get a rickshaw to take us there with our piles of heavy luggage.

No sooner had we crossed the border into the Punjab than we began to see large caches of military equipment draped in huge olive drab camouflage nets woven through with vines all along the roadside. Jet fighters streaked overhead. Military Jeeps sped up and down the road in both directions, sending up small clouds of dust like smoke from tiny fires. The sky was clear and blue. A woman walked down the roadside barefoot, a bundle of firewood on her head, a shy three-year-old child clinging to her faded turquoise sari, ducking behind her as we passed. The wind caught her sari and billowed it out like a sail. When I turned to look back, her sari was still billowing and I imagined her a sailboat sailing toward the shores of home. A tiny sailboat riding out a storm, she carried the daily life that must go on—wood gathered for the stove, water hauled, meals prepared, children fed, no matter that there are cannons and tanks along the road, no matter what the conflicts that rage.

We arrived in Pathankot just before dark. Now there were soldiers every few feet. I wanted to take pictures but did not. Photographing might draw unwanted attention to our presence and then requests for our nonexistent papers. The presence of so much military in the middle of a civilian population left a palpable tension in the air. We drove straight to the train station where Prema tried to buy tickets. "Just wait in the car," she suggested. There were half a dozen heavily armed soldiers patrolling the entrance. One of them saw me waiting in the Jeep. I smiled. He did not. A childish urge came up and I wanted to take pictures *because* it was forbidden, but I refrained.

Prema came back to the Jeep. No luck. "Please come back just before eight o'clock, madam," she was told. Now to the hotel just off the main street on a narrow side road. The driver and his assistant quickly helped to carry our bags up three flights of narrow stairs, said something in Tibetan to the proprietor, and got ready to take off. I followed them back down the stairs determined at least to photograph our driver and the aging beast of a Jeep that got us to Pathankot. Off on this side street no one would notice. The driver stood proudly next to his vehicle with the young Tibetan and smiled. He was missing most of his teeth. I squinted into the viewfinder, barely able to get a light reading at twilight, focused and shot. When I looked up, there was a military convoy waiting to pass. A soldier jumped out of the cab and strode toward me. I took my camera from around my neck and tried not to show my surprise.

"What are you taking a picture of?" he demanded gruffly.

"Our driver there," I said pointing to the two Tibetans who were now climbing into the Jeep.

"I am driver too! Take my picture," he suddenly commanded with a smile and positioned himself in front of his truck. I laughed with relief. "Of course. You are a driver too. Good. Bigger smile!" The soldiers in the back of the convoy began to laugh. He climbed back up in his truck and they took off. I raced back up the three flights to the waiting room, filled with others, mostly Tibetans, who'd come to take the train to Delhi. Prema was unpacking her water bowls, getting ready to make her evening offering and prayers.

"It's the Twenty-one Praises to Tara in English," she explained, handing me a sheaf of green Xeroxed papers. "Would you like to chant with me? It's a translation that a friend of mine did. I have a copy of it, you can follow along," she said, rummaging through her bag. She was prepared for all occasions, down to carrying her own stove so that she could boil water and cook for herself.

Every morning and evening, no matter where she was, Prema would stop, fill the offering bowls with water, and chant the praises to Tara. I was happy to join her. Public prayer is a part of everyday

Tibetan life, whether people say their beads (*malas*) as they walk along the street, turn the big prayer wheels that are found wherever there's a Tibetan community, or twirl a miniature prayer wheel in one hand as they walk. That we were in a small hotel lobby was no issue. No one found what we were doing strange. Not only was the chanting freeing, but the fact that we could do it without feeling odd was equally liberating.

The Westernized English translation was lovely, making Tara more accessible to me than ever. Green-golden, dispeller of all fears, her laughter defeated and subdued all enemies, the entire universe was under her sway. She sits in a garland of fire, in one verse, ablaze with her brilliance; in another, a mere stamp of her foot shakes all the mountains on the earth. The crescent moon serves as a diadem on her head, her face radiates the light of a thousand stars, she holds the moon in the palm of her hand, like the ocean of gods, the praises said. She protects all beings, heals sickness; even if one has drunk poison, should you call out to her, you will be cured. She fulfills all desire, removes every obstacle, Mother, Protector, Saviouress, with eyes of the moon and sun. Chanting these praises three times was calming.

Back to the station just before eight with our bags in tow, Prema searched the chalkboard in the hallway to find the Delhi train number. "There it is," she said to my surprise, pointing to all the scrawls. I could make out nothing.

"Now this way." She picked up her bags and disappeared into a small crowded room full of men talking loudly to the one ticket taker sitting at the desk. I watched from the doorway by our mound of luggage. The tickets were neatly rolled up in his half-open drawer. The wooden fan turned slowly overhead beneath a dingy light bulb. Prema could hardly get near the desk. Many people wanted to travel on the Delhi express. Wives, children, and relatives had spread out on the waiting platforms. People just put some kind of ground cover down on the concrete and established their turf. Families were sitting talking or perhaps sleeping, others boiled water for tea or packed up the evening meal which they had cooked right on the platform in the station. The men were in the ticketmaster's office waving their hands in the air, pounding the desk, and in general doing whatever they could to coerce the ticketmaster into giving them tickets. Place in line, money, whether or not one had reservations—nothing seemed to matter from the outside. The whole operation was governed by rules invisible to me as a foreigner. Who received tickets seemed completely arbitrary, based on the ticketmaster's internal fluctuations in bile and stomach acid.

Prema was patient. She knew what she was doing. My heart sank. I wanted her to charge in with her Hindi and be aggressive, but that would never have worked. The man on the street in India did not necessarily find the assertiveness of strong Western women compelling. Pleading or cursing was more productive. Prema did neither. She had gauged the situation carefully and slowly worked herself up in the pecking order, where she now was conversing with the man at the desk. She had a commanding presence. It was not a matter of putting your money down and being handed a ticket; it was more like a courtroom where one pleaded a case. Politely, she convinced the man to sell us two tickets. The ticketmaster reached into the drawer ceremoniously and pulled out regular second-class tickets, $2 apiece.

"That's all that was available," Prema explained, "and we were lucky to get that. Let's go."

When we climbed on board the yellow train car, the conductor shepherded us into the "Ladies Compartment," a metal box about seven feet long and five feet wide with a solid sliding metal door and two barred windows. I felt like I was being shown to a cell. With the utmost graciousness he showed us how to pull down the "beds," wooden platforms suspended by chains from the wall, and warned us not to sleep with our heads by the open windows.

"We make some stops during the middle of the night. Sometimes a thief will reach in and rip your jewelry off your neck. That's why the windows are barred in the first place."

Though it was evening, it was still very hot, so hot that we were already perspiring. The windows had to stay open, though the door to our compartment would be closed once we started. A Punjabi matron boarded and was shown to the same compartment. She was followed by four daughters and a ten-year-old boy. They had bags as well as food and several stalks of bamboo or cane. Soon every corner of our tiny compartment was filled. How we would all manage in this tiny cell for fourteen hours, much less sleep, escaped me. One of the daughters turned out to be a New Yorker visiting her mother.

"Don't worry. The youngest ones will sleep on the floor on top of the luggage. That leaves us each one platform to sleep on," she explained sweetly. Once the platforms were pulled down from the walls, you could not sit up. There was no standing as the floor was full of children and luggage. Outside, the larger car was full of men who stared in the most discomforting way. We were two Western women traveling without men, still a questionable enterprise in some parts of the world.

Claustrophobic or not, I was trapped and could do little but lie down. Prema's platform was six inches above my head when I propped myself up to read by flashlight. At first, with Prema's help in translation, I was able to convince everyone to at least leave our sliding door cracked for circulation of air and a cross draft. (The fan on our side didn't work.) But during the middle of the night the mother closed and locked it. I didn't understand why, but I gave up trying to keep it open. In the morning we were awakened by men pounding on the door and shouting at us, demanding that we open our door.

I asked Prema what was going on. She had begun shouting back louder in Hindi something that sounded like a curse, telling them to go away, we were not going to open the door. People had been getting on the train all night whenever it slowed down or stopped and now the outer compartment was crammed full with no place to sit. People were hanging from the luggage compartment, riding in the places between the cars, on the car steps, everywhere. They were pounding on our door to get in and the women in our car pounded and shouted back. Finally whoever they were went away and the yelling stopped.

I had gotten little sleep under the circumstances. It took great concentration on my part to stay calm in such a small crowded space. I had to practice breathing in a very disciplined way so that I didn't just panic and run. There was nowhere to go in any case. I consoled myself with the fact that no matter how strong my claustrophobic reaction, this compartment was not a jail cell. I would walk out of here within hours. Many people were rotting in real jails, were more crowded, or lived under much worse conditions all over the world, and they weren't getting off in Delhi. Telling myself the truth threw the situation into sharp relief. Gratitude followed. My Catholic background rose to the fore and served me well—"offer it up"—but this time it wasn't for the poor souls in Purgatory or in Limbo, but "for all sentient beings," as the Buddhists say.

Finally I began to relax.

By the time we arrived in Delhi the next day just before noon, I felt like I was crawling out of my first Native American sweat lodge, drained but happy. Contending with crowded conditions, which for many is simply a way of life, an ordinary occurrence, had for me been an accomplishment. I was greatly humbled.

New Delhi, India
October 1986

Preparations for Durga Puja were in full swing when I arrived back in Delhi. Villagers poured in from the countryside to the city.

"Shoeshine, madam?" a young boy asked as I walked down the Janpath, a busy main street in Delhi. I stood next to a cow at the street corner. Taxi horns blared. Scooters, auto-rickshaws, buses, cars, bicycles, pony-drawn tongas clipped by.

"No, thank you." I kept walking.

"Your shoes are very dirty, I give first-class shine, very good," he said, following at my side.

"No."

"You must shine your shoes," he informed me as we crossed the street against the light.

"No," I said, fairly wanting to shout at him with my growing annoyance.

"You can't meet business with dirty shoes, madam," he shot back, still beside me.

"No!" I snapped, swatting my hand with a newspaper at the same time, *thwack*.

The October sky yellows with the dusty wind that barrels through the late afternoon, whipping the curtains out into the room. Below my second-floor balcony are huge pink frangipanis in bloom. It's still hot here in Delhi even though it's fall. Though I have other music with me, I find myself listening to Paul Simon's *Graceland* again and again. It seems written for travel in these times. Even Tibetan monks in Dharamsala had to go through security checks to attend the Dalai Lama's teachings. Searches are becoming part of life. Borders are closing with the increase in terrorism. As of this month, Americans are required to secure a visa to visit France; Indian nationals, a visa for travel to England.

Simon sings about lives catching on fire. Will India catch on fire? The Punjab, Darjeeling, the Tamils, the assassination attempt on Rajiv Gandhi the day I left New York—kindling. The heat is building. News of Chernobyl has exploded. Radioactivity doesn't stop at international borders.

I have spent the afternoon with His Holiness, Tenzin Gyatso, the Fourteenth Dalai Lama, and about forty other people, mostly Indian nationals. There were a handful of Europeans; I was the only American. We will spend from 1:00 to 5:00 p.m. in his hotel suite at the Ashok, receiving teachings from His Holiness on basic tenets and practices of Tibetan Buddhism for the next two days as well. He will focus on implementing basic Buddhist teaching into everyday life.

Now alone in my hotel room with the overhead fan whirring, taking it all in, the music, the contrasts between His Holiness and his talk of peace and the heavy, constant presence of the military in the Punjab that we traveled through the day before. The music holds together experiences that my mind can't grasp: stories of massacres and torture of Tibetans, their children forced to beat their parents and the monks by the Chinese; the life of the leper in Dharamsala, going to visit his daughter for Christmas. Prema told me of a *saddhu,* a holy man, she met on a pilgrimage to the mouth of the Ganges. He is iced into his cave for four months each winter. The remainder of the year he cooks food for pilgrims and will accept no money.

The Dalai Lama's hotel suite is filled with flowers. An altar has been set up to the right of the Dalai Lama, with the traditional seven silver water bowls, butter lamps, incense, and bouquets of flowers— pink and salmon-colored roses—and a statue of the Buddha. Tenzin Gyatso sits in his sleeveless gold and red monk's robes on a beige couch beneath a large tangkha painting draped with a *khata.* There is a bowl of yellow roses in front of him. A car honks insistently outside.

I sit in the back of the room on a chartreuse green velvet couch, comfortably squeezed in with three other people. Nearly all the women in the room have on silk saris, green and yellow, pink and dark blue checks, brown, gold-edged, orange, studding the floor with brilliant colors. Most people sit on square orange meditation cushions on top of white sheets spread over the beige carpet. Several of the men wear only white.

The Dalai Lama begins by pointing out the practicalities of training one's mind.

"Mental attitude is very important. It allows you to face even tragedy. Training our minds is very useful. This life is full of contraditions and problems. How will we meet our problems? That is an issue, yes?

"Violence and cruelty are increasing, so the Buddha's message of nonviolence is very important to this modern time. Like Gandhi, we must take the essence of this message and implement it in our daily life."

The Dalai Lama speaks in motion, fairly bouncing—he's so energetic at moments—punctuating his points in the air.

"Altruism is the key to happiness. Self-cherishing has many disadvantages," he points out. "It can bring up innumerable problems, from family fights to international squabbles. These things come from selfishness. Cherishing others, being open-minded, sincere, and honest, these are the things we need to develop."

He gives us instructions in meditation and visualization, taking us through a series of stages of the meditation. What stayed with me was his discussion of enemies as teachers.

"All beings want happiness and not suffering. Visualize your 'enemies,' those who cause you discomfort, in front of you, just like yourself," he said at one stage of the meditation. "Think of all beings as having once been your mother. She treated you with great love and kindness. We should think about everyone with this conviction. We should be deeply grateful.

"We are all dependent on the kindness of others, not just from our close relatives or close friends, but from all beings: the laborers who built this building, the people who raised the food we eat, made the clothes we wear.

"The very existence of our life is entirely dependent upon others. . . . In order to practice these things we've been talking about— compassion, love, kindness, altruism—we must have other beings. Your ability to make progress on the path is dependent upon others. To develop compassion, we must have tolerance, a key factor. Anger and hatred are the greatest obstacles to love and compassion.

"Tolerance is the key to compassion, and for this we need enemies to give us the opportunity to practice tolerance. Enemies are very important, they give you the opportunity to develop and grow."

The Dalai Lama was quick to point out that it's easy to be patient and kind toward people we like and care for. But it's our enemy that makes us develop virtue, grow. Being kindly and tolerant toward those who cause us discomfort or harm, reflecting upon them as people just like ourselves, as members of our own family, was a challenging thought. Like Christ's oft-unheeded dictum: "Love your enemies, do good to those who harm you," the Dalai Lama's message is not for the fainthearted.

The most compelling teaching he gave was the one not spoken. He himself had great cause to be angry and embittered toward the Chinese government. Yet he was not. Some Tibetans I met were dismayed by his insistence on nonviolence, and a few want armed revolution, but he refuses to countenance such a path for his people.

This was the lesson that seemed the most difficult and the most important to take to heart, whether I liked it or not.

In the dining room of the YMCA-Delhi, where I was staying, tea was served in hot nickel-silver pots that must be handled with a heavy white cloth napkin. Languages swirled around me: German, Norwegian, Hindi, American, British, colonial English.

The air was thick this morning in Delhi. I sat across from a couple from Munich at breakfast.

"We're still feeling the effects of Chernobyl. We still can't eat mushrooms," they told me. "At first they said don't drink milk, eat salad, spinach, or mushrooms. Now it's just the mushrooms."

I told them that I was on my way to Switzerland after the teachings and from there, I hoped, to Poland, to begin my research on the Black Madonna, the patron of Poland.

"Poland received some of the fallout from Chernobyl, too. Watch out."

The hotel telephone switchboard continued not to work for the third day in a row—no outgoing calls—my day lurched off to a slow, dry start. I was waiting for a call from Sunil Roy, former Indian Ambassador to Mexico, Nicaragua and other countries, now a consultant to the U.N. on the Environment. He was first sent to Warsaw in the 1950s, when India established an Embassy there. Poland was his favorite post.

Sunil arrived at the Y, having given up on the phone system. He insisted on driving me to the library where he pulled out two encyclopedias, motioned me to a table, and had me begin to read the entries on Poland. In the meantime, he went off to find a paperback copy of James Michener's book, *Poland,* somewhere on the streets of Delhi, for me to read on the long journey still ahead of me.

"It will help you begin to get a feeling for Poland's history, whether or not you approve of Michener," he said when he returned to pick me up from the library and handed me a copy triumphantly an hour later.

"There's an old story about India and Poland, I don't know where it comes from. It's an Indian story, oddly enough," he told me later that evening over dinner with his family.

"When the world is destroyed there will only be two places that will be safe. One is a temple in Ujjain, southern India, and the other a tunnel underneath the Wawel Castle chapel in Krakow, Poland. I've never been able to find out anymore. Isn't that a curious tale?

"But you see, you're right, you're onto something, my dear. There *is* a connection between India and Poland. Something about the spirit of the people. It wouldn't occur to most people to put those two countries together, but let me tell you, I loved my years in Warsaw and I was completely at home with the Polish people. You must study the history of Poland. It is heartbreaking, but you must learn it."

On the flight from Delhi to London en route for Switzerland, I decide to put off reading *Poland* and instead finish *Freedom at Midnight,* an account of India's struggle for independence, the fateful history with the British and Mahatma Gandhi. The words had a vividness now that leap to life. Independence was gained only in 1947, and the country is still gripped with the conflicts between Sikhs and Hindus. After just being in India, this brief, popularized history had a palpability that ordinary prose lacked. Monks in saffron robes had walked past me on the streets, off the page.

I remember the shoeshine boy I impatiently refused. The beggar children that I did not give to still haunt me. "Why this one?" I asked myself. There were so many and some clearly had no other way to survive. I gave to many, but to some I did not.

CHAPTER 8

The Ravens of Einsiedeln

◆

Einsiedeln, Switzerland

In the seed, the genes whisper: stretch out for the light
  and seek the dark
And the tree seeks the light, it stretches out,
  for the dark
And the more darkness it finds, the more light it discovers....

—Reidar Ekner[1]

Küsnacht, Switzerland
October 1986

I have come to Switzerland to see the Black Madonna at Einsiedeln. The statue of Kali in Varanasi, India, had reminded me of a photograph of this Madonna. I could not forget the strikingly similar quality of peacefulness in them both. For the first time in ten years I am letting myself look back into my own cultural tradition of Catholicism.

When I first left the United States to travel overseas, it was to Asia. I had never been to Europe before. I had turned away from my own spiritual and cultural tradition, assigning it little value. Now I no longer believe that to be true.

Scattered throughout the European continent there are hundreds of dark or black Madonnas: in Spain, France, Italy, Austria, Switzerland, as well as other countries.[2] But the Madonna at Einsiedeln intrigued me for two reasons: first, the sense that she is related, however remotely, to the peaceful Kali that I had seen in Varanasi; and secondly, the fact that she is painted coal black. This is not a Madonna that blackened because of smoke or was carved out of a wood that darkened over the centuries. She strikes me as one of the clearest examples of an unequivocally black deity venerated by a white population, and this fascinated me. Clearly this is not a matter of ethnicity; Switzerland is unremittingly caucasian.

I've come to Küsnacht because the Jung Institute is here and because of its convenience to Einsiedeln. The small town of Küsnacht is almost halfway between Einsiedeln and Zurich, on the shores of Lake Zurich, the Zürichsee. I had been given an excerpt from a dissertation written at the Jung Institute on the Einsiedeln Madonna and I wanted to do further research here. I was directed to a lakeside hotel nearby, a ten-minute walk from the Institute.

It's late Sunday morning, the first chance I have to see the Madonna at Einsiedeln, and I am on the verge of getting sick. I slept with a cobalt blue woolen muffler wrapped around my neck and a brown wool shawl from India over my shoulders, as well as all the blankets the hotel provided. My throat is raw.

Gulls wheel and squawk outside my window on the Zürichsee. The wind is high and cold this morning, noisy in the big evergreen outside my window and shrill as it whistles through the window shutters. The clouds are jagged and moving rapidly, the sky lead-colored broken up with patches of azure blue. Two gray swans were swimming just outside my window when I first got up but now the waters are rough and whitecapped. Church bells ring continuously.

Downstairs at breakfast, purple mountain heather blooms outside in the dining-room window box. Inside, pink begonias turn toward the light.

I make a meal of thick brown bread spread with butter and apricot jam, milk tea, and crackers in the Hotel Sonne dining room.

The waiter speaks only German, the housekeeper Italian, and the people at the next table French. My years of Latin and grade-school French allow me to understand a word here and there, but I am without the ability to converse. A handful of French and Italian phrases help me move through the day, but I can go no further and am embarrassed to speak only English.

By midafternoon I'm on the train to Einsiedeln. The rain is falling hard by the time I finally arrive. The big church bells of the Benedictine monastery can be heard booming, even from the train station. Equipment bag over one shoulder, book bag over the other, rolls of film, pens, watercolors, colored pencils, and paper stuffed in every pocket, I put up my umbrella and set out briskly. Laughing at myself for dragging all this equipment with me everywhere, I hurry through the rain, happy, not knowing exactly how to get to the church but sure of the direction.

Within six blocks I come to the large Baroque church with a fountain in front and the Virgin standing on a crescent moon in the center. It can only be the Monastery of Einsiedeln. Up the long flights of steps to the large doors on the side, I open first one heavy set of doors that creaks softly on heavy wrought-iron hinges into the vestibule, then a second set, and I am inside.

The Madonna's small black chapel stands directly in front of me, completely enclosed within the nave of the larger basilica. I make my way to an empty pew and kneel down. Bells ring, Latin echoes from the distant back of the church. A group of monks and priests walk down the nave of the church to the front of the tiny chapel of the Virgin, their chant reverberating softly through the cavernous basilica.

I am craning my neck to see the Black Madonna set against a cloudburst of beaten gold with thunderbolts and lightning shooting out from all sides. Her expression is serene and lovely. She is a young Mary, perhaps sixteen to twenty, painted coal black. The black Christ Child she holds in her arms looks almost playful in his gaze. A bird sits perched on his hand, about to peck his thumb. Mother and son

Monastery of Einsiedeln, Switzerland. (Author)

are ornately robed in heavy cream-white satins, thickly embroidered
with a crust of flowers of colored silk threads. The Madonna holds
a royal scepter in her right hand.

Forty black-robed priests and monks begin to line up in front of
the black marble chapel. Everyone rises to their feet. The Catholic
monks and priests look so somber all in black with their serious faces,
no smiles, their eyes cast down, a striking contrast to the cheerful
faces and bright robes of the Tibetan monks I've just left in India.
It has been nearly ten years since I stood in front of the Madonna
in the side chapel in Abiquiu, New Mexico, and began to follow this
path. I have come so far to see her again!

Now the monks are lined up. An expectant silence falls. After a
moment they burst forth into the gorgeous medieval melody of the

Latin hymn *Salve Regina* in perfect harmony, unaccompanied. The outpouring of their devotion to the Madonna transforms them. I am stunned. When they sing to her they are no longer somber, nor seem so foreign. Every afternoon at four o'clock for the last four hundred years they have sung the *Salve Regina* to this Madonna.

The hymn echoes throughout the enormous nave and sweeps me back into my own childhood, thick and overgrown with a Catholicism I found impenetrable as an adult. Now standing here in front of this Madonna their song cuts through the years and gives me a way back to a place that had been lost. Memories rush up.

Daily mass and communion, visits to chapel, seasons of Lent, Fridays without meat, Advent wreaths, the world of saints like the bird-covered Francis—crazy for God—and Theresa who taught her nuns to dance, whispers floating out of confessionals soft and blurred, the smell of incense swung from the altar, the mass sung in Latin, Gregorian chants, the soft tinkle of bells at the consecration, "Say but the Word, O Lord," making rosaries by hand, bottles of holy water, "Remember O Most Gracious Virgin Mary," the wonderful celebration of Mary's month, May—all wash over me as I stand here before the Black Madonna of Einsiedeln, listening. A childhood that I could only turn my back upon, had considered lost, inaccessible, had to walk away from, had no way back to, is redeemed in this moment by their song.

I am flooded with feelings. Each day in May we would sing to Mary and crown her statue in our classroom at the Ursuline Academy in Dallas, Texas. By May it was already hot. The large paned windows were opened all the way, angling out into the room almost horizontally. A large electric fan on a green-based metal stand blew from the corner.

Grade school—drawing names on ragged paper scraps out of a navy blue felt dress uniform hat—the day would come when it was my turn. Filled with excitement I would go home with a run through the door to make my announcement, "Mother! It's my turn! I have to bring the crown tomorrow, help!" Did she help me make the crown or did she do it for me, I no longer remember, only the wandering comes back, through our yard, through our neighbors', stopping, bending down to look for small enough flowers to make a tiny crown two inches in diameter. Sometimes we would have to get in the car and drive to my grandmother's a few miles away by the creek, for pansies or tea roses—did my grandmother help then too?—and we would weave whatever flowers we'd collected into a tiny circlet. Carefully we would wrap the ring of flowers in waxed papers and put it into the refrigerator for the night.

The next morning I would carry the wax-paper-covered crown to school on top of all my books for everyone to admire. Then, after the first bell, just before time for classes to begin, we would all stand up beside our desks singing a hymn to Mary and take our turn to walk up the aisle, slowly, to our classroom altar and to crown her.

◆

Father Matthew guides me through the basilica of Einsiedeln after the service. His humble devotion to this Madonna and his helpfulness begin to tear down the walls I had built between myself and Catholic priests. When I ask him about the miraculous healing powers that this Madonna reportedly has, he assures me that the greatest miracles that take place here are those inside the human heart.

I asked him why the Madonna was black. No reason, he replies, unwilling to make much of it. There is a way in which this is a correct and true answer. It stays with me. "For no reason." There are many reasons and there are no reasons.

Now I am standing here in front of this Madonna about to light candles and pray, something I haven't done in many years. An underlying issue arises: for whom will I pray? Can I really do what the Dalai Lama said in Delhi—regard my enemies as my greatest treasure? Friends in recovery tell me something similar, I must forgive anyone who has harmed me; not to do so means that I harm myself today.

Black Madonna at Einsiedeln, Switzerland,
"Our Lady of the Dark Forest." (O. Baur)

Though in my morning meditations I envision both loved ones and those I find difficult—"enemies"—to light these candles is a different act. It requires more on my part.

I thought I had let go of the past, but the level of interior discussion that is set off in this moment tells me again that I have not. Will I light candles for those who have harmed me? I like to think that I am justified for my bad feelings, but this must stop. Am I ready to look at my part?

I feel a small current of warm air as I step up to the banks of burning candles set along the sides of the Madonna's black marble chapel. There is no reason. Regarding one's enemy as a treasure goes against reason. Forgiveness goes against reason. The blackness of this Madonna, the teachings of the Buddha, Christ, and my friends in recovery all tell me that I must go deeper, beyond reason. This Madonna is a healer, but how can she work if I won't listen?

After a moment of wavering, I finally genuflect and light candles for everyone I care for, as well as those for whom I bear enmity. I ask to become willing to give up my resentments. The first step is willingness. There, as I light the last taper and put the match out, I have made another beginning.

When I push open the heavy wooden doors of the church to leave, I see that it has been snowing all afternoon. Now it is after dark and still the snow falls, thick and silent. It spirals and swirls in gusts of wind, sparkling in the circles of light made by the tall street lamps.

◆

I had been told to contact Dora Kalff, one of Jung's students and protégés. Now in her mid-eighties, a native Swiss like Jung, she revered the Black Madonna at Einsiedeln and sometimes sent her patients there.[3] A visit to Frau Kalff seemed imperative when I found out that she was not only a highly regarded Jungian analyst but also a Tibetan Buddhist. She and her son, Jungian analyst and Tibetan Buddhist scholar Martin Kalff, had established the Yiga Chözin Center for the Study of Buddhism and Psychology in Zollikon, between Küsnacht and Zurich.

Frau Kalff received me in a room carpeted deep red with a small dark blue oriental rug in the middle. The walls of her study were bursting with books and toys, the tops of the bookcases lined with bright-colored papier-mâché masks. She tells me that the Black Madonna is appearing in the dreams and fantasies of some of her clients.

"When the Black Madonna comes, I usually see this as the first impulse of the good feminine. When she appears, then we can guess that the psyche is beginning to grow in a spiritual direction, spiritual as together with everyday life, with the body, the earth. Not separate. Many people speak about spiritual development as though it's high up, somewhere else.

"Tara and the Black Madonna are the carriers of this development in the psyche. We're seeing a dawning of the feminine *now*. Women are beginning to realize that to follow the man's way is not working. We must develop our own capacities, not follow men. The Black Madonna is beginning to break through."

I am shown into a small but elegant dining room. It's now the first of November. I'm in Winterthur, on the other side of Zurich. The table is set for three on a white linen tablecloth. Purple asters stand in a crystal vase in the middle of the table. The silver is old, heavy sterling, simply styled. At the end of the generous oval table is a formal silver tea service with a white-porcelain-lined brown teapot. In the corner is a stately large rectangular heating stove made of squares of emerald green tiles and polished brass.

Only an hour ago Carol Savvas and I were standing in the middle of a field of dry grasses at Rikon laughing as we picked special long-life grasses for a Tara retreat she will soon leave to make. I had met Carol recently at Dora Kalff's. An American as well as a student of

Tibetan Buddhism, she was in Switzerland to work on her doctoral dissertation for the University of Wisconsin at Madison. Fluent in Tibetan, she was translating the biography of Machig Labdron, the famous eleventh-century Tibetan woman master who had transmitted the *chöd* meditation practice. Machig had thousands of disciples as well as her own children. Machig is also considered to be an important manifestation of Tara. The moment Carol found out that I was interested in Tara, she generously offered to help me with introductions to scholars, Tibetan lamas and to translate.

Black hair, black eyes, light olive skin, Carol's finely featured face was set off by a purple and gold-trimmed scarf. The fall trees were pale red, gold, orange, and green on the distant hills in the falling light. The sky was cloudy, the sunset full of reds and violet, a storm on the horizon, and the wind biting cold.

"We must hurry back to Winterthur. I have to finish cooking dinner and introduce you to Dr. Lindegger," she said. "Hurry, that's our train coming now," she cried as we made a dash back across the field to the tracks. We got on board, catapulting into our seats out of breath.

Peter Lindegger is a classical philologist and Tibetologist in Winterthur; he teaches ancient Greek, Latin, and Tibetan at Zurich University. Carol suggested that I meet with him because he is familiar with both Tara and the Black Madonna. I am invited to dinner as well.

A stack of books sits beside the place setting that Carol is motioning me to once dinner is ready to be served. Dr. Lindegger has been making notes all afternoon to review at dinner and has pulled down a few books from his shelves for me to look at, "some of the ones you should know about," he tells me. Some are in German. I am immediately intimidated by the amount of scholarship stacked in front of me. Fortunately he speaks English fluently and he assures me that it's all right that I don't speak or read German. Now I am merely embarrassed. But my discomfort is quickly dispelled by Dr. Lindegger's graciousness and Carol's call to dinner. She has baked chicken tarragon with rice, is tossing salad in the kitchen, and needs help getting plates to the table. We no sooner sit down than Dr. Lindegger begins.

"You have picked a very difficult, complicated subject, very complicated and full of questions that are not yet solved. I can only give you my particular viewpoint on the matter. Tara and the Black Madonna are not connected historically or geographically but they have the same archetypal roots. Jung's term 'archetype' is a dangerous word, subject to much misunderstanding, misuse, but in this case there is a high possibility that it is the correct word to use.

"Won't you have some chicken?" he broke off, as he sliced a leg. "Do you prefer dark or light?"

Jung gave the name "archetype" to the myth-forming elements that seem to be present in the human psyche after he encountered variations of the same story motifs again and again in disparate cultures around the world, such as the hero who journeys into the underworld, the divine child, the enchanted princess, the Great Mother, the wise old woman or man, the evil sorcerer, and the wise fool, to name a few.

Jung is careful to point out that an archetype is not the fact itself.[4] These are psychic forces with their own dynamic energy found alive and operative in some form, dependent upon the culture, in every human psyche. For Jung, the archetypes were "the real but invisible roots of consciousness,"[5] threads that came up from the instinctive, primitive underworld of the collective unconscious, that vast timeless pool of human experience that seems to be transmitted in our very genes. The Great Mother, the Divine Child, the Virgin Birth, and the Dying God are some of the archetypes found in the Madonna's story and in many stories around the world, much older than Christianity's. On one level, Mary herself is a composite figure, as Dr. Lindegger would explain, formed by a process that began long before Christianity.

"Please, enjoy your dinner," he urged.

"First, the Madonna is rooted in Mesopotamia. This you must

understand. There are two roots of Mary, some say even more. There is Ishtar and there is Isis, but first we will speak of Ishtar.

"Ishtar was called the Queen of Heaven, a Sumerian-Babylonian goddess of vegetation and a moon goddess. (Called *Inanna* by the Sumerians, of which Diane Wolkstein and Samuel Noah Kramer write, Ishtar is her Semite name.) She was worshipped prior to the third millennium B.C. as the goddess of fertility and love. She was worshipped not only in Mesopotamia but along the western coast of what is now Turkey, where the Greeks had established colonies. It was actually the Hittites that brought the cult of Ishtar to the West. The inhabitants of these colonies on the west coast were sailors and merchants. When the Greeks took over her worship, they called her Artemis. Both are unmarried goddesses. It was believed that in order to become cultivated, one must sleep with Ishtar or Artemis. Then one was no longer a barbarian. In the epic *Gilgamesh,* Enkidu knew all after sleeping with Ishtar, like Adam coming to consciousness after eating the apple in the Garden of Eden.

"Ishtar belongs to the chthonic world, the world below, the underground. She becomes known as the goddess Cybele around the fifth century B.C., some say earlier. Her face is black, the emphasis with her in the form of Cybele is on devouring. Just as I told you Mary has two roots, Ishtar also has a second origin. Ishtar's was from the underworld. Before Ishtar became Cybele, she had also passed through a period of worship as the goddess Astarte."[6] (Astarte was the goddess worshipped by King Solomon in his old age,[7] also known as Asherah in the Hebrew tradition.)

"But in her form as Cybele, the focus is on the descent into the underworld. She was very popular until the second century after Christ. She ruled with her son Attis, another god who died and was resurrected. She was the goddess of death. The Roman soldiers brought her cult back from their wars and it spread throughout the Roman Empire.

"Would you have some salad now?" he asks, passing me a bowl full of crisp greens and tomatoes.

"Not yet thank you," I reply, putting the bowl off to the other side of the books on my left. I write as quickly as possible, stealing a forkful of rice, now cold, in between making notes.

"Let me draw something for you, do you mind?" he says, taking a pen out of his freshly pressed white shirt pocket. He draws a map of the Mediterranean across the top of my notepaper, and then makes a wide arrow from the fertile crescent of Mesopotamia[8] out across the Mediterranean, past Greece, Italy, Sicily, and up through Spain and France to the north, then turning back to the east across Central Europe to Russia, to show the route of migration of cultural values.

"The Black Madonna is the most contemporary form of the idea of a very old goddess, whether we are talking about our Madonna here in Switzerland or one in France. She had different names, forms, and functions in different cultures. This map I have drawn shows the route she followed. To study her, one must understand the tradition or belief in the fact that the ground her shrine or temple was built on was itself holy.

"One cannot make the ground holy, it simply is. Knowing this, one culture would incorporate the sacred sites of the preceding culture, building one temple over another temple or calling the same statue by a different name. If you didn't do this, the people would worship there anyway.[9]

"In 205–04 B.C., the cult of Cybele was introduced into the Roman state," Dr. Lindegger went on to explain. "Called *Magna Mater,* the Great Mother, by the Romans, she arrived by ship from Asia Minor in the form of a black meteorite and was passed hand to hand by Roman matrons to the throne awaiting her sixteen kilometers inland in Rome.

"The Romans thought that the *Magna Mater* could help them conquer Hannibal, thereby beating the enemy with his own deity.

"Remember that I'm still telling you about Ishtar as one of the two main sources I see for the Black Madonna. You must also keep in mind that though Ishtar became known as Cybele in the Roman Empire, she was known as Artemis to the Greeks.

"Artemis is mentioned in the Linear-B script, the earliest Greek text extant, the oldest text of the Indo-European language, older than our earliest Sanskrit texts. There is a black-faced Artemis, associated with Hekate.

"The most ancient Artemis that we know of was found on Sparta and she too is black. We have only the mention of her in Pausanias, an author comparable to the modern guides to famous places. So, even though I said Mary had two roots—Ishtar and Isis—when you begin to examine Ishtar, you find you must also go back and look at Astarte, Cybele, and Artemis. This is a little of what I mean about the complexity of the subject you've picked."

I nod my head with a growing understanding.

"Now we come to the development of the motherhood of the deity," said Dr. Lindegger, "the Egyptian aspect, Isis. Now we have the Mother Goddess depicted in paintings and in statues suckling her son Horus. Isis was worshipped from around 1800 B.C. and, like Mary, was a virgin who brought her son forth 'of herself.'

"These elements all meet on the island of Sicily. The cults were carried there by sailors. For Sicily, the sacred places are worshipped regardless of the pagan names, for example, 'Maria sopra Artemide.' An especially important place is Erice, called Eryx in Greek and Roman times. Here the Carthaginians worshipped Ishtar, the Greeks worshipped Artemis, and later the Romans, Venus. In the middle of the Mediterranean, this is a passage that almost all ships had to make that sailed the Mediterranean. It was close to Africa, it was the passage to Spain. Used by the Phoenicians and Greeks, it was very important."

He stopped for a moment to consider the map he had made of the Mediterranean on my notes and then drew into place, quite precisely, the island of Sicily.

"The temple to Ishtar was seven hundred fifty meters above sea level on a very steep rock face, on which a bonfire was burned. About 800 B.C., after it had been a sanctuary to Artemis, it was changed into a temple of Venus. One can easily see the different archeological layers or strata here. Aeneas is said to have built a temple to Venus there in honor of his father Anchises who died there.[10] The Romans worshipped her as 'Venus Erychina (or Erucina).' This gives us a very good example of the way a sacred site was respected and used over and over by different religions."

Our dinner conversation is cut short by the Zurich train schedule. The last train out of Zurich for Küsnacht leaves at 12:05 a.m., allowing me an hour to finish dinner and get to Zurich by train from Winterthur. We clear the table and get the dishes rinsed and stacked. Dr. Lindegger assures me that we've only begun to scratch the surface of Mary's story and little was said about Tara. I will have to come back, we will correspond. Carol tells me to hurry now, we still have to walk to the station. I give my thanks again to Peter Lindegger and am gone.

The next morning the railway car sways gently from side to side as we race down the tracks to Einsiedeln before dawn. Now the tracks climb, gaining altitude gradually, and the sun breaks behind the snow-covered peaks overlooking a blue-gray lake in the mountains outside of Rapperswill. The whistle blows and a flock of gulls explodes from a green field below. They bank, turning away in one motion, their undersides flashing white for a split second as they arc away from the sunrise, then suddenly they're gone, blended into a dull gray sky.

The whistle jolts me out of my reading. I have been sitting absorbed in the dissertation from the Jung Institute on the Black Madonna of Einsiedeln. The paper is a mine of information, beginning with the history of the monastery from its origins in the ninth century on up to the present day. I had narrowly assumed that it was written by a woman but later, at the Jung Institute library, found that it was the work of Dr. Fred Gustafson.[11] I rely on his telling here.

The story of the Madonna at Einsiedeln begins with St. Meinrad, a ninth-century Benedictine hermit who passed this way over one thousand years ago. At thirty-one, he retired from the world of teaching in a monastery school to seek solitude on Mount Etzel, overlooking what became Einsiedeln, in the year 828. Over the next seven years more and more people came to pray with him and hear him preach from his homemade altar. Word of his special piety grew.

Needing greater solitude, he left the mountain and retreated to the forest, called the Finsterwald, across the Sihl River, in A.D. 835 when he was thirty-eight years old. *Finsterwald* means dark wood, or dark forest. He took little more with him than the Rule of St. Benedict, a missal, and a statue of the Virgin for whom he built a small chapel adjacent to his monk's cell.

Meinrad noticed two hawks threatening a nest of young ravens in a fir tree as he walked into the Finsterwald. The good priest chased off the hawks and saved the two fledglings in the nest. Thereafter, the legend goes, the ravens lived with Meinrad at his tiny hermitage.[12]

During his years in the Finsterwald, Meinrad's sanctity grew. Surrounded by terrifying demons at one point—so many, it was said, that he could not see the light of day—he fell to the ground, commended himself to God in prayer, and an angel from heaven appeared to drive them away and to console Meinrad.

Meinrad's death was divinely revealed to him while he offered mass on January 21, 861, after twenty-five years in his forest hermitage, as Gustafson relates the legend. His ravens shrieked, setting off the whole forest with their cries, as the two men who would club him to death made their way toward his simple cell. When they arrived, Meinrad greeted them courteously, fed them, gave them clothing and the following instructions, much to their surprise.

" 'When you have killed me—and I know you have come to do that—light two candles and put one at my head and the other at my feet.' "[13] They proceeded to club him to death—we are not told why—but before they could set a match to the candles, the candles ignited themselves, "lit by heavenly fire," a sign from heaven that they had murdered a saint.

The ravens screeched and cried, flapping around the heads of the murderers, and followed them from the forest. Thinking themselves safe in a local inn beyond the forest, the men began to drink. But a local farmer who knew Meinrad and the ravens had heard the birds' cries and, sensing that something was wrong, set off to Meinrad's cell while sending his brother to follow the birds. When he found the hermit dead, he returned to the village to find his brother, who was standing outside the inn the murderers had entered. As they opened the door, the ravens flew in at the murderers, knocked over their tankards, and pecked at their heads, thus identifying them. The murderers were subsequently convicted of their crime, tortured and killed, their bones broken, their bodies burned, and their ashes thrown into the water. Today the monastery's flag bears the two ravens. It is from this "dark wood," the Finsterwald—so Gustafson contends—that the Black Madonna, the "Schwarzemüttergöttes, the Black Mother of God," emerged.

The chapel of the Black Madonna is reportedly located over the original hermitage of Meinrad in which he was murdered. Until recently his skull lay in a small gold casket near her feet.

Meinrad retired to the forest, withdrew from the bounds of civilization, and confronted the demons of hell itself. He left the sunlit mountaintop retreat that he first built on Mount Etzel. He too was longing for darkness, the broken, shadowy light of the forest beneath the trees, a shelter of greater solitude.

Meinrad's story follows the pattern of the stories of many, whether the desert fathers, the Buddha, or Christ: the retreat into the wilderness, temptation and torment by demons, and, if one survived, consolation from God. The wilderness, be it desert or forest, becomes the crucible in which the transformation takes place.

Alchemy was the medieval analogue for the process of transformation, and Jung studied it at length. Gustafson draws on Jung's study of alchemy to make the argument that the development of devotion to the Madonna at Einsiedeln parallels the process of alchemy. A striking emphasis is placed on darkness or blackness as the initial stage of the alchemical work. And that blackness, Gustafson notes, in medieval times was called the "Raven." The legend of Meinrad and the ravens takes on another layer of meaning.

The blackness with which the alchemical process begins is also known as the *nigredo*. It carries many levels of meaning. The *nigredo* is a symbol full of ambiguities. According to Jung, the "crow or raven" or "raven's head" is the traditional name for the *nigredo*. "To nourish the ravens is to nourish the contents of the dark experiences of one's psyche and life,"[14] Gustafson tells us. The possibility of wisdom and insight comes from including the dark, chthonic secrets of life. Citing Jung he points out that "it is of the essence of the transforming substance to be on the one hand, extremely common, even contemptible . . . but on the other hand, to mean something of great value, not to say divine. For the transformation leads from the depths to the heights, from the bestially archaic and infantile to the mystical *homo maximus*."[15]

Jung's description of this essence reminds me of addiction. The disease draws one into an increasing loss of self-respect, to the point where, at bottom, it is felt that hardly anyone could be more "contemptible" than oneself. Yet in recovery, the very wound that drains one's life is the greatest source of healing and transformation, "from the depths to the heights . . ."

Jung's use of the word "mystical" fits precisely my own experience. One has a chronic, medically verified disease and yet there is no known medical cure, nor has there ever been. The surest, most demonstrably consistent recovery, year after year, comes through abstinence combined with abandoning oneself to a life of the spirit. The body recovers, visibly and dramatically, physical health returns, through commitment to the spirit, however one might define that for oneself. The mystical experience of the sages and saints, no separation between oneself and the divine, or in Buddhist terms, the experience of nonduality, can come through the back door of addiction turned inside out by the recovery process.

Many people are able to stop drinking or using drugs initially, but the harder issue is to "stay stopped" and to transform one's life into a source of joy and pleasure rather than remaining in the painful state that fueled the need for the anesthesia of choice.

This is the great alchemical formula; it takes spirit to cure spirit, Jung said. The phrase comes back to me again.

"Self-knowledge is an adventure that carries us unexpectedly far and deep . . . [it] can cause a good deal of confusion and mental darkness. . . . For this reason alone, we can understand why the alchemists called their *nigredo melancholia,* 'a black blacker than black,' night, an affliction of the soul, confusion . . . or, more pointedly, the 'black raven,' " Gustafson tells us, drawing again on Jung.[16]

The construction of the chapel of the Black Madonna within the larger church of the monastery at Einsiedeln directly over Meinrad's cell and place of death takes on a larger resonance, and points not only to an event but to the alchemical process itself. The Black Madonna of Einsiedeln grew out of Meinrad's decision to live with the "ravens," to pursue a deeper meaning in life, to go "the way of the *nigredo,* the Finsterwald," to inhabit his own dark places.

To say that one is "longing for darkness" is to say that one longs for transformation, for a darkness that brings balance, wholeness, integration, wisdom, insight, I now realize. For so long I didn't know what I meant when I said that, when I felt it—a longing for darkness. I remember standing in front of that statue of Kali at Varanasi and thinking of this Madonna at Einsiedeln. Now I find not only the Madonna but the beginning of words to name that longing and desire.

Late one night over coffee, when I said that I was longing for darkness, a friend said, "Watch out! It's dangerous to say that. You don't know what you are calling to yourself."

The association of the word "darkness" with something negative, with evil, is precisely the problem I am naming. That kind of association is one of the cornerstones of racism. Racism is evil, not darkness. There is a redeeming darkness and this is what I seek.

Seeing the Madonna of Einsiedeln proved to me that the longing for darkness is a deeply felt human need that cuts across, goes beyond, and at the same time includes issues of ethnicity. This is a multivalent darkness. This is the darkness of ancient wisdom, of people of color, of space, of the womb, of the earth, of the unknown, of sorrow, of the imagination, the darkness of death, of the human heart, of the unconscious, of the darkness beyond light, of matter, of the descent, of the body, of the shadow of the Most High.[17]

Like light, darkness has a wide range of symbolic meanings. The color black can signify the stage just before enlightenment in Tibetan Buddhism—imminence; space; burning; the final stage of the soul's journey to beatitude in a Sufi tradition; wisdom;[18] fertility in Old Europe; purity in a Turkish tradition; mourning in the West; and the first step in the medieval alchemical process, the *nigredo*.

The scientific disciplines of astronomy, astrophysics, particle physics, and cosmology have turned the world inside out in the last decade, metaphorically speaking. The world that we see, called the "luminous world," is now believed to be only a fraction of what exists. Ninety percent of the universe is apparently made up of dark matter,[19] about which we know very little.

Though the ancient Greeks maintained that heavenly objects consisted of a fifth element, or quintessence, that was essentially different from matter as we know it in the forms of earth, air, water, and fire, the predominant theory in astronomy until recently was that cosmic matter radiated measurable light and was composed of matter as we ordinarily think of it, with known chemical elements and physical properties. In the 1930s, this perception was questioned. Evidence began to suggest that to explain the workings of the universe as we know it would require a form of matter that was nonluminous, that did not radiate light, was virtually undetectable, but that exerted a gravitational force that would explain the motions of the galaxies.[20]

Called "missing matter" initially, the discovery of laboratory evidence of dark matter became an accepted and important field of scientific research in the 1970s.

Science speaks of the hunt for this invisible universe, the detection of which promises to set off "a new Copernican revolution."[21] Gradually the scale of our accomplishments recedes. The earth is not the center of the universe, the sun does not revolve around us, not only are we merely one planet of many but the galaxy to which we belong, the Milky Way, is only one of an infinite number of galaxies in what seems to be an expanding universe. This elusive dark matter that cannot be seen, only felt, as we observe its gravitational effects on galaxies, is 90 percent of what exists. We cannot see it, know it, or measure it, yet science maintains that it's there. Whether new discoveries will render the existence of dark matter obsolete, paradigmatically we have reached the limits of light. The world is not as it seems. What is, is not evident. The lessons of darkness.

On the train rides back and forth to Küsnacht, I thumb through some of the books on the monastery's history and continue to read Gustafson's paper, which by now I am carrying with me everywhere.

After Meinrad's death in A.D. 861, other priests and monks came to live as hermits, building their cells around the chapel Meinrad had built for the Virgin. But it was almost nine hundred years before the cornerstone of the great church that stands at Einsiedeln today was laid, in 1704. In the meantime, the evolving monastery was placed under the protection of the Virgin as "Our Lady of the Hermits," and by the tenth century there is evidence that the pilgrimages to her had begun.

There were several fires over the course of the centuries, but according to legend, each time, the Holy Chapel of the Virgin was spared. For some, this served to explain why she was black. (Anthropologists Moss and Cappannari remarked that often they were told that a particular Madonna they were inquiring about was black because of smoke.)

There is obvious merit in the explanation of smoke making the Madonnas black, I have seen it for myself in observing the restoration work that goes on in the basilica at Einsiedeln. But while candle smoke can be a factor—as can be paint, pigments used in centuries past, or the aging of wood—why haven't all the statues and crucifixes in the churches with Black Madonnas become black? Only the Madonna has been left to darken.

The statue of the Madonna in the chapel at Einsiedeln today is apparently not the original statue from the ninth century. Whatever its age—some say fifteenth century—it is known that this statue was restored in the eighteenth century. The written testimony of the artisan who did the work in 1799 lies in the monastery library. Gustafson had access to the account and included the story.

The French invaded Einsiedeln in 1798 and captured what they thought was the prized Swiss Madonna, which they shipped back to Paris, signalling victory. (At that time, the abbot of Einsiedeln also functioned as a political leader for the region.) The Black Madonna of Einsiedeln had a strong regional association and functioned as political symbol as well. (Black Madonnas tend to have regional or even national associations, for example, the Black Madonna of Czestochowa, Poland, and Our Lady of Guadalupe in Mexico, to mention two.) But the Benedictine fathers had wisely removed the real statue, supplanted it with a copy, and had their Madonna smuggled into Austria for safekeeping. When the chest containing her was opened nearly a year later, the statue was found to have been damaged, perhaps from moisture.

Fuetscher, the restorer, wrote that in his opinion the Madonna had originally been fair-skinned, like the inhabitants of the region, Gustafson reports. Though he tried to refurbish the Madonna to her previous dark state, he took the liberty of adding blue to the eyes and a little red to the cheeks and lips. The result was that people questioned the authenticity of the statue. In the end, Fuetscher had to paint over the faces, eyes, cheeks, and lips, and make both Mother and Child completely black.

Now the blackness took on another dimension. People demanded that she and the Christ Child be completely black. To be like the people of the region, could she not even be allowed blue eyes? It was 1799, the end of the eighteenth century, the Age of Reason. Logic and rationality had prevailed; on the surface, philosophers hailed the "Light of Reason." The restoration of the Madonna's darkness was an eruption of the nonrational element necessary for meaning in human life. The basic psychic need for balance, paradox, complexity, and color finds its balance and expression in the blackness of the Madonna.

Reading through Gustafson's paper that night in my room I was excited to find that he too connects the Madonna of Einsiedeln with Kali, with Isis, and adds the Greek earth goddess, Demeter. The ravens always associated with Meinrad and Einsiedeln were also a symbol of the Terrible Mother, the Goddess of Death,[22] another form of the Great Mother.

I sit up in bed reading late. I had heard that Jung maintained that this Madonna is a manifestation of Isis, as Lindegger had said. The cult of Isis was popular in the Roman Empire and continued well into the second and third centuries A.D. It had spread from southern Eygpt where her main temple was at Philae, near the top of the slender river valley that begins at the Nile's First Cataract near Aswan. This was Nubian territory, reaching down below the Nile's Third Cataract into what we know today as the Sudan.[23] Nubian-speaking peoples, who were black, lived in this gold-rich valley for five thousand years, playing a powerful role in Egyptian history.

Isis, out of the Nile Valley, bringing the influence of Africa and Egypt to the West throughout the Mediterranean into Italy, Spain, and France and as far north as Germany, Switzerland, even England, some say. Called "the Star of the Sea" and "Queen of Heaven," Isis, like the Black Madonnas, was renowned as a miracleworker and healer. Some scholars claim that some of the early statues of the

Madonna and Child were actually Isis and Horus, renamed as Mary and Jesus.[24]

The waters of the Zürichsee lap gently at the shore outside my window. I pull my shawl around me more tightly. I have come to Switzerland solely to follow out the intuition that came to me in Varanasi a year ago: Kali and the Black Madonna at Einsiedeln are somehow connected. And because Kali and Tara are connected, the Black Madonna is connected, however remotely that might be, to Tara as well. The uncovering of her roots in Isis, often depicted as black, deepens and includes the obvious: the possibility of an African source as well for the Black Madonna. I turn off the light by my bed after midnight and fall asleep satisfied.

Letting myself reconnect with the Madonna through Einsiedeln is galvanizing, I begin to try to articulate why this is so early the next morning.

I make notes, tear up pages, start over, cross out sentences, get up from the desk, walk away, leave the room, go outside by the water, come back, and fight with these words. Some of them, such as "God," are so charged that an explosion goes off in my head. An old presence, punitive and harsh, which I have long tried to cast out, is evoked.

One moment I am full of certainty about these matters; the next, I realize that I must be slow to posit these connections of the Black Madonna, Tara, and Durga-Kali as anything more than what they are: a direction to explore, a road to walk down, nothing more. Though I've not met Gustafson, I feel as though I've found a traveling companion. I laugh at having assumed that the paper could only have been written by a woman. Such an automatic assumption contradicts one of my own interior premises: the image of a dark Mother God is just as vital an image for men as it is for women. I must constantly work to be rid of my own sexism.

The Black Madonna presents us not with an issue of sex or

gender, but of life, life with all its teeming diversity of peoples, our different colors, our fullness.

Seeing the Madonna at Einsiedeln gives me the sense that she is a Western remnant of the ancient Dark God—be she the Indian Kali, Durga, lesser-known forms of the Tibetan Tara, the African-Egyptian Isis, the Roman Cybele, or the Greek Artemis or Demeter (Ishtar or Inanna) all contain aspects or have manifestations of the Black Mother.

I use the word "God" fully intending to draw on the resonance and power that such a term can carry in Western culture. The word "goddess" connotes a mythological time past rather than actual present time. It tends to allow one to dismiss this manifestation of God as little more than a concern of feminist scholars and a vestige of a lost and sometimes hypothetical past.

Mary is also God: unacknowledged, female and dark. She is the Mother God. God, as I am using the term, is both what we describe as female and male, both dark and light, and neither male nor female, nor dark nor light, nor any other term that we can use. God the Mother is just as real and as present today as any other human conception of a power which no human term can fully describe.

Saints, poets, mystics, philosophers, believers, and theologians throughout the ages have wrestled with the dilemma of description. The language of paradox seems the most accurate: God is both and neither/nor, both is and is not. The mind is pushed beyond conceptual limits. I restate what to the mystic is obvious. But we can no longer afford for this to be an insight of a few. It needs to become our common understanding. Without it, we fall too easily into polarization, duality; we imagine that there is an "other." It is our mistaken notion of the *other* that threatens to destroy us as we imagine ourselves separate from and different than the world of nature, and from each other as beings who together share this fragile planet's fate.

Tara is described as a Buddha by the Tibetans, not only as a goddess or a bodhisattva, giving her existence a weight, a fulfillment, and an order of being that is altogether different from Mary's. Institutionally, Mary is identified only as the Mother of God and, at that, primarily by only certain churches within Christianity such as the Catholic, the Anglican, and some of the Episcopalian churches. The Eastern Orthodox Church is famous for its devotion to Mary, but there too, she is not seen as a Godhead in her own right. Other churches within Protestantism may maintain a belief in Mary as well, but again, it is most often within tight conceptual limits, if she is included meaningfully at all. Mary is depicted as a powerless and derivative force. The Church of Rome, for example, insists that she can only *intercede* with God, that she is only a petitioner on behalf of the faithful. In and of herself, Mary can do nothing. Only her son or his father has any power.

But whether it's condoned or not, the worship of Mary is practiced by many people, acknowledging a reality in her much greater than is admitted by the institutional Church. Rome claims that Mary can only be venerated, not adored. She can have a special veneration, *hyperdulia,* more than the saints, who are allotted only veneration, *dulia,* but she cannot have adoration, *latria.* Yet the dogma of the Church and the religious practices of the faithful have often been in unspoken conflict. The actual practices and understanding of the faithful are sometimes quite different from the formal teachings of the clergy. The worship of Mary is evidence of this phenomenon.

But Mary does not belong just to certain belief systems. She belongs to everyone who longs for a richer, more vital conception of a power greater than ourselves, which some choose to call God. She presents a challenge and an opportunity for anyone who talks about the "reemerging Goddess" or a Goddess religion and yet for many she is too bound up with Rome. I long to liberate Mary from the Catholic Church. We all need her. Perhaps then we can consider what it means to have the presence of God the Mother in our midst today.

The difficulty and necessity of enlarging the concept of God would be confirmed when I returned home. The Rev. Lee Hancock, the Seminary Pastor at Union Theological Seminary in New York, a

Presbyterian minister would tell me of her sermon on "Christianity and the Loss of the Goddess," delivered in a leap of faith after years of quiet, private struggle. In one of the most powerful experiences of her life, she confided to her congregation that it was no longer enough to tell herself that God transcends male and female, she needed an *incarnate* female presence in the Christian tradition. She received a standing ovation.

Delivered again to a larger, unfamiliar congregation, the sermon was perceived as controversial. Some loved it, others were clearly frightened. Many thanked her for "naming the unnameable." Protestantism had almost thrown out the feminine altogether in the Reformation, she noted, and yet what held Lee Hancock was the whole notion of incarnation in Christianity, "the Word became Flesh." But for her locating it in one gender is problematic. Symbols communicate authority and power and shape people's lives; we need them, but if the symbols are devoid of a female presence we don't have anchors. The need for a female image of God is there, but people are nervous about expressing it. For women in the clergy, she said, this is a burning issue.

The Rev. Jane Henderson, Associate Rector at New York's Episcopal Church of Heavenly Rest and Episcopalian priest, would tell me that the experience of God can become much fuller by exploring the feminine side of God. Yet by and large, she said, established churches discourage this and in doing so are missing an opportunity. Intellectually many people understand the need for a more inclusive liturgy, but when the pragmatic realities of preaching and changing the language of the liturgy are presented, people get upset.

To suggest that God is female requires a male cleric to reconcile himself with his own femininity, Matthew Fox, O.P., the Catholic theologian would tell me. For some this is merely awkward and new, for others, very threatening. No longer can the Virgin serve as a projection for that aspect of the self. The very notion of God the Mother requires integration. Changing the image of God has enormous implications, he assured me.

Fox would remind me of the great medieval creation mystics, Hildegarde of Bingen, Julian of Norwich, Meister Eckhart, and others, of whom he has also written.[25] These mystics drew on scriptures. They did not make up the idea of God the Mother, Fox said, for it has been there all along within the Christian tradition—neglected, sometimes condemned, and forgotten by many.

Just to change the language doesn't solve the problem though, Elisabeth Schüssler Fiorenza would say, pointing out how Mariology in the Church has also been used to keep women in their place. The change to a female God language must also be psychological. She reminds me of the related figure of Wisdom, the builder of the world in the Old Testament.[26] Wisdom was also an appellation of the early Gnostic Christians for the Mother.

Mothergod. I would write to Meinrad Craighead, who uses this term. The inspired painter and great-great-niece of Brother Meinrad of Einsiedeln, Meinrad has created a whole world of stories and images of God the Mother that she would periodically feed me.[27] This Black Madonna at Einsiedeln is another image of the Mothergod to her, forever unfolding and coming to us in her many forms. She dreams of her often: always dark, always beautiful, in the fullness of age, sometimes old beyond understanding, heavily and beautifully robed in layers and layers of cloth, sometimes even in the skin of a mountain lion.

God's "loving breasts" and "the milk of the Father" are allusions found in the early Christian writings of Clement of Alexandria, Elaine Pagels would bring out.[28]

I had come to a holy spring known by many.

Rootless, refusing to go home again, to wrestle with where we come from in our own Western culture, like so many I had overlooked the backyard in which Mary has quietly grown like a flowering tree. A forsaken image as I looked to other cultures, I now find in Mary a taproot that reaches to the center of the earth and a root system that stretches around the globe. Paradoxically, I could not discover this by staying at home. Only by finding Tara and Kali could I begin to look again at Mary, and then only at the black or dark image of the Madonna.

The hotel restaurant has just opened for breakfast, at 7:00 a.m. the next morning. I stuff croissants, rolls, honey, and jellies into a bag for long train rides. Rock music blares on the kitchen radio, dishes clatter. I finally succeed in communicating to the waitress that I want soft-boiled eggs and coffee for now. Outside, the light flickers in the trees. It is a crisp, sunny day, windy and cool; welcome after the last two days of fog and cold. I'm on my way to Winterthur.

The day I met Carol Savvas, she introduced me to the Venerable Geshe Champa Lodro Rinpoche, a Gelugpa monk who had made his way to the Tibetan community in Switzerland from India after fleeing Sera Monastery in Tibet in 1959. (The title "Geshe" indicates an advanced degree, akin to our doctorate of philosophy.) He taught and led meditations weekly at the Kalffs' Yiga Chözin Center for the Study of Buddhism and Psychology. Carol is also a student of his. Geshe Champa Lodro speaks German, and a little English.

"Geshe Rinpoche will be happy to know you're interested in Tara," Carol assured me. No sooner had she made the introduction than he asked if I would like to know more about the Twenty-one Taras. It was two weeks ago, nearly to the day, that I was to have met Lochö Rinpoche in Dharamsala for an explanation of the Twenty-one Taras. He had been unable to meet me again. Now I had come to Switzerland to find the Black Madonna and I find not only her, but once again, always in front of me, the Buddha Tara.

The moment of meeting Geshe Champa Lodro Rinpoche—his back to the window in Dora Kalff's study, saffron yellow and red monk's robes contrasting with the gray fall sky behind him, the smile on his broad open face as he asked if I wanted to know about the Twenty-one Taras—became etched into my mind with photographic clarity.

Carol Savvas met me at the train station and we walked to Geshe Champa Lodro Rinpoche's apartment two blocks away, where he lives with his mother and several other family members who escaped from Tibet. Geshe Rinpoche has been very busy today, she tells me, but we will see how long he has for talking.

We enter a room full of deities, painted, cast, and carved. Tangkha paintings hang across one wall, on another wall sits a glass-enclosed case with shelves full of statues of Buddha and other deities. Geshe Rinpoche wears a maroon sweater over his claret robes and a deep pink-red shawl. The yellow silk cover of the text he will read from is spread across his lap. He receives us with a broad smile and I feel warmed.

He speaks in Tibetan to Carol for a long time, his voice rising and falling softly. Carol and I sit on a Tibetan rug on the carpeted floor by the window. Geshe Rinpoche combines warmth and formality in an unusual way. He does not simply talk to me about Tara, but refers me to ancient texts, insistent that I hear an accurate version of Tara's story.

Now Geshe Rinpoche begins to explain Tara's origin in the traditional style of Tibetan stories.[29]

"Many countless aeons ago, in another *kalpa* [time] altogether, in the time of Buddha Ngadra, there lived a princess named Yeshe Dawa, Wisdom Moon. She made innumerable offerings to Buddha Ngadra and the spiritual assembly, as the result of which she grew very close to becoming enlightened herself.

" 'If you pray for a man's form, you will be enlightened in this very lifetime,' the monks told her."

Though I have heard different versions of this story before, this is the most complete telling. The spirit of Tara that comes through Geshe Rinpoche and Carol inspires me. I imagine Yeshe Dawa in formal debate, like the young monks I saw in Dharamsala outside under the trees, moving their bodies in a proscribed way, assuming traditional postures as they debated in their graceful intellectual argument-dance. Red robes flashing, they whirled and clapped in a kind of tai-chi form of danced debate. I imagine Yeshe Dawa making a full turn, with the energy of a storm gathering. She claps her hands together loudly once, a thunderbolt.

Carol's voice, translating for Geshe-la, cuts through my imaginings.

"Man, woman, the 'self,' the person—all these phenomena have no true existence," said Yeshe Dawa. "They only exist as projections of our incorrect conception of the world.

"In actuality, they do not exist in and of themselves. They have no separate, independent existence, so there is no need for me to change myself into a man. Ideas of 'male' and 'female' always delude worldly people. Many wish to gain enlightenment in a man's form, but few wish to work for the benefit of sentient beings in a female form."

Carol and I both chuckle as she translates Yeshe Dawa's comments about how worldly people are always being confused about sex. Male and female. There's a kind of fantastic perspective on gender here, couched in this story reputedly so old that it predates our evolution as humans on this planet. Geshe Rinpoche smiles at our obvious enjoyment and goes on with the telling of Yeshe Dawa's vow.

"Therefore I will remain in a woman's form until reaching enlightenment and thus I will turn the wheel of Dharma, working for the benefit of all living beings, until the world of samsara is empty and all suffering ended."

These words are like clean, cold water from a high mountain stream being poured over me. Geshe Rinpoche then told how it was many millions of years more after taking this vow that Yeshe Dawa spent meditating on "the six perfections of generosity, moral discipline, patience, enthusiastic perseverance, concentration, and wisdom," before she herself reached the state of mental concentration called "free from samsara." After this achievement, she helped millions of beings, every day, be freed from suffering, the world of samsara.

"Each day she liberated millions of beings from the sufferings of samsara through the power of her mental concentration and teachings. She taught them how to have love, kindness, and compassion, she changed their minds from having anger to having patience. Because so many beings were rescued by Yeshe Dawa they began to call her the Rescuer, the Mother Who Rescues, *Drolma*, the Tibetan word for Tara. Tara is her name in Sanskrit."

Every day when Yeshe Dawa woke up, she would not eat breakfast until she had freed over a million beings from suffering. And then she would not eat lunch until she had freed at least another million beings. Then she would refuse dinner until at least another million were free, even if night had fallen.

The power of the mind, single-pointedly concentrated on the great altruistic desire to become enlightened for the benefit of all beings, *bodhicitta*, is not to be underestimated in the Buddhist system. This image of Yeshe Dawa freeing millions of beings each day through her mental concentration and perseverance gives me a sense of the Tibetan concept of mental activity being not unlike our description of radioactive materials with powers so concentrated that only a few pounds are necessary to affect millions of people.

" 'You, Yeshe Dawa,' the Buddha Ngadra prophesied, 'will reach enlightenment in the form of Buddha Tara.' Just as he foretold, she became fully enlightened and worked to free all living beings from the sufferings of the world."

Finally I hear how Tara became a Buddha. Her different titles have been confusing—Goddess, Bodhisattva, and Arya, which means Transcended, Gone Beyond. She had reached increasingly advanced levels of attainment during her various incarnations in different ages or time periods—kalpas. Reincarnation, infinite universes, concepts of time, matter, and space that we generally confine to astronomy and quantum physics make grasping Buddhist texts a challenge.

Geshe Rinpoche went on to give us some idea of how central Tara is and has been to Tibetan Buddhism.

"The Lord Chenresig, Avalokitesvara, the Bodhisattva of Compassion, recited many hundreds of thousands of verses about Tara in the Tara Tantra. In the present aeon, Buddha Sakyamuni reached enlightenment by relying on Tara. After that, all the mahasiddhas, the great adepts, from India relied on Tara and in this way became very advanced spiritually.

"All of the great accomplishments of Lord Atisa came out of his complete reliance on Arya Tara for the answers to his questions. When he was invited to come to Tibet from India in the eleventh century, she told him that it would shorten his life by twenty years, but that it would greatly benefit the Dharma, the teachings of the Buddha, and the Tibetan people, so he went."

The visit of the great Indian pandita (teacher) Atisa went on until the end of his life seventeen years later, setting off the second flowering of Buddhism in Tibet after a long period of persecution. Buddhism in Tibet was nearly extinguished during the time before Atisa's coming.

Geshe Rinpoche told me that "it is said that Atisa saw Tara's face, directly, all the time. Always she was there to answer his questions. Likewise, all the great lamas of Tibet relied on Arya Tara. Their virtuous activities spread far and wide as a result of their reliance on Tara. The Dalai Lamas especially have relied upon Tara," he assured me.

Geshe Rinpoche clarified many things about Tara for me that day and in subsequent meetings.[30] Most of all, I enjoyed his generosity, equanimity, and humor. Both he and Carol were very kind to me. But the days grew shorter, the season colder. Soon I would have to leave Switzerland and this well of the Buddha Tara that I had found.

This morning I am torn between going to Bern to secure a Polish visa or giving up the idea of Poland altogether this trip. I had wanted to begin the research on the Black Madonna at Czestochowa, but time, money, and introductions are lacking. Today is the last day I can get a visa and the Polish Consulate in Bern closes at noon.

I can't get a train to Bern that arrives before 11:15 a.m. It seems that regardless of the difficulties involved, I am here in Europe and it would be simpler to go to Poland now than to return to the States and have to make a special trip to Poland next year. But time makes the decision for me. The train I'm on to Zurich runs fifteen minutes late, and by the time we arrive, I have missed the connection to Bern. Now it is impossible for me to get a visa to Poland. The matter is settled. I will have to go next summer, for the pilgrimage that I was told takes place each year. It will be better, I'm sure, to walk to Czestochowa than to visit the shrine by train or car. When I saw a copy of the Black Madonna of Poland in the church at Einsiedeln, Father Matthew explained that pilgrims walk each year from Warsaw to Czestochowa, a distance of nearly two hundred miles, to reach the shrine for the Feast of the Assumption of Mary, August 15. The way turns.

I go to the French Consulate instead. I will go to a cousin's home in Belgium by train, which means I will have to pass through France. In the tiny village of Hondelange, three generations of my cousins still live in the same farmhouse, now modernized, that was pictured on a turn-of-the-century postcard that turned up in a closet in my grandparents' house in Texas.

The landscape of Western Europe feels familiar, though I see everything for the first time. I am always going home. The shape of the land makes me burn with homesickness suddenly as the brilliant red, yellow, orange, vermilion, purple, gold, brown, darkening trees of fall fly past the train window on the way to Belgium, to these cousins in Hondelange who will tell me family stories of World Wars I and II and show me the graveyard on the outskirts of the village where unknown relatives lie fast.

Back home in California three months later, just before I remarried, I dreamed of the Dalai Lama.

In the dream there were three Japanese-style wooden hot tubs outdoors. The Dalai Lama was sitting fully dressed in his red and yellow saffron robes in a tub full of very hot, soapy water. He liked his water so hot and soapy that my husband and I, also fully clothed, had to sit in a separate hot tub. None of us were wet.

The Dalai Lama was very happy and jolly, enjoying himself with the innocence of a child. He playfully performed somersaults, doing complete flips back and forth in the air, laughing, turning upside down, every which way, robes flying. It was wonderful to be with him. He was full of joy.

Then he became quiet and looked at me. We sat in our separate tubs just looking at each other. I began to feel an immense vastness, the vastness of the ocean, of endless sky, pure space. Nothing was said. There was only the full looking into each other's eyes. I was aware that something momentous was occurring in the silence. I could not say what it was, for whatever it was was beyond language. I looked at him without reservation, without shyness, without fear, and he gazed at me similarly. There was nothing between us, only pure being. It was a vivid and real exchange.

Suddenly a blue sword came out of the crown of the Dalai Lama's head, over and across the distance between us and down through the crown of my head, all the way down my spine. I felt as though he had just transmitted some great wordless teaching. The sword was made of blue light. I was very happy.

Then he climbed into the third tub, where I was now sitting alone. We sat side by side in silence. I was on his right. Our faces were next to one another, faintly touching, looking in the same direction, as though we always looked at the world this way. We were still sitting in water, still not wet, and fully dressed. It seemed perfectly natural to be with him this way.

The Dalai Lama got out of the tub and I followed him. I wanted him to verify the experience I had just had with him. I wanted him to confirm the power and intensity of the time that we sat looking into one another's eyes. I wanted him to tell me that he had transmitted some form of teaching. I wanted him to acknowledge everything that had happened, to tell me what it meant. I wanted him to explain the sword that came out of his head into mine. But every time I asked him a question, he changed forms, like Proteus, the old man of the sea, and said nothing. He would walk along and I would ask a question. Rather than answer, he would change forms and keep walking, impervious to my interrogation, each form getting smaller and smaller. By the end of the dream, he had changed into a tiny, exquisite, brilliant, turquoise blue creature, perhaps an Egyptian scarab or some kind of rare and valuable beetle. He began to climb up a whitewashed brick wall as I stood below on an upside-down empty wooden flower tub, watching him ascend into an alcove high on the wall above me, out of reach. Then I woke up. At that moment the private audience with His Holiness the Dalai Lama, Tenzin Gyatso, of the prior October was completed.

I wrote to the monk who had been my guide in Dharamsala about this dream. Surely this had happened to others who had seen the Dalai Lama. Did the Dalai Lama give teachings this way deliberately or was the dream just one of the effects of his presence on people? What did it mean? What was the sword of blue light?

Even as I wrote the letter, I knew better than to expect a reply, the dream had told me as much. Nor did I receive an answer.

CHAPTER 9

The Way to Poland

◆

Switzerland and France

Darkness within darkness.
The gateway to all understanding.

—Lao Tzu[1]

California
June 1987

I had pulled into my driveway after a trip to the grocery store and was suddenly overcome with grief. A darkness came over me, just before I was scheduled to leave the country for Europe. I was going back to Switzerland, then to France, and finally, Poland. I would take part in the annual pilgrimage to the Madonna of Czestochowa, the Black Madonna of Poland. Pilgrims walked from all over Poland to the monastery of Jasna Gora in the town of Czestochowa in south central Poland. I was going to join them. The car was hot and the smell of broccoli in the grocery bags strong. Why was I so disturbed?

Going to Poland means that I am leaving everything and everyone familiar behind. I have never been separated from my children for as long as I will be now. I am leaving my husband, my friends, the garden, the familiar trees, the hills I walk, everything I know, to go to strangers, to be with people I have never met or spoken with, to go to an event I must not say that I am going to attend. Poland is still under a totalitarian regime, no matter what the surface appearance. It is 1987. Solidarity is still outlawed. Adam Michnik, one of its chief architects, was writing from his jail cell only months ago. Many other leaders of the opposition were recently in and out of prison as well.

The world-shaking events of the spring and fall of 1989 in Eastern Europe that would tumble the reigning Communist governments of first Poland, then East Germany, then Rumania and Czechoslovakia were yet to come. Solidarity would not be a legal organization again until April of 1989.

Now, as I travel to Poland in 1987, fear of the central government, their net of informants, and the Polish secret police is still widespread. Paranoia is jokingly referred to by some as a Polish national pastime, but the Poles have good reasons for their fears. Often phones are tapped, mail—especially from the United States—opened and delivered in plastic bags weeks later. Secrecy reigns. A telephone call cannot be made to or from outside Poland without going through one central switchboard, available for monitoring by the authorities. There are no newspapers from the outside world for sale in Poland. My husband is Jewish, his father's family from Poland. I know what happened there. The question of whether or not I will go to Auschwitz-Birkenau lies in the back of my mind.

I tried unsuccessfully to get a visa as a writer. The Polish Consulate lost my passport, can't find my visa application. I submit an application again and am told that clearance will have to come from the foreign office in Warsaw and now there is no time, "Surely you can understand?"

I must accept what friends who have lived there tell me.

"Lie. Do not tell authorities what you're doing. Apply for a tourist visa, go as a housewife. And for God's sake, don't tell them that you're going on the pilgrimage, much less writing about it. You won't get a visa. The government doesn't like the pilgrimage, it makes them nervous. It's so large that there's nothing they can do to stop it."

A Polish tourist agency has mistakenly told me that the pilgrimage begins on August 26. Luckily I know that it begins in the early part of August, though I can't find out precisely when.

"It would be unwise to bring a tape recorder. People will be suspicious of you if you want to tape what they're saying. Take notes, but don't take them in any systematic way. Scatter them on pieces of paper that are not in any obvious order. Don't let people see you taking notes.

"Be very careful taking photographs. Do not photograph the Solidarity banner, Solidarity is still outlawed. Last summer I saw two Westerners arrested for just taking pictures at the shrine. I don't know what happened to them. It's difficult to take a picture of the crowd there without photographing the Solidarity banner, there're so many . . ."

"Of course you know not to photograph the airport, train stations, soldiers, or any problem you might see. If trouble breaks out, do not take pictures of it. Walk the other way. I didn't and I landed in jail for a few days. Not something you'd like. I was strip-searched. You don't want to get mixed up with the police . . ."

"You will be approached by the secret police on the pilgrimage. Do not tell them anything. They are always on the pilgrimage. Also there are informers. These are people who are quietly being black-mailed in some way by the government. They must be informers if they want to get housing, a passport, permission to attend the university, such things as this. They don't like what they're doing. They are not the secret police. They are compromised, in a trap themselves. The government has something on them. You will not know who they are, the informers or the secret police . . ."

"Only say that you are a pilgrim and you've come to do penance and pray. Especially be suspicious of the person who asks a lot of questions."

"Stay in the background, be invisible . . ."

"Say that you are trying to find a relative. Explain that you were already in Europe with your husband and that you wanted to see

Poland. He couldn't come because of business. Lots of Americans do that, but hardly any Americans ever go on the pilgrimage, that's rare. Just don't let the authorities know.

"If they search your bags and find your tent and camping gear, tell them that you're going to visit the Tatra Mountains. Yes, tell them that you've always wanted to see Zacopanie, yes, say you are going to the mountains, lots of tourists do that . . ."

"People still disappear in Poland, though you don't hear about it in the news. I know. Martial law is over. This is 1987, not 1982, but it still happens I tell you.

"But you shouldn't worry, you're an American. Everything will be fine. You'll have no trouble, don't worry."

"It's completely arbitrary. There's no particular pattern or sense to what gets enforced and what doesn't from what I could see. I lived in Warsaw for three years. That's how they keep everybody off balance, the inconsistencies, the arbitrariness of it all. Me, I was so careful, I never even took a letter out of the country for somebody else. One moment everything is fine, and then the next moment, for no reason, I am being strip-searched at the airport."

What identity I have, at least in my own mind, must be hidden. All the warnings people have given me echo in my mind this afternoon as I sit here in the car. I don't know what to make of them, have no idea how to weigh them, have no context. Why am I doing this, what am I going to or for?

Then I realize that if I am going to write about darkness, all the permutations of darkness will come up. I was naive to imagine that I could look only at a redeeming darkness, the darkness of divinity, the darkness of the Madonna, the darkness of Tara, or the darkness that is associated with the earth, with rest, with fertility. Of course. I say that I am longing for darkness and this is what I get, another kind of darkness: racism, the secret police, Auschwitz, my own endless fears. Beauty doesn't come without the beast. I can expect no less.

Though I am still disturbed by all the leavetaking, I am relieved to understand that feeling upset is to be expected. My fears are both rational and irrational. I cannot make this journey comfortably or from a distance. I lean over the seat, grab a bag of groceries, and get out.

Walking to get ready for the pilgrimage in Poland. I walk up to the ridge tops that flank Mount Tamalpais, up to the East Peak, to the top and around the mountain. From here, one can see the Farallones Islands thirty miles at sea, fog-ridden. On the coast, the sky is cloudless, the mountain sunny. Goldfinches dip into the air like water.

Pffafikon, Switzerland
July 1987

Back in Switzerland, I walk up from the town of Pffafikon on Lake Zurich over the thousand-year-old Pilgrim's Way (*Pilger Weg*) to Einsiedeln, up a wooded hill with steps of root-crossed stones smoothed with age, the day is clear and warm. Above, in the open fields, the cherry trees are heavy with fruit. Up past St. Meinrad's Chapel on the Etzel Pass, the Alps become visible in the distance. Then the way is down, to a stream with a covered bridge near where Paracelsus, the great medieval doctor and alchemist, lived. Up to hilltop fields where farmers pitch pale wheat around a central pole and the air is sweet with clover, then down to the great Monastery of Einsiedeln far below, across the Sihl River, now a lake dotted with sailboats, to arrive with hair wet, face red and damp from the heat and exertion, just in time for the *Salve Regina,* sung at four o'clock. Walking . . .

Again I go to see Champa Lodro Rinpoche and Carol Savvas.

"Come to Zug, you can take the train," Carol says. "We are having a weekend retreat on the lake at a summer cottage. Geshe Rinpoche will give you a Green Tara initiation."

A sailboat is pulled into the reeds along the lake where a summer cottage sits. Inside, a small group of Tibetan Buddhists sits quietly in meditation. I arrive in time for the lunch break. With his warm smile, Geshe Rinpoche picks up a honeydew melon from the picnic table and explains through Carol, teasing us, that it is just about the size of the dragon's egg that was kept in the Potala, the Dalai Lama's palace, in Tibet when he was a small child.

When lunch is over, we go inside. I have brought a bright red begonia in full flower for Geshe Rinpoche, which I place on the small table in front of him and then sit down. On my right, Carol sits translating and explains to all of us the initiation of Green Tara. Then it is my turn to go before Geshe Rinpoche and bow as he places an image of Green Tara briefly on the crown of my head and gives me her blessing.

This is the Tara who sits with her right leg slightly extended, ever ready to step out into the world to help quickly. This beautiful Green Tara comes to you down through the top of your head. She becomes you, you become her. Simultaneously a tiny Green Tara sits on a moon disk in your heart, radiating out love and compassion in every direction, *Om Tare Tutare Ture Soha,* her mantra spins, radiating like the spokes of a wheel, rays of jeweled light going out all over the world. Every place the light touches, suffering is relieved and healed.

The Green Tara I take away over time grows leafy, vine-covered, and wild. The moment I imagine her descent into my body, I feel the wind moving in the trees. The water of the mind moving through the cleansing filter of the image. She is the great protector, Khadi-ravani Tara,[2] who dwells in the forest, the joyful beauty who roams free, arrayed in precious silks, pearls, and coral, drawing beings to her through her infinite compassion like bees to the hive.

Les Saintes-Maries-de-la-Mer, France
July 1987

The Camargue in the South of France is comprised of a huge delta in which the Rhone River empties out into the Mediterranean. I have taken the train from Switzerland. Now I drive through Arles, through the honeyed light of southern France, through field after field of enormous, heady sunflowers, some still in bright yellow bloom, others done, dark green now, down to the church of Les Saintes-Maries-de-la-Mer.

The Black Mary that I was told to find here turned out not to be Mary but St. Sara. Father Morel, the pastor, tells me that the Gypsies call her Sara-la-Kali, though no one knows why. "It is a mystery."

The original language of the Gypsies is derived from an old Indian language. Even today many of the words used are a corrupted form of Sanskrit called Prakrit. In the language of the Gypsies, the word *Kali* means both "gypsy woman" and "the black one," he explains. It is Sara-Kali, Queen of the Gypsies, who resides in the crypt of this ancient church by the sea.

Each year in late May, the Gypsies gather from all over Europe to venerate St. Sara. "The poor are honored, the rejected welcomed, and the unloved comforted" at this feast, I read in a booklet Father Morel gives me. In a grand procession culminating in days of praying and feasting, they dress the statue in layers of clothes and jewels and take her down to the sea.

"Most of the stories center around the three Marys—Mary Jacobe, Mary Salome, and Mary Magdalene—though often there are only two Marys depicted, standing in a boat without sails, like you see in the church. In one tradition, Mary Jacobe and Mary Salome are considered Jesus's aunts, sisters of his mother Mary," Father Morel tells me.

"According to one legend, Sara, the Queen of the Gypsies, was already in the Camargue in the first century when the boat full of Marys arrived. Sara waded into the sea to greet them. Yet historically it is believed that the Gypsies didn't enter Europe until as late as the fifteenth century. In another version she was Sarah of Egypt and she came as a servant with the Marys on the boat as they fled persecution.

"No one knows really," he assures me. The reasons have been

lost to time, blown out to sea. "There is some evidence that there was worship of Ra, the Egyptian sun god, here as well.

"The side altar on the left in the church is pre-Christian and dates back to the fourth century B.C. This has been a pilgrimage site since at least the sixth century A.D. When this church was built in the ninth century, they simply built it around the old altar and columns. Relics were found here from the first century, women's skulls, from the Middle East."

The net of stories that carried Sara and the Marys was knotted with a variety of sources. Was this Sarah the Egyptian, or the Sara who was with Mary and Martha at Christ's tomb the morning of the Resurrection, according to yet another tradition? Were the Marys Mary the mother of Salome and Mary mother of Jacobe, or were they Mary Magdalene and Mary, Christ's mother, as yet more fantastic legends hold, forming the basis of stories of Mary Magdalene carrying Christ's child to France?

The advent of the Marys arriving here in "a boat without sails" marks the first-century entrance of Christianity into what is now France, Father Morel said. I go to look for Mary and cannot find her without the stream of stories that carried her from one part of the world to another. Seldom have I had a more vivid sense of all the different strands that make up what we call Christianity than in my visit to this ancient church.

It is hot outside, nearly 100 degrees. The Mediterranean is a brilliant cold hard blue. There are white horses and heavy black bulls everywhere; and though I looked for them, I did not see the pink flamingos for which the Camargue is famous.

Inside the church, the light is dim. Steps lead down to the crypt below the main altar in front. I descend into the curved low ceilinged room of another world. The room is blackened by hundreds of years of candle smoke and the lack of ventilation. There are no windows. The banks of three-foot-high white tapers burning are the only light, the air is hot from all the candles burning and smells of wax and the odor of bodies.

St. Sara, Sara-la-Kali, Patron and Queen of the Gypsies, at the church of Les Saintes-Maries-de-la-mer, the Camargue, France. (Author)

To the right of the altar is St. Sara, dark-faced, smiling. She is about five feet tall, slightly elevated on a stand. She is dressed in blue gauze over a gold brocade. She has a lovely deep brown face, almost black, and black hair. There are children's crutches laid up against the wall behind her, canes, metal braces, testaments to her healing. As I stand in the back letting my eyes adjust, a family of Gypsies walks in. The man lights a candle and then approaches the statue, while his family watches.

He is a tall man, with unruly dark hair. He wears ordinary black cotton pants and a white shirt, half open from the heat. He goes up to St. Sara with a complete lack of self-consciousness, and as he must have done many times before—the movement is so intimate, so familiar—he parts her elaborate robes and finds a way through her dress to the statue underneath. She is suddenly flesh, the way he touches her underneath and gently strokes her. Then he leans over closer, whispers something to her, kisses her on the lips, and steps away.

I am breathless.

Now the moment of leaving has passed. It is August 1, 1987. I am on the train from Arles in the south of France to Geneva, from where I will fly to Poland.

I realize that when I went to Asia for the first time, I had a brochure to look at, lists of clothes to bring, but not so for this trip. Making my own arrangements has proved to be very complicated. What bits of information I've gleaned about the pilgrimage to Czestochowa in Poland have been contradictory: "Bring a tent," "Don't bring a tent." "It will be terribly hot," "It will get cold," "It may rain the whole time." "You will be given or be able to buy food along the way," "Bring your own food, often there isn't anything available."

At the Polish consulate in Bern I met a Swiss woman from Geneva who invited me to call her on my way through to Poland. I would do so. She would pick me up from my hotel by the train station in Geneva and take me to dinner. Over dinner I would discover that she had friends in Warsaw. She would call and arrange for a driver to meet me at the airport when I landed in Warsaw. She was raised and schooled at the Benedictine Monastery at Einsiedeln. She too loved the Black Madonna.

I spilled out all the contradictions about Poland that I was contending with. She added a few of her own but said one thing with which everyone agreed: I would find Polish people absolutely unique.

"What spirit!" she told me. "You will fall in love with them, you won't want to come home."

CHAPTER 10

We Go Now

♦

Warsaw, Poland

Ayiasma

The black image
Framed in silver worn to shreds by kisses
The black image
Framed in silver worn to shreds by kisses
Framed in silver
The black image worn to shreds by kisses
Framed in silver
The black image worn to shreds by kisses
All round the image
The white silver worn to shreds by kisses
All round the image
The very metal worn to shreds by kisses
Framed in metal
The black image worn to shreds by kisses
The Darkness, O, the darkness
Worn to shreds by kisses
The Darkness in our eyes
Worn to shreds by kisses
All we wished for
Worn to shreds by kisses
All we never wished for
Kissed and worn to shreds by kisses
All we escaped
Worn to shreds by kisses
All we wish for
Kissed again and again . . .

—Gunnar Ekelof[1]

Warsaw, Poland
August 1987

I am sitting in my hotel room, having just arrived, talking on the phone to Josef Zalecki in Czestochowa. It's the third of August. "The pilgrimage is very difficult. Many things can happen to you. I am surprised that you would undertake this, much less by yourself," he tells me over the blurry sound of a long-distance telephone. "It is very daring." I have never met Josef, only shouted to him through a pay telephone in the tiny village post office in LaSalle, France, while covering my other ear in hopes of hearing something back.

Easily distracted from our phone conversation, I notice that the ochre curtain in the room is actually a patterned damask tablecloth like the sheet on my bed, only the sheet is white. The curtain is pulled back now, and though the sun is out, still the sky here seems gray.

"Are you very strong?" he goes on. "I don't know if you can do it, thirty kilometers, often more, day after day. But I shouldn't say that, children do it, old people do it. Yes, maybe you will do all right. People have babies, die, all kinds of things can happen. The pilgrimage is very hard. In case you cannot finish the walking, you will call me and I will come to fetch you. Tomorrow morning I will catch the express train to Warsaw and meet you about ten o'clock at your hotel if you like. Then I can help you find a group to go with. We can catch the train back in the afternoon to Czestochowa and you will stay with our family. The village we live in is nearby.

"It would be good for you to visit the shrine before the town fills up with pilgrims. It will be impossible to see the Madonna for more than a moment once everyone arrives. Nearly a million people will be here and they all have come to see this Madonna. It's a madhouse! We're only three hours away by train. You can stay until the morning of the pilgrimage and then take the early morning express back to Warsaw to begin walking," he finishes up cheerfully.

The logistics sound draining. It has taken two days of travel by trains and planes just to get to Warsaw from the South of France.

"I don't know what to say, Josef, just come. It would be good if you would come tomorrow and we will go from there. I am very grateful for your help."

More than thirty-five thousand people will leave from Warsaw alone two days from now. Hundreds of groups of pilgrims are forming to go from different churches all over the city. Pilgrims from Gdansk are already on the road. It will take them two weeks of walking, sometimes fifty kilometers a day, to reach the shrine at Czestochowa. From Wroclaw it takes six days to walk to Czestochowa. By the time we reach the monastery on August 14, nearly a million pilgrims will converge, having walked from all over Poland. I am both relieved and nervous that Josef is coming.

Suddenly I remember being warned that all the phones in this hotel are tapped. Did we say too much? It is hard to remember all the precautions I have been told to take. My heart is pounding.

All my luggage must be broken up and repacked quickly into two bags that will go with me on the pilgrimage, and another one that I can leave in Czestochowa for after the pilgrimage. I have a tent, sleeping bag, rain gear. Any item that someone mentioned I brought, preparing as one would for the Himalayas: rolls of toilet paper, silver duct-tape, water-purifying tablets, antibiotics, Bandaids, moleskin, a full first-aid kit, dried food, vitamins, gifts, down vest, mittens, wool cap, long underwear, can opener. I begin to unpack the bags and fall into a doze on my bed sorting out gear.

The next morning I am just about to close my bags when Josef arrives at my door, a man in his forties with warm brown eyes. He is a university professor. His English is very good and soon I am put at ease. When Josef asks me why I've come to do the pilgrimage, I'm caught off guard and despite warnings to the contrary, I tell him that I'm writing a book. Now I must trust him.

We go quickly, there is little time for talk. We must find a group of pilgrims for me to join, as well as make arrangements for my luggage: now two very large and heavy bags. Leaving the bags at the hotel, we set off on foot for the Pauline Church on Dluga Street.

The Pauline fathers were entrusted with the care of the Black Madonna at Jasna Gora when Ladislaus, duke of Opole, brought them to Czestochowa from Hungary in the fourteenth century. "Jasna Gora" means "Mountain of Light" or "Bright Mountain." One of their members initiated this pilgrimage from Warsaw 276 years ago when the city was filled with the plague. The Pauline fathers have kept the pilgrimage going each year, no matter what wars, famines, or governments, including those of Hitler and Khrushchev, have arisen to stop it.

Josef explains my situation to the brother who greets us at the door. After a moment, he suggests that I join Father Dominik's group since one or two people in it speak English. A young man walks up behind Brother Januz as Josef is speaking to him. Januz motions to him to join us. He has on a tie-dyed T-shirt, a leather change purse around his neck, slacks, and tennis shoes. His haircut looks very modern. Josef introduces us. This is Father Dominik.

"This is no priest," I think to myself. I begin to laugh with surprise as we are introduced, blurting out, "You're not a priest!" They must be teasing me.

"I am too priest!" he tells me in a heavy Polish accent, feigning wounded feelings and grinning. Now everyone is laughing.

"Yes, he is a priest, this is Father Dominik, head of Group Fifteen, Gold. Every group has a color; number Fifteen's is *zloty*, gold. I know him. I taught him English in school," Josef says, "he was a student of mine."

Aside from this brief introduction, everything else is taking place in Polish. People are walking in and out of the hallway as the conversation goes on. Josef tosses me tidbits of English when I begin to look perplexed. Suddenly I am acutely aware of being alone, in the midst of strangers. Josef takes me aside and suggests a plan. I can join Father Dominik's group, leave my belongings here in this hallway, go to Czestochowa with Josef this afternoon, and return to Warsaw by train the day after tomorrow. It will be the morning of the pilgrimage. I will be met by a driver who speaks no English and amidst the crowd of thirty-five thousand people, I will somehow find this Dominik, this priest whom I have only just now met, this priest who can't be a priest who is a priest, who, despite the chaos and numbers of people in our group, will have remembered to put my bags on the lorry for Group 15, Gold.

"Well, it's up to you, what do you want to do?" Josef asks. "The train leaves soon."

My head is spinning. I have no context in which to make a decision. The potential for such plans going awry is enormous. I take a deep breath, make an invisible leap, and reply, "I'll leave everything here, Josef, let's go."

Settled in our compartment on the train to Czestochowa, I respond to Josef's inquiries by showing him pictures of my family. The compartment is warm with the afternoon summer sun. It has brown upholstery with six seats; only one other seat is occupied, by an old man nodding, full of sleep.

"Your first two children look so different from the third one, the youngest," he remarks matter-of-factly. I cross my legs, pull my blue skirt down further over my legs, and turn to look out the window, pretending to be absorbed in the scenery roaring by. Being their mother, I never see the difference. It hadn't occurred to me in this situation that anyone else would notice, much less comment on this fact. He presses further.

"Why do your first two children look so different from the third. Did they have different fathers?"

"Well, yes. Yes," I repeat, wanting time, trying to think of how I am going to handle this. I feel myself flush. He is very direct. I realize that he is Catholic and assumes that I must be as well.

"Did your husband die?"

"No. My husband didn't die," I reply, looking into my handbag for something quickly. An answer? A card with instructions as to what to do? Why can't I just say I don't want to talk about this? I feel a heat rising inside me, I can't find the words.

I'm in Eastern Europe. Raised in the Cold War era, I think of it as being more remote than India or Nepal. The term from my childhood, "Iron Curtain," though no longer used or appropriate, suddenly makes itself felt. Ever since I entered Poland and had to surrender my passport at the hotel desk, I have felt as though some door had closed behind me to which I no longer had the key. The door of this compartment is closed, there is no place to go, no simple way out.

"Well, what happened?" he says.

"My first two children do look very different from my third. They have different fathers. My first marriage was annulled by the Church, the second one wasn't in the Church in the first place," I said, hoping that would settle the matter.

"But you're married now, aren't you? Now you are married in the Church, eh?" Not only is he Catholic, he is a conservative Catholic, I realize.

"No, we decided not to marry in the Church. My husband is Jewish."

"Oh.

"Well, how is it that you met my brother who told you to stay with us?"

"I've never met your brother, I've only spoken with him by phone." I turn to look out the window again as the pale yellow of farmlands at summer harvest whirls by. Here the wheat is stacked in a conical style. "Didn't he tell you that when he was visiting you last spring?" I ask, turning back to him, shifting in my seat.

"No. Well, he did mention something about someone coming once, but he was very busy. He was celebrating his twenty-fifth anniversary as a priest. He had many people to see. I didn't realize that you'd never met." He looks back again at the stack of pictures in his hands and continues through them.

Now he is looking at my pictures of the Dalai Lama, followed by a photograph of a Green Tara, then a White Tara, and various Tibetan teachers and friends of mine. It had never occurred to me to conceal them. Suddenly I realize that they will seem strange to him, foreign beyond belief, reprehensible, pagan. They are scattered throughout the stack of my family pictures.

"Who is that?" he asks with a slight frown, pointing to the picture of His Holiness.

"That's Tenzin Gyatso, the Fourteenth Dalai Lama of Tibet, whom I went to India to see last fall. I became a student of Buddhism ten years ago. This deity is Tara," I explain, taking the photograph of a tangkha of Green Tara out of his hands. "She is like the Madonna to the Tibetan Buddhists," I say, trying to bridge the gap that is so quickly widening between us. "The Dalai Lama's like the Pope of Tibetan Buddhism, you could say."

"Oh," he says, his brow furrowing deeper.

His head is cocked to one side as he looks at White Tara, then my grandfather, then a Tibetan friend in India. I try to point out my mother, still lovely, my brothers, aunts, uncles, father, cousins, so that he could see that I'm from Texas, not from Mars. By the end of the family pictures, his head is tilted back from me altogether, he is frowning, his face troubled. There is a long and uncomfortable silence.

"What kind of person are you?" he asks finally in exasperation.

How is one to answer such a question? Keenly aware of my vulnerability as a foreigner who has failed to register with the police as required, I turn to look out the window again and find myself embarrassingly close to tears. I turn around again.

"Tell me," he insists.

"Look, I can't make my life make sense to you. How can I answer such a question? I don't understand altogether why I'm here myself."

To my embarrassment and surprise, I begin to pour out my story. The pain of over twenty years ago is suddenly apparent, bright and fresh. I am shocked at what pours out of me. "I'm a recovering alcoholic. I was raised Catholic, went to Catholic school for fourteen years, was a daily communicant. I did it all by the book, including getting married at nineteen and having children. But it was a terrible marriage, horrible fights. I was pregnant with our second child. They thought I would lose the baby. The doctors put me in the hospital. Then they called in a Catholic priest to talk to me.

"It was a Catholic priest who told me to get divorced and to file for an annulment simultaneously. I wanted nothing more than to stay in the Church. I didn't know anything else. I thought that people who got divorced went to hell. I couldn't believe that it was a priest telling me to file for a divorce. But after I got out of the hospital, I did just that.

"After a year of waiting I was told that unless I had the money to send a canon lawyer to Rome, it could take seven years. That's when I left the Church. I had two children under the age of two. I was twenty-two years old. I had done everything the way I was supposed to do it. What was left?

"I didn't know how to handle the situation. I remarried three years later. My second husband and his father tried to save us, gave us their name, their loyalty, but I was beyond help. That's when I began to drink. That was my way of coping. It was a disaster. I didn't know it but I was already on my way to becoming an alcoholic."

Now I am red-faced, crying as though it all happened yesterday. It's like a bomb going off inside me, all this that happened so long ago that I never understood, couldn't make sense of, and drank over for years, now it feels like it's running down my face, oozing out of my pores. I am mortified and stripped bare. I have no defenses left.

I want to change the subject. I had no idea of the emotional impact this trip would have on me and this encounter with a Catholicism that I thought I'd left. Why couldn't I be silent? Why did I disclose so much? Josef seems to understand and keeps handing me Kleenex. Truth makes a place where a seed of friendship is planted.

After a few moments, I catch my breath and try to continue. "I can't practice Catholicism anyway. The Church won't allow women to be priests."

"That's a preposterous idea!" he exclaims. "There were women priests in pagan times. Paganism. That's the association. It's impossible, you just can't have them."

I would discover that Josef's attitude about women priests was not unusual or extraordinary for Catholicism in Poland. It belongs to another world and is markedly different from the Church in the Americas. At least he was honest.

"Josef, what kind of a person are *you*? Would your life make sense to me?" I ask. He shrugs with a smile and stops asking questions. Beyond our differences he now understands that this pilgrimage is also a homecoming. He accepts the fact that I honor the Virgin Mary. Here we have something in common.

When we arrive at the train station, Jadwiga, Josef's wife, is there to greet us. She hurries us into their car. A pretty woman with blue eyes, short brown curly hair, my height and age, she immediately makes me feel welcome and at home. Once at their house, she shows me to my room, the bed made up with fresh linens, towels laid out, and tells me I have a moment to rest and freshen up before dinner. She will call me when it's ready.

One by one after dinner, the children play the piano. The two girls dance a mock tango while their brother plays a melody. Barely able to keep straight faces, they begin at one end of the living room in the open curve of the black grand piano with their backs straight, cheek-to-chest (the youngest girl comes to just above her older sister's waist). With a crash, their brother hits the signal chord and they take off, arms extended, in a flurry of giggles, dancing their tango to our end of the room where we sit. Just before careening into the dinner table, still heavy with plates of pork slices, potatoes, home-grown tomatoes, cucumbers, and cups of hot tea, they shriek, wheel into an abrupt turn, and tango back to the piano. Josef and Jadwiga are doubled over laughing, as I am.

Then the girls play the piano, each playing one piece from their lessons. Now it's my turn, I'm informed. Falteringly, I play *Für Elise* and the first few bars of one of Chopin's mazurkas, the extent of my repertoire, which is badly out of practice. But like the children, I am credited for trying. Then Josef plays and plays well, he is passionate and practiced.

"Enough of music. It is late," Jadwiga insists. "You must be up early in the morning!"

My hosts provide me with background material on the Madonna I will see tomorrow. I lie reading in the freshly made bed. The Madonna of Jasna Gora is an icon, a painting, not a statue like the Black Madonnas I have seen in France and Switzerland.

My room upstairs overlooks the family's vegetable garden and greenhouse full of tomatoes. In the distance I can make out the spires of Jasna Gora. The moon shines half full through storm clouds blowing across its face. Rain threatens. I turn back to the book and continue reading.

An icon in the Byzantine tradition is much more than a likeness or representation of the saint or deity honored. The icon is considered a vessel that conveys the sanctity of the saint depicted. Veneration by the faithful is believed to create an actual contact with the saint. The life of the artist who painted it was a spiritual life, filled with prayers and fasting; the artistry with which he or she executed the icon was considered to be a direct result of the level of personal holiness attained.[2]

I know little about the Eastern Church. What is the difference between Russian Orthodox and Greek Orthodox, or are they the same? Do the phrases "Byzantine" or "Eastern Orthodox" refer to them both? I pencil questions to myself into a tiny pocket notepad that I will carry on the pilgrimage and wish that I could fall asleep; it's 11:00 p.m.

One of the legends about the Black Madonna at Jasna Gora is that the icon was painted by St. Luke on the wooden planks of the table the Holy Family ate upon in Nazareth, thus for many it ranks with the Cross as a first-class relic. Through its veneration, one stands in the living presence of Mary and the infant Jesus themselves. This mystical approach is characteristic of the Byzantine Church, maintains the author, Marian Zalecki, O.S.P., Josef's brother. Zalecki writes that in the Byzantine tradition of icons, the image is not separate from the saint depicted. The Virgin of Jasna Gora, as long as she is seen and venerated with fervent conviction, *is* the Virgin herself, if one understands the Byzantine tradition.

The icon hanging in the chapel is a fifteenth-century copy of the original. Art historians and scholars still debate its origin. Some maintain that the original might have been painted as early as the sixth century A.D. Others suggest that it may have been done as late as the twelfth or thirteenth century. There is some agreement that the icon was painted from a fifth-century Byzantine prototype long worshipped in Constantinople, the *Hodegetria*, "The One Who Leads the Way." The *Hodegetria*, one of the most famous images of the Madonna and child, was particularly revered by ships' pilots. Destroyed by the Turks in 1453, the original *Hodegetria* was widely copied and many of the paintings modeled after it still exist, the most famous being the Madonna of Czestochowa and the Madonna in Rome's Santa Maria Maggiore, Our Lady of the Snows.[3] I fall asleep in the midst of reading their arguments.

The following morning is August 5, the day before the pilgrimage begins from Warsaw. Josef will take me to the shrine to see the Black Madonna and try to arrange for me to photograph her.

"You must photograph today. It will be impossible for you to take pictures once the pilgrims arrive. The Madonna is only visible three times a day for half an hour at a time, the rest of the day she is covered by a shield of silver."

First, Josef takes me to the Knights' Hall in the monastery to point out a series of paintings that help one understand the import of this Madonna to the Polish people. In the seventeenth century, Poland was invaded by Russia, Sweden, and had an uprising of the Cossacks. By the middle of the century even Krakow had fallen, and Polish troops had been forced to recognize the king of Sweden as their overlord.

Suffering defeat after defeat, the Poles were nearly devastated by the Swedish forces. The Swedes had won over most fortified resistance, as well as plundered every church and monastery they could along the way. Then came a turning point in Polish history: Swedish troops attacked the Monastery of Jasna Gora in November 1655. Jasna Gora was surrounded by some six thousand Swedish soldiers and twenty-five hundred cavalry.

"The monastery had two hundred fifty soldiers and less than one hundred monks to defend against the Swedish forces with their artillery," Josef tells me. The prior of the monastery, Augustin Kordecki, was not about to turn over Jasna Gora to the Swedes. He had foreseen the coming attack and prepared for a long siege. "When the Swedes attacked with their artillery, Kordecki led a procession of monks displaying the Holy Sacrament along the battlement walls to show the Swedes they weren't afraid. He was not going to surrender, no matter what the odds."

Monks and soldiers, with the help of mercenaries attacking from the rear, successfully fought off the thousands of Swedes until just before Christmas, when the Swedes finally withdrew. The victory against such enormous odds was considered miraculous. The protection of the Virgin was believed to be the reason for the spectacular defense, and upon his return from exile, the king, John Casimir, placed Poland under the protection of the Madonna of Jasna Gora and declared her "Queen of the Crown of Poland." News of the monastery's success spread like wildfire and helped fuel the resistance against Sweden.

The Czestochowa Madonna is also credited by the Poles for their victory against the Bolshevik Army in 1920. After one hundred and twenty-five years of having been partitioned between Prussia, Austria, and Russia, Poland achieved its independence again. Poland had literally been wiped off the map of Europe and did not exist again until this "Miracle of the Vistula" that occurred in the defense of Warsaw.[4]

Wandering through the halls, we finally reach the Gothic chapel of the Virgin with the altar and presbyter set behind ornate black wrought-iron open grillwork. Framed in silver, the icon is set high above the altar into a massive, ornate Baroque altarpiece veneered in ebony. Cool and impersonal, the faces of Mary and the infant Jesus are a dark brown, burnt sienna color, set off by heavily jeweled robes. Hers is blue encrusted with jewels, diamonds, rubies, sapphires, pearls, and other precious stones sewn onto the fabric over the centuries. The infant's robe is rose, elaborately embroidered with gold. Thousands of necklaces of amber and coral hang on the adjacent fabric-covered walls. The riches of the dark.

The chapel is full of people, a wedding in progress on the altar itself as well as the normal course of pilgrims. I don't see how we will even get in, much less be able to photograph. Josef leads me off to a door on the right and I find myself in the sacristy. Josef finds a priest he knows to explain my request. While they talk, I look around the large room bustling with priests, monks, and pilgrims. On one wall is a large painting of St. Sarah, the Egyptian, hanging on the sacristy wall among the other paintings, and a statue of Our Lady of Montserrat, another famous Black Madonna, sitting over a doorway. This St. Sarah was an actress in the fifth century who repented and became a desert anchoress, like St. Paul I, the patron of the Pauline fathers, I am told.

I wonder whether this figure could be related to the St. Sara of the Camargue that I had seen in France. There St. Sara, the Queen of the Gypsies, is brown-black. Could St. Paul I, a third-century Eygptian, have been dark-skinned or black? Could I be mistaken about the Madonna over the doorway, is she from Montserrat in Spain or Tindari in Sicily? There are so many Black Madonnas. There is no time to find out now for Josef is beckoning me away from the painting.

"The Madonna will be showing for only a few minutes more. I don't know when the screen went up. It closes after half an hour. We're in luck! Hurry now, I don't know how much time we have. This priest will take us into the chapel and you can photograph. Come *now*," he says.

Josef helps me find a space by the railing where I set up my tripod. I am pushed up against the brass railing that marks off the presbyter. Barely able to move, I screw the camera on top of the tripod and set it on the railing, intermittently jostled and bumped as pilgrims, some on their knees, circulate around the altar. The wedding service continues in Latin and Polish, a tiny island of calm amidst a sea of motion. It is hot with all the people crammed in here, I begin to perspire. Looking at the Madonna with one eye through the viewfinder, I struggle with the focus. Her face is dark, the altar surrounding her is black, the chapel dimly lit; I'm unsure of what light reading to use. Is the focus clear?

Josef sees how nervous I am, tells me to relax, take my time. But I don't know how much time I have, only that it is *now*. Soon the silver shield will be lowered over the icon and the Madonna will disappear in a matter of minutes. With no flash, the camera is set on long time exposures. Every time I am bumped, I lose a frame. Yes, I want to do this, to take these photographs, but what is it that I'm after, I wonder, as I shoot one picture after another. Squint, focus, change exposure, shutter speed, what did I just have it set on? I stop for a moment, just to look at her. I can't see her when I'm taking pictures.

The Madonna is mysterious, unmoved by all the emotion before her. I cannot penetrate the secret of her face. I had the same experience at Einsiedeln. I begin shooting again, I cannot take enough pictures of the Black Madonna. I am hungry for her, want to devour her, incorporate her. My eyes are teeth and I am chewing up her image, ingesting her, making her part of my being. I want to receive her as a wafer in communion, I want to swallow her, whole. Can a photograph be a wafer? If you take a picture of something sacred, is the image of the sacred image sacred?

Trumpets begin to play as I am changing film, signalling the lowering of the shield. Now it is a matter of seconds before I lose her. Slowly a line of silver appears at the top of the icon and the shield begins to slide down over her face. I finish loading, shooting as fast as I can as the shield is coming down. Now it begins to cover her forehead, down, now her eyes are gone, down, her nose, now the mouth, gone, now the Child in her arms, the jeweled robes, blue, gold, diamond-studded, rose, her hand gone, down, down, the final flourish of trumpets, and the picture is closed.

I am shaking and wet with perspiration. The intensity of what I

Our Lady of Czestochowa, Jasna Gora Monastery,
Czestochowa, Poland. (Author)

am trying to do and the concentration required drains me. What I
am doing, I only begin to understand.

After dinner that night, Josef too warns me again about the pilgrimage. "Do not draw attention to yourself. You are already a curiosity because you are a Westerner. Don't make matters worse. Don't
trust anyone, even someone you think is a friend. The secret police.
There are stories. But still . . . I shouldn't tell you these things. Martial
law is over. You shouldn't worry, you're an American. It would be
too much trouble for them to harm you. I shouldn't talk like this.
Don't worry. Everything will be fine. This is not Central America.

"Most Polish people are very polite, they wouldn't lay a hand
on you even if you are arrested. They like Americans. They would
interrogate you, take your notes and your film, but that's all. You
would have to leave the country, but they wouldn't hurt you."

The next morning, I'm up at 3:00 a.m., filled with apprehension and
excitement. The pilgrimage begins today, August 6. I have a three-
hour train ride and thirty-eight kilometers of walking to do on four
hours of sleep. "Sleep!" I tell myself, but I am wide awake. It's cold
and rainy outside.

By 7:00 a.m. I am on the train, leaving. Jadwiga runs alongside
the car as the train pulls out, cupping her hands to her mouth,
shouting, "Do not fear, don't worry." She has such authority in her
voice that my mind is eased. The stories I had heard, the warnings
we had talked about last night fade like a bad dream she is waking
me out of, shaking my shoulders, leaning over to whisper, "Do not
fear, don't worry. Everything will be all right!" She is still waving,
growing smaller as the train picks up speed.

I fall asleep, waking just before it reaches the outskirts of Warsaw.
When it pulls into the central station, there is Jurek, the driver,
waiting for me on the platform.

My heart sinks as we drive down the streets of Warsaw. We
have found the pilgrimage, but it stretches out for miles. I knew

there would be thousands and thousands of people, but I didn't know what thirty-five thousand people stretched out in lines looked like. It will be impossible to find Father Dominik and Group 15, Gold. Everyone is a stranger, everything is unfamiliar. Jurek drives along at ten miles an hour while I crane my head out the window looking. I can't believe I have done this, that I am here, the pilgrimage is beginning. But the further we drive, the more people I notice singing and laughing. Others line the roadside, waving, clapping, handing out flowers for pilgrims to carry as they walk by. The more pilgrims I see, the more I like them and the happier I grow that I have come this way. Yes, this is a good thing to do.

Still driving slowly, we have passed over twenty groups now, all carrying signs for Group 17. There are thousands of people in Group 17 alone, and still no sign of Group 15. I begin to get a sense of how large an event this is. We pass two pilgrims in wheelchairs, a couple with two baby carriages wired together face to face and two babies inside. Just behind them the outlawed red and white Solidarity banners snap in the wind. Several people fly them, despite the risk of arrest for doing so.

I had counted more than thirty groups of number 17 when suddenly a young man runs up to the taxi, raps on the hood, and yells something in Polish. Jurek stops and motions for me to get out, indicating that this man is from my group, 15. How could this be? I haven't seen their sign anywhere. Jurek and the man converse in Polish. I show Jurek the note that Josef wrote in Polish saying to help me find Father Dominik and Group 15, Gold. "Yes," he says in English, "Yes." This is it. I get out, sling on my daypack, lean back into the taxi window to shake Jurek's hand to say thank you, "*Dziekuje,*" and goodbye.

Taking my hand, the young man leads the way through the moving crowd and in moments I see Father Dominik. He sees me too, walks briskly to my side, and greets me warmly in his best English. Yes, he remembered my bags. "Of course," he says with a laugh, "of course. It is all right, everything. All right. Please come. We go now."

CHAPTER 11

The Pilgrimage to the Black Madonna

◆

The Road to
Czestochowa, Poland

"Solvitur ambulando." It is solved by walking.
—Bruce Chatwin[1]

Outside Warsaw
August 1987

We sit in tall grasses by a lake, sprawled out resting and eating lunch this first day, the sixth of August. The sky is full of thunderheads and a wind blows fitfully. I feel joyful as a group walks past us singing. Why not be walking and singing together as we are? There is nothing better in the world to do, it seems today.

There are two young women in our group studying to be translators who speak English fluently, Jola and Aska. Dominik speaks some English and Vesa, a young man from Finland, speaks English as well, so there are at least four people with whom I can communicate in some way, lessening the initial sense of isolation.

Walking together after lunch, Father Dominik and I understand each other enough to find out that we share a love of the Black Madonna. He has great feeling for Our Lady of Jasna Gora, seeing her as an ecumenical symbol capable of uniting both the Eastern and Western branches of the Church. He does not understand why I fail to be excited by such ecumenical possibilities. We have run out of words with which we can communicate with one another. I am relieved that we have to stop talking. Now we are just walking together in peace.

It takes us the rest of the afternoon to get beyond the environs of Warsaw, the gray cement-block buildings, into the countryside. We have one rest stop and reach the farm where we will camp out just after dark. Rain begins to fall just as I am putting up my tent in an apple orchard. We have stopped walking just at the moment I thought I would keel over. I've walked over thirty kilometers on top of the three-hour train ride and hardly any sleep!

August 7, 1987.

Midafternoon, we are somewhere in the fields of Poland. People still line our way, waving and smiling as they did in Warsaw. An old man who reminds me of my grandfather waves to me. I cannot help but weep. How I miss everyone! A nun reaches over and takes my hand without a word. She is a sister who's been wearing a tambourine on her head like a halo. I liked her immediately and am grateful for her unspoken warmth. Everyone is saying the rosary in Polish and I swim in a sea of sounds that I cannot understand.

The walking began at 5:30 a.m. this morning. Thin white clouds brush wide across the sky. I walk as in a dream, exhausted. Jola sees how tired I am and knows that I will not make the thirty-five kilometers we have to go in such a state. She suggests that we take a ride to the next stop, cutting off seven to eight kilometers of the walking. I agree. It is only 9:00 a.m. and I can hardly stay awake even though I am walking. We ride to the next rest stop the group will take and I collapse on the ground, exhausted, too tired to talk or eat. I can only sleep.

Thunderclouds fill the sky again, threatening more rain. The day is chilly and the wind picks up, good weather for walking. The countryside is flat and golden with the harvest of wheat being cut. Farmers work their fields with horses here, there are very few tractors.

On the pilgrimage, Group #15 Gold. (Kryziek Sarnowski)

The frequent roadside shrines to the Black Madonna that we pass remind me of chortens and temples along the roadside and trails in India and Nepal. Some are built of roughly curved and whitewashed stones, others are wooden boxes atop poles with the Madonna of Czestochowa's image painted inside, some are tiny shrines where one can actually enter and kneel. All through the day people are singing, all through lunch the singing never stops. I join in as we walk along, at least I can learn the melodies.

Military helicopters fly overhead, checking our location, and we all wave. The government is nervous. There are nearly a million people now out on the roads all over Poland, walking, threading their way through the countryside, singing, praying, playing music. People play guitars, violins, tambourines, recorders, harmonicas, whatever is at hand. It is an event outside the authorities' control.

Last night we slept in an apple orchard. I ate dinner with Dominik, George the seminarian, and Vesa, the young man from Finland, the one other Westerner on the pilgrimage that I meet. Dominik insisted that we join him and George in the farmhouse where we are given hot tea, tomatoes, cucumbers, and meat. The priests are put up in the farmhouses, given beds, a shower or bath, and treated like visiting royalty.

This evening we are in another farmyard, scrambling to get up our tents before the rain that's just beginning. Aska and Jola help at every turn, reducing what seems impossible to the merely difficult. The farmer comes out to pitch hay for sleeping into the loft for people without tents. Four young women dance in the barn, full of good spirits. Long braids flying, skirts billowing, whirling around and around they swing each other until they fall down laughing into the hay. I sit watching from the door of my tent, too tired to move.

10:10 p.m. I am sitting in my tent writing by flashlight, both feet wrapped in bandages from toe to ankle. The nurse at the first-aid station opened and cleaned eight blisters. I set my alarm for the work of my water-purifying tablets to be done so I can have a drink of water, then reset it for 3:30 a.m. Most people won't rise until 4:00 a.m., but it seems to take me longer to get my tent down by myself, dress, rebandage my feet, pack, and be ready to walk by five.

August 8, 1987.

The nurse has told me that I cannot walk this morning, I must get off my feet or they will be so bad that I will not be able to finish the pilgrimage. There is a week more of walking to do, so I ride in the back of a lorry full of luggage this morning. It's 7:15 a.m. and

I'm bouncing around with six Scouts my oldest son's age, singing "Oh, Susannah" in Polish and English.

We come to the village where we are to meet up with Group 15, Gold, but it will be at least an hour before they arrive.

Polish Scouts help keep the groups together and direct traffic, placing themselves at junctions to point the way and to keep traffic moving, ensuring passage of vehicles and the safety of pedestrians. We take up at least half of whatever roadway we are on. With the pilgrims far behind us, there is time now to rest and sing. The Polish store of music seems endless.

A priest appears who speaks English and invites me to come into the monastery courtyard across the street for food. There we find huge pans of hot fried meat and enormous pots of cabbage and potato soup on long tables lining the courtyard. The priests and brothers have been cooking for days. They circulate through the crowd, serving us generously. It is their way of taking part in our effort and gaining merit. Though it's early morning, I have two servings of everything— meat, cabbage, potatoes—not knowing when I will see such good hot food again. My usual vegetarian preference of diet has little place here.

Today is Dominik's name day, the Feast of St. Dominic. Name days are celebrated more than birthdays in Poland, I am told, and there is much merriment. Two of our group members have hitchhiked back to Warsaw to purchase a leaded cut-glass bowl, plate, and glass to present to Dominik upon their return, right in the middle of the road, stopping all traffic. Before we can go on, Dominik is thrown up in the air, long white robes flying, his protests and resistance no avail; he belongs to the group and is tossed in the air like a favored child.

At lunch, Dominik is presented with flowers and songs from the sisters and then tossed in the air again. The fun is inescapable. Someone at the microphone is playing the melody for "Oh, Susannah" on a guitar. A song from my own language—home! Drawn like a magnet, I run through the crowd and ask if I can join in the music and sing. None of the musicians speaks English, yet everyone understands and nods, smiling, handing me the microphone. Their friendliness was so inviting that though there were several hundred people sitting in this field where we had stopped for lunch, I felt like I was in my own living room singing with friends. I was completely caught up in the moment. Only later would I remember Josef's warning.

I fall back behind the group as we walk after lunch to talk with Dominik again. It takes a great deal of effort on his part and mine to communicate, but we manage. When we get lost, we call on Jola or Aska to come translate and go on.

"Women priests? Impossible. No, this is not possible!" he says, when I ask him if he thinks the Church will change its position on the priesthood.

It is close to midnight and still the group is up singing. The energy is building. Today is the third day. I found myself drifting in and out of prayer and meditation much of the day, singing the melody when I can to the "Hail Mary," beginning to remember two or three Polish words of the prayer. Despite the rain that stops and starts tonight, we sit around a fire singing out from under our various umbrellas or ponchos. George and Dominik improvise animal characters as everyone plays a game that I can't understand, only watch. They are hilarious in their white robes in the center of the sandy circle pantomiming—a raccoon? a monkey?—in the firelight. I have never seen priests behave like this: warm, funny, natural, spontaneous, playful. No wonder everyone loves them.

August 9, 1987

The poorer the villages, the more colorful they become as we walk deeper into the countryside. Now the cottages are made of wood with thatched roofs. There are lavish flower gardens in the yards full of hollyhocks, purple and white cosmos, marigolds. The gold of the wheat fields is broken up by the sudden green of marshes, a pond

Morning break, Father Dominik and pilgrims dancing. (Author)

or a stream. This is Old Poland, where the field work is done by horses and hand-held plows. One of the few signs of our age is the use of automobile tires on a horse-drawn wagon.

Midmorning Break. There is singing and dancing in the field, the music of tambourines, and an uproar of laughter as one group sings a song about Chernobyl, which Jola translates: "We are so grateful to have Chernobyl. Now we will all die of radiation instead of Reagan's missiles, hey, ho . . ." they sing and periodically burst out with laughter. The Polish humor is black, dry, and sharp. "Life is brutal" is a favorite phrase, always delivered with a hearty laugh and enormous smile. The sky is overcast, the day cool, gray and windy, as we sit by the river eating and singing.

By 3:00 p.m. we have already walked twenty-seven kilometers and have seven more to go. This is an intensely physical experience. Lunch is in a pine forest where I am sitting on my rain poncho with my new companions. We eat while Robert, a paramedic, pops the blisters on Vesa's feet and paints them with a bright purple ointment, guaranteed to stain your skin for at least two weeks. Then he wraps them in gauze. Both my feet are wrapped in gauze as well.

Tonight I promised Dominik that I would mend his daypack that's falling apart. I go to the farmhouse where the priests are staying so that I can sew in some light. Soon Dominik and I have exhausted our ability to make conversation. He asks me if I will sing again tomorrow when we have a fire. I begin to hum a melody that he recognizes and knows too. I sing the song in Hebrew, then he sings it in Polish. Though the languages are different, the melody is the same.

"I will sing again if you will sing with me," I tell him. He agrees. I write out the refrain from "Rock My Soul in the Bosom of Abraham" and begin to sing the melody for him. He learns it quickly and soon we are singing "Rock My Soul" and I am no longer sewing. Suddenly I see how late it is and finish the mending quickly. Dominik is inexhaustible, but even George, the seminarian with our group, twenty years my junior, looks tired. We finally say goodnight.

It is nearly 11:00 p.m. by the time I get back to my tent and make some notes. Again today someone asked me where I was going after the pilgrimage ended at Czestochowa. I am anxious whenever this happens, no matter how innocent the question. I am uncomfortable writing in my own journal. I try to devise abbreviations and codes for words rather than writing out whole sentences. But within minutes even I find it hard to understand what I just wrote. My respect for writers who persist under authoritarian regimes grows. The first censor to get beyond is the fear in oneself. It is debilitating if one listens to it. Deadly. I don't live here yet I see how quickly I am affected by the idea that these notes might be confiscated, read from another point of view, bring harm to someone else, and I have nothing to hide. My attempts at writing in code are absurd. I resolve to take notes as though I am at home in my own country, only not to include people's names or ways for people to be identified.

Being told that I am automatically suspect because I am a foreigner leaves a residue of suspicion in me every time I am asked a question. The only clue I have as to whether or not someone might be the secret police or an informant is the fact that they will question me.

I am so careful that it's exhausting. I lock everything, my bags, my tent when I leave it, and I am tired of it. Just now, when I went to the farmhouse to mend the daypack for Dominik, I left my tent open. When I return, I can't find my knife and am left to wonder if someone stole it. I go to check my rain poncho left stretched over a fence to dry and find some toilet paper on it. Since the practice on the pilgrimage is that people leave toilet paper to alert others as to where they went to the bathroom, does that mean that someone urinated on my poncho as a way of letting me know that I am not liked or accepted, that I am an outsider? Am I paranoid? Is this my imagination, or did some unused paper simply fall out of someone's pocket onto my poncho? I have no way of knowing.

The more I sing, the friendlier people are to me. Three more people are talking to me with the little English that they have. I am grateful. Though Josef warned me about being visible, I have no context, no clues, no indication as to where the boundaries are in this situation. I pray that I can complete this walk. Just walking is so hard, so very, very difficult. I think of Thich Nhat Hanh, the Vietnamese Buddhist monk who came to visit Green Gulch and taught us walking meditation. I try to focus on my breath, notice how many breaths I take to a step. Walking these distances at the pace we keep is in itself a rigorous spiritual practice.

I cannot bear to think of what time it is or how much further we have to go. "Take refuge in the present moment," Thich Nhat Hanh said. Present moment. If I can just stay in this present moment, but it hurts! I try only to plod along, singing or praying, giving up any sense of time, distance, and place. Such information only fuels the difficulties of the walk, the pain of the blisters rubbing in my shoes on the tops of the toes, on the sides of the toes, between the toes, on the heels, on the balls of the feet, and then the burning of rashes on my ankles and calves from stepping into nettles. Only singing takes the pain away.

This afternoon Dominik told us that a child from Group 10 was hit by a car and killed. Tonight a father carried in his arms his swooning fourteen-year-old son, on fire with fever, to the first-aid tent, while the sister bandaged my blisters. I watched as the doctor rushed to his side—pulled out her stethoscope, elevated his feet, and called for help—I tried not to cry.

Jola wrote down the complete Polish phrase I keep hearing, and translated it for me into English: "Life is brutal and full of traps."

August 10, 1987.

We waken at 4:00 a.m. this morning. A car drives along the road next to where we are camped in the fields with its horn blaring and someone in singsong repeating a phrase in Polish over and over on an electronic bullhorn. Today there is a mass at five, then a 6:30 a.m. departure for the road with over thirty-two kilometers to go. My feet are very bad this morning. It's still dark and I cannot organize myself inside this tent until light. I roll out of my sleeping bag and do some exercises for my aching back, then rebandage my feet.

The soft sound of voices rises invisibly around me as others begin to get up. Gradually they grow louder, like birdsong at sunrise, the first few hushed tones become fuller and are soon joined by others. I am lost again, floating in a sea of language that I do not understand. Buoyed by inflection and tone, carried by emphasis, I am left to the ear alone, swimming in sound. I grow infinitely more sensitive to the tone of the human voice. Yet I am grateful that I do not know the language. Words could easily cut me off from the experience of the pilgrimage.

I fail to understand how and where people have found water for washing. At each stop it is different. Some farms have a well in the yard that you draw your own cold water from for washing. Some have faucets inside or even hot water to use for washing—luxury! But one has to rise extra early to find these things out. I have taken to borrowing Jola or Aska's washpan, getting up before they do, finding water, and washing crouched in the privacy of my tent rather than trudging off to the roomier nearby—and sometimes not so nearby—forest. There will hardly be anyone waiting in line at the outhouse at 4:00 a.m., if there is one. Someone is usually up in the farmhouse where there is occasionally hot water, if you ask or are willing to pay a few zlotys.

The day's walk normally begins by 5:30 a.m. Before this I must dress, repack my two bags, take down my tent, eat breakfast, pack a lunch for the day, and get my gear to the lorry in time to begin. Often one of the Scouts or young men takes my bags to the lorry for me. The Poles I am meeting are extremely polite, even the young people, and the young men consider it their duty to help an older woman. I am not used to thinking of myself as so much older, but I finally accept their kindness (it is pointless to oppose them, I discover) and relax. The logistics are a challenge in themselves and I am grateful for the old-fashioned ways of the Polish people.

Getting into camp, getting my feet attended to, setting up the tent, cleaning up, and having dinner all before dark, when I'm exhausted by the day's walk, is equally challenging. In the mornings I have more energy, but it is always dark when we get up. In the evening there is usually light left during which to set up camp and make dinner, but I have no energy. Either way, it is a feat of no small measure to accomplish the most basic tasks under these circumstances. Often Jola and Aska are nearby and we share the evening meal.

August 11, 1987. Morning

I hear the sounds of water being drawn from the well across the road. In the dark I am scribbling these notes on what I hope is a blank page. I can't find my flashlight. Already there is the sound of tent poles coming down and laughter. The music is beginning, someone is playing a recorder.

This morning a great remorse comes over me. The days without a language of my own drive me deeper and deeper inside, until underneath all surfaces an endless sorrow appears. I have hours each day to think, to remember, and to pray. We walk to the point where I am dizzy with the intensity of physical effort. There is no question of stopping walking, despite what the sisters tell me each night about my feet, "No walk tomorrow." Each morning I resolve to go to at least the first rest stop and see how I do. Each morning I make my way to the rest stop and then I don't want to quit. After a few days, continuing to walk has become a case of national honor and international diplomatic relations: can the Westerners, that is Vesa from Finland and me, keep up with the Eastern bloc, or are we too soft? Vesa's legs are severely cramped and he walks in great pain, often asking when we will stop. I am in pain as well, but it is only needles and fire I seem to have under my feet, my legs are fine. I try to sing and to know as little as possible about the distances left to go. Singing takes the pain away.

When I see other people's feet at night at the first-aid stations, they are as bad as mine and many are worse. Some women are walking these distances in high-heeled shoes. They have no others. Shoes are a very scarce commodity in Poland. Two young men walk the way barefooted. There are people in wheelchairs. A man pulling two rusty baby carriages roped together with two infants—one sick inside—gets stuck, a carriage wheel has fallen off. Four of us help push him through a long section of sandy forest floor. I am selfishly relieved when he drops behind.

One man in our group is eighty-two and has only a thin coat for protection—no tent, no food, only what he can find along the

Lunch stop. (Author)

way or is given. Then there is little Dominik, age six, from whom I draw inspiration. Little Dominik's mother was unable to have children, so she made this pilgrimage to the Madonna seven years ago. She became pregnant and made the pilgrimage the following year during her last month of pregnancy. Little Dominik was born during the pilgrimage on August 8, the feast day of St. Dominic. This is his sixth year of making the pilgrimage, and at age six, he is walking every bit of the way, very proud of himself.

When I see what other people have to work with, whether it's their shoes or physical condition, and the effort they are making, my own blisters become very small. Am I being masochistic? Catholicism can veer so far in that direction, but I don't think so. For most people in the world, life is hard. We forget. I had no context at first, but after days of walking I am discovering that if I just make the initial effort in the morning to start, then I don't want to stop. The hardest part is putting my shoes back on in the morning; that hurts. But after the first few kilometers, the pain becomes like a background noise and is, in truth, bearable. Seeing what others are contending with and the fact that they are contending spurs me on.

The physical energy expended during the day begins to take its toll, my defenses wear down, I feel stripped emotionally. The isolation from everything and everyone I know is having an effect. I have tried to keep up my morning meditations on Tara, but it would be impossible to get up any earlier to sit quietly before we walk, so I do it while we are walking, much more difficult for me to stay concentrated. Afterwards I say her mantra on the finger rosary I've brought from Switzerland.

Today I watch as people drop behind the group with Dominik to make a confession during the day. I have had no thought of going to confession. I want Dominik as a friend; further, what little communication we have is clouded by our lack of language. Often I am unclear as to what he has understood of the brief conversations we have been able to carry on.

But as I walk this morning I see each of my children's faces and realize that I have not forgiven myself for mistakes I have made as a parent, most of all for having been an alcoholic. The lack of forgiveness creates an underlying intolerance, a thin, hard rind around my heart. Unable to forgive myself, I can hardly forgive anyone else. To forgive means to cease to cherish displeasure in another. I have not included myself. Further, forgiveness means that I have to be willing to give up any version of my story in which I depict myself as a victim. The self-righteous anger that I derive from cultivating such a position, whether justified or not, is poisonous. I have to rid myself of it and to take full responsibility for my life. I do not want to do this, I do not know *how* to do this. Hours of walking pass, rain comes and goes, the sorrow deepens, the pain sharpens, and my inability to understand *how* I can forgive myself becomes more and more evident. Finally I am willing to do anything to break through this dilemma, even talk to Dominik, as a Catholic priest, despite my years of enmity with the Church. He must have gleaned some insight into this process of forgiveness. I can actually feel the weight of hardness in my heart. I will go to confession after all.

I fall back behind the line I am walking in, find Dominik, and signal to him. "I want to talk to you about forgiveness, Dominik. I think that I want you to hear my confession."

"Yes?" he says, looking at me puzzled, knowing what difficulty we have in understanding one another.

"It's very simple," I assure him in my slowest English. "You must talk to me about forgiveness, about how to forgive oneself. You must help me; please, hear my confession."

We fall behind the others. Thunderclouds pile up overhead, the air is cool and the wind gusting hard. He takes out his purple stole, the vestment a priest wears when hearing confession, places it around his neck, and we begin.

We are walking behind our group, one hundred feet or so, and an equal distance from the next group behind us. The wind is so cold now that I have to loan Dominik a wool-knit watchcap. At each revelation I fear Dominik's rejection. He will tell me I cannot receive communion. He will tell me what I must believe; but such words never come. This man is different. He listens carefully. He hears out my anger, the resentments, the pride and bitterness that I would be done with and have tried unsuccessfully to be rid of. I tell him the story of my alcoholism.

"You are forgiven, of course. I don't forgive you, Christ walking here between us forgives you. I am only person, I am only human. I cannot do such a thing, Christ does this. He understands. Please, your penance is to finish pilgrimage. It is enough difficult."

The confession has lasted over two hours as we struggled to understand each other. Sometimes Dominik could not understand me at all and I had to repeat myself again, slower, find different words. Sometimes I was not sure he followed me and I had to question him closely. By the time we finish, we are both exhausted emotionally. It has taken great effort and concentration on Dominik's part to speak only in English for two hours. It has taken a great deal from me to acknowledge that despite the years and the depths of my rejection of the Church, there are ways in which I am Catholic still.

I have not had a conversion experience. I am still a student of Buddhism, yet it is wonderfully freeing to acknowledge that I am Catholic too. I don't fit anywhere and for the first time that feels correct. I am walking along a nameless path. This walking creates the path, is not separate from the way. Walking becomes the way to weave together the threads that I hold of different traditions. The way of the pilgrim is always to walk, no matter what the country or culture. Pilgrimage knows no boundaries, crosses over the borders. There is only the nameless way, and to find it one must walk, feel one's feet on the ground, let the way lead. I only begin to understand this as we walk on through the afternoon. All the praying in Polish during the afternoon leaves me time for thought.

Dominik asks me to say the rosary with him over the loudspeaker after confession this afternoon. Each day the rosary is sung as we are walking. He explains, "You say first part English, we sing rest in Polish. Now say 'Hail Mary' for me."

"But, Dominik, no one will understand. People won't like it. Please don't ask me to do this."

"China, you must. It is good, English. Say for me, please," he says with his warmest smile.

Can I remember the prayer? It has been so many years since I said the rosary. It comes back to me as I begin:

"Hail Mary, full of grace, the Lord is with Thee. Blessed art Thou amongst women and blessed is the fruit of Thy womb, Jesus."

"Good. I tell you when to say. It's okay."

All the while we are walking, walking. There is no end to this walking. Rain begins to splatter us and everyone pulls up a hood or throws on whatever rain gear they have simultaneously and walks on. The sound of stiff plastic crinkling ripples through the air.

Now Dominik signals me that it is time to begin the rosary and hands me the microphone.

"Hail Mary."

It is good to hear the words so clearly and in English.

"Full of grace."

Yes, I mean this, Mother Mary, hear my prayer.

"Blessed art Thou amongst women."

Yes, how great you are, greater than the Church has ever admitted you to be. You are not just the Mother of God, you are God the Mother, I know who you are, and I am happy to sing your praises, Mary, hear my prayer.

"And blessed is the fruit of Thy womb, Jesus."

Yes, you too, Christ Child, you are a ripe fruit, raspberry, apple, plum, something red, something red with blue, a purple fruit that stains the mouth, marks the lips, is sweet, fragrant, full of liquid, juicy, tender, soft, inviting to eat. Yes, you too, I can say these things in truth about you. I love you. I have always loved you and I thought I had no way to love you. Hear me now. I have come all the way to Poland to sing to you.

I hand the microphone back to Dominik to complete the prayer, "*Matka bozska* . . ." he sings in Polish to the accompaniment of the sisters on tambourine and guitar. Then he hands me the microphone again. I can do this. I am happy walking next to Dominik singing these prayers. What better thing to do as we walk under this storm-filled sky.

It has rained off and on during the afternoon and by the time we get to our campsite for the night it is very muddy. We have walked over thirty-four kilometers, some say it was thirty-eight kilometers because our route was changed at the last minute. This is the sixth consecutive day of walking. I stumble with my bag and decide to set up my tent where I am rather than look further.

I find a place near Jola and Aska along a narrow lane that leads to an open field. Vesa is in the farmyard barn. I go to find him to see if he can help me set up my tent as I can do little more than walk. When I step into the barn, a man begins to laugh at me. I look down at what I'm wearing, an ochre rain poncho over a skirt, a blue scarf fallen around my neck, tennis shoes and gray leggings, and laugh myself. "I guess I look pretty funny," I say, trying to go along. The man's tone suddenly becomes sinister and in very good English he says, "You don't know how funny." He is distinctly unfriendly. I am cut to the quick, embarrassed, and feel foolish. I am surprised to hear him speak English. He has never spoken to me before and is hostile. Have I seen him before? I turn quickly and go back to my tent site to begin to set it up alone.

Five minutes later I am standing by a corn field dumping the tent stakes out of the tent bag onto the ground, when two young men walk past. With a derisive tone and in very good English, one says, "Water, please, Darek, water, water," openly mocking the times I've asked Darek, one of the young Scouts, to help me find water as we've walked past farms. Whoever this man is, he has been watching me. I feel scalded and turn red. Here is a second man who is sarcastic and unfriendly. Until now, everyone I have walked with or had any form of communication with has been polite and friendly. This behavior is completely out of character with the pilgrims I know so far. What am I to make of this?

Tears well up and I begin to cry, I can't stop myself. Why should I be crying? I must be exhausted. I don't know what's happening. I duck into Jola and Aska's tent to try to get hold of myself, but still I cannot stop. Two men were rude to me, is that any reason to fall apart?

"Please stop crying, I can't bear to see you so sad like this," Jola says, but I cannot, no matter how hard I try. I have never walked so far in one day as we have today. Having Dominik hear my confession deepened the intensity of the day beyond the sheer physicality of the experience. I was able to speak fully to him of the sadness hidden inside that I had over leaving the Church twenty years ago. I had never spoken of this, nor even recognized it before. I am raw physically and emotionally.

"You must tell me who these two men are," she says.

"That's absurd! They may have been tired too, who knows how they're feeling? Everybody isn't going to like me and not everyone likes Americans. In some countries people are rude to you simply because you're an American. I've been spoiled because so many Poles like Americans. There's nothing to it. I don't want to make something out of it, I'm just exhausted."

"No, you don't understand, you must tell me," she says insistently.

"Jola, I wouldn't think of telling you who they are. I don't know myself. I would have to go find them, point them out, that would only make matters worse. And then you would scold them. That's absurd, don't you see? If anything is to be said, I will say it, and I won't do it tonight when I'm so worn down and upset."

Jola refuses to accept my answer. She gets Dominik. Soon he is crouched inside the little tent as well.

"China, you must tell me who it was. It is not right that they speak to you like this, you are our guest," he says.

"No, Dominik. I wouldn't think of telling you."

"You must, you must point them out to me," he says with unexpected authority in his voice.

"No. Can't you understand, I'm just exhausted? Worn out. It's nothing. Why won't you stop talking about this? It is nothing, nothing!"

"China, we think is maybe secret police. We must know who it is. We cannot have them in our group. I will ask for identification and have it checked. We cannot allow this. They always make trouble. They spy on people. They are rude, they—how you say?—break up things, they drink, they make pilgrims unwelcome again at the farm we stay at or in the villages. We know they are on the pilgrimage. Please, point them out to me."

My heart sinks. When Dominik says this, I crumple up inside. The secret police. A whirlpool of feeling sucks me down, is drowning me, washing over me, leaving me without air. I gasp for a breath the second I'm tossed up to the surface of these feelings again, then down I am pulled, down, tossed. I know there is nothing to do but remain calm, yet I cannot. I am devoured by fear. It takes me over completely, stealing my life from me, my wit, my humor, my presence of mind, gone, and I am left feeling like a child crying, terrified to be left alone. The secret police. All the warnings I have ignored come back to me. How do they work? Were they only letting me know that they are watching and then later, when I am alone and the pilgrimage is over, will they arrest me? What for? I do not remember ever having been as frightened as I am at this moment.

"Of course, Dominik, the secret police," I repeat as Jola and Dominik's insistence suddenly becomes reasonable. "It never occurred to me that they might be the secret police. They are not men I have seen with our group before. They are strangers. Yes, I will try to point them out to you. I understand."

"China, you must not travel alone after the pilgrimage like this. You are safe as long as you are with us on the pilgrimage, but then you must come to me in Warsaw," Jola says. "It's just my parents and me. We have a very small apartment, but you are welcome. Tell me you will come."

"Yes, China, please, not be alone like this after pilgrimage. Go to Jola," Dominik says, "is better."

"But I have plans to go to Lublin and Krakow. I will come for one night, Jola. I will come, once I get back to Warsaw," I say, beginning to calm down. "I promise to call you as soon as I return, thank you." It is a strange relief to know that these men might be the secret police. To me that means that I'm not crazy, that there was something sinister in the interchange.

Now the doctor comes, an older woman, whom Dominik has sent for. A heavyset woman, she lowers herself slowly into the tent while asking cheerfully in Polish if I am constipated, Jola explains. Many pilgrims are, but fortunately I am not. She pats me on the head, tells me to chew two tablets of valerian root, drink juice, and rest.

"Come with me, you need hot food, we will go to priests' table now," says Dominik. "When we walk to the house, see if the man is still in the barn and say to me which one. Come," he says, taking my hand and pulling me up to my feet outside the tent.

Hot tea, hot soup, a plate full of meat and potatoes, served generously by the mistress of the farm, help calm me down further. Not yet ready for sleep, I go with Aska after dinner to bandage a woman's knee who took a bad fall today. It grows late, ten o'clock. I walk back to my tent alone now, down toward the lower fields from the barnyard. The moon is rising. I am stopped, held by its extravagant beauty. Standing by the fence rail overlooking the corn fields I watch this enormous moon rise full over the countryside. The clouds lie thin and drawn out across the horizon at three separate heights, making the moon take on the shape of a pale golden egg as it rises up through them. I have never seen a moon like this, stretched thin at the top, taut and full at the bottom like an egg.

I have a decision to make. Being fearful, whether with good reason or not, is enormously painful. I have nothing to guide me here but my own intuitive response to people. Will I trust my own sense or will I be tormented by all the warnings I have been given, even though there is good reason? Will I withdraw from people now, be invisible, or will I trust my own sense of who is friendly and who is not?

It has been an extraordinary day. Is this moon the dragon's egg of Geshe Champa Lodro's Tibetan tale? Seeing the moonrise in this moment feels like a blessing, protection. Far across the field a bonfire and circle are going on. Laughter and music drift across the field, covering me like a blanket as I lie down inside my tent. I choose trust, a different kind of reason, and fall asleep content.

August 12, 1987.

I see one of the men we suspected as the secret police this morning, walking quickly past our group, disappearing into the crowd ahead. He is gone by the time I find Dominik to point him out. The other man has disappeared from our group as well, confirming Dominik's sense that they were secret police. They vanish and are not seen in our group again.

The energy continues to build as we walk deeper and deeper into the countryside. A kind of cleansing and toughening up is taking place, rather than a wearing down. We have more energy after the days of walking rather than less.

I have the sense that I am putting together some enormous puzzle: Poland, India, Nepal, Switzerland, France, each place representing an enormous journey out of which I am able to glean one more small piece. It is good to be on foot, walking briskly instead of flying through time, geography, cultures, hurtling across oceans, mountain ranges.

The countryside begins to roll and dip, beautifully shaped into simple rectangles of green, brown, black, and gold.

Midnight, turning into the thirteenth of August. Soon we reach Czestochowa. The moon is full still, the night brilliant and cold. We walked over twenty-five kilometers today. Tonight we have a circle and bonfire. Dominik keeps his promise and sings "Rock My Soul in the Bosom of Abraham" with me in his thick Polish accent. There are more duets, solo performances, instrumentals on guitars, harmonica. Then the dancing begins. First it is Dominik and a handful of others who start with a circle dance around the fire. The next round is a larger circle. I jump up, throw off my boots, socks, down vest, and run into the circle, putting my arms on the next person's shoulders for a traditional folk dance. The grass is cold and wet on my bare feet. Soon we are circling around the fire to the music going faster, the momentum of our circle stronger and stronger, I am lifted up and carried in and out of our line which now begins to reel crazily as more and more people join in. The circle grows, the laughter grows, and soon we are bumping into an even larger circle.

We get hot as we go faster and faster around the bonfire. Blisters and all, I am dancing, singing, arm in arm, the energy grows, the circle casts a trance, we are whirling, burning up the night, still the circle grows, the music plays even faster. The concentration and energy the dancing takes is more than I can keep up and soon I am dissolving into laughter, I cannot stop laughing, we are all laughing, the circle break open, falls apart, we are falling, down, it is over.

After the bonfire I walk back to the campsite with Kriezek with whom I've shared my camera as we've walked. We stop to photograph the moon. Placing the camera on a low fence, we take turns holding our breath for the timed exposures with the hope of catching the moon and stars streaking across the sky. But it's not the moon that I want to keep, it's the night, the dance, the mood, the singing, the moon and stars, the laughter, the chill in the air, the warmth of the fire, the cold wet grass on my feet, the sense of belonging, drawn around me like a shawl that together we have all woven of song.

August 13, 1987.

Jola brings a young woman to me who is not well. "She speaks no English," Jola explains, "but she wants to ask you for help. She is very sick, diabetes. She is losing her sight. There are drops that can help, but she cannot get them here in Poland. It is very difficult. She wants you to get the eyedrops. Also she wants to be able to give herself the shots she needs, but it is very difficult for her to get needles and syringes. She cannot get disposable needles. Will you help her?"

My heart leaps to my throat. This woman is my daughter's age, twenty-one, and clearly unwell. Her skin is a sallow yellow. I want to help, but how can I?

"Jola, you must explain to her that I may be of no help at all. I will have to send medical supplies from the United States. What if I can't get what she needs, what if it doesn't get through to her in time? I won't be back in the States for another three weeks as it is. It may take some time to find a doctor who would give me the medication and syringes she needs. It takes weeks for mail to get to Poland. I have no idea what this will cost. What she is asking is not so easy, but I will do what I can. Perhaps I can find help in London before I go back to the States. But she must understand that this is risky and a very complicated way of getting the medicine she needs. It may not work. She must still try to get medicine for herself in Poland."

Jola explains this to her. "Yes, she understands. She is happy that you will try. She has been very ill. She is losing her sight rapidly. See, she is getting yellow even. She has been very sick on the pilgrimage. It is very difficult for her, but she wanted to come anyway. The doctors give her so little hope. She is counting on the Black Madonna to help her."

August 14, 1987.

The sky grows cloudy and the air turns chill. The weather is moody, unpredictable. The day can begin warm or cool and will change half a dozen times from then until nightfall. Few people seem prepared for the variation in temperature and the frequent shift from dry to wet. It begins to sprinkle again.

This is the day we arrive in Czestochowa. I waken at 6:00 a.m. It is a cold, beautiful day with a hint of the warmth to come. We have only eleven kilometers to walk today. I am up an hour early. There is no line at the outhouse and I am able to find warm water for washing. I feel lucky and return to my tent with a borrowed yellow dishpan of Jola's full of warm water.

It sprinkles off and on all morning. We stop and start. Dominik and the sisters weave, braid and tie a cross together out of sheaves of wheat and bunches of red gladiolas that we will present this afternoon when we arrive at the Monastery of Jasna Gora.

After only two kilometers we stop in a clearing for a ceremony. We are to go up to anyone that we might have offended or hurt in any way during the pilgrimage and apologize, saying *"Przepraszam,"* which means "I'm sorry, please forgive me for anything I may have done to hurt you." We walk from one to another, saying *"Prze-*

praszam," kissing three times on alternate cheeks and embracing in the traditional Polish manner. Saying "I'm sorry" is a simple and powerful act. As I move from person to person, most of whom I have been unable to speak with the entire time, I realize that I am connected to more of these people than I had thought. Someone with whom I had wanted contact but in whom I had sensed an aloofness comes up to me and says *"Przepraszam."* I find a young man with whom I had felt impatient, say *"Przepraszam,"* and feel cleansed.

After we are through with the ceremony we still must wait before proceeding the last nine kilometers to Czestochowa. We are told that the crowds will be enormous and that our mass will be held at 2:00 a.m. in the chapel. This will be a long, full day.

Finally we begin walking again, greatly slowed as nearly a million pilgrims are converging from all over Poland today. It begins to rain again as we walk slowly past the fields in harvest. As we crest the next hill we see Czestochowa below, belching enormous black billows of smoke from industrial furnaces. Suddenly we are walking back into civilization and heavy industrial pollution. We stop before going further. The Scouts make a person-by-person count of the members of our group. Darek tells us that we are to walk ten abreast and to stay in the lines we're in once we've been counted. The crowds will be enormous and it is all too easy to get lost.

Immediately fear arises again. I remember the story of Westerners being arrested for taking photographs last year in Czestochowa. One can hardly photograph the crowd or the monastery without getting a picture of the outlawed Solidarity banners. They are everywhere, carried openly by many of the groups. Though the pilgrimage is too large for the government to be able to stop everyone from flying the banner, the authorities clearly don't want the outside world to see how alive Solidarity is still within Poland. The authorities would have you believe that Solidarity has been eclipsed. The disdain of the Poles for the authorities is strong, their dislike of the Russians palpable. Solidarity's strength is evident everywhere on the pilgrimage.

I am afraid of becoming separated from the group in this enor-

Solidarity banner and the Polish flag. (Author)

mous crowd. We seem to be preparing for a tidal wave the way the Scouts are lining us up ten abreast and being so insistent about staying together. Their sudden strictness only escalates the anxiety. I am at the end of a line in the back. I break away to find Dominik in the middle of our group just as we begin the long walk down the main boulevard into Czestochowa. The Monastery of Jasna Gora lies at the end of this walk. We are in the city with a million pilgrims, as well as several thousand of the population turned out to watch or cheer us these last three miles. I have never been in a crowd this size.

"What if I lose you? What should I do, where would I go to try to find you? What would I say?" I ask Dominik.

"China, say the rosary with me, please?" he responds, smiling, ignoring all my questions.

I have a choice: hide myself in the crowd and be devoured by fear or accept Dominik's invitation and trust that nothing will happen. To speak English over the public-address system as we are walking into Czestochowa with police everywhere is precisely what I was reminded again last night not to do, it makes my being a Westerner so obvious. But now I find the fear so painful that I would rather do anything than let it hold sway.

"Yes, Dominik, all right."

I fall in the line next to him on my right, a young boy on my left, the sisters with their guitars and the singers just behind me. I have my tiny wooden finger rosary, ten beads long, which fits over my thumb, from Einsiedeln. Dominik has his long brown beads that he wears looped over his wide leather belt. He hands me the microphone and nods for me to begin. I am still flustered at first and say softly:

"Hail Mary, full of grace."

Yes, I am already more comfortable, this is right.

"The Lord is with Thee."

With each step down I am a little less afraid and I speak louder.

"Blessed art Thou amongst women."

I am walking into a state of trust.

"And blessed is the fruit of Thy womb, Jesus."

My voice grows calm and stronger still, and soon I am no longer afraid, but happy. Exposed and vulnerable, paradoxically this is precisely where safety lies. The rain comes down harder.

People line the boulevard in the city for the last two kilometers. Some have no expression and only stare, others wave and smile. Many have brought flowers and thrust them into our hands as we go by. A woman pilgrim from Russian-occupied Estonia hands me a single long-stemmed red rose. She speaks no English, but has sought me out because I am from the West, Aska explains. "It is her offering, you must take it." I give her a red carnation in return, feeling that we have just signed an international peace treaty.

It takes us all afternoon to walk these last kilometers. We are slowed down, often to a stop, by the sheer numbers of pilgrims who have to funnel down this one street. Finally, at the monastery which we now see ahead, each line of ten pilgrims is stopping and making a full prostration bow as they step onto the monastery grounds.

At the last intersection before the monastery, the lines separate. We stay behind thirty paces or more to allow the group in front of us to stop and make their bow. The sky is gray and drizzling. There are flowers everywhere lining our way now as we inch forward, mounds of bright red, yellow, blue, white flowers, roses, gladiolas, carnations. Flowers are offered outside the church along the path we walk, the church we will enter empty-handed.

Now it is our turn. Crowds of people press along the edge of our path. The way broadens as we reach the open field below the monastery walls. The Solidarity banners are everywhere draped across the walls beneath a huge copy of the painting of the Black Madonna. Her portrait is set between two halves of the Polish eagle, towering above the sea of pilgrims. We kneel down on the wet ground, stretch out our bodies full length, hands and arms extended, each of us making a cross. The earth is cold, wet and gritty on my forehead. Up on our feet again, we begin moving to the left through the first of three gates that we must enter before reaching the inside of the monastery walls. The lines are broken now and people are packed tightly as we begin to move toward the narrow gate.

The sky blackens suddenly and the wind comes up with a blast. A storm threatens as we inch our way along. The closer we get to the gate, the tighter the crowd gets and the faster it moves. Soon I am overpowered by the crowd and carried along like a leaf on a stream through the narrow gate, then quickly the pressure subsides as soon as we pass through the portal. Then a second gate, a third, and with each the compression which takes my breath away for a moment; then we are inside the courtyard. The storm breaks and rain pours down on us.

Inside the monastery walls people are crammed, hardly able to move along. How will I ever find Jadwiga in this crowd? Then I see her, there she is, standing out in this rain, waving a bouquet of red carnations for me, by the door of the museum that we will soon pass. I break out of the line and make my way to her, giving her a big hug. "I am so proud of you," she says, handing me the flowers, "you did it! Meet me here after you go inside the chapel."

The entry to the church, like the gates, takes my breath away. The most important thing to concentrate on in a crowd this size seems to be remaining upright. There is a final push and I am swept over the threshold, carried by an energy far beyond my strength.

Now we are inside and still we can barely move. I can see the Black Madonna at the far end of the chapel. There are no pews in this outer chapel, and only a few behind the grillwork that separates the shrine proper from the rest of the church, in the tiny chapel of the Virgin. There is a solid sea of people, some kneeling on the stone floor, others just standing, others, like myself, trying to move through it all. Slowly we move closer to the icon, step by step, finally winding our way around the side, then behind the altar and back down the other side, only able to catch glimpses of the Madonna as we walk past. One cannot stop at this point, there are thousands and thousands of people behind us, waiting out in the rain, miles of pilgrims still arriving, kneeling, bowing, passing through the gates, one, two, three. I am grateful that I have had a chance to stand here before the Madonna and look at her before the pilgrimage began. She is so mysterious, unmoved. There is so much tumult and feeling around her. Amulets, jewels, the necklaces of amber and coral, silver, rosaries, crutches, medallions hang throughout the larger chapel and line the walls to testify to the healing power of this Virgin. She is stunning in her silver and jewels, set into the black altar. And yet so remote! I cannot begin to fathom this image. I walk outside to find Jadwiga.

We make our way through a huge parking lot full of lorries looking for the sign Group 15, *zloty*, in the driver's window. We find my bags, and drive home to Jadwiga's. There she has hot food waiting,

Arrival of the pilgrimage, "My Chcemy Boga" ("We Want God"),
Jasna Gora Monastery, Czestochowa. (Adam Bujak)

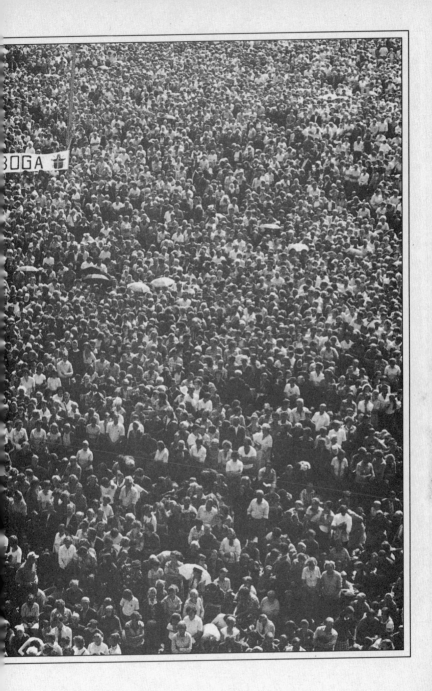

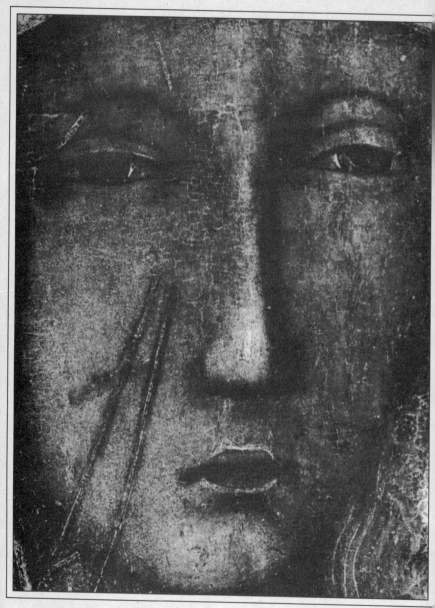

Detail of icon of the Black Madonna, Our Lady of Czestochowa.

plates of pork slices, potatoes, cabbage, tomatoes and cucumbers from her garden. Hot tea, hot water. Luxury! We put my dirty clothes into the wash and I take a bath, the first in days. Though exhausted, I am still full of excitement and talk.

"You must eat," she insists. A devout Catholic, when I bring up the subject of women priests, she shrugs her shoulders. Then she tells me what a friend of hers, a professor known for her independent thinking, says.

"Why not have women priests? How is a grown woman to confess to a man who is completely taken care of, who has no children to raise, no money to earn? If the men are so like God, like the Church says, they should bear a child and then we would believe them," her friend told her. I could hardly stop laughing.

We stay up talking until nearly ten o'clock, when Jadwiga reminds me that I must get some sleep. She will wake me up at 1:00 a.m. to get me back to the church for our group's mass. Masses go on all through the night and ours is at 2:00 a.m. Many people in my group will leave from the monastery back to Warsaw on the next train, so I will not see them again.

Both Jadwiga and I oversleep. She runs into my room at ten minutes of two to wake me, saying, "Hurry, hurry, we have both overslept, there's no time to do anything but get your clothes on and get into the car." I had agreed to meet Aska and Jola at one-thirty at the pilgrim's house and walk with them through the crowds to the chapel from there.

We race off to the church, one headlight out on the car, in the dark. She insists on taking me into the monastery courtyard, where I will be almost at the door. Inside, in a blur of exhaustion and drizzle, I make my way into the chapel where our mass will have already started. The church is packed so tightly, I don't know how I will get through the crowd to the tiny chapel in the front where mass is going on.

"*Przepraszam,*" I say, softly over and over, "*Przepraszam,*" excuse me, as I inch my way toward the front. I see no one who looks familiar. When I get to the chapel, I see a different group there having mass, it is 15, Blue, not 15, Gold! Where is everyone? I make my way back into the sacristy and pointing to my watch and then alternately to the chapel, I say to a young priest, "*Zloty?* Gold? Father Dominik?" He understands, and after complicated sign language and an occasional word here and there, he manages to convey to me that the time of the mass has been changed for my group, that I should sit and wait. He indicates that our mass will begin at 3:00 a.m.

I sit and wait and still no one I know comes. Something is wrong. I go back out into the night and walk over to the pilgrim's house across the road to try to find Jola and Aska. But I can find no one I know and no one who speaks English. Though people seem to understand that I am looking for Father Dominik's group, Group 15, *zloty,* I cannot understand their replies. I grow increasingly agitated. It's now two forty-five, so I go back to the church. How can I have come so far with all these people only to lose them, all of them, everyone, at the last moment like this? I have to find them, no matter what. Back in the main part of the church I walk slowly through the crowd, but there is still not a single person I know, only strangers. What has happened? How could our entire group disappear?

I go back into the sacristy, to try to find someone who speaks English. If our mass had been changed and was to start at 3:00 a.m., then Dominik or George will be in the sacristy by now putting on their vestments for mass, but they are not there. I walk up to each new person that enters and ask them if they understand English. No. No. No. Finally one man nods, indicating that he has a friend who knows English, who is coming to the sacristy shortly. We wait. It is now almost 3:00 a.m. I have lost them, every one! I sit in the chair by the door waiting as I've been told, feeling as though I have lost my family, barely able to hold back tears.

Finally the friend comes who speaks English. I explain to him my predicament, then we find the priest who has been trying to help me and he tells him again in Polish. It is just after three.

"Ah, Father Dominik's group, I know. They must be in St. Paul's

Chapel. Their mass is not in this chapel or even in this part of the monastery. We must go to St. Paul's," the man translates from Polish. The priest takes me by the hand out of the sacristy into the large basilica that adjoins the chapel, past numerous side altars and clear to the back, where off to one side, behind a black iron grillwork doorway in another chapel, I see Darek, Jola, Kriezek, Valdek, another Scout, Aska, the sisters, our group! They swing open the door and I step inside just as Dominik is giving the final blessing at the end of the mass. Home.

No one leaves though mass is over. One of the sisters picks up the guitar and begins to play a song from our walk. After the song, we start to say goodbye. A woman whose presence I had sensed all along and whose smile always cheered me comes up to say goodbye. I do not know her name, nor many of the others who say goodbye, and yet I know these people so well. This woman with the curly blond hair and radiant smile who embraces me now is crying, as I am. Every night she would set up her tent near me. Every morning she would smile at me warmly. She encouraged me in wordless ways. She would share some of her traditional Polish food, made by her mother. The first time I said the rosary in English with Dominik over the loudspeaker, she came up to me afterwards and said, "*Dziekuje, bardzo dziekuje!*" Thank you, thank you very much. Much of my discomfort about being a foreigner dissolved in the warmth of her response. Though we had no language of words with which to communicate, we have communicated a great deal.

Now we are at the end, standing here in this chapel, laughing and crying, saying goodbye in a language I can't understand. How do you say goodbye to someone with whom you have stripped away all facades? The intensity of the walking has broken down all pretense, left us transparent. I am grief-stricken to leave these people with whom I have had this experience, whom I have seen in this way, from this place. If only more of us could walk with one another, singing and praying for days and days, if more of us could stop, there, toward the end, and say "*Przepraszam,*" "I am sorry, please forgive me for anything I have done to hurt you," "I am so sorry," if more of us could sit around the fire at night singing and dancing, if more of us could bring each other flowers, let our care show, be known, just walking, day after day, under the moon, the sun, in the wind, the rain, the heat, the cold, at harvest time, by the water, through the forests, sandy-floored, mushrooms growing, past the red holly-hocks, pink gladiolas, red carnations, purple and white cosmos in the garden, the clippety-clop of a horse-drawn wagon along the road under the blue bowl of the sky, crow calling, hawk diving, people waving, some only staring, the land rising now, rolling softly, ever so gently, past the gold of the wheat being cut for the harvest, past the long green rectangles of farmland, plowed by hand, next to black, and gold the wheat, the heavy horses pulling a load of new-mown hay green and sweet, the air golden and thick with the honey of love, can you smell it?

Our name is Gold, Number 15, Gold. I carry a note in Polish in my pocket in case I am lost that says, "Please return this woman to Group 15, *Zloty*, Group 15, Gold. Father Dominik." Please return me. Find them for me again, take me by the hand through a crowd of strangers, lead me to the place where they are gathered, where they too will be relieved, as I am, to find out that I am not lost. If only more of us could be found.

CHAPTER 12

After the Pilgrimage
•
Krakow, Poland

True prayer and love are really learned in the hour when prayer becomes impossible and your heart turns to stone.

—Thomas Merton[1]

Krakow, Poland
August 1987

Afterwards, Dominik, Vesa, and I made our way by train to Krakow, standing in the crowded narrow corridor of the railway car for the several hours from Czestochowa. Dominik wanted to go to the Pauline monastery in Krakow, and Vesa and I were invited to come with him once he had been given permission to have us as guests.

Krakow was not bombed during World War II. It stands, an intact medieval city. It is Dominik's favorite city in Poland and we are lucky to have him as our guide. We tour Wawel Castle where all the kings and queens of Poland were crowned and lie buried, Wawel, which the Indian legend holds would be one of the two safe places to be when the world is destroyed. We go to the Church of St. Mary's with its rare altarpiece, a triptych, that portrays the life of Mary in sculpture, we have coffees and sweet cakes at the old Market Square with its fourteenth-century clocktower. Vesa brings up the subject of Auschwitz over dinner that night after the day of sightseeing.

"How far away are the camps?" he asks Dominik.

"Half a day by train," he replies, "but only a little more than an hour by car."

"Then we can hire a taxi," Vesa said, turning to me. "I'll split the cost with you. Do you want to go?"

"Yes," I said, wanting and not wanting to go. "No, I don't *want* to go and, yes, I must. We are so close."

"Will you go with us, Dominik?" Vesa asked.

"Yes, I will go too, of course. I have been before, maybe five times," he said. "We should leave early tomorrow morning. We must go not only to Auschwitz, but to Birkenau too. It is very close together."

It is settled. We are going to the camps. It feels like the inexplicable desire to jump that I've felt when nearing the edge of a very high cliff or on top of a tall building, this need to see for myself. I have always been haunted by pictures I saw of the concentration camps when I was in grade school.

World War II affected me in ways that I continue to discover. My own father was in the Air Force, taught flying, was a bomber pilot. Over the years, as he ages, how much that war is still alive for him becomes clear. I knew that as a child, but I didn't have the words for it. Now it is known both to him and to me as we go through the picture albums of flight school. Stories from Guam continue to make their way into conversations.

I was no longer afraid to look into the darkness of Auschwitz. But I could not have gone had I not felt that Mary and Tara were real presences who were with me.

August 18, 1987.

By midmorning we have set out by taxi to Auschwitz-Birkenau. *Oswiecim*. The weather is terrible, hot, humid, and heavy. The pollution here from the nearby mines is among the worst in Eastern Europe. The air is sour. We ride into the void, windows down, hitting potholes at high speed. Vesa tries politely to make conversation, but it is impossible.

I got up early to hear Dominik say mass. I was touched that he would go with us to the camps, a Catholic priest, with all the differences of opinion he and I have. He is respectful of the fact that I am married to a Jew. He honors the importance of this visit to me. I honor the importance of the Church for him.

As soon as we arrive, we go straight into the camp, spending little time in the museum in front.

"This way," Dominik says, "this is very big place. There are certain things you must see. Come."

We walk through a wide gate down a graveled walk. The buildings are neatly kept. Everything looks deceptively "normal." Auschwitz had been a model camp which the Nazis held open for inspection by the International Red Cross. Dominik takes us into a nearby two-storied brick building. Young people are planting flowers in the beds outside.

The first room I walk into looks empty. Then I look to the left and behind glass is another half room filled with shaving brushes, toothbrushes, and hairbrushes. Nothing else. I am shocked, unprepared for the effect of so many inanimate yet personal belongings. I could almost hear them talk. I had expected pictures of railroad cars, people like skeletons, mass graves, Nazis. I had seen them before, since grade school. But I had never seen anything like this.

Upstairs, we walked into a long narrow room that held only people's shoes on either side. Shoes, thousands and thousands of shoes, men, women, and children, all thrown together in heaps indiscriminately. No order. Shoes.

There was the room of suitcases. Names were scrawled in large black letters on the old leather cases: Breuer, Frank, Kafka, Neumann, Harner, Oppenheim, Gibian. I jot them down as we walk along. Then a display of prayer shawls, a display of thousands of eyeglasses, another room, a display of hundreds of artificial limbs, of corsets, of pots and pans. Piles and piles of people's belongings. No people, only their effects. What was left.

I had brought my camera after much interior debate, knowing that no picture could capture what I would see. Yet I was glad to have it. I wanted to be able to show my children, to say the camps are real, this happened. I went there. See. But I run out of film after the first dozen shots and I am relieved. The pen will have to be my camera, these fragmentary notes the pictures I take. We walk through room after room of displays. We do not speak.

There is a room full of paintings done by prisoners at the camp. These tell more than any photograph of what it was like. A Christmas scene in the snow, at night, under street lights, outside: prisoners lined up in the snow, naked, the Nazis hitting and killing them. Another painting shows the Nazis laughing and jeering as prisoners are dragged to work. Another shows prisoners pulling a cart of dead bodies in the snow while being whipped by Nazis. Some of the Nazis are smoking cigars and laughing while others do the whipping.

In the hallway between the rooms the walls are lined with photographs of faces with shaved heads in prison uniforms. Their names, professions, dates of birth all listed: poet, mechanic, priest, house-wife . . .

The Room of Children is lined with photographs of young children photographed in this same way. All the photographs, in the hall outside this room, and these children's photographs as well, are strangely passive, no expression. Except for one girl in this Room of Children. She has no name, only the number 27129 on her picture. Her eyes are full of tears, as are mine when I see her.

One room has a display showing the sleeping arrangements. There were three wooden tiers of straw, with six to eight people (men and women were kept separately) in each slot, making a total of eighteen to twenty-five people "sleeping" virtually on top of one another on these shelves. One could not roll over.

Dominik explains that though Auschwitz was the showplace for the International Red Cross, Birkenau, where we will go later, only a short drive away, was not shown. There, the situation was worse. We saw photographs of the latrines at Birkenau: a row of cement holes upon which one was allowed to sit for a total of ten seconds—someone was timing you—before being pulled away. From there we walked into the room of Hitler's medical experiments. By now I was silently weeping.

We go to Block 11 for prisoners who resisted. It was here they were sent for "correction." The most difficult prisoners were kept in cells in the basement, six feet by six feet, eight feet by eight feet. There was a word in Polish crudely scratched into the wall in one of the cells. Dominik explains what it means, "*Remember.*"

Off to one side, in the back of the basement, there was one more small room that I must describe. Inside this room there were three or four bricked-in cells three feet by three feet, one square yard, into which prisoners who had been part of the Resistance or had tried to escape were forced to crawl from a small door near the floor and remain standing with three other people all night. In the morning they were taken out to work all day and then returned to this cell. It's wrong to even dignify this tiny block of torture with the word "cell," it was so small.

Think of it like this. You're in a crowded elevator where everybody is pressed together like sardines and you feel a little anxious, it's so tight, there's no room, you can't move an inch, people's bodies are packed against you. Take the three people crammed in there closest to you and build brick walls around your foursome on all sides. That's where they put the ones they wanted to break the most, Dominik tells me. People couldn't survive this treatment very long.

I walked into one of these cells, where the brick had been knocked out so that you could see inside. Nothing. There you stood, just you and three other people. In the dark, all night, no room to sit down. You just had to stand there. I got claustrophobia looking at these cells. When I stepped into the dismantled cell itself, I had to catch my breath, it was being squeezed out of me. It was like stepping into a fire. I immediately leaped out.

Dominik pointed out the different buildings used to house Jews of different nations as we walked out of Block 11. There was a block for each country, for Jews from Russia, for Jews from Denmark, one for Austrian-Hungarian Jews, one for Yugoslavian Jews, and so our walk went, block after block. In 1943, the population of Auschwitz was 90–95 percent Jews. Today, one rarely sees a Jew in Poland. It is eerie, especially for me. There are less than fifteen hundred Jews in Warsaw, only a few thousand in all of Poland, in what had been the flowering of Eastern European Jewry before the war.

I go alone into the Jewish Museum. Dominik waits outside. My notes become increasingly fragmented as I move from one photograph to another. There are photos of Kristallnacht in Germany, photos of Bernard Swierczyna, prisoner #1393, organizer of the Jewish Resistance—killed. Photos of hundreds of naked women marched to the edge of an open pit grave to be shot, their faces looking confused, in shock, completely broken-spirited. My attention was riveted by one naked young girl among them standing in line with her shoes on, her hand outstretched to the viewer, her mouth open, pleading. Photos of broken bodies. Photos of the Jewish Resistance. Photos of Hannah Senesh, the Jewish woman from Palestine who parachuted behind enemy lines to bring a message of hope to her people—she too died in Auschwitz. Photos of naked women standing in line for the "showers," the gas chambers. I stumble out of the darkness of the display, back into daylight.

Dominik is waiting. Though we do not talk, it is good to be together. This is too much to be with alone.

We walk over to the crematorium, where I go inside alone. It was built below ground, of cement, and even now is very cold. This crematorium ran from 1940 until 1943, the year I was born.

I walk through the gas chamber without even knowing it until I step into the next room with the ovens, the extra long ones that could cremate two bodies at once. That's when I realize that I must have just been in the gas chamber. I go back into the big concrete room and look at it again. There are no showerheads, nothing to give one a clue as to what you are standing in, what you have walked inside of. I expect to feel something but I feel nothing, even after I realize what it is. Now it is just a big empty concrete room.

I turn around and go back into the room with the ovens. One brick oven in particular is draped with flowers and notes from visitors around the world. I look at it for some time and then I decide that all I can do is stand here on the tracks in front of this oven and write.

It is important for you to understand this. I am writing to you from the now cold ovens of Auschwitz. The ovens are cold, this room is cold, but I grow hot trying to take in the knowledge of what happened on the precise spot where I am standing. I cannot. I can take only the simplest notes, feverishly. There are pink gladiolas and red carnations laid in the open oven door, there is a trough full of flowers, white zinnias, pink carnations, yellow sunflowers now where bodies once were laid. Other people come and go, talking in whispers, I am only dimly aware of them, I'm in such a heat. The oven door. On the top oven tray is a sign. It is the memorial pledge of a group called C.A.N.D.L.E.S.

We are the voices of the children saved from the ashes. We pledge to do the following. We will not let the world forget what happened here in Auschwitz. We will remember that a part of humanity perished here. This soil is soaked with the blood of our mothers and fathers, our sisters and brothers. We will show our children where their grandparents hugged us for the very last time. We will work together to eliminate prejudice from the face of the earth. . . . We will appeal to the conscience of the world never to let this happen again.

The placard is dated January 27, 1985.

Outside the crematorium the air is warmer now and the wind

has picked up. Dominik has been waiting patiently. I am glad that I looked.

Now Birkenau.

Huge. Rows of wooden barracks, most of them burned down by the Nazis. We go into one, full of empty beds. Birkenau. Burned. Now quiet open fields of wildflowers and crickets. Four million people died here alone.

We walk down along the tracks to the memorial at the end by the crematoria. There has been a stone laid down in the earth for each person who died here. I find it disquieting to walk on them.

The gas chamber at Birkenau, blown up by the Nazis at the end, now open to the sky, is full of rubble, weeds, and water, purple thistles and wild iris.

Crematory II at Birkenau, the sign reads, had a room for undressing, a gas chamber which held and killed two thousand people at once, a room where the hair of women was cut off, a room where gold was removed from teeth, stoves for burning personal documents. The women's hair was used to make chair stuffing.

The Germans planted poplars so that you couldn't see the crematoria here. Human ashes have been scattered all over this ground. There are purple thistles everywhere. Yellow and white wildflowers, I am too distracted to notice what kind. I am walking over this ground in shock from even the little I've seen of just these two camps. Dominik points to the poplars by Crematory II. Now, nearly half a century later, the poplars are still stunted on top from the fires of the crematoria of Birkenau.

CHAPTER 13

There Are Roses of Fire
*
California

As I dig for wild orchids
in the autumn fields,
it is the deeply-bedded root
that I desire,
not the flower.

—Izumi Shikibu[1]

*California
September, 1987*

Near sunset, at home in California, walking the ridges of Mount Tamalpais, the grasses were dry, most of the wildflowers gone but for the orange monkey flower, a few bright stalks of clear red Indian paintbrush, and the California poppy. Long after returning from Poland, I would think of Auschwitz-Birkenau and the problem of evil that it presented on these walks below and around Mount Tam. Buddhism doesn't talk about evil, the term is "ignorance." Intellectually, I understood this, but the word isn't strong enough when I apply it to Auschwitz. It has no stench.

I was confronted with a major cover story in the news on the rise of neo-Nazis after returning to the States. In a town nearby, a young man was thrown through a plate-glass window by skinheads for trying to tear down an anti-Semitic sign. I read another story of a young neo-Nazi, in California, who had fallen in love for the first time. He was so transformed by the experience that he renounced the hatred he had preached and tried to retract his former racist positions, publicly stating that he had been wrong. His fellow neo-Nazis beat him up, nailed him to a plank and slashed his chest with razor blades, being sure to leave him alive. He cried for help for a long time. All the white people who saw him turned away and passed him by. A black couple, who knew him to be a racist, came to his aid.

This was in America, 1987, taking place while I stood next to the ovens in Auschwitz. In London, on the way home, a well-intentioned friend assured me foolishly "the harm is past, gone, done, over. It's all a thing of the past. We should bury the camps, tear them down, and go on."

Having seen the camps, even briefly, gave me a visceral sense of how much agreement it took to create the madness that Hitler lived out. Hitler was popularly elected. Thousands of people, not just Hitler, made the choices that led to Auschwitz-Birkenau. Many were well-meaning people.

The evil that culminated in Auschwitz was cumulative, participatory, and involved choice, even if the choice was only to deny what was happening and to personally do nothing.

The sun is low on the horizon now, half sunk into the sea, the rays brilliant in the last flash of light that comes this evening just before it sets. I stand on the hilltop to watch until the last sliver of light is extinguished before turning back. The dirt trail leaves the open hillside and winds downhill gradually, through bay laurel groves, a stand of redwoods, and the dark green coyote brush, before it becomes a wider fire road that at the bottom meets the blacktop road I take toward home.

Within a month after coming home from Poland, my youngest son would turn seventeen. After seeing Auschwitz, I resolved to speak more openly to Ben and his friends about war. Soon they had to face the military.

At Ben's seventeenth birthday party, after the cake and ice cream had been eaten, the dishes done, I asked the living room full of teenagers if they were aware that by law all the young men there had to register with the selective service, by the age of eighteen. I was afraid they might laugh, that I would embarrass Ben. But it was just the opposite, they wanted to know more.

"I don't believe in war. I don't want to kill anyone," they said one after another, "What do you mean, I *have* to sign up?" They were astonished when I reeled off the consequences of not knowing about the law or paying attention to it: no financial aid for college, possible fines up to $250,000.

No, they were not aware. They wanted to know more about the law and their alternatives. We began having monthly, sometimes bi-monthly pot-luck suppers to explore what it meant to want peace in the world. We talked with combat veterans, conscientious objectors, Buddhist priests, lawyers, parents, and a woman veteran, Lilly Adams, who was a triage nurse at nineteen. Lilly's story of running a hospital behind the lines on the battlefields of Vietnam stripped away any romanticism about the military. We talked with each other. I turned to works of Mennonites, Buddhists, and Quakers.

A format established itself. After supper we would read the fourteen ethical precepts written by Thich Nhat Hanh, the Vietnamese Buddhist monk who created an order of pacifists in Vietnam during the Vietnam War.[2] The reading was followed by silent meditation. I was continually surprised and moved by these young people. They were mostly teen-age boys, who on the surface might look as though they had no greater concerns than skateboarding, cars, jobs, school, dating, and surfing, but who in fact cared deeply about our world, other people, the environment, and the future.

At the group's instigation we went public and held a successful community event. The group baked cookies, designed and printed up flyers, paid the community center rent. They gave speeches about how our group had started and why we continued to meet. Each member stood up and read one of Thich Nhat Hanh's Precepts,[3] which had been copied and placed on each audience chair. Then they asked the audience to observe five minutes of meditation for peace with us. I sat in the back, my heart singing, so proud of them I could burst. All of us, beginners, together. We called ourselves "The Peace Project."

Walking the hills at home. Out of the ashes of Auschwitz, out of the pilgrimage to the Black Madonna, out of following the Buddha Tara, this was the way I was shown.

Spring came, 1988, bringing Geshe Lobsang Tsephel, whom I had met in Dharamsala, to San Francisco. He had come to give a Green Tara initiation which I attended in the city.

I thumbed through my notebooks from India and Switzerland, finding notes from the days of teachings the Dalai Lama gave in Delhi. The paper was colored by the flowers I had picked at the Lodi Gardens and pressed between the pages. They lay there still. Some had stuck to the pages, others fallen loose. The paper was mottled with blues, yellow, pale brown, and light rose; one page spilled out dried blueberries and a stalk of tiny pink flowers.

The Tibetan teachings are like flowers to me: fragrant, uplifting, delightful. They bring great consolation and joy to hear. There are many elements I don't understand, some I may not agree with yet inevitably I feel as though I am walking into a well-tended garden in bloom when I hear the teachings. The Tibetans have a wild, luxuriant imagination that fills the air.

As I turned the pages, being careful not to disturb the flowers, I was reminded of the Green Tara initiation that I had just received from Geshe Tsephel. One of the instructions he gave during the meditation was to imagine that the pellets of rice in our hands were flowers.

Imagine that this rice pellet is a flower, that we have many flowers. Throw the flowers into the air, shower this room with flowers. The Buddhas and bodhisattvas are always throwing flowers in our path, showering us with flowers. So we too should scatter flowers.

Imagine that this room is not ordinary room. Yes, it is ordinary room, but it is also Tara's heaven. Imagine that all the Buddhas and bodhisattvas are being drawn into this room on rays coming from your heart. See with the mind's eye the Buddhas and bodhisattvas filling this room. Imagine Tara as big as a mountain and as tiny as a speck of dust in the air. Imagine this room filled with Taras. This room is blooming Buddhas, bodhisattvas, and Taras.

See Tara sitting on a moon disk that rests on an open white lotus blossom. See her, all green, jewels on her head, beautiful silk garments flowing over her body, and a blue utpala flower, the lotus, in full bloom by her left ear. She holds the stem of the lotus in her left hand between her thumb and her forefinger, over her heart. She is smiling at you. She has a beautiful smile. She has a beautiful, gentle face. She is looking at you with loving kindness, she is pouring out her compassion to you, she will come the instant you think of her, call out her name, no matter who you are, where you are, or how unbelieving you have been. She is the hearer of the world's cries, she is the boat that carries us across the river of the sufferings of this world, samsara, she is the guide, she is the energy of all the Buddhas, she is the mother of the Buddhas, she is the Bodhisattva of Compassion, she is the fully enlightened one, she is mother of us all. *Om Tare Tutare Ture Soha.*

There was a vase of huge red and yellow roses open on the carved red lacquer table in front of the Venerable Chos Kyi Nyima in Nepal. There was a bowl of yellow roses on the glass-top table in front of His Holiness the Dalai Lama, Tenzin Gyatso, in Delhi. There was a small vase of roses on the table in front of Champa Lodro Rinpoche in Switzerland by the lake where he gave the Green Tara initiation. There were yellow roses on the altar as Geshe Lobsang Tsephel chanted the prayers to Green Tara that night. There was an enormous blossoming tree of open yellow roses outside the second floor window where Geshe Tsephel sat the next day when I went to see him. The rose tree had grown up to meet him, to frame him in this way, as though he was another blossom on the tree of roses.

On the desk in my room, my grandmother's crystal bud vase is filled with tiny pink tea roses. Two days ago they were tight buds. This morning they are fully opened and their fragrance floats through the air, drawn by the open window next to me as I write of roses. My great-grandfather loved roses. As nurseryman he helped bring commercial rose growing to East Texas in the late 1920s. Did he know how I would grow to love roses, that I would wear only the scent of roses, would find roses on these altars in India, Nepal, and California, make an altar of my own, offer roses? That his son, my grandfather, ninety-seven last summer, would keep a rose garden in Hope, Arkansas, by his wooden bushel basket mill? That he would grow one hundred fifty varieties of roses?

A climber rose growing outside my window this past winter forced its way through a crack, pushed open the window, and began to grow inside the room, toward my altar. Respectful of such boldness in a flower, I let it grow. Wild audacity. The strength of a rose, determined to bloom, beyond reason.

Who planted this rose? Was it my great-grandfather, my grandfather, my grandmother? My grandmother received the roses my grandfather brought from Arkansas, filled the house with them, gave them to friends and neighbors, the roses brought home in barrels tied down in the open trunk of my grandfather's car.

Roses. Legend has it that in Mexico, on December 9, 1531, the Virgin of Guadalupe miraculously appeared and told the Indian peasant Juan Diego to pick roses where Juan Diego knew only cactus could bloom on Tepeyac Hill. This Virgin had dark skin and black hair like Juan Diego. She wore a black belt above her waist, traditional Indian style, indicating that she was pregnant. He was to take the roses in his cape to the bishop and to report this vision. He was to tell the bishop that the Virgin wants a church built here.

Juan Diego is turned away three times. Trying to hide the roses from the bishop's attendants to no avail, he opens his cape and the roses have become part of it. Juan Diego is then admitted to the bishop's presence. He kneels and reaches for the roses to hand the bishop and his cape falls to the ground. On the cape is the image of the Virgin of Guadalupe imprinted on the cloth. The roses have fallen to the floor and lie scattered everywhere, their scent filling the air.

This is one telling. Eduardo Galeano tells us another in *Memory of Fire*.[4] The apparition Juan Diego saw on Tepeyac Hill spoke to him in Nahuatl, the Aztec tongue, when she told him that she was "the mother of God."

It was the bishop, Zumarraga, who decided that the apparition was Guadalupe, the Dark Madonna from Estremadura, Spain, that was appearing to Juan Diego. It was Zumarraga who had the Aztec codices set on fire, tore down the Indian temples, destroyed their idols—twenty thousand of them. Bishop Zumarraga, the Indian's protector, was the keeper of the branding iron that stamped the Indians' faces with the names of their proprietors, Galeano says. Zumarraga knew that Tepeyac had been the site of the Aztec worship of the earth goddess, Tonantzin, who clad herself in snakes, hearts, and hands. The Indians loved Tonantzin, Galeano tells us, they called her "our mother."

Tonantzin, whose name meant "mother" in Nahuatl, had the crescent moon and the maguey or century plant as her sign.[5] The maguey was quickly pre-empted by the Church for the Dark Virgin of Mexico, whether in the form of Guadalupe or another favored Madonna, *Los Remedios*, The Remedy.

Juan Diego's *tilma*, his cape, still exists. It is said that if one looks very closely into the eye of the Virgin imprinted on the cloth, the figure of Juan Diego, standing before her, can be discerned still.

Our Lady of Guadalupe, the Dark Madonna who appeared as a pregnant Indian woman, is the Madonna that Pope Pius XI declared to be the patroness of all the Americas, from Alaska to the tip of Tierra del Fuego in South America.[6]

There are roses of fire.

CHAPTER 14

The Madonna's Face

•

Rio Grande Valley, Texas

> . . . while birds and warmer weather
> are forever moving north,
> the cries of those who vanish
> might take years to get here.
>
> —Carolyn Forché[1]

Dallas, Texas
July 1988

There is a famous shrine and pilgrimage site to a Black Madonna in South Texas, the Rio Grande Valley, just north of Mexico, I am told. San Juan, Texas, between Harlingen and McAllen, is the home of the Madonna de los Lagos, famed as a healer and miracleworker. Called *morenita,* the little dark one, she is a brown Madonna, not black, I find out, though some refuse this distinction and continue to call her black. Most simply refer to her as "Our Lady." I go to see for myself, stopping first to see family in Dallas.

Circling back. I take my grandfather for a drive down along Hackberry Creek after dinner one night. Lightning breaks up the sky and the wind comes up. I pull over and stop.

"Mind waiting for a few minutes, Pop?" I ask.

"Not at all, you go right ahead," he says as he always does.

I took my shoes off as soon as I got out of the car and ran down the grassy hillside to the creek. I need to stand barefoot in this creek, on its slippery limestone bed, to know that I'm back in Texas. Out in the middle of the stream in the moonlight, with the water softly flowing over my feet, my grandfather nearby, I feel a quiet sense of release. I turn back to this creek, to the cedars, the mockingbirds, the fireflies, the heat, the cicadas, and the family; turn back to a landscape washed by memory, droning with the resonance of lived and recollected life. At ninety-seven, my grandfather's memory of the turn of the century grows sharper, while yesterday can be lost. It was in my grandparents' house, across the street from this creek, that I spent much of my time growing up.

The wind blows hard through the cedar branches, scattering the shadows cast by the moon across the ground. Though the creek runs low and quiet tonight, the moment I step out into it, I remember it flooding, swollen and crashing, tearing apart the raft a cousin and I had built out of fireplace logs. In a flash, our plans to float Tom Sawyer-style down Hackberry Creek to Turtle Creek, out into the Trinity River, and down into the Gulf of Mexico were taken out of our hands by its sinking.

I drive this certain route with my grandfather almost every night when I'm in Dallas, along the creek, down Drexel Drive, past "3600," as we called it, my grandparents' house, now sold, as though it creates a mandala, a protective pattern, a labyrinth or circle in which I enclose the fragment left of this world we shared. I do not know what I will find when I leave for the Rio Grande Valley.

Rio Grande Valley
August 1988

Storm clouds drift above us, shadowing the gray-brown-green land below as we begin the descent in our small plane, buffeted by high winds. From the air, the landscape is unrelentingly geometric. Agribusiness ruled off the Rio Grande Valley into the precise square grids of farmland cut up by the straight, fast roads that we see from the air.

The Valley is not actually a valley since there are no hills on either side. It's a hot, broad coastal plain, 27 degrees north of the Equator, with a growing season of three hundred forty days a year— that's three crops—making this land immensely valuable for fruit and vegetables.

The land here has been heavily irrigated and fertilized, and but for few exceptions, largely stripped of its natural vegetation. A handful of state parks and wildlife refuges contain the remnants of native plants and trees that grow in the Valley. As the central flyway for the North American continent, thousands of species of migratory birds fly through here, increasingly endangered, as are we, by runoff from the chemical fertilizers and pesticides used in agriculture that wash into the ponds, *resacas,* and waterways. But it's the Rio Grande River, snaking across the desert landscape, that controls this Valley, as the Nile does Egypt. Its water can be dammed, drained, dredged, rechanneled, blessed, and cursed, but ultimately, it's the Rio Grande River that gives the Valley its essential character, creating hundreds of miles of permeable border between the United States and Mexico.

"You don't have to go to Europe to find a Black Madonna, for heaven's sake, we've got one right here in Texas," my Uncle Peter said in true native Texan style.

"You ought to see her shrine. It's a big place, thousands of people go there for mass on Sundays, the place is packed. There's a room full of *milagritos,* photographs, letters of thanks to the Virgin for being cured, and all sorts of things that people have left behind, like crutches, because they believe she's healed them. It's wild. I go to mass there when I'm in the Valley."

The research I'd done on this Madonna during the months preceding the trip surprised me. I'd been able to glean little about this particular Madonna herself. I thought she might be another form of the Virgin of Guadalupe, but I was wrong. The Madonna at San Juan, the *Virgen de San Juan del Valle,* is a replica of the *Madonna de San Juan de los Lagos* in Jalisco, Mexico. Though not as well known internationally as Guadalupe, she is famous within Mexico and within the Hispanic community in the United States. Each year, at the Feast of the Purification of the Virgin in February, the Candeleria Festival takes place at San Juan de los Lagos in Mexico, I read.[2] Brilliantly costumed societies of dancers come from all over Mexico on a kind of perpetual pilgrimage or *promesa* to dance for the Virgin. Another source said that the name of the village was *Lagos Moreno,* the dark lake. I could gather little more information than this. Even the bookstore at the shrine did not have a published history.

The geographical location of her shrine in Texas was another matter. It was a political minefield. Thousands of Central American refugees were trapped in the Rio Grande Valley, pouring over the border at a growing rate of two thousand a week[3] to apply for political asylum in Brownsville at the federal offices of INS, the Immigration and Naturalization Service.

The refugee situation compounds the problems of the already strained border community, home to thousands of Texas families who live in the *Colonias,* residential areas that lack the basic services of sewage and water. Poverty, high infant-mortality rates, unemployment of up to 35 percent, and poor school districts make this area one of the most economically depressed in the United States.

The Rio Grande Valley had seen the Sanctuary movement take root with the arrest of volunteer church workers Stacey Lynn Merkt and Jack Elder in 1984 in Brownsville. Merkt and Elder helped feed and shelter refugees at the Casa Romero, the Catholic Church's open house.[4] Casa Romero was the response of Bishop John Fitzpatrick of Brownsville to the refugees' obvious needs. It was named for the outspoken Archbishop Oscar Romero of El Salvador, who was assassinated as he offered mass in San Salvador on March 24, 1980. Archbishop Romero sided openly with the poor of El Salvador as an outspoken critic of U.S. policy. Well over $4.5 billion of aid, almost $900 million of which went to the military, has been poured into El

Salvador, a country of only 5.2 million people, since 1980.[5] Aid continues.

Merkt was arrested for "transporting illegal aliens" while riding in a car with Brenda Sanchez (a Lutheran Church worker from El Salvador), a nun, another Salvadoran, and a reporter on February 18, 1984. Reading about Stacey Merkt and the Sanctuary trials in Texas and Arizona had pricked my conscience, but I let it go no further. Now through a series of coincidences I would be staying in a refugee shelter myself while I researched the Madonna at San Juan.

The storm that hovered over the Valley as we flew in continued to threaten, darkening the sky, breaking into short bursts of rain and hail and then quickly subsiding. I was expected to arrive by supper at the Casa de la Merced, a project of the Sisters of Mercy which provides temporary food and housing to men, women, and children from El Salvador, Guatemala, Honduras, and Nicaragua. Space was at a premium. I had a place to stay, if there was room.

By the time I arrived in the Valley, I was feeling increasingly uncomfortable with the direction this Madonna was taking me. The variance between the information I gathered myself about the refugees in the Valley, the unprecedented numbers seeking asylum, and the news provided by Washington grew.[6] The erratic coverage of Central America in the American press made following events dizzying. There were stories of stories not being published. Classes were offered in "reading the news"; it was now considered a skill. What was termed "democratic reform" in one country, our government called "Communist influence." What Washington described as "fragile democracy," others called oligarchies held together by terrorism, torture, human-rights violations, death squads, and the aid of millions of U.S. tax dollars.

I picked up a car at the airport in Harlingen and drove to McAllen, puzzling over how this fit with the Black Madonna. Resistance, apprehension, excitement, amazement—all kinds of feelings came up during the drive. The fact that the Casa de la Merced was run by the Sisters of Mercy was reassuring. Underneath I found a faith in the Catholic Church that I had long forgotten. I took for granted the fact that the members of the clergy would not be involved in the refugee issue if something wasn't deeply and morally wrong. Whether or not this was a naive or an accurate assumption remained to be seen.

The cotton standing in the fields gave comfort as I sped by. Stately palm trees—fan palms, date palms, over fifty varieties grow here—feathery mesquite trees, slow-growing native ebony, sabal, mountain laurel, oak, groves of oranges and grapefruit, hot pink-maroon bougaïnvillea, and bright-blossomed oleanders provided respite along the road. By six in the evening it was still close to 100 degrees. The landscape was unfamiliarly flat. When I got to the turnoff at McAllen, all the road signs were in Spanish; I had entered another world. Only a few more miles to the Sisters of Mercy.

"*Buenos noches,*" a woman called from the porch of the Casa de la Merced when I drove up and got out of the car. "Come on inside, you're just in time for supper." Big Rio Grande Valley ash trees surround the house, protection from the hurricanes that sweep through here.

Inside the comfortable two-story frame house the overhead fans whirl slowly, an old air-conditioning unit pumps out its pittance of cool air, throbbing in the background. The downstairs was pleasantly cool. Dinner was simple—rice, beans, and eggs Mexican-style—eaten at a long table with the nuns and brothers who share the house.

The Casa is run by Marian Strohmeyer, a Sister of Mercy and native of the Rio Grande Valley. This house is the home she grew up in. Now with all the family gone it has one simple function.

"Border hospitality," Sister Marian explained, "that's all we provide. Border hospitality was just part of the way of life down here. That's one of the hardest things about what I've seen happen in the Valley. Lived here all but ten years of my life—that means over fifty years, I'm sixty-one now—and I've seen our way of life begin to unravel.

"Neighbors have turned against neighbors, lots of people have become afraid to offer th : hospitality that was part and parcel of our way of life. They're afraid to give somebody a ride to the bus, to the store, down the street. Afraid that the INS will say they're transporting illegal aliens. People on the street have come to believe that it's a crime to offer hospitality. That's no crime!

"The border is no longer the border, it's wherever there's a border patrolman," Marian explained in her no-nonsense manner. Short silver hair, blue eyes, medium height, with a solid body, Marian has a straightforward approach to life.

"I heard that INS is planning to put in a hotline with an 800 number you can call anonymously if you're suspicious that somebody's employing refugees illegally. That reminds me of the movies I saw as a kid on Nazi Germany," she recalled over dinner. Her two dogs bark as someone comes to the back screen door. Marian goes to the door and a sister from Boston picks up the conversation.

"We usually have about sixteen refugees here, in addition to the nuns, brothers, and lay volunteers who staff the house. Often there're a lot of children. The refugees here right now are from Honduras, Guatemala, and El Salvador. They usually stay one to two months, get their paperwork done for the INS, and then move on. Two women came in Monday from El Salvador. They walked across the river and then got caught, a mother and her seventeen-year-old pregnant daughter. They were taken to the *corralon,* the detention center. There's a children's detention center a few miles away from the *corralon.*

"I just came down here from Boston not long ago. I was surprised to find that there were no signs in Spanish at the INS office. They were all in English. Most refugees don't speak English, much less read it.

"Two women and two men came yesterday from Honduras. They had taken a bus through Mexico. Twice they were robbed. At one point they had to go without food for five days. These people endure great hardships just to get here, that should tell you something about how bad things have gotten where they come from.

"We just had an eighteen-year-old boy from Guatemala who fled because his father was murdered. His father had told him that if he was killed to leave the country immediately because he would be next."

Marian came back to the table to continue our talk. Over the next hour the conversation shifted and turned, my trip to Poland mentioned.

"Did you know that there's a Czestochowa, Texas?" Marian asked.

"Never heard of it."

"Oh, you'll have to go," she said emphatically.

"It's outside of San Antonio. There's nothing there but this big church, out in the middle of nowhere, with a copy of the Madonna of Czestochowa. It's right near Pannamaria, Texas, where Chevron has a big open-pit uranium mining operation that they're closing down.

"If you get to San Antonio to see Stacey Merkt, you can get over to Czestochowa, no problem."

After the dinner clean-up, Adella, the sister from Boston, and I go outside in back on the lawn where some of the refugees are singing. There are oak trees and a Chinese tallow, with chairs set around on the grass in a restful setting.

I join a circle of people sitting on the ground and the steps in front of one of the trailer houses. A handful of women and children sit on the front steps. Adella translates and explains that Ricardo, the guitar player, is from Honduras. I realize that he's the same age as my oldest son.

"You can tell who is telling the truth after a while and I have the feeling Ricardo is," added Jack, a Little Brother of the Good Shepherd who's come to help.

Ricardo plays *La Bamba* and I start to laugh. Every day on the pilgrimage in Poland someone in our group would sing that song. With Adella and Jack's help, I explained how young people in Poland

The Black Madonna, Our Lady of Czestochowa,
Czestochowa, Texas. (Author)

sing "Hey hey la bamba, hey hey la bamba . . ." and we all laughed
for a moment to think of people in a country so far away, singing
this same song and dancing.

Ricardo spoke a little English and said, "You play?" offering me
the guitar.

"Un poquito," I assure him, *"un muy poquito,* very little, but I know one song in Spanish, in Ladino, let me sing that." *Bibilicos* is a song about how the world suffers for love.

For as long as the song lasted I was part of this patchwork of makeshift community, then it was over. A few people smiled and clapped politely. Others had no interest. I handed Ricardo back the guitar. Adella nudged me.

"It's late, after ten. I have to get up early. What time are you going over to the shrine in the morning?"

"Early. Let's go. I'm tired, too." We say goodnight to everyone and walk back toward the main house, calling out, *"Hasta mañana, buenos noches. Gracias,* Ricardo, and good luck."

As we're walking back in the soft night air, Adella tells me that Ricardo just found out that the INS was going to deport him because of an error made while filling out the forms. Apparently it wasn't his mistake but a volunteer's who was helping him. It happens, she says. So many refugees arrive penniless, either robbed along the way, their money extorted, or having had to spend everything just to make the trip across Mexico. There is only one group in the Valley that offers free legal aid, *Proyecto Libertad* in Harlingen, and they are badly overloaded.[7] Ricardo believes that he'll be killed if he's sent back to Honduras, so he's very anxious.

"He's going to try to fight it and start the paperwork all over again. He's applied for political asylum," she said. "See you in the morning. I'm in the room at the end of the hall downstairs if you need anything. Goodnight."

I was given a room at the top of the stairs with a window air conditioner and told to be sure to turn it off in the morning if I used it. The room was clean, simple, and stifling hot. It faced west and the windows had been closed all day. The air conditioner was not on, but I quickly found the switch. It was an older unit, but it worked. There were two single beds freshly made, one covered with a homemade quilt. A towel, a washcloth, and a fresh bar of soap had been laid neatly on top of it. I felt welcomed.

The Shrine of the *Virgen de San Juan del Valle*. The Madonna, that's what brought me here, I keep thinking as I fall asleep. Tomorrow. Before I see anything else, I have to see her.

The next morning as she goes out the door to work, Marian calls back as I'm walking down the stairs, "You can't miss the shrine from the highway. Ask for Father Pete Cortez, he's the priest there in charge. He'll help you with whatever you want to know about the Madonna. Hot coffee in the pot," and she's gone.

◆

The large modern shrine is full of people coming and going. Some pilgrims walk on their knees down the aisles to the Madonna. She is tiny, this one, less than two feet tall, but set dramatically in the center of a large circle over the main altar that is the focal point for the entire church. Though no service is going on when I arrive, the shrine is half full with people praying quietly, lighting candles. Confessions are being heard, so Father Pete is not available.

I genuflect and kneel down in one of the pews to look at this Virgin. I am relieved that Pete Cortez is not available. I am still working through where this root system has led me: South Texas, a refugee shelter, now this Madonna in front of me. *Morenita,* the little dark one. She has long black hair that flows over her satin robes, Spanish-style. She stands alone, without the Christ Child, on a crescent moon, Our Lady of the Immaculate Conception, *La Purisima,* Mary Most Pure, as the Immaculate Conception is also called in Mexico.

In 1519, the Spaniard Cortés placed a statue of the Immaculate Conception at what had been the site of the Mayan moon goddess when he landed at Cozumel. Many of the Mexican Madonnas are the Immaculate Conception, characteristically portrayed standing on a crescent moon,[8] linking her both with the woman in the Book of the Apocalypse and the moon goddess of pre-Columbian Mexico.

I wandered around the shrine and found the room off to the side where there were thousands of photographs people had sent in thanks to the Virgin for their healing or her answer to their prayers. Similar to the *ex-votos* or *retablos* along the back walls of the monastery at Einsiedeln, paintings depicting the miracle of healing by the Virgin, the photographs were a more contemporary expression of this ancient practice. There were *milagritos*—little metal charms of arms, legs, hands, hearts, eyes, different parts of the body that had been healed or needed healing—just as on the walls in the Madonna's shrine at Czestochowa. There were also actual crutches and leg braces, like around St. Sara's statue in the crypt of Les-Saintes-Maries-de-la-Mer in the Camargue, as well as sports trophies, ribbons, letters of testimonial, and beautiful shiny long dark braids of hair that had been cut off straight, at the nape of the neck.

As I came around a corner, Father Pete was walking out of the confessional, a short, energetic man with a mustache, his collar slightly askew from the heat. A big smile spread across his face as I introduced myself. I liked him immediately. He invited me into his office where he told me a little about this particular statue of the Madonna.

The story of the Virgin of San Juan goes back to 1623 in what was then known as the village of San Juan de los Lagos Moreno in Jalisco, Mexico. Spanish missionaries had built an adobe shrine for Our Lady of the Immaculate Conception there shortly after they arrived in Mexico. This Virgin of San Juan of the Valley is a copy of the one in Jalisco.

According to seventeenth-century legend, a family of traveling acrobats were in the village of San Juan de los Lagos in Mexico rehearsing for a performance. One of the young daughters fell to her death on pointed daggers below. The child was taken into a home and lay dead, her body being prepared for burial, when an Indian women entered the house carrying the statue of the Virgin. As she placed the statue over the girl's body and prayed to Mary, the young girl was restored to life.

Thereafter this *Virgen de San Juan de los Lagos* was beloved by the villagers and became renowned throughout Mexico as a miracle-worker. The story breaks into more than one version when the devotion to this Virgin is brought to Texas. Father Jose Aspiazu from Spain, member of the Oblate fathers, to which Pete Cortez, O.M.I., belongs as well, was the first pastor of the San Juan Catholic Mission, begun in 1949.

Early in the 1940s, Mexican Americans in the Valley had begun to make the long and sometimes dangerous journey to Jalisco, Mexico, to make a pilgrimage to the Virgin of San Juan. To save them this journey, he told me, Father Aspiazu ordered a replica of the statue to be made in Mexico and subsequently established the now-famous shrine to her in the Texas Valley, first dedicated in 1954.

A second version of the story intrigued me more. Around 1940, an image of the Virgin was reported to be growing out of a rock northeast of San Juan, Texas. People started bringing candles and going there to pray. The Church did not approve of the growing devotion to the rock Virgin in the fields. Bringing the Madonna de los Lagos from Mexico brought the faithful back into the parish church. However the devotion to her came to be in the Rio Grande Valley, it is now well established and has become a major pilgrimage site for many, especially Mexican Americans from all over the United States.

After visiting with Father Pete, I met Pedro Rodriguez, the head sacristan at the shrine, who had been with this church for thirty-two years. Rodriguez told me the strange story of the shrine's destruction in October 1970, when a crazed single-engine plane pilot radioed the control tower saying that he was going to destroy the church. In kamikaze fashion the pilot headed straight for the church tower, having timed his attack to coincide with a special mass that was being concelebrated by priests from all over the diocese. School was in session and the attached building was full of children. The pilot crashed into the tower, killing himself and setting the church on fire.

"I helped the priests save the statue of Our Lady," Pedro told me. "It was eleven forty-five in the morning when it happened. There were over forty priests in the church to celebrate mass. The ceiling came down in flames all around us. The school lunchroom next door was full of children, but nobody was hurt except for the pilot. It was a miracle."

The old shrine was completely destroyed by the crash. Years went by with activities in a temporary structure while donations from the people, primarily migrant workers, steadily accumulated to build this striking, new, and much larger shrine, seating nearly two thousand, which was dedicated on April 19, 1980. Fifteen thousand people visit the shrine each weekend, more in the summer months.

Rodriguez explained that this Madonna has a special relationship with the migrant workers. It was their nickels, dimes, and dollars that poured in to build this shrine. They marched with the Virgin of San Juan de los Lagos on their banner to the state capitol in Austin. Before they leave for the fields and orchards of the North or the West, many come here with their family to light a candle, a ritual repeated upon return. Father Pete had mentioned this too, spoken of seeing families sleeping overnight in trucks and cars, before and after their journeys as migrant workers, to pay a visit to *la Virgen,* to light a candle and fulfill a *promesa,* give thanks for a prayer answered. The strength of the workers' devotion in turn taught Father Pete Cortez, opened his heart more to see, as it did mine in his telling. The life of the migrant worker is hard with often little or no drinking water, plumbing, or decent housing. He knows, Pedro Rodriguez assured me, for he was once a migrant worker himself.

◆

Walking out of the shrine in the early evening, I am hit by the strong winds that seem to prevail here. At 8:00 p.m., it is still 92 degrees F. Driving back to the Casa de la Merced, a pale gold ball of sun gives off its last nearly blinding light as it sets over the brown, furrowed fields, behind the palm trees, beyond the mesquite. The crickets are quiet now, the land lies flat for miles and miles, the road deserted as I speed along. By the Mile 3 road sign, the sun has become a perfect fiery ball of molten orange. By Mile 4 Road, only the top half glitters gold and bright; by Mile 5, it is gone.

The driveway at the Casa is lined with crimson red and pale pink oleanders in bloom, the ash trees surrounding the house electric with buzzing of insects. Marian's dogs bark as I walk up to the screen porch.

"Had any supper yet?" she asks as I walk into the kitchen. I am excited about the parallels I see between the Madonna de los Lagos being a patron of the migrant workers and the Madonna of Czestochowa having a similar role for Solidarity in Poland. Marian quickly points out at least one major difference. "Americans consider unions heroic in Poland, but not in the United States," she says without expression, and changes the subject.

Four more people arrived today, this time from Guatemala. Over supper Marian attempts to explain the INS system for the Valley, one that was unique in the nation. Those who applied for asylum directly to INS, if considered eligible, were permitted to travel to the city of their destination for the processing of their application. Those who were apprehended and able to post bond were allowed to travel as well. This was all standard procedure. What was unique about the policy in South Texas, Marian explains, was that refugees who were unable to post bond were required to stay in the Rio Grande Valley until their hearing, a process which could easily take three to four months, sometimes up to five or six as the court systems became increasingly clogged.

While on the surface it might have seemed a kindness to release a refugee on their own recognizance, because they were classified as illegal aliens they were not permitted to work. The policy created increasing hardships as the numbers of people grew rapidly.

Unable to meet the financial requirements of a bond, ranging anywhere from $500 up to $7,000, growing numbers of people not permitted to leave or to work were stranded in the Valley. In addition to those unable to post bond, there were untold numbers who had not been apprehended who were caught in the net, complete with road blocks, as well. Total estimates ran into the thousands.

By the following winter, with two thousand people a week applying for asylum, INS policy changed. They would no longer allow even those who had properly applied to leave the Valley.

The story broke into nationwide headlines when the National Refugee Rights Project in San Francisco filed a class-action challenge against the attorney general and INS.[9] The result was that over twelve thousand refugees were allowed to leave the Valley and travel in January 1989.[10] But INS changed its policies again and went to simply detaining everyone who applied, even those who had approached them voluntarily.

By the end of winter, early 1989, nearly five thousand of those fleeing Central America would be detained by the INS. The *corralon*, detention center, would be overflowing, and circus-size tents and Red Cross shelters would be set up to accommodate the overflow that turned the Rio Grande Valley into a state of chaos.

The situation in the Rio Grande Valley would deteriorate to the point that the Texas Conference of Churches and the Catholic Bishops of Texas would publicly denounce the newest INS plan to stop the flow of refugees as "the largest concentration camp on U.S. soil since the Japanese-Americans were incarcerated during World War II."

Bishop John J. Fitzpatrick of Brownsville summarized the refugee plight that would exist by spring.

"These are people who have been impoverished, terrorized, tortured, had family killed. They are fleeing civil wars. Great numbers of the civilian populations have been killed in these countries. Their economies are ruined. They get here and they're not allowed to work, they're not allowed to leave this INS district, and they're given no food.

"There are two roads out of South Texas. Both have roadblocks at which every bus, truck, and car is stopped and checked. Roadblocks. Inside the United States. The border is no longer the Rio Grande. It's been moved sixty miles north of Brownsville.

"The Central American Bishops have asked us to continue insisting that the United States stay out of their countries. They must be self-determined. We support the Bishops of Central America. We must have a change in policy in the State Department," Bishop Fitzpatrick said adamantly.[11]

Increasing numbers of people were deported without being informed of elemental legal rights.[12] The court found that "INS had beaten, drugged, stripped, threatened, lied to and otherwise coerced Salvadorans into waiving their right to seek political asylum" and ordered INS to see to it that people had access to legal counsel and telephones.[13] Contempt proceedings would be instituted against the INS[14] by March 1989.

At issue was the internationally recognized right to seek political asylum.[15] The U.S. Refugee Act of 1980 gave recognition to the fact that persons who have refugee status have the right not to be deported. In 1987, a landmark U.S. Supreme Court decision, *INS* v. *Cardoza-Fonseca,* considerably broadened the standard the INS had been applying in determining refugee status. The 1987 decision bases the asylum application on a "well-founded fear of persecution" rather than on the more difficult proof of clear probability.[16] But as Bishop Fitzpatrick said, to admit that these people deserve the status of refugees or political asylum means acknowledging failure in U.S. foreign policy.

When Stacey Merkt was indicted, she gave a statement that I read years ago and have never forgotten: "We United States citizens will have no excuse. We will never be able to say, 'I never saw, I never heard, I never knew'—that we set a house on fire and locked the door."[17] Her words troubled me then, and now even more that I was in the Valley, beginning to understand what she meant. Now I had been in Poland, seen the camps. Her unspoken allusion to Germans of the Third Reich who claimed they didn't know what their government was doing in the 1930s and 1940s finally penetrated.

I had come to see the Madonna de los Lagos, *morenita,* the little dark one, but I was being shown something else. The work in the Valley had rapidly become a matter of listening, not looking. It was as though the Madonna had led me there, only to point to something else.

At dinner I sit across from Sister Alberta, a gray-haired, soft-spoken nun with a Spanish accent from her years of living in Central America. Sister Alberta offers to translate for me so that I can begin to hear first-hand why people are fleeing. At over sixty years old, she still works full time on behalf of the poor. A woman from El Salvador has agreed to talk with us, though she is too afraid to give her name. She still has family there.

The overhead fan whirrs softly, stirring the warm night air around us as we sit enclosed on the screened porch after dinner. The metal chair I sit in squeaks with every move. Crickets chirp in the grass. El Salvador seems so far away from the languor of this summer night. The woman begins in rapid-fire Spanish. Sister Alberta translates.

"She tells you that there is much poverty and danger in El Salvador. She lived in a zone where is was impossible to live. There were kidnappings, bombings—it was impossible to stay there. She says that the guerrillas are trying to protect the poor against the army and the death squads, but they are often crushed by the land-owners, the army, and the government."

The woman goes on in Spanish, throwing her hands up in the air in a gesture of frustration. "Where can we go? we asked ourselves. There was nothing for us to do but leave."

"She said that even the very young boys have to go to the army now even before fifteen. They kidnap many children, it's horrible. Some they even sell," Alberta says.

Alberta turns to me to explain. "These people worry all the time about their children. We have no idea of the suffering that they are going through in their minds. I know. I know what kind of country they left.

"I was in Guatemala and there are many from Guatemala here.

I left in 1982. You would find it hard to believe how they tortured the people they kidnapped, so many children," Sister Alberta said, putting her face in her hands, "even old ladies, they would put them on a truck and take them just to rape them. It was unbelievable! I lived in Guatemala. I know these things firsthand.

"One day they took about sixty men to a certain place in the countryside. Then they cut off their arms and legs and left them to die just like that.

"They took nearly one hundred people another time. Whole families. The men had to dig their graves and then they shot all the men. The children had to watch their fathers being shot and the wives had to cover the dead husbands.

"I worked with the poorest people, the ones who lived in the ravines, the hopelessly poor and the drug addicts. But even this bothered the authorities, was an offense. People began to tell me that the police were looking for me. Being a nun was no longer any protection. They were kidnapping and torturing Sisters, too. I went into hiding in a big convent, but every convent had spies around. I belonged to a team of Guatemalans who worked with the poor, but they became afraid because now I was a danger to them. That's when I decided to leave. I didn't want anybody to be hurt because of me. I was sixty years old then. Many thousands have been killed in Guatemala.[18]

"Now it seems that the worst place is El Salvador."

The next day I drove to Harlingen to *Proyecto Libertad,* the one source of free legal aid for the refugees. Founded in 1983 by attorney Lisa Brodyaga, *Proyecto* had nine thousand open files at the time. There were three lawyers and five paralegals, with the support of small secretarial and volunteer staff to handle the crushing load.

Jim Cushman, one of the paralegals at *Proyecto,* showed me the offices. Jim was particularly concerned about the children being held in detention.

"They can be held indefinitely. Most of the kids are fourteen to seventeen years old, though sometimes they're younger, like the seven-year-old that was brought in this week. Immigration [INS] had the attitude that they're defending our national security. They operate like the CIA, with whom they share files, in bad faith. I find them really hard to deal with, they have an attitude of 'plausible deniability' and will do as little as possible to help you and your client."

I walked through the *Proyecto* offices, crammed with files, so full that one had to turn sideways to allow someone else to pass, past two couches of refugee families. I was going to meet Brenda Sanchez. Brenda was the former Lutheran Church worker in El Salvador who was in the car the night Stacey Merkt was arrested.

Stacey Merkt pleaded innocent. She was adopted by Amnesty International as a Prisoner of Conscience for her refusal to plead guilty. She was indicted on a legal technicality that was later dismissed. In a subsequent incident she was ordered by the judge to prison. She voluntarily surrendered herself to a prison term while pregnant in 1987. She was the first person in the United States convicted for participating in the Sanctuary movement.[19]

Brenda speaks English but is more comfortable in Spanish. Jonathon Moore volunteered to translate. Brenda's voice is soft but firm. Jonathon's sentence-by-sentence translation echoes and gives a resonance to her words.

"I was going home," she said, "*mi casa,* I had to get the bus from the school. I was fourteen. I got out of my school. It was yet miles from there to where I had to take the bus. There was a march at that time. It was known that after a march, the military comes, repression occurs.

"It was a peaceful demonstration asking for better living conditions. Everybody was out on the streets—peasants, students, teachers. But that time when I was heading for home, we began to hear bullets whine. So I ran to a garage, it was the only thing that was open. When I went inside, it was full of people. Whoever's garage it was, he pulled down the metal gate in front just after I ran inside.

"He was looking outside through a crack to see what was going on. He was telling the rest of us what was happening because the bullets kept raining. 'There is the National Police outside. They're shooting at the demonstrators.' He said to get back, a tank was coming down the street. It stopped. A soldier on top of the tank yelled for him to open the door because he knew there were people inside.

"The soldier was saying that there were subversives hidden in the garage, that someone had been shooting out of the garage, which wasn't true. Everyone started shouting, 'No!' But the soldier kept insisting in vulgar language that they should open the door so that they could see that no one was armed. Finally they opened the door so that the soldier could see that none of us were armed.

"But the solider began shooting with a machine gun from on top of the tank. He didn't ask anything when they opened the door, he just opened fire.

"It began to rain pieces of flesh. They used explosive bullets. I couldn't see how many survived or how many died. Only thing I did was throw myself down on the floor. Pieces of bodies were everywhere. My blouse had been white. Now it was red.

"When he finished shooting into the garage, he said that nothing had happened here and the first person that said that something *did* happen there would die. Then he left. The tank rolled on down the street.

"I crawled out from under the bodies around me. I left and I ran back to school. This was about eleven-thirty in the morning. I didn't get home to my house until about eleven o'clock that night. My family thought I was dead.

"When we were in the garage, before the tank had even come, the person whose garage it was had already had the women and children go to the back and the men in front. That's why I lived, because there were people in front of me that were shot.

"The ones who died were in front, the men, some students, some old people, people who had just been in the streets doing their routine things of the day. They hadn't participated in the march, they just happened to have been on the street, just the same as me, I was going to catch the bus."

Brenda left El Salvador in December 1983. "When we left, it was seven young people from the Lutheran Church. I was the only woman and I also had a one-year-old baby, my daughter Bessie.

"A friend that I grew up with was murdered not long before I left El Salvador. A close friend, like a sister. She was eighteen years old and five months pregnant. They came at two in the morning and took her out of her house. She wasn't found until a week later, outside. Her head was cut off. Her womb had been cut open, she had been cut into parts. Her baby had been taken out of her womb and cut into parts, too. When the body was found, the dogs had already been eating it. Fifteen days later they killed her husband."

"The baby, the baby too?" was all I could say. She nodded her head and explained their offense.

"They were Catholics. Both belonged to a Catholic base community. Her principal Christian mission was to help those who needed it. A young wounded man came to her house and she helped him. She bandaged his wound and gave him some of her husband's clothes. She had never even asked his name. He left.

"Three days later they came to get her. They killed her brother, too.

"If you are a Christian there and you really practice, it costs you a lot. She carried out her Christianity in practice and it's a crime.

"In El Salvador, before we left, neighbors from our community, more friends of ours, were killed. This happened. This is the truth. On this same day they were looking for Pedro, my husband; they were going to take him away but he wasn't at home when they came to look for him.

"The neighborhood was near the air force base. They surrounded the community. They didn't let anybody go in or out. Between midnight and two in the morning they began to knock on specific doors. They had a list. Sometimes they marked your house with the print of a hand that had been dipped in white paint. That was a warning. Leave or be killed. The death squads of El Salvador. It was like their signature. They took two women and three men. They were looking for four men, Pedro was one of them, but he wasn't home. I wasn't home either."

I breathed a sigh of relief, dug in my bag for more Kleenex. Brenda went on in her simple, calm way, Jonathon sitting behind her on the desk in this office the size of a closet, the only room empty in which we could speak privately.

"They took a girl fifteen, a girl eighteen who was pregnant six months, another they took was a fourteen-year-old boy, then a sixteen-year-old boy, and a boy who was nineteen. They took them to a football field nearby. They raped the girls in the football field. Then they took them to a public park in Ilyapango. In that park, they shot the three men and the girls they continued to rape. The fifteen-year-old girl tried to run, so they shot her. The girl that was pregnant, when they were through raping her, they put a gun up her vagina and killed her and her baby."

"Wait a minute," I said naively, "this was in public?"

"It was on the plaza, *si,*" said Brenda, "other people saw it. They saw everything but nobody said anything. If somebody says that they saw it, they get killed. The soldiers have guns, and what do the people have? *Nada,* nothing. The person with the gun has power. They killed the men at five in the morning while everybody was going out to work."

"You left El Salvador in December 1983, and came to the States. You were caught, but now you are free?"

"Not completely. We're still waiting for a deportation hearing."

"She's still out on bond, waiting for a hearing here on her petition for political asylum," Jonathon explained.

"I'm still waiting for my destiny."[20]

Brenda and Jonathon were calm when she finished talking. I was deeply shaken.

◆

I drove straight from *Proyecto* to the airport at Harlingen to get a flight to San Antonio. I came close to missing the late afternoon flight by making wrong turns, I was so disturbed by Brenda's story and leaving Casa de la Merced that morning. Though I kept checking a map of Harlingen in my hand I could not orient myself east, west, north, or south. My sense of direction had temporarily evaporated. I returned the rental car as if by accident and hopped on a shuttle bus to the airport, settling into my seat on the flight just in time for takeoff.

I was going to stay in a house run by Catholic religious in San Antonio, then drive to Czestochowa, Texas, the next day to see the Black Madonna.

Sitting in the backyard later in San Antonio at dinner, nothing political was discussed. Everyone made small talk, to my relief. Stacey Merkt, her husband John Blatz, and their baby Daniel Guadalupe were there to visit with two church workers who had just returned from five years in Nicaragua. I had intended to ask Stacey about her trial in Texas, but I had no stomach for such talk. She herself was tired of being asked about it. Rarely have I so much appreciated the little things people talk about, like the weather and the weight of a child. I sank into my chair under the trees and watched with special pleasure as baby Daniel gleefully ran after a rooster that lived in the backyard.

The room I was given to sleep in was simple, with two single beds, no air conditioning, an electric fan, and a set of bunk beds, dormitory-style. It was clean, pleasant, and hot.

I was invited to join the residents for prayer in the morning. Just before going to bed, I walked into the study to ask what time we would meet, and on the wall I saw a poster of Robert Lentz's icon of the Madonna for El Salvador, *Madre de los Desaparecidos,* the Mother of the Disappeared.

Painted in the traditional Byzantine or Greek icon style against the nontraditional backdrop of a Central American jungle, the image of this dark brown-skinned Mary was stunning. But when I noticed the white handprint smudged in the lower left-hand corner of the painting, I was brought up short and felt a visceral punch. "The white hand," one of the death squads in El Salvador.

Brenda had told me how sometimes when you are marked, you will find the imprint of a human hand that's been dipped in white paint on your door. If you find this hand on your door and you do not leave, you too will disappear.

The Madonna with the white hand of a death squad on her icon. She too was marked, in solidarity with the disappeared. Suddenly it hit. This was the Madonna I'd come to see, this was what I had been led to by the Madonna de los Lagos. Everything I had not understood began to fit. There's a point at which the spiritual and the political intersect. The icon of the *Madre de los Desaparecidos* exploded out of that junction.

I stared at this image for a long time before going back to my room to sleep.

It occurred to me that there was something false about the way Mary was so often depicted as a passive sufferer. I no longer believed that.

Mary is not passive. The image that we've been shown has truth in it, but it is a limited truth. I derived great comfort in the fact that Mary was an earthly mother, that she went through a pregnancy as a teen-age mother, that she had known homelessness, that she had borne at least one child. She had witnessed that child's suffering and death, she knew the depths of a mother's sorrow.

But Mary's passivity may be all that we've *allowed* ourselves to see. A woman rising up against authority, a woman strong and fearless, a ferocious woman, an independent woman, an heroic woman, a

MADRE DE LOS DESAPARECIDOS

Madre de los Desaparecidos. (Robert Lentz)

physically courageous woman—to have seen Mary this way would not have served the social order. I began to imagine Mary differently.

I imagined Mary as a fierce mother one morning in my prayers and meditation. I imagined her protecting Christ. The Mary I saw stepped in front of his tormentors. She did not stand passively as he made his way to Golgotha, at first she hurled herself at the Roman soldiers, "Stop, stop, stop!" trying to wrench their whips away from them, then to remove his crown of thorns. She was fiercely protective and she was greatly outnumbered. They shoved her away and formed a phalanx around Christ.

She denounced the soldiers, she defied them. She did not faint, she was not helpless, she did not retreat, she was not polite. She was a tower of strength, she did not take her eyes off her Christ. She walked with him, outside the phalanx of soldiers. She was his most powerful witness, she suffered with him mentally and physically.

This is a Mary we have not seen in the West. This is a Mary that we need now, a fierce Mary, a terrific Mary, a fearsome Mary, a protectress who does not allow her children to be hunted, tortured, murdered, and devoured.

"Mary, the poorest people, the most vulnerable, the weakest who suffer the most are devoted to you. Why do they pray to you?" I asked. "Why don't you protect them? Would it be worse if they did not pray to you? We need a mother who protects us, who is like a lioness defending her young, is terrible when crossed.

"Show me your face."

I see the Grandmothers of the Disappeared, *Abuelas de la Plaza del Mayo,* I see the Mothers of the Disappeared, *Madres de la Plaza del Mayo.* I imagine these women of whom I have only read.

Fourteen women defied the Argentine military's ban on demonstrations in April 1977, and came to the Plaza del Mayo demanding to know the whereabouts of their children and loved ones who had "disappeared." They were dismissed as crazy, called "*las Locas.*" The Mothers refused to be intimidated. They did not go away.

The Mothers returned, every Thursday. By December 1977, they had become a target of the military themselves in Argentina, and nine of their members, including a French nun, were taken away by plainclothesmen after a meeting and never heard of again. They disappeared, along with thirty thousand other Argentinians. The Mothers returned to the Plaza to demonstrate the following Thursday. Nothing stopped them.

By 1984, *las Locas* had become national heroines. The Mothers of the Disappeared had continued to demonstrate, week after week, year after year. Bearing witness, powerful witness, witness that has become known around the world. *Las Madres.*

In Chile, Maria Acevedo's son and daughter were taken by the military in 1984. Involved in demonstrations against the government put in power by the CIA-backed military coup against Allende, her children were targeted by the National Police.

Maria and her husband Sebastian were at home when the police kicked in the door and took first their daughter. The son they took from his work place. At first Maria and Sebastian went looking for them at the police stations and military headquarters. They were not to be found. Rape and torture often accompanied arrest. Sebastian grew increasingly distraught.

"On the second day, my husband said that he wanted to crucify himself in front of the church. . . . He asked the priests to nail him to a cross . . . but they would not. So at four o'clock on the third day, Sebastian Acevedo set himself on fire in front of the church. . . ."[21]

He died that night.

The Sebastian Acevedo Movement Against Torture has become internationally known for its nonviolent direct-action groups in Chile, in which Maria plays an active part. In 1987, her son and daughter were released.

In El Salvador, we have *CoMadres,* Committee of Mothers and Relatives of Political Prisoners, Disappeared and Assassinated of El

Salvador, inspired by the Grandmothers of Argentina. *CoMadres* was awarded the 1984 Robert F. Kennedy Memorial Human Rights Award for its work on behalf of the disappeared and political prisoners of El Salvador. Started on December 24, 1977, still they are demonstrating, protesting, witnessing, refusing to accept that their children, husbands, friends, and loved ones are neither dead nor alive, "disappeared."

The witness is one who looks, who does not turn away, who does not despair or give up, who is willing to be called upon, who will speak up and testify in public, who will take an oath, who will bind themselves to the truth, "so help me God," to the community, for the community, for without the witness there can be no community.

I begin to understand the strength it takes to make even the first step, to be willing to see and to listen, even when it is terrifying. It appears that one is doing nothing.

In these women, I begin to see Mary's face.

CHAPTER 15

Walesa's Prayer

♦

Gdansk, Poland

"The path is straight. We are at the edge.
Down in the village the little bell chimes.
Roosters on the fences greet the light
And the earth steams, fertile and happy.

"Here it is still dark. Fog like a river flood
Swaddles the black clumps of bilberries.
But the dawn on bright stilts wades in from the shore
And the ball of the sun, ringing, rolls."

—Czeslaw Milosz[1]

California
September 1988

I came back from Texas with these stories burning in my ears. There
are many more than are told here. I woke up with them at night
and walked with them in the morning. I could not unhear them.
What is one to do with this kind of knowing? The Mothers of the
Disappeared and the *Casa de la Merced,* the House of Mercy, put the
ease of my life in sharp perspective. My admiration for people like
Sister Marian Strohmeyer and Sister Alberta grew. They lived every
day with an awareness of which I held only the smallest fragment.

It was easy to be outraged by what I had seen and heard and

yet I knew unequivocally that anger was part of the problem, not the solution. Ultimately the problem isn't "them," be it the government, the INS, Congress, anything or anyone objectified, separate or outside. The problem lies in the hardness that threatens to grow around my own heart, lies in my own thinking that wants to imagine that there is an "other" that is the enemy outside myself. If only "they" would change, then all will be well. No. If only I will change, then all will be well, must be my position. This means neither that injustice is to be tolerated nor that I will be silent. It means simply that the solution begins with looking at my part. Let the change I see so needed begin with me.

It was not easy to put the awareness and spiritual teachings I've received into practice. I failed often and continue to do so. I had no easy answers to the enormous complexities of South Texas, but I had a new willingness to live with the questions that it brought up.

The greatest consolation was the continued meetings of the Peace Project. This gave me hope. This was what I kept in front of me, a circle of young people asking, together, what does it mean to "be peace"? Thich Nhat Hanh's question deepened.

When the chance came to go back to Poland I eagerly accepted. Poland had continued to reverberate through my life. Without the pilgrimage to Czestochowa, without the Black Madonna, without the glimpse of Auschwitz, I would not have become part of the Peace Project, I would not have stayed at the *Casa de la Merced* in South Texas. I might have gotten a hotel room, driven out to the Shrine at San Juan and left the Valley, too blind and frightened to be willing to begin to see and hear what I did.

Poland was shaking itself out of the nightmare of totalitarianism that the U.S. seemed to be backing into from sheer moral decay. I was inspired by my friends in Poland and what was happening there. I longed to see Dominik. I had had no time or inclination after the pilgrimage was over and the visit to Auschwitz to inquire about the pre-Christian culture at Jasna Gora. I was still curious. I wanted to find Lech Walesa to ask about the Black Madonna. He wears a badge with her picture on it everywhere. The pilgrimage the summer before had been a great show of resistance to the authorities and an outpouring of support for Solidarity while Solidarity was still outlawed. Few seemed to know about or understand the relationship of the Black Madonna to Poland, Walesa, and Solidarity.

I wanted to go to Yugoslavia where the Virgin is reported to be appearing now, like in the past at Fatima or Lourdes, I wanted to meet one of the visionaries who speak with her. The apparitions would not last indefinitely.

Above all, I wanted to get to the surface. I needed perspective and air, I was so uncomfortable, so saddened, so disturbed by what I had found in Texas, no matter how philosophically I could view the situation. What I saw and heard was wrong and it was tragic. I packed and left for Poland six weeks later, reeling.

Gdansk, Poland
October 1988

"Yes," Monsignor Jankowsky said, "the Black Madonna. You want to know about the Madonna and Solidarity. She is our patron, she is the Queen of the workers. This is a very special relationship, very important. The workers believe that she will take care of them in every situation. This devotion is very important. She is the hope of the Solidarity movement and now today, with the latest political developments, Poland finally has a chance.

"Now it is most important to act, not to say. Words cannot change the situation here in Poland," he tells me; "it is very difficult now, but the Polish people are powerful.

"Send Poland your moral support. The change is inevitable. No one can stop it. Czestochowa's Madonna is a great symbol, which helps us to live here. It's a sanctuary in which millions of people get protection. In this northern part of Poland, the copy of the Madonna in St. Brygid's makes this church in Gdansk like a small Czestochowa sanctuary. We draw our strength from it.

Czestochowa pilgrimage 1988 and Solidarity banners. (Photographer unknown)

"Come Thursday at one-thirty and you can speak directly with Walesa about this."

Lech Walesa's devotion to the Black Madonna was well known within Poland, but I could find no way to arrange a meeting with him from the United States to ask him about it. Solidarity was still outlawed. I conferred with a Polish friend.

"Just go to St. Brygid's Church in Gdansk," Wiktor Osiantinski told me. "You must ask for Monsignor Jankowsky. Tell him that you want to talk to Walesa about the Madonna and see what happens," he said in his characteristically understated fashion.

"You will stay with us in Warsaw. Call my wife Ewa. She's a writer too, she knows everyone. If anyone can help you, she can. It's very simple what you must do. Go to Gdansk and find St. Brygid's, that's Solidarity headquarters, and ask for Jankowsky. Maybe he will be there, maybe not. It will be up to him whether or not you see Walesa."

Having been in Poland before, I knew he was right. Everything would work out, I sensed. The hospitality provided by people in Poland is exceedingly generous. I wanted to see Dominik and friends in Warsaw and go to Gdansk no matter what. Whether I got to see Walesa or not was not so important.

Go. See what happens. I joined a small group for the first part of the journey.

As life became more complicated in Poland with the crumbling of the government in power, it simultaneously became more straight-forward. One had to act directly. There was no lengthy advance correspondence with people in Poland, no getting through secretaries, assistants, or answering machines. Phones, especially at Solidarity headquarters, might be tapped. Mail was oftened opened still. Wiktor was right. There was nothing to do but go to Gdansk and attempt to make the contact directly.

What was happening in Poland was enormous, something on the scale of an Arctic glacier breaking loose in a surge and suddenly traveling at a hundred times its normal speed or the pending breakup of a glacial dam that is about to loose massive roaring torrents of icebergs, water, and debris.

Solidarity, still outlawed, was at the bargaining table with the Polish government, headed by Rakowski, an arch enemy of Solidarity's in the early eighties. Agreement had been reached to hold roundtable talks, yet no one could agree under what circumstances they would take place. It was a stunning development.

Gdansk with its *Stare Miasto,* the old city, with its graceful fountains and medieval buildings now reconstructed along the Vistula River had much historical significance. I wanted to find St. Brygid's. Every time Solidarity or anything remotely political was brought up, our government guide would change the subject. The day before in Warsaw, we had passed a large demonstration in front of the Warsaw City Hall with police ringing hundreds of protesters waving banners, and people still pouring in from side streets to join the gathering. As we drove through the middle of the crowd-filled street in our Mercedes-Benz tour bus, our guide tried to convince us it was a student prank, to be taken as a joke.

The buildup of pressure was palpable. The country was on the verge of breaking apart. The discrepancy between what I could see with my own eyes and our guide's official description made me increasingly tense, until I wanted to grab him by the shoulders and say, "Are you crazy? Surely you see what's happening? Do you imagine that we can't?" Officially it seemed that he could not acknowledge the obvious. Best to find St. Brygid's on my own, I decided, and walked off alone that afternoon in Gdansk, not having any sense of its location. I went up to anyone who looked friendly and said, "St. Brygid's?" Soon a young couple overheard me and walked me directly to the door, only a few blocks away from the market where we stood.

At St. Brygid's there was noticeable enthusiasm in the crowds of people going in and out of the church. Flags fluttered in the air, long strings of them suspended from the church spire to the ground like a country fair or Tibetan prayer flags. People milled around outside the entry, while inside the church the sale of Solidarity souvenirs went on briskly in the back. There I was able to get directions as to where I might find this Monsignor Jankowsky.

I went out of the church and around to the parish house and rang the bell, not knowing what to expect. Within moments I was ushered in to wait while the housekeeper found someone who could speak English. Someone came, we talked, I waited again, then some time later I was told that Jankowsky was in and would see me. Please be seated. More people came into the hallway. Within half an hour, I was ushered into a vistors' room as three men, smiling and shaking hands, walked out.

Monsignor Jankowsky was a large, portly man, with gold wire-rimmed glasses. He was not sure of the purpose of my visit as he motioned me to sit down in a large carved black wooden chair and sat down across from me, looking slightly puzzled. There were red and white carnations, the colors of the Polish flag, in the cut-glass vase on the black table where we sat. He asked me if I spoke German. No. He spoke very little English, so explaining my visit was difficult.

I pulled out pictures of the Madonna of Jasna Gora and the pilgrimage and he smiled, no words required. He understood something now. He bounced up, walked out of the room saying something in Polish, and soon returned with a young man who spoke English more fluently and could translate for us.

The new cabinet was to be announced that week. Everything was in a state of flux. There were talks of strikes everywhere, whether called by Walesa or not. Young workers were fed up. It was not clear that they would follow Walesa. The government made threatening statements about not allowing anarchy. Poland's mood was volatile.

Yes, Jankowsky promised me, I could speak with Walesa alone for fifteeen, perhaps twenty minutes, the following Thursday. It is agreed. Once the group tour is over I will somehow have to make the 700-kilometer round trip from Warsaw to Gdansk. The phones at the church were out of order and there was no indication of when they might be fixed. His translator ventured, "The government? Maybe they cut the phones off, maybe they just are broken. No way to know. No way to confirm the appointment. Just come." I thank the good Monsignor and his translator and take my leave. The hallway is full of people waiting to see Jankowsky.

The next morning we went to the Solidarity monument by the Lenin shipyards, built in memory of those who died in the strikes of the 1970s and 1980s. Formed in the turmoil of August 1980 as an expression of the cooperation between the steel mill workers and the shipyard workers, Solidarity was not just another political party.

To begin to understand Poland I had to learn something more about Solidarity and what set it apart from other political movements. No matter what would happen in the future, Solidarity had had an irreversible impact on the country and its rise was instructive. Jonathan Schell's essay on Solidarity and interview with one of its chief architects, Adam Michnik, is instructive.[2]

Solidarity's genius lay in its choice of nonviolence and the arena of everyday life in which to resist the authorities, Schell points out. Rather than resist the totalitarianism and repression of the Polish government with an equally violent response, Solidarity completely sidestepped the usual revolutionary process.

Michnik's finely honed philosophy was grounded in his own actions. Often he wrote from prison. The philosophy he articulated was direct and straightforward.

". . . start doing the things you think should be done, and start being what you think society should become. Do you believe in free speech? Then speak freely. Do you love the truth? Then tell it. Do you believe in an open society? Then act in the open. Do you believe in a decent and humane society? Then behave decently and humanely."

When KOR, the Workers Defense Committee and spearhead of the democratic opposition, was founded in 1976, members wrote a public statement of purpose to which they affixed their names, phone numbers, and addresses, an unheard-of action for the opposition of a totalitarian regime. Early on, KOR made openness, truthfulness, and trust a matter of policy. This was not naive idealism. In their political situation, with the danger of infiltration by informers and the secret police, they knew that fear and suspicion would destroy their movement. They chose trust, within the bounds of common sense, as a matter of public policy. This was the kind of building block out of which Solidarity was constructed.

Despite the declaration of martial law in Poland in 1982 and the banning of Solidarity, resistance continued and grew. When Michnik was released from prison in 1984, he found his dreams of a free people in Poland more than fulfilled, exceeded, he told Schell. Resistance and repression existed side by side. People were arrested but not intimidated. Poles refused to consider themselves defeated by the government, despite tremendous repression, and so they were not defeated. This affirmation of autonomy and decency in the face of repression seems to be key to the survival and to the future successes, whatever they might be, of Solidarity. This acting "as if" they were a free people, coupled with the strict discipline of nonviolence, helped bring Solidarity into its position of strength.

The policy of nonviolence also made it possible to have the support of the Church, Jankowsky told me, so crucial to the opposition's survival. The Madonna of Czestochowa had long symbolized the triumph of a free Polish spirit against all odds. A copy of the icon of the Black Madonna at Czestochowa circulated through villages in Poland during martial law but it sparked so much resistance that the authorities placed the painting under house arrest. More than a religious symbol, the Czestochowa Madonna is an archetype of freedom in the Polish psyche.

The sense of freedom here is building rapidly. In part, I feel freer being in Poland because I've been here before. Every single situation and person isn't unfamiliar. But the other part belongs to Poland. As the economic system and the government's authority continue to break down, something else opens up. Exhilaration, confusion, sorrow, frustration, excitement, exhaustion, relief, cynicism, and resignation, all mixed together, linger and fill the air.

I returned to Warsaw early the next morning.

◆

Professor Andrzej Wiercinski kindly received me in his office on the first day of classes for the fall semester, amidst the bustle of student conferences and scheduling changes. I make my way to his office hoping that, as an anthropologist at the University of Warsaw, he will tell me about pre-Christian use of the site of Jasna Gora.

Wiercinski is a man of medium height with wavy white hair and glasses. He wears a white coat like a physician. He tells me that he has not yet made a god of his health and smokes heavily, do I mind? I am in his office and feel that I can only say that I don't, but he is kind enough not to light up during our conversation and make me prove it.

He has no interest in the pre-Christian Slavic culture, he informs me bluntly when I ask him about the site of Jasna Gora. Slavic culture, he assures me, was very patriarchal. He is interested in Hinduism, in the Great Mother Goddess, he says, pulling down a translation of the *Hymns to the Goddess* from the Sanskrit off his bookshelf. I am thrust back on what I already know.

"She will ruin you if you devote yourself seriously to this problem," he says ruefully.

I do not know what he means by this remark. I have felt delivered rather than condemned by this pursuit. I know that I am in unmarked territory, at least for myself. I fit nowhere and everywhere. This is both liberating and disorienting. I begin to discover the depth of my need for approval, the desire to fit in, to be a part of, to belong, but I don't belong. I search for a label that I can grab onto but there isn't one.

Perhaps this is what Wiercinski meant: to seek and to worship these images of divinity, to claim the darkness as well as the light of the Buddha Tara, of Mary, of God the Mother, is to pit myself directly against Western culture, which would just as soon she was left out. But this is old thinking again, to see myself embattled, in conflict. My enemy is my own way of ignoring the authority of my own experience. There is not a person or an institution outside that I must fight, there is only my own thinking.

The dream of the Dalai Lama: no one can verify your experience for you, not the Dalai Lama, not the Pope, not all the professors, lamas, rinpoches, teachers, friends, family, or people one considers wise in the world. There is only the effort to be in relationship with what some might choose to call God.

"We live under the spell of the Great Mother," Wiercinski went on, pacing back and forth in front of the window in his office, the Warsaw sky outside gray and threatening.

"The material world is the female side of God, *mater*. The problem is that we don't recognize it, so we are consumed by it rather than nourished. We are under the spell of *mater*-iality; if we don't recognize this, we will be devoured."

Late that afternoon I went on to meet Professor Janusz Pasierb, who is a Catholic priest, and the art historian in charge of preserving the icon at Jasna Gora. Early for the appointment, I sit outside on a stone wall next to his apartment building, watching as the late afternoon light softens and pearls, casting a milky pink over the stone walls along this Warsaw street.

I had been directed to Pasierb by Professor Anna Iracka, an art historian with a special interest in folk art and roadside shrines of the Madonna. Over tea and cookies, she informed me that some art historians objected to the Madonna being called the Black Madonna, *Czarna* Madonna. I was completely surprised by this remark. She was dark, yes, she was dark brown. In black and white representations of her she was black, yes, but still, not everyone approved of this term, "Black Madonna."

Janusz Pasierb received me in his spacious book-lined apartment. Yes, he told me, Anna Iracka was correct, the expression "Black Madonna" is inaccurate. It is a recent turn of phrase, possibly sparked by the popularity of a song written by a nun in the sixties. He concedes that perhaps it became popular because it was a linguistic way to oppose the authorities, resistance grows subtle under totalitarianism, but still, it is an incorrect term, in his opinion. Black represents something negative in European culture, he tells me.

"She is not black, she is cosmic red, the color of blood, of life!

Cosmic red comes from the painter's intuition that as these figures descended from above the earth, they would have to burn through the atmosphere, thus the term 'cosmic red.' Cosmic red is actually a deep red-brown. Red in Byzantine art represented the fluid of life. Black was not used in icons."

Red. I was astonished to hear this description. There is something wonderful about it. The Black Madonna is cosmic red.

Mary, Star of Heaven, burning through the atmosphere, the descent fiery and glowing into the earth, now rising darkened, deep red-brown, some say scorched, black. Tara, Morning and Evening Star, growing out of the rock, colored brilliant blood red with *tika* powder.

Glowing and molten, the image shifts from black to dark earth brown-red. Black symbolizes the first stage of the alchemical process in the West; red, the crucial moment of transformation.

Tomorrow is the interview with Lech Walesa. Before we leave for Gdansk, I go to visit Dominik at the Pauline Monastery in Warsaw. We sit upstairs in a large receiving room. He has brought a copy that he painted himself of the famous Russian icon *Ikona Wlodzimierska* to show me, another Dark Madonna. I hadn't realized that Dominik is an accomplished painter. The copy is small in scale but beautiful. We open the large double windows to let in the afternoon sunlight so that I can see it fully. The lower windows are the color of amber and fairly glow with a kind of ancient, honeyed, autumnal light.

"The *Wlodzimierska* Madonna means to the Russians what the Madonna at Czestochowa means to the Poles."

Dominik had been allowed to be alone with the icon of the Madonna of Jasna Gora one day at Czestochowa. "Did I tell you about this?" he asked. "It was quite wonderful, really." The painting had been removed from the chapel for some restoration work and he was given permission to see it by himself for just a few minutes.

"Face to face, not somewhere up above. Yes, it was a very great experience, really. The picture is like the earth. Very strange, very old, like someone with a very old body with a lot of scars. You can see the ages on this picture. The picture was completely dark. I know from having studied it that in this certain place there should be green and in another place should be red, but it looked completely dark. Then the Father switched off the overhead light for the room and it was completely different, mysterious—the picture was light! The colors were very bright. It was wonderful.

"It is very difficult to tell you what it was like. It isn't a normal picture. It isn't just wood and paint and gesso. It is something else altogether. The painting isn't an 'it' but someone, do you understand me?

"But for that time I was surprised, I couldn't really pray, you know. I was only staying and looking, because for me, my presence was my prayer. I kept thinking I should be praying, maybe saying the 'Our Father,' but I was praying in my way.

"The pilgrimage we went on a year ago began on August 2, 1711. Twenty people took part, arriving in Czestochowa on August 14, 1711, two hundred seventy-seven years ago.

"The Warsaw pilgrimage used to be the most famous pilgrimage, but now that's changed. From all over Poland now, everywhere, people are walking, since 1978. Every group has the Solidarity banner. You saw. This way unofficially people are showing others and showing our government that Solidarity still exists, is alive in Poland, even though it is still outlawed. Solidarity is inside everyone who is really Polish, whoever is free inside and independent.

"Walesa has done this pilgrimage, too. Yes, Walesa started from his relationship with the Black Madonna, from God, for Solidarity. Every time he would go to Jasna Gora for a very important feast and pray to the Black Madonna.

"Ask Walesa about his relationship with the Black Madonna. For him, she is very important. Most people from abroad ask him only political things, but there is something else here in Poland, more than politics. In our nation there are not only political problems but spiritual problems. We have a war between the authorities and the life of the spirit.

"This prayer of Walesa, if I remember well, he made during martial law when he had been arrested. When he was in prison he always had the little badge of the Black Madonna with him. Afterwards he came to Jasna Gora. He gave to the Black Madonna a little plaque with a broken heart. He made the gift of the broken heart. He gave the Black Madonna his life, totally. His prayer was always 'My life is yours, you should be working in my life.'

"It was a very wonderful prayer of Lech Walesa. He gave his Nobel Prize [for peace] to the Madonna, it's in the monastery at Jasna Gora. He's a very famous person in Poland, but he didn't make the prayer for that reason. It's really his love for her and his spirit. It's a private matter of his life, not for show. He said this prayer in Jasna Gora and asked for her protection for our country.

"The portrait of the worker in the museum at Jasna Gora is Lech Walesa. You can see him with the little painting of the Black Madonna pinned over his heart. He wears it to this day."

We leave Warsaw for Gdansk just after dark. It is 350 kilometers each way. Our taxi driver has brought delicious little cakes from Blikle, the oldest bakery in Warsaw, founded in 1869. "Sweet ones for you, *pani,* and salty ones for the men."

Tomasz Sikorski, the friend who accompanies me, is a painter I had met in Warsaw after the pilgrimage. One of my favorites is his "Black Madonna and Child Fleeing Warsaw," done in 1982, during martial law. A tall, blond man with an attractive, angular face, Tomasz has a capacity for optimism unusual for anyone, much less Poles, who seem characteristically more inclined toward irony. Soon he will be coming to the States to marry a woman he met while teaching.

After the first hour of the drive, we are quiet. It's well after dark, nearly eight o'clock. I fall asleep despite being bounced around, and wake up not long before we arrive in Gdansk at eleven o'clock.

Bogdan, the driver, delivers us to a friend of Ewa Osiantinski's who has generously opened her home to us. She has waited up for us and insists upon spreading a full dinner over our useless protests. In moments she is opening up tins of meat and fish, slicing tomatoes, cheese, bread, setting out butter and tea on the table. I eat three sardines, some bread and cheese, and have to say goodnight.

October 13, 1988

We visit the archeological museum in the old city. Suddenly it is nearly time to be at St. Brygid's and I still want to buy flowers for Walesa. We dash out to Bogdan, asleep in the taxi parked off the square. In Poland flowers are given at every occasion: from women to women, men to women, women to men, it is the custom.

"Wait here, then we'll drive to the church," Tomasz explains quickly in Polish, as he bends over, leaning into the cab. Walking quickly to a nearby flower stand, I buy red and white roses, a dozen, six of each, the colors of the Polish flag.

We drive into the parking lot at St. Brygid's. Bogdan insists on staying with the car. It is illegal for him to have driven his taxi to Gdansk. He is nervous since he is obviously not a local. *Warzsawa* is painted on the doors of his bright yellow taxi. We are right on time for the interview at one-thirty.

We are walking across the courtyard to the parish house when Walesa himself drives into the courtyard alone, at the wheel of a new gray VW van. He gets out, a short man with a gray mustache, sandy brown hair, dusty black shoes, a blue shirt, and gray pants, and is about to go into the parish house when I walk up to him to give him the bouquet of roses. He is used to receiving flowers from strangers, smiles politely, thanks me in Polish, and hurries inside. By the time we make it through the small group that has gathered inside the hallway waiting for him, Walesa has disappeared into a meeting room with Jankowsky and others. We wait. Soon it is 1:45 p.m., past time for the meeting.

Just then Jankowsky's translator bursts through the front door and finds me. "I'm very sorry to be late. Let me find Monsignor," he says as he walks past, and he too disappears into the meeting room. Moments later he comes out.

"It is impossible today. He cannot see you now. Impossible. The government. They just announced the new cabinet today. In Warsaw. Come to the press conference he's giving at two o'clock in the church tower. Go around to the back. You'll have time with him there. It's the best we can do. Sorry," he says sweetly, and dashes off.

I imagined trying to get a word in edgewise between the various wire services and newspapers' seasoned and aggressive reporters, or jostling for space with television crews. I am startled at the idea of having to ask questions about the Madonna in public.

At two o'clock sharp, Walesa comes out of a meeting in the parish hall and strides quickly across the courtyard to the church. A group of us follow, up the narrow circular staircase into a room in the tower. There are nearly thirty of us in the room with him, once everyone is seated. He sits with his translator in front, the eagle of Poland patterned on the wallpaper behind him. No television crews, to my relief, no radio, few reporters. I don't know who the other people are. His translator announces a few ground rules, asks how many of us he must translate for, and then Walesa is open to questions. The room is quiet.

Will there be more strikes, what is his response to Rakowski's cabinet appointments, what will happen to Poland?—these are the questions of the moment. My question about his relationship with the Madonna seems small and abstract in comparison, yet no one else will ask it. She is not a "news" subject. Whether Walesa speaks to this or not, it is clear from my conversations with Father Dominik and Monsignor Jankowsky that his relationship with the Madonna, indeed, Solidarity's relationship with her, has a great deal to do with the events unfolding in Poland. How to get to this level of discussion will be difficult now, if not impossible. Still, I must try. Finally I raise my hand. "Would Mr. Walesa speak about his relationship and Solidarity's to the Madonna?"

Contrary to Jankowsky and Dominik's comments, Walesa lets me know immediately that his relationship with the Madonna is a personal affair and has nothing to do with the movement. But they are priests, Walesa is a politician. The question puts him on the defensive. He points out that Solidarity has many members who are not believers or who belong to other faiths.

"We are very pluralistic in our organization and we are not oriented by what religion you are or are not as far as trade unions are concerned. This is a separate, private matter.

"The badge I wear with her image was given to me by Cardinal Wyszynski during the Polish workers' pilgrimage to Jasna Gora. I was very happy because of this and I have worn it ever since. It's a very long story and a complicated issue," he assures me, at the same time letting me know that he is not going to go into it.

For a moment I am disappointed. This "complicated issue" is precisely what I had wanted to hear him talk about. Here is one of the most internationally significant political movements of the century, a nonviolent revolution, and unbeknownst to most people outside of Poland it grew and survived precisely because it was nonviolent and, because for many, though not everyone, it had a spiritual dimension. The Church provided a bulwark of freedom and has been a safe harbor for much of the underground press, the intelligentsia, the arts, Solidarity, and all manner of resistance to the authorities.

What is happening in Poland is tremendous, its significance extends far beyond its borders, one can know this, being here. Naively I want him to acknowledge that the Madonna has something to do with this wave of freedom that's building. But Walesa is not Gandhi, nor Martin Luther King, Jr., nor the Dalai Lama. He stays on the political side of the intersection he occupies and only alludes to what I had hoped to explore. Yet on balance he is wise and correct to do so. The intersection of politics and religion is also occupied by fanatics.

Lech Walesa, Gdansk, Poland. (Author)

It is a dangerous place. With Poland's history of anti-Semitism, Walesa and Solidarity follow a prudent course in keeping the relationship of the Madonna and Solidarity separate, so that Solidarity doesn't become too closely aligned with the Catholic Church.

"Poland cannot be understood without the issue of the cross and belief," he says now. "Many times, especially in very difficult periods, Poland was saved by the Church and the Polish nation was much better off because it was a nation of believers. We believe in miracles and that makes people heroes. Sometimes *only* a belief in miracles led us to survive—especially at the very crucial points of our history in the fight for independence. We go to the Madonna and beg her to help us when something is very important for us."

Walesa gesticulates strongly with both hands as he talks. He's an emphatic speaker. Clever, diplomatic, cheerful, so energetic that he has a quality today of nearly bursting. More questions about strikes and *perestroika* follow, his voice rising with feeling and excitement, his words tumbling out faster and faster. Again and again I discern the words for pluralism, revolution, reform, individualism, effective economic reform. I don't need Polish to understand Solidarity's demands.

"The situation in Poland is particularly difficult, there is a climate for strikes," he explains. "We are very much afraid. So far we have been saved from explosions, but people's patience is strained. It may not be possible for this situation to continue. The talks may go well, but afterwards is unknown. We are not trying to take over the government. It is a dangerous moment. Our problems will not go away overnight. We hope that our Madonna will help us to survive."

After the press conference, Bogdan, our driver, is anxious for us to leave. His wife is worried about the long drive and he himself is nervous because two strange men were in the parking lot taking down all the license numbers of the cars there, noting the time of entry and departure from the church's parking lot while Tomasz and I were at the press conference. He tells us he is afraid that they are the secret police and that tomorrow they will telephone him in Warsaw or call him in. They will want to know who we were and what we were doing. I try to reassure him. "Tell them whatever you like," there is nothing for him to hide. The fear of the authorities is a plague. I too have had it. Everyone becomes captive in the dance.

"We should feel sorry for them," Tomasz says. "What a terrible job, taking down license plate numbers!" Suddenly Tomasz and Bogdan are caught up in a heated discussion in Polish that continues off and on until well into the night.

Should one pay attention to the authorities or simply ignore them, regardless of their threats and posturing? Bogdan is married, with three children. He is subject to losing his livelihood if he has a run-in with the police. He evidently despises the authorities. He tells us that many taxi drivers have become informants, especially the drivers who work the big hotels and airports. Not that they want to be informants, but they are often required to report to the police in exchange for their license to operate. So, to avoid being drawn into this situation, Bogdan drives his taxi illegally and doesn't take fares from the airport or the big hotels. Being tracked down from this trip to Gdansk could endanger his situation. But I had American dollars and could pay him good money. He hadn't counted on being noticed by the police in Gdansk. Now there is nothing to be done.

By the time we eat and drive out of Gdansk for Warsaw, it's twilight. There is a low-lying fog over the countryside, the trees look like lace against the falling light. Ground fog obscures the trunks and the tops appear to float across the landscape above the ground as we hurtle past.

It is nearly two hours now since Tomasz and Bogdan began their discussion in Polish. They are so passionate, Tomasz no longer stops to translate. I don't know what they are talking about. I wouldn't be surprised if Bogdan stopped the car at any moment and they came to blows, their discussion is so heated. Tomasz has leaned over the front seat from his place in the back, Bogdan keeps his eyes on the road, but the conversation is excited, their voices louder, more emphatic. Now it is completely dark. There are no lights on the road. I grow more and more anxious traveling at such high speed with the two of them going at each other with such intensity. Suddenly a villager on a bicycle looms in the headlights, then a tractor with no lights shows up lumbering along the road at 20 kilometers while we bear down at 100 with a truck coming toward us on the other side.

I can't look. Leaning my head back into the rear-window well, I say the beads that I've unwound from my wrist over and over as fast as I can.

Before we get into Warsaw, the conversation stops. Tomasz explains that their discussion was strictly philosophical, they were not angry, they had different points of view as to how one is to live in a country like Poland. They have learned something from each other, he says. Tomasz has been arguing for what I later recognized as one of the keys to Solidarity's success—acting *as if* one is free, whether the government says so or not.

"One must refuse to be intimidated by the regime at all costs," he said. "If they want to listen in on telephone calls, open your mail, find out where you've been and with whom—let them! Do not hide. To hide is to be the mouse to their cat. One must simply step into another world altogether and refuse to be afraid, regardless of threats. It is the only way out."

CHAPTER 16

The Mystery of the Messages

•

Medjugorje, Yugoslavia

Moses and the Shepherd
[God speaking to Moses]

I have given each being a separate and unique way of seeing and knowing and saying that knowledge.

What seems wrong to you is right for him.
What is poison to one is honey to someone else. . . .

I am apart from all that. Ways of worshipping are not to be ranked as better or worse than one another.

—Rumi[1]

On the Way to Medjugorje
October 1988

It was nearly midnight by the time I got back to Ewa's from Gdansk. There was only time for three hours' sleep, then the waking up in the dark to finish packing and be ready for a 5:00 a.m. taxi. I would sleep on the plane to Yugoslavia.

My destination was the tiny village of Medjugorje, in western Herzegovina, where Mary was reported to be appearing daily to a group of young people. The appearances had been occurring since 1981. I hoped to meet one of the visionaries who had been seeing Mary.

Though I had first heard of the events at Medjugorje in Switzerland two years earlier, I was not inclined to go. The description reminded me of afternoon movies of Lourdes and Fatima, shown by the nuns in their heavy starched collars at Ursuline Academy during thunderstorms when we were forced to stay inside. But after the experiences in Poland and Texas, I felt less biased, more open and willing to look. Time was running out. Two of the original group of six young people no longer saw her.

Janusz the taxi driver knocked softly on the apartment door precisely at five o'clock. I was almost ready. Ewa poured a cup of tea for me which I hurriedly finished as Janusz gathered the luggage. The bulging camera and recorder bag went over my shoulder; Ewa kissed me goodbye on each cheek, then once again, Polish-style; Janusz picked up my duffel and we were off.

Janusz spoke a little English.

"Don't worry," he said, as we drove out the boulevard of linden trees to the airport, "the borders, Yugoslavia closed maybe, but is okay. You come back to Poland.

"Rakowski said the government will talk with Walesa, but not to forget, the government strong is, has the military. Not anarchy like before, he is saying, government will not stand for it."

There were no English-language newspapers available in Poland, so I had little information about what's going on in the rest of the world. Though civil war was rumored in Yugoslavia, their economy had gotten a tremendous boost from pilgrims going to Medjugorje, over 11 million so far. Medjugorje would probably be one place in the country that people would continue to be able to get to, no matter what happened politically.

On the flight out of Frankfurt to Dubrovnik there were groups of Western pilgrims going to Medjugorje with plastic name tags pinned to their clothes. I was full of questions. I didn't know how to get to Medjugorje nor had I been able to reserve a room in advance. I had the name of a family that takes in boarders from a friend who stayed with them two years ago, but I had not been able to reach them.

I introduced myself to a woman behind me who was a tour leader, hoping to ask her how to get to Medjugorje from Dubrovnik.

"No English," she says in a thick German accent, then laughs. She is from the States—but she does not offer her name or any information, instead telling me that I will be able to get information at the airport in Dubrovnik.

We stop in Budapest for nearly an hour. The plane sits on the ground away from the terminal and I am allowed to stand at the bottom of the steps, but can go no further. An armed guard stands at the end of the gangplank, as in Poland. In the Eastern bloc, soldiers have become an unobtrusive part of the landscape until moments like this. It has been a long day of traveling and sitting, sitting, sitting. I need to go for a walk, but I have no way to communicate, so I stay put.

The day is mild, with high winds that wrap me in their sounds, drowning out all noise. I stand buffeted on the bottom step, realizing that I'm homesick. A flight to San Francisco was being called in Frankfurt just as I was finding my gate for Yugoslavia. I wish that I was on it. The coolness of my fellow pilgrims reminds me of what it's like to be a stranger. Another pilgrimage has begun. Anonymity and loneliness are part of it.

By the time we land at the airport in Dubrovnik, other pilgrims on the flight have befriended me and the sense of isolation has eased. A couple from Tennessee struck up a conversation with me while waiting in the customs line. When I discover that there is no bus from the airport and the local taxi driver wants $180 to drive me, one way, I turn to the tour group and ask if I can pay my way in their chartered bus. The leader is friendly now, yes, there is room. Twenty dollars will be enough.

As we pull away from the airport, I ask the Yugoslavian guide aboard how to find housing in the village. I show him the card with the name of the family I was told to stay with and he begins laughing: it's his aunt whose name I have in my hand. She lives next door to him. He will take me there himself once he has deposited the tour group at their respective houses.

We wind up the coast along the Adriatic Sea in the late afternoon light. There are palm trees, hot pink and purple bougainvillea, wild olives, tall, thin dark green cedars-of-Lebanon, lemon trees, pink and white oleanders, deep and leafy arbors overhung with grapevines in front of homes overlooking the sea. Sycamore trees, pines, roses, neatly tended vegetable gardens line the drive. The limestone hills reach down to the sea, the water turns pink, the limestone rocks take on a pale rose touched with the faintness of gold. The warm light turns to a cool blue and finally darkens to red-purple in the falling light of sunset. Only two more hours to Medjugorje.

From the bus after dark, the road still hugging the sea, I glimpse a small wooden fishing boat anchored out with a lantern hung from a wooden pole over the water. A lone fisherman holds his line taut in the translucent lime green water that gleams like a glittering stone in the inky sea.

The light in the water is radiant, seeing it inexplicably buoys me with hope. We rarely know who or what we are to one another. The fisherman will never know how he affected a passing stranger. The light blue boat rocked gently in the back of my mind, floating into the last moment of dusk as the thinnest crescent moon hung low and silvered above the blue-black sea. Beyond his small circle of light was only the dark. Gray pearls were strung along the shore wherever there was a village. Light.

A priest traveling with the group leads everyone in the rosary. The bus is quiet but for the chanting of prayers and I am glad to be with pilgrims again. Dragan, the Yugoslavian guide, tells us a little of the history of the apparitions at Medjugorje and the lives of the visionaries.

Mary first appeared to six peasant children on Podbrdo Hill— known as Apparition Hill—on June 24, 1981. She has continued to appear daily since then to them, though now only four still see her.

Two have received whatever messages she was to give them and have gone on with their lives. Four continue to see her, every day, at least once, at 5:40 p.m. sharp, in the choir loft of the village church.

Witska, one of the visionaries, says that the basic message is to pray, more and more. Dragan assures us that the visionaries and their families are, in his eyes, legitimate. He too is from Medjugorje and has known the visionaries since childhood, long before Mary's appearance.

"It's a very hard life they have," he tells us; "there is no material gain involved. The visionaries have no privacy whatsoever. People are coming from all over the world. Sometimes people don't even knock on their door, they just walk into their homes to see them. Please have consideration for them.

"Mary's appearance may be explained like this. When children want something, they go to their mother. When children are in trouble, their mother goes to them. She is our Mother, she is concerned for us. The world is in trouble. She brings a message of love and of hope. She asks for peace and reconciliation. We must pray and listen to her."

Is Mary appearing in Medjugorje, is Tara growing out of the rock in Pharping? My mind balks. I pray for an open heart and the willingness to look.

The sky is gray, the air cool on my face the next morning as I make my way into the village to the church, three miles from where I am staying with Dragan's aunt and her family.

The English speakers' mass is going on when I arrive at the church, packed with over two thousand people. At least one thousand more stand and kneel outside, following the service over loudspeakers. Services go on in a variety of languages during the day. In the evening the mass is in Croatian, the villagers' mass. Inside the church, people are standing and sitting everywhere. Every inch of space is taken, including the bare floor, making it very difficult to move.

After mass I go toward the parish house to find one of the priests. I am told that I must speak with Father Slavko in order to meet the visionaries. Though Father Slavko is not in, I am fortunate enough to meet a woman who helps take care of Marija Pavlović, another of the visionaries as well as the woman who is Father Slavko's assistant. Father Slavko is the gatekeeper; he decides who can and cannot be in the choir loft with the visionaries when Mary appears at 5:40 p.m. A handful of people, about ten, are allowed in with them each evening.

I am invited to meet Marija and told to come to her house by 2:00 p.m. Marija's helper and I walk a mile or so through the open fields, stopping to pick fresh tomatoes and peppers for Marija's supper.

When we arrive, Marija is on the front steps talking to at least two hundred or so pilgrims who have gathered outside her house to hear about the messages from Mary. There is no way to get through the crowd. I decide to walk up Podbrdo Hill instead where Mary first appeared to the children, just behind Marija's house.

The hill is similar to the one I walk at home, but rockier. It takes perhaps twenty minutes to reach the top, depending on how often one stops. There is a constant stream of people going up and down, sharing the path with goats and an occasional vendor.

Within an hour I am back at Marija's. I've been shown into the living room to wait. Another group of pilgrims has arrived just after me and she has gone out to pray with them and answer people's questions about the Madonna, again. Meeting with groups of pilgrims goes on each day and is a large part of Marija's life. I glimpse what Dragan meant about the lack of privacy and the difficulty of their lives.

Marija Pavlović is a pleasant young woman with an easy, good-natured smile, despite the constant swirl of people around her. She is tall and thin, with large warm brown eyes, short curly brown hair, and wears a pair of khaki slacks and blouse. She lives in her family's home, comfortably and simply. Her lifestyle has not changed because of the apparitions. Another day, I found her taking out the garbage in a large pail. Her mother was tending the cow. Marija has not an ounce of pretension.

There are three or four others in the living room with me where she asks me to wait. Two more people are busy cooking in the kitchen. A large, opulent woman from Rome sits at the other end of the couch from me. She wears rhinestone-studded eye glasses and a large tortoise-shell and rhinestone comb in her hair.

The man in the chair next to me is a friendly American, Terry Colafrancesco, from Alabama, who has been here over a dozen times. In his mid-thirties, visiting with one of his young children, he offers to be helpful in whatever way he can. He is an enthusiastic believer in the reality of the Virgin's appearances at Medjugorje.

"Medjugorje is a new Bethlehem, if you ask me. Even up to my seventh trip here, if someone had said what I'm about to say to you, I'd tell them they were crazy. But this is my fourteenth time here and I'm beginning to understand what is really going on, underneath the surface.

"Medjugorje is going to go down in history with Noah and the Flood, with the Flight out of Egypt, maybe even the birth of Christ! It's an event of that magnitude," he tells me in his soft Alabama drawl.

"Mary's practically living here, she comes here every day. The fact that she's coming and that she's been coming every day for over seven years is a strong message in itself. Our Lady's been so hidden in the scriptures, I think that this age is being given to Mary, this is her time."

I am taken aback by the depth of his enthusiasm. I have no reply and can only respond with a long "Hmmmm."

I had to think back over my decision to come here. What made me curious about Medjugorje was the ecumenical nature of Mary's message. Brendan O'Reagan, a neurochemist working on a documentary series for public television called "The Healing Mind," told me about his trip to Medjugorje to examine medical records of cases claimed to be "miraculous" healings.[2] It was Brendan's talk with Ivan, one of the visionaries, that finally piqued my interest enough to come. According to Brendan, Mary was calling people to a life of the spirit, not necessarily to become Catholics. Not only had the Yugoslavian government been disturbed by the events at Medjugorje, so had the Catholic Church. Many were put off by Mary's insistence on respect for all religions; further, there had been a bitter controversy between the local bishop and the parish priests as to whether or not to believe the young people.

I asked Terry if what I had been told of Mary's message was his understanding—a call to a life of the spirit, not to a specific religion. His answer, like much of what I was told and would later learn about Medjugorje, was mixed. Yes and no.

A Frenchman, Cyril Auboyneau, sitting across the room from us, joined in the conversation. Refined, witty, a slender man in his early forties, he had been living in Medjugorje for four years. He was very familiar with the visionaries, the messages, and the ongoing events at Medjugorje. He also spoke Croatian, the native tongue in the village, and often served as a translator for Father Jozo Zavko, the Franciscan priest who first believed the children and spent eighteen months in a Yugoslavian prison for doing so. Despite the orders of the authorities, Father Jozo refused to close the church to the thousands of people who immediately began streaming to Medjugorje. Civil authorities feared revolutionary plots, church authorities feared challenges to power.

While we waited for Marija, Terry and Cyril told me more about the messages of Mary at Medjugorje. Cyril reviewed the ones that he felt were the most important.

The conversation reminded me of some of the talks with Tibetan lamas and friends in Buddhist practice. Mary's existence, like that of the Tibetan deities, was spoken of with as much confidence as we have in our perception of the person sitting next to us. There is no question about their reality. Both Mary and Jesus were included in conversations at Medjugorje as though they were relatives coming to visit, or someone who had just stepped into the next room.

For those who believe, the kind of intellectual distance that I might hold does not exist. Being in Medjugorje was something like the experience of being in Kathmandu or Dharamsala, or being with pilgrims in Poland. This is the landscape of belief. I enjoyed the stories people told, their complete confidence in Mary, whether I could share their devotion or not.

"The main message is to pray, pray, pray," Cyril assured me, "pray to be enlightened by the Holy Spirit, pray for an outpouring of the Holy Spirit, for when you have the Holy Spirit, you have everything.

"Perhaps her most important message up to this time," he continued, "was given in August 1984. Our Lady asked that people pray and say the rosary every day; fast on Wednesdays and Fridays, preferably on bread and water; read the Bible every day and meditate; don't just attend the mass, live it. Live the mystery of the mass, live the mystery of the Redemption. And go to confession once a month. These are five things Our Lady asks of us."

This is where I get confused about Medjugorje. It sounds as though one has to be a Catholic to respond to Mary's messages. When I asked Cyril about this, he gave me what I later realized was the wisest reply, "The messages are a mystery. One must pray to come to understand them."

Prayer, fasting, and reconciliation are traditional spiritual practices widely used throughout the world, not limited by belief. This I could easily grasp. Perhaps it is the language of the Church of Rome in which the messages come clothed that puts me off, not the messages themselves.

"Our Lady wants us to pray as a family and to read the Bible every day," Cyril said. "She wants us to have togetherness in prayer and communion, brotherhood, and love. Since July 1986, many messages have been about holiness. She said that we cannot live without holiness. Holiness means to overcome all sin with love, to overcome all difficulties with love. She said that God has given us the gift of holiness.

"In 1987, Our Lady talked to the visionaries about saving the world through Medjugorje. She encouraged them to pray more to understand God's plan to use them as a tool to save the world."

Central to the idea of saving the world is the premise that it is on the verge of destruction. There is an apocalyptic overtone at Medjugorje that gives me pause. I wanted to ask more about this but now Marija has time to talk. Just as we sit down at the table a woman walks up slowly to the doorway, accompanied by friends who help her stand just inside. They are very excited. She wants to tell Marija the story of her healing. "It was a miracle!" they exclaim. Can I please wait a little longer? We draw chairs around the table to listen.

She is a woman named Nada, in her forties. She wears dark glasses, taking them off as she sits down. Through a combination of disease and complications from a serious car accident, she had been confined to a wheelchair, unable to walk, for nearly the last fifteen years of her life.

She tells her story in a simple, moving way. Her hands shake as she speaks. Her healing has only just happened yesterday. She was in the church, at mass, when the priest said, "There is someone in a wheelchair here who will now stand up and walk."

Suddenly she found herself on her feet. She rises to her feet, trembling as she tells this story. I feel a surge of excitement as she stands up. Is this a miracle, or the power of suggestion? Was her illness psychosomatic? There is no way to know which, if any, it is. There is no objective context.

They tell us that no one could believe that Nada was standing, much less walking to the altar. Her family and friends with her in the church began to weep. Today is her first real "walk." She has just gone up Podbrdo, Apparition Hill, to the top and back down here to Marija's house. Her face is flushed.

By the time Nada finishes her story it is too late to speak with Marija. She needs to rest briefly before the afternoon apparition. We put off our talk again until tomorrow.

October 16, 1988

The weather is beautiful this morning. The sky is a crisp, clear, cool blue. Women in elaborate traditional black and white Croatian ethnic dress arrive for Sunday mass, weaving in and out of the crowds of tourists and peasants in their simpler dress. I am determined to walk up Podbrdo Hill with only my rosary and candles to leave burning like the other pilgrims. I will take no camera for photographs, no money for gifts along the way; no decisions to make. I am exhilarated!

The soil is deep red in this rocky limestone country. The older houses are fitted together of cream-colored limestone rocks, the newer ones are whitewashed and of simpler construction. Shiny yellow squashes and ochre pumpkins lie in the fields; green and red peppers are ripe now for picking. Grapevines, climber roses, morning glory vines—pink and blue flowered—abound. Cows low, tethered here and there in scattered fields. The paths worn by peasants and pilgrims are shot through with the white of limestone polished by footsteps breaking through the dark brown brick red, cosmic red soil. Just before I reach the bottom of the hill, I pass a woman carrying a large round pan full of uncooked bread dough in her hands.

On the hill, I stop at the first cross placed where Mary first appeared to the children. I bow low, my head to the earth, light a candle, and leave it burning on the pile of rocks with other candles. I write the names of family and friends on the back of the wooden cross as others do for a blessing. At the top of the hill, I stop again, bow low, light a candle, placing it on a rockpile covered with hundreds of candles, some still burning, some melted down, the rock blackened. I find a place on a suitable rock to sit down and be quiet.

Hundreds of people mill about on this rocky hillside, speaking softly, sometimes not speaking at all. Instinctively people leave each other alone. Some kneel in prayer, others sit with their eyes closed, some are weeping, some stand looking out over the valley, others simply stare. Occasionally someone is insensitive to the mood and arrives at the top huffing and talking at the top of their voice, but the reflective mood is inescapable and soon they too are quiet. Cameras click and whirr, different languages drift across the air. People come and go, helping each other along the rocky way: elderly people, people with canes. Some are crippled, but still they come with their crutches. Goats wander up and down, looking for garbage. Candle wax runs all over the rocks, many blackened and charred from the burnings. It is peaceful on Podbrdo Hill, overlooking the valley, the church, the fields of vegetables, grapes, and tobacco.

I have been granted permission to be in the choir loft with the visionaries this evening when the apparition appears. I pray that all judgments and defenses be removed, that I am able simply to be present.

Many people are profoundly moved by Medjugorje; some describe it as a conversion experience. Sitting on top of this hill I remember the *converso*, the heart-turning experience I had with Chos Kyi Nyima in Nepal after my first Tara initiation. And though I may not become a convert as some do at Medjugorje, I have had similar enough experiences to have an abiding respect for people's feelings here.

Overlooking this valley, thinking about Mary and Tara, I recall a prayer to Tara which I love.[3] In it she is said to come in whatever form a person needs her to assume in order for her to be helpful. True compassion. Buddha Tara, indeed all the Buddhas, are said to emanate in billions of forms, taking whatever form is necessary to suit the person. Who can say that Mary isn't Tara appearing in a form that is useful and recognizable to the West? When the Venerable Tara Tulku came to Green Gulch a few months ago, we spoke of this. From the Buddhist perspective, one cannot say that this isn't possible, he assured me. "If there is a person who says definitely no, the Madonna is not an emanation of Tara, then that person has not understood the teachings of the Buddha." Christ could be an emanation of the Buddha. I am comforted remembering this. This is not to say that Mary *is* Tara or that Christ *is* Buddha. Buddhism gives me a different context, another way to reflect upon this experience. Such thinking gives me room, provides spaciousness. I draw no conclusions.

Whether Mary is appearing in the choir loft this afternoon or Tara, whether anything or anyone is actually appearing, may never be known. Some think it's fabrication and dismiss it altogether. I know only that sitting here on this hilltop on a rock, the sun warm on my face, I am comforted by the outrageous notion underneath it all—that heaven cares—whether we understand, believe, or not.

When I come down from Podbrdo Hill, I see the young woman with the round bread pan again, returning from a neighbor's where she's been baking. The odor of freshly baked bread sweetens the air as we pass.

I go back to Marija's as planned, but there are too many pilgrims outside clamoring to see her today. She cannot talk now. People have come from many of the neighboring towns and villages for Sunday mass, as well as the usual crush of tourists from around the world to see the visionaries. We make plans for tomorrow morning and I go off alone into the fields and vineyards, Marija to her room to rest before the apparition.

Birds warble cheerfully, crickets sing in the grass, children's voices float across the field, cows low, there's a faint sound of a radio in the distance and a rumble of cars, but mostly it is peaceful here out in the middle of this vineyard. I spread out a poncho on the ground and sit down under a large oak. In an hour I have to be at the church, by the belltower, in order to meet Father Slavko and to be admitted to the choir loft with the visionaries. There is little time to rest. I could have slept for a good two hours. I want to do a watercolor of this vineyard. I want to sit and do nothing. I must remember to allow twenty mintes to get to the church from the fields; that leaves twenty minutes to rest and twenty minutes to paint. I set my alarm.

I begin to feel frantic. Tension races up the back of my neck, my lower back pangs and tightens, I catch myself holding my breath. This is not the way to prepare for the apparition. Stop. Take a breath. Take refuge in the present moment.

For a while I sit quietly in the mild warm weather and do nothing. The grapevines in front of me are turning red, the light behind them sets them on fire. Then I pull out my watercolors and begin to paint. Soon I am lost in trying to mix colors like the ones in front of me. Though I can rarely, if ever, match a color, this effort gives me a deep and satisfying pleasure. I am happily defeated by trying to paint a tiny faint gold line around the edge of the burnished copper red, brown, and vermilion leaves, backlit by the sun. It is a kind of giving up that I don't mind. I lie back and give my weariness to the ground.

At 4:45 p.m. sharp, I meet Father Slavko at the doorway to the choir loft. By 5:00 p.m. I'm inside the church at the top of the stairs outside the apparition room—choir loft. Three men are standing in the stairwell saying a rosary and I join them. Minutes later, someone signals us to go in and take our places. Now I am in the choir loft alternately praying and mentally taking in every detail that I can. I want to memorize this picture, the white walls of the choir loft, the large painting of Mary at one end of the room, the folding chairs. Ivan Dragicević, another of the visionaries, sits in the doorway, wearing black slacks, a checked sports coat, and black tie. It is the first time I've seen Ivan. He's an attractive, black-haired, fair-skinned, clean-shaven, medium-height-and-build, utterly normal-looking young man in his early twenties.

I find a brown leather kneeler to sit on next to a man who is filming for local television in Atlanta. Since the choir loft is visible to people inside the church below, we have been asked not to make ourselves visible. We are told not to stand up or to walk upright if at all possible. One must hunker down and move quickly from position to position. We speak in whispers. The cameraman and I are motioned to where we will be facing the visionaries as they pray, off to one side, maybe ten feet away. The apparition appears in front of the painting of Mary, before which the visionaries will kneel and pray.

The man from Atlanta has been in the choir loft before and is more relaxed. Father Slavko has asked me to photograph the visionaries during the apparition. I nervously check the camera, get a light reading, then the cameraman leans over and asks me what speed of film I have in the camera. "Too fast," he informs me, "won't work. All the lights are switched on when the visionaries come in. It won't be this dark." I dig into my camera bag, hold up a roll that he glances at and nods, yes, it would be suitable, and reload. How much time do I have? Done. I try to calm myself again and focus on breathing. There are still a few minutes before the apparition will start. Being in a choir loft in Yugoslavia waiting for Mary to appear seems very strange, and at the same time, perfectly natural.

The cameraman and I are up in front by a chest below the painting of Mary. He explains that the half-dozen large plastic bags sitting next to the chest are full of petitions to Mary from people all over the world. There are two plastic rose bushes on the chest, some slightly dust-covered pink and blue silk imitation flowers, and more little piles of letters of petition.

"Quick," the cameraman advises, "if you have any pictures of your family with you, write a prayer for that person on the back of their picture and put it on the table with the other petitions."

I always carry a packet of pictures of family, friends, and teachers when I travel; luckily it's in the camera bag, side pocket. I pull it out. There may be thirty pictures. I quickly thumb through to see who's there and to think of what I would wish for that person. There is no time to go through the entire stack. I scrawl something quickly on the backs of my children's and husband's photos. Luckily I find a group shot of my entire family in Texas; that takes care of about forty people at once. Would my brother laugh at me or care? Which friends? Definitely Father Dominik. What about the pictures of my

Tibetan teachers and the Dalai Lama? No time for decisions. I put them all back in the pouch they're carried in and put the pouch with every one of them in it on the chest, just under where I calculate Mary's feet will be.

Below us people inside the church are saying the rosary, people outside are saying the rosary. One plastic bag full of prayers says "Personally Yours." Through the doorway stacked over six feet high in the corner of the stairwell, I see extra-large gray garbage bags piled full of more petitions. Camera flashes are going off below. There are perhaps ten of us in the fading light of the choir loft. It's nearly time.

Suddenly the lights are switched on. Marija walks in. She and Ivan are the only two visionaries who will be in the choir loft this afternoon. Marija wears a blue and white-striped sweater and a blue skirt. Looking neither left nor right, they go directly to their places in front of the painting, kneel down on the floor, and begin to pray. Those of us in the loft kneel down with them. The television camera whirrs softly.

Marija and Ivan are praying out loud at first, softly, I can hear them, then I feel a clammy heat sweep through me and I no longer hear them. They are looking up, intently, at what appears to be the same spot in the air. Then their lips stop moving. They nod their heads as though indicating that they understand something that's just been said to them. Ivan seems to ask a question, but no words are uttered out loud. Marija nods. I take a picture quickly, but don't want to be distracted. Something clearly has come over them, though I cannot see or even sense anything of what is going on for them. In this moment I have no doubt that they are seeing Mary. I am present for—and very close to—a remarkable event, and I give thanks. I put the camera down on the floor next to me and bow low, touching my forehead to the floor out of respect, then kneel quietly with them until the apparition is over, perhaps five minutes later. Then they make the sign of the cross, stand up, return to themselves and begin to leave.

Marija and Ivan stand by the doorway talking softly. I move around to just behind where they were kneeling to take a picture of the painting of Mary. A Japanese man sits there openly weeping. I put my hand on his shoulder to reassure him that all is well and I am suddenly aware of how happy I feel, light and joyful.

Then the lights are turned off and Ivan signals to us that we must leave. I zip the camera into my bag, take the packet of photographs off the chest, and file into line to descend the spiral metal stairs of the tower. Ivan and Marija step aside, letting those of us who were with them in the loft file out first into the early evening.

I am caught off guard when my turn comes to walk out. There is a very large crowd waiting. Now I see why Marija and Ivan wanted others to go first. We must walk through a gauntlet of people ten deep on either side and over fifty people long. They were waiting for a glimpse of Marija and Ivan, or better yet, a chance to touch them. It took my breath away to think that the visionaries live with this intense focus day after day, year after year.

I am through the crowd in moments and looking around for an empty spot on the lawn where I can sit and collect myself. But before I can sit down, one of the men who was in the loft with me comes over and wants to talk. I have no words for the experience and know better than to try to find them now. They will come later. Now it is important not to talk.

It's only six o'clock in the evening and it feels like an age has passed. The moon rises to the south over Krizevac Hill where a fire burns on the cross-topped hill. Church bells peal, people stand in line all around the building walkway for confessions being heard in Italian, English, Croatian, French, and German. I spread my shawl on the grass a respectful distance away and sit down with this experience.

I was in front of Marija and Ivan the whole time they were seeing the apparition. I watched them closely from the start. Marija is guileless and strong. Yes, they seem to see something, why can't it be Mary? What may seem far-fetched to many seems possible to me.

I am grateful to have been allowed into the presence of the Mother of God, or God the Mother, as I think of her, but we are always in this presence. Only rarely do we become aware of it.

Now all around the church the doors are opened and mass begins. Crowds spill out onto the walk. People sing the mass in Croatian, the unfamiliar, haunting harmonies of Eastern Europe. Outside, confessions continue whispered, the penitent kneeling on walkway stones next to priests sitting in folding chairs. Sins float and vanish into the thin night air.

◆

The next morning when I go to Marija's, we are finally able to meet as planned. Sitting at one end of a long dining table, Marija peels a tangerine, offering the translator, Nives Jelich, and I each a section. Marija has on a turquoise blue sweatshirt and a polka-dot apron over her skirt. Her mother stands in the adjoining kitchen cooking; three more people sit on the couch waiting to see Marija. Dragan, the tour guide, pops his head in the door: would Marija come outside for a moment to pray with his group of pilgrims? The phone rings for Marija. She takes the call, talks for a moment, then puts her tangerine down and politely excuses herself to go pray with the pilgrims. She is easy in the midst of a constant commotion that I imagine would have broken many. The calm and cheerfulness with which Marija lives in this daily intensity is perhaps the strongest evidence to me that whatever is going on with her is authentic. The apparitions have been occurring daily for over seven years at this point.

We resume talking again after the pilgrims have left. I asked Marija what is important for people to understand about Medjugorje. She is soft-spoken but animated.

"Fasting, prayer, peace, conversion, and mass—this is the main message of what Our Lady wants," she says.

"The strongest connection with our Lord is through the mass. Our Lady is very emphatic that the center of our life is the holy mass."

"But, Marija," I ask, "what about people of other faiths?"

"Our Lady said that she is the Mother of all children and other faiths come here. We are not in a position of separating them. She is inviting everyone. We have free will. It is up to us if we want it or not. . . . She's not saying that your faith is not good because you're not at mass, but she is giving us a chance to have the best."

Nives, who translates for us, is a devout Catholic. I have no way of knowing if "best" was Mary's word, Marija's word, or Nives' choice, and no way to find out. Over the last two days, people who come to Medjugorje often have said that there are five main elements or principles in the messages. (These are separate from the five requests of Mary that Cyril explained the first day at Marija's.) I decide to move on and review the list which I had been told Mary had articulated.

"Marija, did Mary say that 'God did not create religion,' or that 'God did not create division in religion,' which is it?" I ask.

"God did not divide people into different religions, He meant for us to be one," she replies.

"Now which one? We should ask that," Nives interjects pointedly.

"Let me ask her about the second principle, Nives, as I understood it. 'Whatever faith people have, they should practice with a complete gift of self.' Is this correct, Marija?"

"Our Lady didn't say that," she begins to tell me, then she and Nives talk between themselves in Croatian.

"I was told that Ivan said that, to a man I know who spoke with him directly. Several people have told me this. What is Our Lady saying that is giving people this idea?"

"She doesn't remember that," Nives explains.

I go on. "The third one, 'It is the fault of Christians to look down on people of other faiths.' "

"Yes, that is correct. Our Lady said that. She said that we must respect everyone as a person, as a human being. We must not look down on other faiths."

I am relieved to have understood this correctly. I had heard the story of Mary telling the visionaries that there was a holy woman in their village whom they should seek to be more like.[4] When they inquired as to whom this might be, to their surprise, the woman Mary identified, Pasha, was a Muslim.

"The fourth one: God works in different religions, but not every religion has the same amount of grace?"

"Our Lady didn't say that. That's what the visionaries as a group decided in reflection from what Our Lady has been saying. They concluded as a group that the Catholic faith has the most grace available."

Given that they're all Catholic, this comes as no surprise. It is good to know that Mary didn't say this herself, that this was the visionaries' interpretation of a series of her messages, not her words.

"The fifth principle was that it was no accident that Mary is appearing in a Catholic Church. What can Marija say about this?"

The answer is unclear. Was it the translation or the question? I can't tell. Marija goes off on what seems to be a tangent, explaining that the Muslims don't reject Mary's appearance here because they have had an apparition of Mary Our Lady as the Mother of Jesus whom they consider a prophet.

I move on to the secrets. This is the side to the messages of Medjugorje that I can least appreciate: the ten secrets. Each of the visionaries will receive ten secrets from Mary, it is said. Once they have received them, they will stop having the apparitions, except for perhaps once a year. This has been true for two of the visionaries so far.

The little I know about the secrets concerns the future and what is to come if people don't heed Mary's requests for prayer, fasting, and conversion, as it's often called.

The apocalyptic overtones of earlier Marian apparitions are es-

pecially strong at Medjugorje. Mirjana Dragicević, one of the visionaries who no longer sees the Madonna, was told the tenth and last
secret on Christmas Day, 1982, according to Mary Craig's account.
Some months later,

> she was deeply pessimistic. The world would be given three
> warnings, in the form of three dire events, before the visible
> sign would appear; and three days before the first warning,
> Mirjana would announce its imminence to a priest of her choice.
> The short intervals between the three warnings would be, she
> said, "a period of grace," but if, once the great sign appeared,
> the world did not turn to God, the punishment would come.
> There was no use expecting the whole world to be converted,
> she conceded, but prayer could alleviate the extent of its pun-
> ishment. The seventh secret had already been annulled. But:
> "the eighth secret is worse than the seven before it. I begged
> for it to be made less severe. Every day I beseeched the Madonna
> to get it mitigated, and at last she said that if everyone prayed
> it might be averted. But then she told me the ninth secret and
> it was even worse. As for the tenth, it is terrible, and nothing
> can alter it. It will happen."[5]

The only preparation people could make would be spiritual, they
had to give their lives to God, Mirjana told her interviewer. The
Madonna told her that this was the last time she or Christ would
appear on earth. There would be no more apparitions after Medjugorje.

"Marija, there is an apocalyptic tone to Medjugorje, an implication
that if the world doesn't respond to Mary's messages and requests,
we will all be destroyed. I find it hard to imagine a loving God and
Mary threatening us like that.

"I thought Mary's message was to have peace in our hearts, to
bring peace into our families and into the world, that the emphasis
was on being peaceful and joyful. How does that fit in with hints of
the destruction of the world?"

"Our Lady said that fasting and prayer will even stop the wars. Our Lord gives us love and peace to help us, he doesn't want to destroy us. *We* make the choice.

"God is the God of love. Our Lady has come asking us to pray and fast, not because of her. She loves us, she wants us to be joyous, she wants us to be happy. She wants us to have the Spirit. She's coming because she loves us, but it's our choice. May everyone who reads this find that Our Lady is our Mother."

Our talk is cut short by the arrival of another group of pilgrims, wanting to see Marija. Soon I must leave to meet Father Jozo. Marija steps outside once again to pray with the pilgrims and answer questions.

I'm still full of questions. I speak with a woman close to Marija, a friend who has been with her through much of the last few years. She asked not to be named. Marija's friend's explanation of the messages was broader. She was a Westerner, a native English speaker, who had spent a significant amount of time traveling abroad and had lived in Asia before finding her home in Medjugorje years ago. We stood in the kitchen talking while Marija was outside with the pilgrims.

"Our Lady has never specifically said that our only way back to Jesus is the Catholic Church. She did say that she was 'the Mother of All,' and this on more than one occasion."

Marija's companion told me that Mary is teaching the visionaries on a day-to-day basis to live the gospel. She wants people to turn back to the Good News of the gospels. She has told the visionaries to read the gospel many times.

Marija's friend said that the way the word "conversion" was used by the visionaries simply meant choosing God. It didn't necessarily mean conversion to a specific religion. Many people were afraid of Christ because they associated him with Christianity or the Catholic Church, but that's too limited a concept.

" 'Jesus is the light of the world,' she said. Anyone looking for light is looking for Jesus, is looking for the Christ, is looking for their

God, is looking for this contact with their God. I don't think we should worry about what they find.

"People don't realize that we make our ideas about God into a god and then this idea of God becomes a problem. We think we know who God is and we don't."

Marija moves in and out of the conversation as more groups of pilgrims come and go. Nives, Marija's friend, and I continue talking for some time in the kitchen. Marija gives me a beautiful smile from the kitchen as I finally prepare to go. I take one last look at her standing in the sunlight in front of her kitchen window, the light framing her, and I leave.

♦

Leaving Medjugorje, I reflect on the apocalyptic undercurrent. Whether we live in "the end days" or not, I cannot sanely entertain this kind of thinking. I only know this present moment; what will come, comes out of this present moment. Thich Nhat Hanh's phrase, "take refuge in the present moment," consoles me.

The simple aphorism "take what you need and leave the rest" releases me from imagining that I have to resolve or understand what is happening at Medjugorje. As I leave I'm acutely aware of how different this experience has been from earlier ones. People stare at the sun in Medjugorje. There is talk of miracles and more mention of Satan than I've heard in years. Yet the quiet flood of joy and happiness that I experienced in the choir loft is a clear indication that something true and good has happened for me here. Many moments here have moved me. Of some I remain wary.

After leaving Marija, I go to meet Father Jozo and to hear him speak at his nearby church. His words to all are "Do not fear, do not be afraid." Even his physical presence, joyful and loving, conveys this message.

The secrets, which sounded so frightening, I had only read of, I heard nothing about them firsthand. Marija confirmed nothing about them of which to be afraid, I realized.

Cyril's words, "the messages are a mystery, they must be approached with prayer," I took with me from Medjugorje.

I thought back to the journeys that came before.

Poland—to which I was originally drawn because of stories of the Madonna growing in the bark of trees, only to find the Madonna growing in me. Switzerland—the song of the monks' *Salve Regina* opened the door back into the overgrown, wild, walled-off garden where her image stood untended and unwatered in my heart. Green Tara planted in me.

Poland—the pilgrimage to Jasna Gora cut wide the swath through the weeds, released a floodgate, let loose a stream of feeling that courses through my heart.

Nepal—going to see the Tara growing in the rock at Pharping, meeting Chos Kyi Nyima Rinpoche, Buddha Tara taking root in me, breaking my heart open with her vow to have only a woman's body until all suffering in the world is ended. Becoming enlightened in a woman's body, they said it couldn't be done. Buddha Tara chooses this body, chooses to be a woman. Sisters, dance and beat the drum, take up the practice of rejoicing.

Texas—flying to see the Madonna of San Juan de los Lagos, finding the Mother of the Disappeared, *Madre de los Desaparecidos.* The political dimension of the Dark Madonna: Brenda Sanchez's stories, Marian Strohmeyer's merciful house, *Casa de la Merced,* and *Proyecto Libertad.* Finding the Sanctuary movement—"we are locking the door on a burning house, there are people inside"—Liberation theology, the assassination of Archbishop Oscar Romero in El Salvador, the Maryknoll sisters, forty thousand civilians alone killed, all cut through me. The murder of the six Jesuits, their housekeeper, and her daughter was yet to come.

Back to Poland—Gdansk and Walesa, the Black Madonna on

his lapel. The river of Mary coming up from underground at Jasna Gora; changing to cosmic red from intergalactic black.

Struck by the Madonna in Texas, like a meteorite falling out of the sky, I didn't see her coming, I didn't see that following Tara would take me back through Mary, would knock me off a solitary path into the heat and controversy of community. The *Madonnas de los Lagos, de los Guadalupe, de los Desaparecidos* let the world in. Burned.

Mary is dark from entering lives on fire.

The Indoeuropean root of the word *black* meant *gleaming*, only later did the meaning darken.

Home—the Peace Project. Meeting for peace, pot-luck suppers, and reciting Thich Nhat Hanh's Precepts for the Order of Interbeing. Again we ask ourselves how can we "be peace"? Robert Aitken Roshi of the Diamond Sangha comes to meditate with us, sits with us, reminds us, "Breathe."

CHAPTER 17

Where the Streams Cross

•

California

Whoever wants to paint the variegated world
Let him never look straight up at the sun
Or he will lose the memory of things he has seen.
Only burning tears will stay in his eyes.

Let him kneel down, lower his face to the grass,
And look at light reflected by the ground.
There he will find everything we have lost:
The stars and the roses, the dusks and the dawns.

—Czeslaw Milosz[1]
Warsaw, 1943

Dallas, Texas
May 1989

Circling. Ever since I returned from Eastern Europe I sense some great slow circle closing. In it is included my grandfather's death.

My family called from Texas mid-spring to say that my grandfather might not live through the summer and that we should come to pay our respects and say goodbye. He would be ninety-eight in August.

I called my grandfather and asked him what he thought about how much longer he was going to live. Should we wait and come for his birthday in August or should we come before? He thought he'd live until August, he always had before, after all. "What month is this? Isn't it July?"

"No, Pop, it's April."

"Oh."

Matthew, Madelon, Ben, and I all arrive back in Dallas the last week of May. It has been years since I have had time like this with my family, now grown, where we stay together for days visiting. We go to see Pop, pack up his wheelchair, and take him with us everywhere: down by Hackberry Creek, past the former family home, to the cafeteria for lunch, to my Uncle Robert's house for dinner. We take him overnight down to the countryside near the Brazos River to the farm where my mother now lives. He is as pleased as a child and though easily tired, still alert and present.

I have learned a song for him. I want to sing it at his funeral, but he won't be there so I tell him that he must listen to it and tell me if he approves. It's a shape-note hymn. My friend Marita Gunther, a voice teacher, had helped me learn it, making me sing it over and over. "No, like this," she would say firmly, then singing a phrase. "Again. For Grandfather," in her German accent.

Now I am standing in front of him in Texas, singing. He sits in his wheelchair, Madelon next to him, it is just the three of us in the front room. Though he is hard of hearing, he is straining to listen. I sing loudly, singing my heart out for him—"Bright Morning Stars Are Rising"—Madelon sits crying, I want to cry, but I want to sing more, so I give the hymn more volume, bring it up out of my feet, let myself move. The last line—"Our fathers have all gone to heaven shouting"—yes, that's him, that's my grandfather, Walter. I can see him now waving his cane in the air, shouting, "Wait, here I come!" as he marches past the gates of St. Peter that my grandmother, Florence, always swore were there.

After we return to Dallas, Ben asks Pop how he feels about dying. "I'm not afraid, Ben, I'm ready. I'm glad you asked me. Ninety-seven is a long time to live. I've enjoyed every minute of it, but I am a little tired and my hearing's not so good. It's hard for me to read. I'll be ready when the Lord calls me.

"I'm so happy you came to see me."

The afternoon we left, we had lunch outside with Pop at my Aunt Sue's—sandwiches—then Pop got tired and went in to lie down for his nap. It was almost time to leave for the airport. I went inside.

The shades were drawn in his room. He was dressed in his gray-striped trousers and a dress shirt and tie on as always. He had taken off his coat and shoes for his nap. Jaki, his nurse, had pulled a light wool blanket over him after he lay down on top of the covers.

"It's me, Pop, and Ben. We've come to say goodbye." He had almost fallen asleep, but he roused himself.

"Oh, good," he said. "It's been such a wonderful visit. Ben, I don't think I'll see you again. Remember that I love you and take good care of your mother."

I just remember my hands on his face, stroking his forehead, now so thin, the bones showing more. My grandfather, shrinking, at 115 pounds now, weighing less than me. Fading. We have said goodbye many times before.

I push the hair back on his forehead. I stand at his bedside. There is nothing more to say or do. I have already made him promise that he'll come back to haunt me, to give me a sign that will let me know that he made it safely to the other side.

"Don't forget, Pop, I love you," I say as I lean down and kiss him goodbye.

♦

When I get back to California, I walk home the several miles from Green Gulch Farm, up over Coyote Ridge. At Green Gulch, Yvonne

Rand had lectured on Death and Dying, her straightforward talk a comfort. Yvonne, learning about the breath from the dying, how to be with someone, now teaching me.

Hands numb, thighs and calfs tingling from the long walk, at home I get ready to bathe but see that my left hand is covered with writing. I had had a pen on the walk but no paper so I used my left hand, wrote all over it, filled it up with words while holding a fistfull of wildflowers and a pen in my right. Now sitting in my room half undressed, I copy them down quickly, straight off the palm: "blue-eyed grass, wild strawberry, blackberry vine, sage, lupine, poison oak everywhere, Indian paintbrush, orange monkey flower, bee hives, wind in the pines along the ridge top, eucalyptus leaves—soft clatter—half a moon, six o'clock, pale in the sky." Then from up the left thumb—"pale silvered grasses ripple in the wind, water streaming." In the middle of the palm, squared, is my oldest son's name, Matt, with whom I mean to talk.

Learning natural history is a form of meditation, reciting the names of wild things, a litany. I say them now to ground myself in a world that without my grandfather will be less familiar.

Santa Monica, California
July 1989

Circling. Those who were far, draw near.

The Dalai Lama comes to Los Angeles to give the *Kalachakra* initiation, four days of teaching and ritual ceremonies for world peace. *Kalachakra* means the Great Wheel of Time. I see several of the Tibetan monks that I met in India again. Geshe Champa Lodro and Carol Savvas arrive from Switzerland for Geshe Rinpoche's first visit to the United States.

As I walk along the beach during a break, I remember that I first learned to swim in Santa Monica at the age of five. My grandmother, originally from Rochester, New York, would sometimes spend the summer in California with her six children to avoid the fierceness of the Texas heat. At least once, I was brought along. Part of the family moved to California before the turn of the century, some to the south, some to the north. I had forgotten that I have roots in California too, not just Texas.

The *Kalachakra* ceremony was nearly complete. Some of us stayed in and around the auditorium to watch the ceremonial disassembling of the mandala that was to take place now that the full initiation had been given. The Dalai Lama would return to the civic auditorium to sweep the granules of colored sand from the mandala into a container, then they would be taken by His Holiness and a band of monks by car to a nearby inlet in the bay to be returned to moving waters in the traditional way.

I stood by an open doorway and looked out onto the lawn. The sight of a Native American sitting alone in a metal folding chair against a gray wall caught my attention. The dark blue velveteen shirt, turquoise necklace, wide pink headband around his gray hair, and a wide-woven red belt set him apart from everyone else. A short, stocky, older man, he looked familiar, so familiar that I walked up to him and after excusing myself and asking if I might speak with him, I said, "Aren't you Thomas Banyacya?"

"Yes," he said. He had come to pay his respects to the Dalai Lama whom he'd met with on other occasions. Banyacya is a Hopi. The Hopis feel a special kinship with the Tibetans, the spiritual understanding is similar, ceremonies are similar, even certain words and prophecies seem to be connected, Banyacya explained.

When the Sixteenth Karmapa, the head of the Kargyu sect, one of the four main schools of Tibetan Buddhism, came to the United States in 1974, one of his stops was Hopi Land (Arizona) where he met with Hopi elders. Tibetans and Hopis have what some consider to be interlinking prophecies. A Tibetan prophecy from the tenth century predicted that "when the iron bird flies and horses run on wheels, the Dharma will come to the land of the red man." In a film of the Karmapa's visit we are told that there is a corresponding Hopi prophecy that "men will come with red hats and reveal themselves to be the friends of the Hopi."[2] The Venerable Dudjom Rinpoche, the now deceased head of Nyingmapa School, also met with Hopi elders in the 1970s.

Hopis do have a prophecy about someone, a person or even a nation, with red hats or red cloaks who will come, Banyacya told me as we stood talking, but he was careful to point out that there are different ways to interpret the prophecies. Suddenly there was a bustle of activity, our conversation was cut short, the Dalai Lama would soon arrive. I went inside.

I turned back from the doorway. Banyacya was by himself again. The sight was painfully emblematic. Here thousands had gathered to honor and hear the teachings of the most revered Tibetan teacher, the Dalai Lama, yet the elders of our own landscape, and their interpreters like Banyacya, we ignore. He sat alone, I sensed, to our peril.

Standing in the auditorium doorway, it occurred to me that we, myself included, rush to aid the Tibetans in their struggle with the Chinese, not seeing that what the Chinese are doing to the Tibetans, we have already done to the Native Americans. We've killed their people, their languages, broken treaties, stolen lands, usurped them, displaced them, imprisoned them, plied them with alcohol, low-paying, unsafe jobs, very much like what the Chinese have done and continue to do to the Tibetans.

One of the Dalai Lama's greatest concerns is that the Chinese are making Tibet a global sacrifice area. It's being used as a nuclear dump and launching pad for nuclear weapons by the Chinese. The Tibetan environment is being ruined, forests and minerals stripped, wild game depleted. Part of the Dalai Lama's Five Point Peace Plan is to have Tibet established as a zone of peace, completely demilitarized, making it a giant global park between India and China.[3]

The Four Corners area of the American Southwest is littered with nuclear test grounds, radioactive wastes, strip mines and above-ground radioactive mine tailings, making it a "national sacrifice area," no matter how much it would be denied. The phrase "national sacrifice area" was used by the National Academy of Science after determining that this arid land with so little rainfall has little, if any, probability of being restored after strip-mining.[4]

The parallel is striking.

When I returned home I stayed in touch with Banyacya to get a clearer understanding of the significance of what he had told me during our brief meeting at the Kalachakra.

I found that though there may be different ways to interpret the prophecies, in 1948 there was one prophecy that the Hopi spiritual leaders agreed upon: "A gourd of ashes would fall out of the sky" that would kill the earth and leave the land unable to grow crops.

When this event took place, the Hopi were obligated to speak up so that we all, the earth included, might live. In 1948, they decided that the time had come to make known their prophecies to the non-Indian world before——the prophecies implied——it was too late.

For Chief Sackmasa and the other leaders who met in 1948 at Shungopovy pueblo on Second Mesa, "the gourd of ashes" was the atomic bomb that had been dropped only three hundred miles away at Alamagordo, New Mexico, in 1945, and then used on Hiroshima and Nagasaki.[5] In the series of councils that followed, the spiritual leaders came to agreement about the meaning of the prophecies and how they were to be presented to the outside world.

The prophecies warn us against poisoning the earth and urge us to turn, each in our own way, back to the Great Spirit, as the Hopis say. We are told that balance with the earth must be restored, or we will suffer the consequences. We must each begin today to purify our own lives and the land around us, Banyacya told me.

Global warming, deteriorization of the ozone layer, polluted waters and lands, vanishing rain forests, acid rain, extinction of species, the proliferation of radioactive waste, just to mention of few of our modern horrors, these are but Western scientific terms for what the Hopi prophecies long ago foretold.

♦

California
July 28, 1989

Two weeks later at home, there are five statues of Tara sitting on the dining-room table crowded with offerings: pyramids of green apples, dark purple-black plums, pale peaches, braided breads, cookies all neatly stacked on white plates, and flowers. In front of her several statues, bouquets of fresh garden flowers—blue iris, yellow spider lilies, pink and magenta carnations, deep purple and white gladiolas, lavender foxgloves, and red roses—all spill out of vases and jars on the table. More flowers sit on the floor in front of the hastily draped piano bench, now incorporated into a temporary altar along with the dining table.

The living room is full of friends and family who've come bringing the fresh fruits and flowers. Yvonne Rand has brought twenty meditation cushions and additional statues of Tara. She leaves me one that has been blessed, the insides filled with prayers, the eyes painted in, "opened." The furniture is moved back against the wall, transforming the living room into a small meditation hall for a *puja,* a devotional ceremony and offering to the Buddha Tara.

The Venerable Geshe Champa Lodro Rinpoche, my teacher from Switzerland, has come to visit. Carol Savvas and his niece accompany him after the *Kalachakra* ceremony.

It is nearly three years since I met Carol and Geshe Champa Lodro Rinpoche in Switzerland; now they sit in my living room, telling the story of Tara and how she became a Buddha.

Geshe Rinpoche begins in the traditional Tibetan way to explain why we make prayers and offerings to Tara. "Everyone wants to be happy, no one wants to suffer. In this way, no matter what our differences, we are all alike."

I sit next to my husband Corey, while Anna, our two-and-a-half-year-old friend from across the street, sits in his lap, thumping her feet. She steals up to the table and takes sugar cookies, one at a time, from the plates of offerings. I begin to be distracted, wondering whether or not I should try to stop her (her parents are seated off in the opposite corner), but Geshe Rinpoche only glances at her, notices what she is doing, smiles unperturbed, and continues talking.

"Many aeons ago, when Tara was the Princess Yeshe Dawa," he says, "she made great collections of merit and wisdom. Her name, Yeshe Dawa, means Wisdom Moon." Though I had heard the story of her vow only to be enlightened in a woman's body many times, now it seems as though I am hearing it for the first time.

The fullness of this circle, this coming home, this roundness, having my root teacher staying in my home, meeting and blessing my children, my husband, friends, and *sangha,* gives me pause: this long arc back from around the globe to where I had set out from in California, by Green Gulch Farm, where I had first heard the fragment of Tara's story that moved me to set out for mountains I never reached. Friends from Green Gulch here tonight, reconnecting after long absence; now after this long journey, out of all this longing, I see into a darkness that is not separate from light. The root of black is gleaming.

"Tara is always coming to us, can we come to her?" Geshe Rinpoche asks. "The Buddha Tara is coming to us. Sometimes she comes as a man, sometimes as a woman. She has many forms, innumerable forms, she sends out many emanations in order to help us. Tara has the power to free all beings from the world of suffering, samsara.

"In India, she was known especially for freeing us from the Eight Great Fears.[6] Sometimes they are called the Sixteen Fears, but it is really from unlimited fears that she can save us. There is no limit or end to her abilities to help us. Tara has the power to grant anything. If we make prayers to her and get no result, it is only from our own lack of effort, not hers.

White Tara. (Line drawing, artist unknown)

"Since Tara is Buddha, she is completely enlightened. There are no greater accomplishments than hers. We have come to meet Tara. If we do this, and if we take Refuge in her, then we can definitely find the happiness of liberation," he assures us.

We begin the Twenty-one Praises, chanting them in Tibetan as best we can, repeating them three times.[7]

Tara's eyes are like lightning, her face fashioned from a hundred full moons of autumn, gleaming like the light of a thousand stars. A stamp of her foot and whole universes shake, just to remember her beauty provides protection like armor.

Is it Geshe Champa Lodro speaking or is it Tara teaching? My whole body grows warm as we repeat the praises again in Tibetan. The concentration required is tremendous. Am I imagining that this *puja* holds the power that it does for me or is this the teaching— the dreaming, the calling forth of Tara. Bringing Tara to the West. Buddha Tara. If we call her, she will surely come.

Over a year ago, I made a small second altar in my son's room on his desk which I use now. On this little altar, I placed a picture of Green Tara that one of Geshe Rinpoche's students in Switzerland had given me for my birthday. I had spent the evening with Carol, Geshe Rinpoche, and his students at the Yiga Chözin Center in Zollikon.

Now Geshe Champa Lodro recites prayers and blesses my oldest son in the room where I made the small altar for Green Tara from Switzerland. It had never occurred to me that he might come to visit, that my whole family would spend time with Geshe Rinpoche. Just before he arrived, I had hung a photograph of Tibetan monks over the bed. The 360-degree panoramic photograph is contemporary, taken in the 1980s of monks from the Sera Monastery outside Lhasa.[8] There are two hundred monks pictured in front of what remains of a monastery that once held six thousand. Sera was one of the four main monasteries in Tibet. When I showed Geshe Rinpoche his room, he became very happy and pointed at the picture for us all to look. Geshe Rinpoche had entered Sera Monastery when he was eight years old.

The circle continues to close.

As I walk up to the top of the hills in a blaze of sunlight, the wind is high and chilled. I wrap a scarf around my neck more tightly and pull my watchcap down over my ears. Two deer graze below. One freezes as soon as she sees me, the other continues to feed as I walk along the hilltop. Suddenly they turn and bound off into a tall stand of poison hemlock, where they blend easily, the dun tan of their coats with the dense growth of narrow, bamboo-like stalks, the dark interior of their ears the same height as the blackened, dried-out flowers on top.

Poland's hold on me is mysterious. Like the patchwork landscape of childhood, half-remembered, only the longing lingers clearly.

As I walked, I thought about all the different streams that come together to make up this being called Mary.

Poland was a river of Mary, fed by hidden springs, some capped off long ago, dammed up, others now swollen ready to burst; some reduced to a trickle or grown stagnant, others still running strong underground, feeding and swelling this stream of the Mother from which I could not get enough to drink. I wanted to go deeper. I hadn't sought the body of Christ but the body of Mary, her mysterious, dark, elusive, multifaceted form. This was the body I needed to eat, the wine to drink.

Drawn from the Byzantine Church, where the icon is an expression of the deity itself, Mary at Jasna Gora is the *Theotokos,* Mother of God. Out of the Byzantine Church came the great Hagia Sophia, (ca. A.D. 535) the Church of Holy Wisdom, the apex of Byzantine architecture. Holy Wisdom is also associated with Isis. Sophia, Wisdom, also an early name for the Mother, was the Holy Spirit to the early Jewish Christians. The Black Madonna at Jasna Gora, our Lady of Czestochowa, draws from the spring of Sophia, Wisdom, as well.

Pouring in from the underground stream of Ephesus, the *Theotokos,* Mother of God and the black Artemis/Diana that came before her. And before Artemis and Diana, the *Diopetes,* "fallen down out of the sky," the meteorite, was worshipped at Ephesus. Ephesus was at the end of the Silk Road to China and the caravan route from India to the West through the Parthian Empire. I had stood in the foothills of the Himalayas at Dharamsala in northern India and looked west, out over the plains that Alexander the Great had crossed. The lines between East and West, left over in my mind from schoolroom maps, cracked. There was dynamic interchange between Alexandria and India in the ancient world.

Could Tara and Mary's streams have crossed? Look at Astar for a possible link with Tara in the area between ancient Persia and India, Peter Lindegger wrote. Some historians of religion believe that Tara might be derivative. Astar or Astarte was one of the sources of Mary, he had told me some time ago. Could she prove to be a common source? To follow out such a notion might well prove unwieldy if not impossible.

Up out of Egyptian Africa the waters rolled. In the sacristy of the Monastery of Jasna Gora, there is the painting of St. Sarah the Egyptian, who withdrew to a life of repentance as a desert hermit. St. Sara of the Camargue came from Egypt in one of the stories of Les Saintes-Maries-de-la-Mer. St. Paul the First Hermit, the patron of the Pauline Order that keeps Jasna Gora, the Egyptian desert hermit, was sustained miraculously by a raven who brought him bread each day. Born in Thebes in Upper Egypt in A.D. 233, Paul fled into the desert to escape persecution, remaining there over ninety years.[9] It is said that two lions dug his grave when he died at one hundred thirteen.

The Marys of the Camargue are venerated in the church of Les Saintes-Maries-de-la-Mer by a statue that depicts them standing in a boat. Isis is associated with a boat. Tara is described as a boatwoman, "the one who leads us across," an epithet that reverberates with the Hodegetria, "the one who leads the way." Tara is also the vessel itself, "the perfect boat to carry the great load of beings" to the shores of peace.[10]

The seal of Jasna Gora Monastery, the palm tree with lions standing on both sides, is a sign of the Great Mother. It also reveals a raven perched at the top of the palm in other renderings. And the raven is a symbol of the Great Mother.[11] The raven, the *nigredo,* the first phase of the alchemical process; the two ravens of St. Meinrad at Einsiedeln come to mind, iconographic code.

A copy of Spain's Black Madonna of Montserrat, *La Morenata,* sits high above a doorway in the sacristy at Jasna Gora across the room from the painting of St. Sara.

A multitude of streams pour into the Madonna at Jasna Gora. *Matka Boskies Zielnes* is another appellation of the Madonna of Jasna Gora and means the Mother of the Good Crops. To her the faithful bring rye, wheat, and herbs as offerings in the middle of August, the ancient grain protectoress in Christian form. Mid-August was also the feast of Artemis/Diana.

Great Mother worship flourished throughout Old Europe, 7000–3500 B.C.; there is no need to look to the Mediterranean or any place else, anthropologist Marija Gimbutas tells me, "The Black Madonna is a goddess of Old Europe, the Earth Mother." Black meant fertility, and white meant death in this pre-Indoeuropean culture.[12] Goddess figures over thirty thousand years old have been found in Europe, from Yugoslavia to France.

In the Camargue at Les-Saintes-Maries-de-la-Mer, the pre-Christian elements taken over by the Church were clearly in evidence, as they were in Marseilles at St. Victor's, the oldest church in Marseilles, with the dark wooden statue of the Madonna, *Notre Dame de Confession,* in the crypt. It is said that it was in Marseilles that a temple of Isis was first converted to the worship of the Madonna.

The symbols of the Camargue are the bull and the mare, drawn from hidden streams, charged with the energy of pre-Christian cults, like Einsiedeln's ravens, like Jasna Gora's palm tree with the lions and the raven.

Ephesian Artemis was the patron and oracle for early tin importers from Greece who brought Black Artemis to Gaul with them in the sixth century B.C. This may well explain the distribution of Black Madonnas in France along the route of the tin portage, around

Boulogne-Marseilles.[13] Where these ancient images were "miraculously" found often became the sites of worship, the most famous of which were the Black Madonnas, such as the *Vierge Noire* at Le Puy, where Joan of Arc's mother went to pray as her daughter rode to confer with the king of France. In Paris, Chartres has a Black Madonna amongst its treasures.

In southern France, the Dark Madonnas swirl in legends of the Magdalene who in certain medieval traditions brought the Holy Grail, the child of Jesus, from Jerusalem to France.[14]

La Divina Pastora, the Divine Shepherdess in Trinidad, the statue of Mary, is also called *Soparee Kay Mai,* which means Mother Kali. The Black Virgin at Regla, the protectress of Havana Bay, is also the African Yemaya, "the silvered goddess of the seas," Eduardo Galeano writes.[15]

No matter where I look, Mary has an earlier, non-Christian source giving her a depth and richness beyond any of the jeweled adornments she wears in the Church. It is deeply satisfying to find all these streams in her, like the sweetness of water after great thirst.

◆

The fullness of this circle holds within it the fullness of what I find at home. I had to go away to become aware of it. In my room I come across the tape I had made at Chos Kyi Nyima's monastery that included his mother's untranslated comments. I have them translated and discover that she had told me stories of Yeshe Tsogyel and Machig Labdron, the great Tibetan women masters, years before.[16] Both were women who raised families, stories for which I had been asking. Further I discovered that Chos Kyi Nyima Rinpoche's mother, Kunsang Dechen, is a respected teacher of chöd practice in Kathmandu. She herself was the kind of woman about whom I inquired, though I didn't understand this then. Years ago, I now learn, she had answered many of my questions, had told me that having a woman's body was no cause for discouragement. There had been many women masters in the past, she assured me.

"One can practice with great results whether you are married, have children or are a nun. It doesn't matter—married, unmarried, children—this is not what's important," she said. "It's your mind that brings results and how much you practice.

"As long as one has the desire to become enlightened for the sake of all beings, *bodhicitta,* having woman's body can be better for spiritual practice than a man's. This is what Padmasambhava told Yeshe Tsogyel when she complained to him about having a woman's body. This was over a thousand years ago, remember, one should never regret being born a woman."

Termas are hidden Tibetan teachings, buried—in a rock, a lake, the sky, or even in the mind—until the time is right to reveal them or until there is a student to receive them. Kunsang Dechen's words. Finally I learned her name, had her comments translated and could read them.[17] Then I realized I was surrounded by women who are seriously involved in spiritual practice who have or have had families. Some are also now teaching.

The ideal model for spiritual practice has too long been the monastery. One "left the world" for the monastery, be it Christian or Buddhist. One had to abandon the family, take up celibacy. Family, relationships, children especially, have too long been viewed as obstructions to be cleared away for the committed person who has truly given themselves to God, the Dharma, the Way or the Spirit, however variously it may be called.

This is no longer so. Spiritual practice for everyday life, lay practice—with or without families—is coming into its own. We are no longer limited to the celibate, monastic model. I have great respect for the monastic life, but it's time to see family life not as "the lesser evil," but as an equally demanding, though different, choice for intense spiritual practice. The realm of the sacred is being rekindled in the home. Keeping an altar, having time for spiritual reading, meditation and/or prayer with our family and our friends, these are practices I found encouraged from Medjugorje to Dharamsala. They remind us of what we already know. The sacred is a dimension of everyday life, not something separate from it.

I begin to go down the list of women I know or had heard teach recently within my own limited experience. All are women who have raised or are in the process of raising children. Some are married, some are not. Some have grown children, some have teenagers, some have infants. Their significance lies in the fact that these are all voices of mothers teaching, giving us new choices.

Maurine Stuart Roshi, Zen master and president of the Cambridge Buddhist Society, came to Green Gulch to lecture and lead a meditation retreat, *sesshin*. I went to hear her, deeply moved to listen to this woman master lecture in the *zendo* where I first began as a student.[18]

Several women at Zen Center, both senior students and priests with families, had begun to lecture and teach while my focus was elsewhere.[19] Wendy Johnson, head of the Green Gulch garden, works in collaboration with other Zen students and parents, especially mothers, on a book entitled *Simple Treasures:* ways to incorporate spiritual practice with family life—work, partners, children—this is being explored at the inspiration of Thich Nhat Hanh. The Buddhist Peace Fellowship sponsors Family Practice Days at Green Gulch Farm. Thich Nhat Hanh's meditation retreats include and invite children. He has a special genius for imaginative application of ancient practices, for example, giving a child a "mindfulness bell" to ring when household tempers rise, to remind us to stop, take a moment, breathe, and return to ourselves.

Yvonne Rand, who came to the Tara *puja,* received full dharma transmission from the Japanese Soto Zen master Katagiri Roshi in Minneapolis, Minnesota. Though Yvonne's main focus was Zen, our paths crossed again in finding ourselves drawn to Tibetan teachings.

Her Holiness the Sakya Jetsunma Chime Luding, also known as Jetsun Kushola, perhaps the highest woman teacher of Tibetan Buddhism in the West, came to the Tibetan Buddhist Center, Ewam

Choden, in Berkeley to give initiations and teachings, including the White Tara initiation for long life and healing.[20] Her center is in Richmond, British Columbia, Canada.

Lama Inge Sandvoss was the first lama ordained by the Venerable Chagdud Tulku Rinpoche when he came to the West. I meet Lama Inge at Chagdud Rinpoche's retreat center in Napa, California, where she was leading part of the retreat. Her own center where she teaches, Padma Amrita, is in Spokane, Washington.

Among the several teachers who trained Chagdud Rinpoche was his own mother, Dawa Drölma, recognized as one of the women masters of her generation in Tibet. Fleeing Tibet in 1959, Chagdud Rinpoche, like so many Tibetan masters, spent many years in India until coming to the United States ten years ago. Married to a Westerner, Jane Trogme, Chagdud Rinpoche has raised children as well. The main practice of Chagdud's students is Red Tara and Tröma, the black chöd dakini who is a fierce form of Tara. Tara in her many aspects, as well as other Tibetan deities, is studied at his main Buddhist center, Rigdzin Ling, in the Trinity Alps of northern California.

I begin to study Red Tara. Her ruby color represents the desire of all beings for the freedom of liberation. She sits on a disk of the sun, full moon behind her. She is known especially to help in purifying speech.[21] I visited Chagdud Rinpoche's community, noted in part for the strength of its women members and its balance of families. I drew closer. Chagdud Rinpoche became a teacher of mine as well.

Tsering Everest, Chagdud Rinpoche's translator, whom I first encountered some years ago, has been authorized to give certain Tara teachings and to teach dream yoga. Tsering Everest too has made a great study of Tara.

Of Tröma, the fierce black form of Tara, I have learned little, her practice for students more advanced than I. But this much Tsering explained: black can also be understood to represent *emptiness,* the complete overcoming of ignorance: the false perception of reality, the illusion of dualism, of anything existing separately.

Emptiness, the true nature of Tara, the womb of enlightenment, can be understood symbolically as darkness or the color black. Emptiness is not *nothing*. This is a great conceptual error that many Westerners make. *Emptiness* refers to the radical insight of the Buddha twenty-five hundred years ago that distinguishes Buddhism from most systems of belief—there is no individually existing, independently arising, separate self. All that is, is in constant flux, rising and falling in relationship to and with something else.

This is darkness to the thinking mind, to the ego that grasps and holds that there is such a thing as "mine." This goes beyond thinking mind, beyond the world of appearances, into the vast direct experience of being. This is not ordinary reality. This is the black of starless midnight, *imminence,* that comes before the pre-dawn of enlightenment, the "clear light," a state of translucence or transparency that is beyond dark and light.[22] This is a radiant black.

Thus emptiness can be said to be dark or black to us. This is the womb of enlightenment. This is Wisdom. This is the Mother of All the Buddhas, this is Tara.

Walking up into the hills, I think about Tara, about the image and the stories I read of her as a joyful, slightly mischievous sixteen-year-old young woman, who would sometimes chide a person whose life she had just saved, or even chide them before she would save them, if they hadn't prayed to her. Fearless Tara, slaying demons with a frown from her brow, her eyes flashing like lightning. Just a laugh from her brings the world and its demons under her sway. I catch myself smiling just to think of her.

But where is the joyful Mary? Walking along this road, the air cool on my face, with the first hint of fall, the sun warm, suddenly I imagine Mary smiling as I remember the magnificent Greek icon, the *Virgin Kardiotissa:*[23] the infant Jesus has thrown his arms up around his mother's neck, his head thrown back in joyful, loving abandon, his sandal dangling from his left foot, as though he had just run into her arms from play; and Mary, smiling at this child, who looks as though he's about to pull her veil off her head.

When I see this image I recognize her expression and I am flooded again with sweet joy of bearing innocence, the sheer, inexplicable, gratuitous joy that pierces mothering, the remarkable sound of a newborn baby nursing at your breast, the feeling of the uterus contracting as you nurse—the growing, visceral understanding that the body, like the earth, has an intelligence so much more vast and complicated than our own—and then that moment of giving birth to a child, beyond the pains of labor, the whole body taken over, and the moment of being launched into an electrifying orgasmic joy that nullifies all separation between body as sexual and body as giving new life, dissolving, for that moment, all being into bliss. A new life has come into the world. New life!

I see the next moment, outside the icon, as I walk past pine trees, past the blackberries, done for this year, past eucalyptus, ever the mountain, Tamalpais, on my right, the top, East and West peaks, clear and distinct, the day bright. I see Mary in the moment after the painter has put down the brush. She has stepped outside the image given to us and she is whirling her child around in the sweet dance that mothers and babies do as one discovers what makes them laugh and smile. So sweet is this joy, that you want to go on with them like this forever and will make a fool out of yourself, fathers too, make yourself dizzy whirling and twirling them around, or bending over a crib cooing or making some face that only an infant or very young child enjoys, or you will be down on all fours barking like a dog or playing hide and go seek, or standing now, tossing them up in the air. Oh, how mine laughed.

So great is the power of joy that women and men will die for it and I feel this morning that I could die for the beauty of this place. The hillside grasses are a dull gold and brown from the lack of rain, two ruby-chested birds chase each other through the air, never still enough for me to make out their markings and see who they are, and the mountain, closer now, dark green in the distance. A redtail hawk hovers high above in the wind, then dives, taking my heart with her. Underneath, the San Andreas Fault is creaking and, slowly, the Point Reyes Peninsula moves two inches further north each year, while the great tectonic plates grind and shift below the sea, the movement of continents deep, in that dark, even as I look though I cannot see it, the landscape is alive. It cracks and shifts ever so slightly, it breathes.

CHAPTER 18

On the Mountain

◆

*The Dalai Lama,
Mount Tamalpais, California*

As a bee seeks nectar
from all kinds of flowers,
seek teachings everywhere;
like a deer that finds
a quiet place to graze,
seek seclusion to digest
all you have gathered.
Like a madman
beyond all limits,
go wherever you please,
and live like a lion,
completely free of all fear.

—Dzogchen tantra[1]

*California
October 1989*

Sitting on the small stage on top of Mount Tamalpais, the Dalai Lama
leans over the arm of a satin brocade armchair to answer questions
for reporters. Thrust to the forefront of the international spotlight
by the award of the Nobel Peace Prize, Tenzin Gyatso, the Fourteenth
Dalai Lama, continues to be himself, earthy, spontaneous, and present.
The press has been flown in suddenly from all over the country to

see him conduct the Lahsang, a Tibetan ceremony for purifying and healing the earth. The Lahsang is also a ceremony for world peace and part of the Twelfth Tai Situpa's worldwide Pilgrimage for Active Peace in which the Dalai Lama participates.

Revered by the Native American Coast Miwok tribe who sometimes called it "Coyote's Round House," Mount Tamalpais provides a dramatic setting for the ceremony as we sit twenty-six hundred feet above a world blanketed by fog, floating. The Pacific Ocean, San Francisco Bay, Point Reyes Peninsula, all are invisible below. Here on the West Peak, the highest point on the mountain, the sky is brilliant blue and clear, the sun hot. Ravens cry, swooping in and out of the manzanita and pines, blue jays squawk and squirrels scold, all adding to the commotion that breaks up the usual quiet of the mountain.

I am locked into a spot a few feet in front of the stage by the crush of photographers, television cameramen, and reporters. Cameras go off like tiny automatic gunfire.

Two questions recur: what kind of impact did the Nobel Peace Prize have on him, and what does the future hold for Tibet in its campaign to regain independence from China.

The clearest, most forthright answer to all the questions is the Dalai Lama himself. His presence is light, cheerful, warmhearted, and genuine.

"I am just a simple Buddhist monk, no more, no less," he begins, "that hasn't changed."

"Human kindness and compassion, that's my personal religion, maybe it is the universal religion.

"I am always optimistic. There is something in the human blood that needs freedom. A repressive system is against human nature. It won't work in the long run. The human spirit cannot stand the negative, evil forces of repression.

"This twentieth century may be the most important century in human history. There are many sad things that are happening, but the positive aspect is that when things become so terrible, so dan-

*Tenzin Gyatso, His Holiness the Fourteenth Dalai Lama,
Mt. Tamalpais, California. (Anne Dowie)*

gerous, people wake up. The nuclear threat is so awful, so powerful, that it wakes up a desire for world peace. So there is hope. We must have it," he adds emphatically. Becoming depressed is not useful, he notes pragmatically, no matter how bad the world situation seems. The Tibetan emphasis is abidingly positive.

"Each individual must take responsibility for the human family. If we cannot eliminate, we can minimize the misfortunes and sufferings of others. Our individual salvation is just that, individual, but society's salvation is everyone's. A genuine altruistic attitude is the seed of a happy future. We must have patience.

"Violence is unstable. Revolutions may overthrow an existing system by force, but they have very little to offer as a new, meaningful way of life. The reason to me is quite clear. These revolutionary movements that use violence mainly come from hatred, not from love. Yes, there is some compassion, some concern for less privileged people, for people's suffering, that's very good: but when you compare the motivation of love to the motivation of hatred, the force of hatred makes up maybe seventy percent of the motivation. Such a force is unstable. It cannot last over time, it only generates more of itself. In the long run, the only motivation that creates stability, lasting change is loving kindness, compassion, nonviolence, and the altruistic desire to help others. These are the answers."

I had seen him in the auditorium at San Jose only days before, giving Dzogchen teachings, I had seen him at the *Kalachakra* ceremony in Los Angeles, but now I am seeing him under the pressure of politics, in the world's eye and there is no difference. His commitment to the way of kindness, compassion, altruism, and nonviolence is completely embodied.

The Chinese repression of Tibetans has only grown since I first met him in India in 1986. Martial law was declared in Lhasa, the capital of Tibet, in March 1989, in response to increased nonviolent demonstrations against Chinese rule. Tibetans continued the call for independence from China and in the ensuing violence, pressure continued to mount for the Dalai Lama to advocate armed resistance and revolution. He would not. Hundreds of Tibetans were killed, thousands more were imprisoned, and the international press was expelled from the country.[2]

Three months after martial law was declared in Tibet, the world saw firsthand the lengths the Chinese government would go to maintain control. The Goddess of Democracy ruled Tiananmen Square in an unforgettable moment until the authorities turned and massacred hundreds, if not thousands, of their own citizens. The numbers will never be known. The gasoline-doused bodies of demonstrators were ignited on the spot.

Like Gandhi before him, Tenzin Gyatso refuses to bow to brutality or to hold the Chinese in enmity. He speaks of the anguish of the Tibetans, yet never does he dismiss or condemn the Chinese people. He continues to put forth his Five Point Peace Plan, again and again advocating reason, love, and compassion.[3]

Now the sweet smell of juniper smoke lingers in the air, an offering from the Lahsang ceremony. The Dalai Lama sits here smiling, closely cropped head to one side, tinted glasses slipped slightly down his nose, his eyes looking over their top, his hand on his chin in thought, red robe over one shoulder, leaning forward now and again as he speaks on top of this mountain that I walk almost daily, this mountain underneath whose shadow I raised my children, this mountain that we have climbed on, played on, slept on, drawn, painted, and loved. This mountain that I bow to on my walks, pay my respects to, the Dalai Lama now sits on top of, speaking. He reminds the world of what we already know—choose love, choose kindness, nonviolence, work for the benefit of all—he is replenishing the store of wisdom and compassion for the entire human family.

I had begun to bow to Mount Tamalpais from the ridgetop where I walked below for some months before I heard the Dalai Lama was coming. Looking around self-consciously at first, to be sure that I was alone, I knelt down on the trail, touched my head to this ground that I hold dear, and offered a momentary prayer. I bowed first to the mountain, to the North, then rose and bowed again in each of the remaining three directions: East, South, and West.

Over time, making these bows when I reached the hilltop became part of my walks, a way of revering this corner of the landscape. The directions grew to have specific meanings. Mount Tamalpais, to the north, is the spirit of this place; the east, my family and community; the west, out over the ocean, the death which soon comes to my grandfather and one day to me. I pay my respects and hope that I will meet it as serenely as does he. I do not yet know what the south represents.

The next morning I walk early down a muddied fire road on the flank of the mountain. Facing east as I turn toward home in the pre-dawn dark, only the softest light has begun to pearl the horizon.

I am perplexed by the tiny flickers of light going off, like matches being lit and blown out, that I see near the ground. After a moment I realize that these are the glimmer of birds' wings as they flit from bush to bush, hop up and down from the ground. Dawn is still so full of night that I cannot detect the birds until they spread their wings. Then the palest light catches the edge backlit and shows me in the briefest flash illumined, not the bird, but the outspread wing.

Notes

Chapter 1. The Unremembered Gate

1. *The Book of Enlightenment,* translated and introduced by Daniel Chanan Matt, The Classics of Western Spirituality (New York: Paulist Press, 1983), p. 55. The *Zohar* is the thirteenth-century spiritual classic and major text of the Kabbalah, the Jewish mystical tradition.

2. Julius Friedrich Sachse, *The German Pietists of Provincial Pennsylvania, 1694–1708* (Printed for the author, Philadelphia, 1895).

3. Walpola Rahula, *What the Buddha Taught* (New York: Grove Press, 1974), p. 61.

4. Ibid. Rahula notes (p. xii) that Theravada is followed primarily in Southeast Asian countries such as, but not limited to, Ceylon, Burma, Thailand, Cambodia, Laos; whereas Mahayana developed later in Tibet, Mongolia, China, and Japan.

5. (Berkeley: University of California Press, 1978).

6. See Hugh R. Downs, *Rhythms of a Himalayan Village* (San Francisco: Harper & Row, 1980), p. 21.

7. For this version of Durga's story I relied primarily on David Kinsley, *Hindu Goddesses* (Berkeley: University of California Press, 1986), and Ajit Mookerjee's *Kali: The Feminine Force* (New York: Destiny Books, 1988).

8. Kinsley, p. 96.

9. Ibid., p. 118.

10. Margaret and James Stutley, *Dictionary of Hinduism* (San Francisco: Harper & Row, 1977), p. 137.

11. Also known as the *Mahanirvana Tantra,* translated by Arthur Avalon (New York: Dover, 1972), p. 50. "Arthur Avalon" was the British barrister, Sir John Woodroffe, who lived in India in the nineteenth century.

12. Subsequently published as *Sky Dancer: The Secret Life and Songs of the Lady Yeshe Tsogyel* (London: Routledge & Kegan Paul, 1984).

13. Mookerjee, p. 28.

14. Anne Fausto-Sterling, "Society Writes Biology/Biology Constructs Gender," *Daedalus,* 116 (Fall 1987), p. 64.

15. The English word *wrathful* is often used in translation to describe a form of the deity that I am choosing to call *fierce.* I am departing from the general use of *wrathful* as "wrath" inevitably connotes "anger" and these deities, in the Tibetan tradition at least, cannot in anyway be said to be *angry,* despite the ferocity or fierceness of their facial expression or general demeanor. Other terms that might be used are *terrific* and *terrible.*

   The fierceness of Tara and the other deities is often likened to the behavior and expression of a mother trying to get her only child out of the path of a speeding car. To the child the mother might appear "fierce" or even angry but in fact the mother's motivation was love and compassion. This is the crucial distinction—motivation.

   The word *fierce* includes *intensely eager; intense, furiously zealous* or *active* and *ardent* in its definition (*Oxford English Dictionary*) and in my opinion, comes closer to accurately describing the motivation of these deities than does the English word *wrathful.* Though more commonly used, *wrathful* is misleading. As in the case with many terms and concepts in translation, it too has limitations.

   The word "fierce" is generally used throughout this text where others generally use the word "wrathful."

16. Arthur Avalon (Sir John Woodroffe), translator, *Hymn to Kali (Karpuradi-Stotra)* (Madras: Ganesh & Co., 1965), citing the Yogini-Tantra. "The

notion of a difference between them has given rise to various Mantras" (p. 34). Vidya is a form of the Mahadevi or the Great Goddess.

17. Leonard Nathan and Clinton Seely, translators, *Grace and Mercy in Her Wild Hair, Selected Poems to the Mother Goddess by Ramprasad Sen* (Boulder, Colo.: Great Eastern, 1982), p. 27.

18. *Tara, Durga, Kali, Mother, the Great Devi*—Ramprasad sang over and over in his astonishing poems. "Listen to this story, Mother Tara," he demanded in one poem; in another he cried, "Tara, Tara . . . You are the mother of all. . . ." Ramprasad said "You'll find Mother / in any house / . . . She's mother, daughter, wife, sister / Every woman close to you."

19. *The Legend of the Great Stupa of Boudhanath,* translated by Keith Dowman (Kathmandu: Diamond Sow Publications, 1978).

20. The amnesiac scopolamine that I was given during childbirth produced what I later found out was an extreme—some said allergic, some said neurochemical—reaction to the drug. At twenty and twenty-one, I knew nothing about medications, nor had I heard of childbirth without it except in foreign countries. At the time I was told that I had a very low pain threshold and poor pain tolerance.

The drug is rarely used any more with childbirth. Many women have had similarly severe reactions.

Chapter 2. Underneath

1. Charles Olson, "These Days," *The Collected Poems of Charles Olson,* edited by George F. Butterick (Berkeley: University of California Press, 1987), p. 106.

2. For further discussion of this topic, see the work of Christina and Stanislav Grof, M.D., *The Stormy Search for the Self* (Los Angeles: Tarcher, 1990).

3. *Letters,* edited by Gerhard Adler and Aniela Jaffe, translated by R.F.C. Hull, Bollingen Series 95, Vol. II; 1951–61 (Princeton, N.J.: Princeton University Press, 1961), cited in Anonymous, *Pass It On* (New York: World Services, 1984), pp. 684–685.

4. See Ernest Kurtz, *Not God* (Center City, Minn.: Hazelden, 1979), pp. 8–9.

5. The National Council on Alcoholism, founded in 1944, has affiliates in nearly 100 cities in the U.S. They provide information and referrals about alcoholism and treatment on the local as well as national level.

> The National Council on Alcoholism
> 12 West 21st Street
> New York, New York 10011
> (212) 206–6770

Alcoholics Anonymous, founded in 1935, is an international fellowship of women and men who share their experience, strength and hope with each other to solve their common problem and help others recover from alcoholism. Numerous other self-help groups have established successful recovery programs modeled after AA's Twelve Steps such as Al-Anon, Narcotics Anonymous, Adult Children of Alcoholics, Cocaine Anonymous, Debtor's Anonymous to mention only a few.

AA is free and widely established with over 42,000 groups registered worldwide. AA can be found in any telephone directory, or contact:

> Alcoholics Anonymous World Services, Inc.
> Box 459
> Grand Central Station
> New York, New York 10163
> (212) 686–1100

Chapter 3. Fallen Down Out of the Sky

1. *The Great Mother: An Analysis of the Archetype,* translated by Ralph Manheim (Princeton, N.J.: Princeton University Press, 1974), p. 321.

2. Leonard W. Moss and Stephen C. Cappannari, in James J. Preston, ed., *Mother Worship* (Chapel Hill, N.C.: University of North Carolina Press, 1982), pp. 53–74.

3. *Newsweek* magazine, July 1984.

4. (New York: Vintage, 1981), p. xvi.

5. *The Secret Book of Revelation* (New York: McGraw-Hill, 1979), p. 120.

6. Ibid., p. 133.

7. Ibid., p. 15.

8. Elaine Pagels, *The Gnostic Gospels* (New York: Vintage, 1981), p. xvi. An excellent source on the Gnostics.

9. Marina Warner, *Alone of All Her Sex*. Warner notes that in Hebrew, the spirit of God was feminine, the *Shekinah*, "neuter in the Greek, *pneuma*, feminine as *sophia* (wisdom), invariably feminine in Syriac, but in Latin it became incontrovertibly masculine: *spiritus sanctus*" (p. 39).

10. Eleanor Munro, *On Glory Roads, A Pilgrim's Book about Pilgrimage* (New York: Thames and Hudson, 1987), p. 145. Ephesus is now part of western Turkey.

11. *The Secret Book of Revelation*, p. 12.

12. Joseph Jablonski, *Free Spirits, Annals of the Insurgent Imagination* (San Francisco: City Lights, 1982).

13. Johann Kelpius's Order of the Woman in the Wilderness is described as one of the early Utopian communities in America in Delores Hayden, *Seven American Utopias* (Cambridge, Mass.: MIT Press, 1977). The Order is written about more fully by Julius Friedrich Sachse in his chapter "The Hermits on the Wissahickon," *The German Pietists of Provincial Pennsylvania 1694–1708*.

14. Julian of Norwich, *Showings*, translated with an introduction by Edmund Colledge, O.S.A., and James Walsh, S.J., The Classics of Western Spirituality (New York: Paulist Press, 1978), pp. 298–299.

15. Martin Buber, *Ecstatic Confessions* (1909), p. 110.

Chapter 4. Where Tara Emerges

1. "Uttama's Song," from *The Therigata, The First Enlightened Women: Poems by and Stories of the Earliest Women in Buddhism*, translated by Susan Murcott. Unpublished manuscript (Marblehead, Mass., 1985), p. 26.

2. Stephan Beyer, *The Cult of Tara* (Berkeley: University of California Press, 1978), p. 4.

3. At the time, Tara Doyle was running the Antioch College Buddhist Studies Program at Bodh Gayā, India.

4. Professor Robert Thurman pointed this out.

5. John Blofeld has commented clearly on this subject in *The Tantric Mysticism of Tibet* (Boston: Shambhala Publications, 1987), p. 199. Many descriptions of actual practices, *sadhanas*, are rarely set forth except in the most

general way, he maintains. Block prints and manuscripts kept privately by lamas may even have certain passages scrambled or left out so that the uninitiated could not use them without proper guidance.

Chapter 5. This Nameless Path

1. *Proverbs and Songs from the Countryside of Castille* (Cambridge: Harvard University Press).

2. By "close at hand" I mean the San Francisco Bay area. Women teachers were emerging out of the turmoil of some of the Zen communities on the East coast and in Los Angeles, but by 1985, I had turned to the study of Tibetan Buddhism where there were fewer women teachers.
   See the *Kahawai* Collective's work, *Not Mixing up Buddhism* (Fredonia, N.Y.: White Pine Press, 1986); Ellen S. Sidor, ed., *A Gathering of Spirit, Women Teaching in American Buddhism* (Cumberland, R.I.: Primary Point Press, 1987); Lenore Friedman, *Meetings with Remarkable Women, Buddhist Teachers in America* (Berkeley: Shambhala Publications, 1987); Sandy Boucher, *Turning the Wheel, American Women Creating the New Buddhism* (San Francisco: Harper & Row, 1988); and Helen Tworkov, *Zen in America* (Berkeley: North Point Press, 1989), for discussion and profiles of some of the women teachers emerging during this period.

3. (Boston: Routledge & Kegan Paul, 1984).

4. Ibid., pp. 52–54. Allione's discussion of the *delog* draws on Mircia Eliade's *Shamanism* and Guiseppi Tucci's *Religions of Tibet*.

Chapter 6. Who Is Leaving, Who Will Return?

1. *Transformation into the Exalted State, Spiritual Exercises of the Tibetan Tantric Tradition*, translated by Carol Savvas and Lodro Tulku, Fasc. 18. (Rikon, Switzerland: Tibet Institute, June 1987), p. 24.

2. John F. Avedon's book, *In Exile from the Land of the Snows, The First Full Account of the Dalai Lama and Tibet Since the Chinese Conquest* (New York: Knopf, 1984), is basic reading on this subject.

3. (Ithaca, N.Y.: Snow Lion Publications, 1985).

Chapter 7. Effort Is Required

1. *Not Mixing up Buddhism: Essays on Women and Buddhist Practice* (Fredonia, N.Y.: White Pine Press, 1986), p. 7.

2. *"Green"* in Tibetan also can mean *dark* or *black*. Cf. Martin Willson, *In Praise of Tara, Songs to the Saviouress* (London: Wisdom Publications, 1986), *"sNgo sangs = syama,* which can mean any dark colour—black, dark blue, brown, grey, green—but is the usual word for the colour of Green Tara *(Syama-Tara)"* (p. 402, n. 82).

3. Ibid., elephants, and demons, pp. 304–306.

4. Believed to be a human incarnation of Tara, the present incarnation of Dorje Phagmo was handpicked by the Chinese, making her authenticity suspect. The Tibetans I spoke with in Dharamsala had little faith in her.

5. I am indebted to Professor Robert Thurman for some understanding of how astonishingly rich and different the Indo-Tibetan view is from the West.
   Lama Anagarika Govinda's *Foundations of Tibetan Mysticism* (pp. 99–110) further clarifies the spiritual basis of the Buddhist image of deities in union, for what to the untrained Western eye might appear to be only sexual (New York: Samuel Weiser, 1977).

6. (Boston: Shambhala Publications, 1987), pp. 84 ff.

7. Ven. Tulku Chagdud Rinpoche's excellent description.

8. Ibid., p. 85. Blofeld cites Edward Conze's *Buddhism* (Oxford: Bruno Cassir).

9. Karma Lekshe Tsomo, *Sakyadhita: Daughters of the Buddha* (Ithaca, N.Y.: Snow Lion Publications, 1989), edited the proceedings and talks from the Bodh Gayā conference.

10. For a discussion of the complexities of this matter, see Dr. Judith Simmer-Brown's article in *The Vajradhatu Sun,* "Mahaprajapati's Daughters: The Restoration of the Bhikshuni Order in Tibetan Buddhism," Vol. 10, no. 5 (June–July 1988), pp. 8–28.

11. Karma Lekshe Tsomo, "Tibetan Nuns and Nunneries," *Tibet Journal,*

Vol. 12, no. 4, (Winter 1987). Reprinted in *Feminine Ground: Essays on Women and Tibet,* edited by Janice D. Willis (Ithaca, N.Y.: Snow Lion Publications, 1987).

12. I have added to Lekshe's telling with material from Susan Murcott's "Women Who Have Grown Old with Knowledge," her new translation of the *Therigata.* Unpublished manuscript (Marblehead, Mass., 1985).

13. See Helen Tworkov, *Zen in America* (Berkeley: North Point Press, 1989).

14. See Hopkinson, Hill, and Kiera, eds., *Not Mixing up Buddhism,* as well as the work of Professor Anne Carolyn Klein, "Gain or Drain? Buddhist and Feminist Views on Compassion," *Spring Wind,* Vol. 6, nos. 1, 2, and 3 (1986), Professor Rita Gross, and others writing at this time whose work I would later discover.

Chapter 8. The Ravens of Einsiedeln

1. "Horologium" (in Swedish), poem no. 11 in *Mellan polerna* I–XIII (Stockholm: Norstedts, 1982), or "Trees," translated into English by the author.

2. Ean Begg's *The Cult of the Black Virgin* (Boston: Arkana, 1985), contains an important gazeteer in the back, giving the location and description of many of the Black Madonnas in Europe and around the world.

3. Dora Kalff died January 15, 1990, at Zollikon, Switzerland.

4. C. G. Jung and C. Kerenyi, *Essays on a Science of Mythology* (Princeton, N.J.: Princeton University Press, Bollingen Paperback, 1973), p. 73.

5. Ibid., p. 79.

6. Cultural absorption was more widespread than many realize. In Egypt and Syria, December 25 was celebrated as the birth of the sun god, brought forth by the Virgin, prior to the birth of Christ. "No doubt the Virgin who thus conceived and bore a son on the twenty-fifth of December was the great Oriental goddess whom the Semites called the Heavenly Virgin . . . a form of Astarte," Sir James Frazer, *The Golden Bough* (New York: Macmillan, 1967), p. 416.

7. I Kings 11:5.

8. Modern-day Syria and Iraq down to the Nile Valley.

9. This fusion of elements from one culture to another is called "syncretism" in anthropology. It is a dynamic, logical, ongoing process. As Dr. Lindegger indicated, many churches are built on former pagan temple sites.

   Anthropologists Leonard W. Moss and Stephen C. Cappannari give one of the clearest descriptions of this process in their essay, "In Quest of the Black Virgin," that of Pope Gregory the Great, writing in A.D. 601 to his priests: "We must refrain from destroying the temples of the idols. It is necessary only to destroy the idols, and to sprinkle holy water in these same temples, to build ourselves altars and place holy relics therein. If the construction of these temples is solid, good and useful, they will pass from the cult of demons to the service of the true God; because it will come to pass that the nation, seeing the continued existence of its old places of devotion, will be disposed, by a sort of habit, to go there." Quoted in James J. Preston, ed., *Mother Worship* (Chapel Hill, N.C.: University of North Carolina Press, 1982), p. 71. Gregory's priests had trouble winning converts, sparking his counsel to use the sites already considered sacred as a means of making conversion more palatable.

   Moss and Cappannari give what they claim was one of the most interesting examples of this cultural diffusion—the case of a church at Enna in Sicily.

   Enna, situated on a steep mountain in the northwest corner of Sicily, was a site sacred to Ceres and Proserpina, the Roman names for Demeter, Great Mother Goddess of the earth and her daughter, Persephone, the Queen of the Underworld. (In the earlier Greek legend, Persephone was called "Saviour" because of her annual death and resurrection.) In the Roman version of the myth, it was believed that Proserpina's abduction by Pluto took place on the shores of Lake Enna.

   "It is at Enna in Sicily that one finds the most interesting adaptation of pagan symbolism by the Roman Catholic Church: until the mid-nineteenth century, the images of Ceres and Proserpina were used in the church as the Virgin and Infant Jesus, despite the fact that *Proserpina was female!* A papal order by Pius IX removed the pagan statues to an adjacent museum that is, somehow, never open to public viewing." Ibid., p. 61.

Ceres had a black aspect, as did Demeter Melaina, the Black Demeter. Both were earth goddesses, sources of fertility, and precursors of the Black Madonna, along with Ishtar, Inanna, Cybele, Isis, Artemis, Diana, and others.

10. Today named *Monte San Guiliano,* according to Dr. Lindegger.

11. I rely largely on Gustafson's substantial research for the story of the Einsiedeln Madonna. The monastery publishes versions of it as well, but his work is the most detailed and analytical for my purposes. The monastery books, those available in English, are primarily chronological histories. Gustafson gives that and more. His work has been revised substantially and rewritten as a book, *The Black Madonna* (Boston: Sigo Press, 1990).

12. Fred Gustafson, "The Black Madonna of Einsiedeln: A Psychological Perspective," dissertation, Jung Institute, Switzerland, p. 4.

13. Ibid., p. 5.

14. Ibid., p. 13.

15. Idem.

16. Ibid., p. 14.

17. The angel Gabriel said to Virgin Mary, "The Holy Spirit will come upon you, and the power of the Most High will cover you with its shadow. And so the child will be holy and will be called Son of God." Luke 1:35.

18. Ean Begg, *The Cult of the Black Virgin.*

19. James Trefil, *The Dark Side of the Universe* (New York: Anchor Books, 1988).

20. See Virginia Trimble, professor of physics at the University of California at Irvine, "The Search for Dark Matter," Part Two of "Our Cosmic Origins," *Astronomy,* Vol. 16, no. 3 (March 1988), pp. 18–23.

21. Marcia Bartusiak quoting researcher in "Wanted: Dark Matter," *Discover* (December 1988), pp. 63–69.

22. Erich Neumann, *The Great Mother,* translated by Ralph Manheim (Princeton, N.J.: Princeton University Press, 1974), p. 165.

23. *Atlas of the World* (Washington, D.C.: National Geographic Society, revised 3rd ed., 1970), pp. 156–57.

24. Cf. Joseph Campbell and Bill Moyers, *The Power of Myth;* Ean Begg, *Cult of the Black Virgin;* Ivan van Sertima, ed. *Black Women in Antiquity;* Geoffrey Ashe, *The Virgin,* et al.

25. *Original Blessing* (Santa Fe, N.M.: Bear and Co., 1985).

26. *Bread Not Stone: The Challenge of Feminist Biblical Interpretation* (Boston: Beacon, 1985).

27. *The Mother's Songs, Images of God the Mother* (New York: Paulist Press, 1986).

28. Pagels was working on her latest book *Adam, Eve and the Serpent* (New York: Random House, 1988) when we spoke the following January, 1987.

29. Geshe Champa Lodro Rinpoche gave an explanation of Tara that included the essential points of the account given by the sixteenth-century Tibetan lama Jo-nan Taranatha. Taranatha's text was called *The Golden Rosary* and in it he clarified the origin of the Tara Tantra. A version of Taranatha's text is published as *The Origin of the Tara Tantra,* translated and edited by David Tempelman (Dharamsala: Library of Tibetan Works and Archives, 1981). Geshe Champa Lodro would have his own center at Rige Champa Chöling in Adligenswill, outside Lucerne, as well as teaching at Yiga Chözin, where I met him.

30. He explained that there are many more than twenty-one Taras.

Chapter 9. The Way to Poland

1. *Tao Te Ching,* #1, translated by Stephen Mitchell (New York: Harper & Row, 1988).

2. Nagarjuna wrote a well-known "Praise of Khadiravani Tara" to this form of Tara. See Martin Willson, *In Praise of Tara, Songs to the Saviouress* (London: Wisdom Publications, 1986), pp. 282–285.

Chapter 10. We Go Now

1. *Selected Poems,* translated by W. H. Auden and Leif Sjoberg (New York: Pantheon Books, 1971), p. 42. "*Ayiasma (Hagiasma): purifying well. 'The water cult is still alive in Greece and the Near East. A glass of cold water is the holy welcoming drink among the people' " (p. 37).

2. Marian Zalecki, O.S.P., *Theology of a Marian Shrine, Our Lady of Czestochowa,* Marian Library Studies, Vol. 8 (Dayton, Ohio: University of Dayton, 1976).

3. Janusz S. Pasierb, *The Shrine of the Black Madonna at Czestochowa.* Photographs by Janusz Rosikon, Chris Niedenthal, Josef Jurkowski. (Warsaw: Interpress Publishers, 1985), p. 6.

4. Ibid., p. 75.

Chapter 11. The Pilgrimage to the Black Madonna

1. *The Songlines* (New York: Viking, 1987), p. 171.

Chapter 12. After the Pilgrimage

1. *New Seeds of Contemplation* (New York: New Directions, 1961), p. 221.

Chapter 13. There Are Roses of Fire

1. *The Ink Dark Moon. Love Poems by Ono no Komachi and Izumi Shikibu, Women of the Ancient Court of Japan,* translated by Jane Hirshfield with Mariko Aratani (New York: Charles Scribner's Sons, 1988), p. 116.

2. Thich Nhat Hanh was nominated for the Nobel Peace Prize by Martin Luther King, Jr., for his work as chairman of the Vietnamese Buddhist Peace Delegation during the war. He is a poet and Zen master and author of numerous books including *Being Peace* (Berkeley: Parallax

Press, 1987). Parallax publishes much of Thich Nhat Hanh's work: P.O. Box 7355, Berkeley, CA 94707.

3. The fourteen Precepts of the Order of Interbeing, in shortened form:
    1. Do not be idolatrous about or bound to any doctrine, theory, or ideology, even Buddhist ones. All systems of thought are guiding means; they are not absolute truth.
    2. Do not think the knowledge you possess is changeless, absolute truth. . . . Truth is found in life and not merely in conceptual knowledge. . . .
    3. Do not force others, including children, by any means whatsoever, to adopt your views. . . .
    4. Do not avoid suffering or close your eyes before suffering. . . .
    5. Do not accumulate wealth while millions are hungry. . . . Live simply and share time, energy and material resources with those who are in need.
    6. Do not maintain anger or hatred. . . .
    7. Do not lose yourself in dispersion and in your surroundings. Learn to practice breathing in order to regain composure of body and mind. . . .
    8. Do not utter words that can create discord and cause the community to break. Make every effort to reconcile and resolve all conflicts, however small.
    9. Do not say untruthful things. . . . Do not utter words that cause division and hatred. . . . Always speak truthfully and constructively. Have the courage to speak out about situations of injustice even when doing so may threaten your own safety.
    10. A religious community should take a clear stand against oppression and injustice and should strive to change the situation without engaging in partisan conflicts.
    11. Do not live with a vocation that is harmful to humans and nature. . . . Select a vocation which helps realize your ideal of compassion.
    12. Do not kill. Do not let others kill. Find whatever means possible to protect life and prevent war.
    13. Possess nothing that should belong to others. . . .
    14. Do not mistreat your body. Learn to handle it with respect. . . .
For the complete Precepts see Thich Nhat Hanh, *Interbeing: Com-*

mentaries on the Tiep Hien Precepts, ed. Fred Eppsteiner (Berkeley: Parallax Press, 1987).

4. (New York: Pantheon Books, 1985), p. 84.

5. Victor and Edith Turner, *Image and Pilgrimage in Christian Culture: Anthropological Perspectives* (New York: Columbia University Press, 1978), p. 47.

6. Zsolt Aradi, *Shrines to Our Lady Around the World* (New York: Farrar, Straus & Young, 1954), pp. 155–156.

Chapter 14. The Madonna's Face

1. "San Onofre, California," *Hauling up Morning. The 1990 Peace Calendar,* ed. Martin Steingesser (New York: War Resisters League & New Society Publishers, 1990).

2. Victor and Edith Turner, *Image and Pilgrimage in Christian Culture: Anthropological Perspectives* (New York: Columbia University Press, 1978), p. 100.

3. My visit in August 1988 took place during the growing buildup of refugees in the Valley that would reach crisis proportions the following winter. Precise numbers are difficult to arrive at and must include not only INS District applications for asylum but also arrests by the Border Patrol and unknown numbers who did not present themselves to any federal agency, voluntarily or involuntarily. By October, November, December of 1988, 450 people a *day* (nearly 10,000 people a month) were applying for political asylum to the INS Director, the Brownsville INS Deputy Director told me. The rate in August was well on its way to 2,000 per week, whether they had that exact number of formal applications or not for the week of my stay. Figures are for "OTMs" only (Other Than Mexicans), INS explained. On December 23, 1988, the *Brownsville Herald* reported that 30,000 had applied to INS alone since the preceding May.

   By January 1990, there would be a dramatic rise of Salvadorans in South Texas again after the rebel offensive of 1989. On February 7, 1990, INS reinstituted the detention policy and began to put up circus-size tents again to handle the influx. INS said that it could handle up to 10,000 people in the detention camp. Robert Suro, "U.S.

Is Renewing Border Detentions" *The New York Times,* February 8, 1990.

4. The Sanctuary movement is a group of faith communities—churches, temples—that have established themselves as sanctuaries, safe havens, for undocumented refugees seeking political asylum from war-torn areas of Central America. In opposition to the United States government's limited interpretation of the 1980 Refugee Act, participating congregations help provide food, shelter, and assistance in applying for proper papers and the appropriate legal status. They also accompany refugees in resettlement.

5. Charles Lane, "The War That Will Not End," *The New Republic,* October 16, 1989, p. 23. Lane covers Central America for *Newsweek* magazine and lives in San Salvador.

6. "Before 1975, the United States Department of Justice adjudicated fewer than 200 political asylum cases per year. In 1989 more than 50,000 petitions are pending in immigration courts. The flow of Central American refugees in the 1980's was simply not anticipated." Central American and Haitians account for the majority of petitions pending. Aurora Camacho De Schmidt, "United States Refugee Policy and Central America," *Christianity and Crisis,* Vol. 49, no. 13, September 25, 1989, p. 284.

7. In July 1989, the American Bar Association began a *pro bono* program for asylum applicants in Harlingen, Texas, called ProBar. After meeting with *Proyecto Libertad* staff and studying the refugee crisis, they denounced the lack of access to legal counsel and established ProBar to help insure proper representation for refugees' asylum claims.

8. Turner and Turner, *Image and Pilgrimage,* p. 51.

9. *The New York Times,* January 7, 1989, "Suit Attacks Policy of Keeping Aliens in Texas," Peter Applebome.

10. *Morazon* v. *Thornburgh,* Civil Action No. B-89-002 (S. D. Tex. 1989).

11. I spoke with Bishop Fitzpatrick in May 1989. Important background reading on this subject is Penny Lernoux's work, *People of God* (New York: Viking, 1989), *Cry of the People* (New York: Penguin, 1982), and Renny Golden and Michael McConnell's *Sanctuary: The New Underground Railroad* (Maryknoll, N.Y.: Orbis Books, 1986).

The statement of the Texas Conference of Churches and Catholic Bishops was issued February 20, 1989.

12. In fiscal 1988, district directors for INS approved 75 percent of Iranian requests for political asylum, 77 percent of Ethiopian requests, 53.7 percent of Polish requests, 5 percent of Guatemalan, and 2.7 percent of El Salvadoran requests for political asylum.

13. Robert Kahn, the *Brownsville Herald,* May 2, 1989. Findings came from *Orantes-Hernandez* v. *Meese,* 685 F. Supp. 1488 (C. D. Cal. 1988), subsequently referred to as *Orantes-Hernandez* v. *Thornburgh.*

14. The INS was accused of violating Federal District Judge David V. Kenyon's permanent injunction which ordered the Service to inform Salvadorans of their legal right to apply for political asylum.

15. The U.S., a country founded by refugees and immigrants, must at least align itself with international standards and honor the U.N. Protocol we agreed to abide by in 1968. See Helsinki Watch Report, *Detained, Denied, Deported, Asylum Seekers in the United States,* June 1989 (New York: U.S. Helsinki Watch Committee, 1989).

16. 480 U.S. 421 (1987).

17. Quoted in *Sanctuary,* p. 72.

18. Over a year later, on October 10, 1989, I would read in the *San Francisco Examiner* an article by Larry D. Hatfield on Archbishop Prospero Penados del Barrio from Guatemala. Penados, president of the Central American Conference of Bishops and member of Pope John Paul's commission on Third World countries, had called for withdrawal of United States and Soviet support from Latin America. Like Archbishop Romero before him, Archbishop Penados had received numerous death threats for becoming an outspoken advocate for the masses. Penados is responsible for the controversial pastoral letter, "A Cry for Land," in which the Guatemalan bishops "denounced as sinful the distribution of wealth" in their impoverished nation. It is public knowledge he is a likely target for right-wing death squads. He was in San Francisco to receive the San Francisco Archdiocese human-rights award and to address the Guatemala refugee community of over 30,000 in the Bay Area.

19. Vicki Kemper, "Innocent in the Eyes of God," *Sojourners,* August/September 1987, p. 22.

20. Brenda Sanchez, her husband, and daughter were granted political asylum on September 22, 1989, after five years of waiting. Asylum was granted on the basis that there was reason for them to fear persecution in El Salvador.

21. Matt Meyer, "Women in Chile Demand Justice," *The NonViolent Activist*, The Magazine of the War Resisters League (April/May 1989), p. 5.

Chapter 15. Walesa's Prayer

1. "Recovery," *The Collected Poems, 1931–1987*, translated by the author (New York: Ecco Press, 1988), p. 54.

2. "Reflections on a Better Today," *The New Yorker*, February 3, 1986. Much of the groundwork for Solidarity was laid down by KOR, the Workers Defense Committee established in 1976. Rather than address the government, KOR offered concrete assistance in the difficulties of daily life to its members—legal help, food, financial aid, whatever might be necessary to assist members who had suffered from government repression.

Chapter 16. The Mystery of the Messages

1. *This Longing. Poetry, Teaching Stories and Letters of Rumi* (thirteenth-century Sufi), translated by Coleman Barks and John Moyne (Putney, Vt.: Threshold Books, 1988), p. 20.

2. The documentary grew out of Brendan's project, the Inner Mechanisms of the Healing Response, at the Institute for Noetic Sciences, Sausalito, California, of which O'Reagan is also Vice President for Research. The Institute has the largest data base in the country of medically reported cases of spontaneous remissions.

3. "Prayers of Request to the Lady Tara," *Transformation into the Exalted State*, translated by Carol Savvas, Opuscula Tibetana (Rikon, Switzerland: Tibet Institute, June 1987, Fasc. 18), p. 21.

4. Mary Craig, *Spark from Heaven: The Mystery of the Madonna at Medjugorje* (Notre Dame, Indiana: Ave Maria Press, 1988), p. 81. Craig's balanced, historical account was written from her experience of working on a documentary film on Medjugorje for BBC television in 1986.

5. Ibid., p. 107.

Chapter 17. Where the Streams Cross

1. "The Sun," *The Collected Poems, 1931–1987,* translated by the author (New York: Ecco Press, 1988) p. 55.

2. *The Lion's Roar,* Center Productions, 1985, a film in tribute to the late Gyalwa Karmapa.

3. The Dalai Lama's Five Point Peace Plan was formulated in September 1987 and has been presented to the European Parliament at Strasbourg.
    1. Transformation of the whole of Tibet into a zone of peace.
    2. Abandonment of China's population transfer policy which threatens the very existence of the Tibetan people.
    3. Respect for the Tibetan people's fundamental human rights and democratic freedoms.
    4. Restoration and protection of Tibet's natural environment and the abandonment of China's use of Tibet for the production of nuclear weapons and dumping of nuclear waste.
    5. Commencement of earnest negotiations on the future status of Tibet and of relations between the Tibetan and the Chinese people.

4. Study Committee on the Potential for Rehabilitating Lands Surface Mined for Coal in the Western United States, *Rehabilitation Potential of Western Coal Lands* (Cambridge, Mass.: Ballinger, 1974).
    Conflicts over the Four Corners area continue. Banyacya arrived at the *Kalachakra* late because of his involvement in the Big Mountain area of Black Mesa, the holy land within the Four Sacred Mountains of the Dineh (Navajo) and Hopi, a territory that overlaps Arizona, Utah, New Mexico, and Colorado. Now the battles continue in U.S. courts, where Native Americans await the outcome in the various lawsuits and appeals they've brought to halt relocating their people.

5. Peter Matthiessen, *Indian Country* (New York: Viking, 1984), p. 78, for an account of this historic gathering. Banyacya helped initiate the Indian cultural revival movement that grew out of these meetings. Four interpreters were chosen to carry the Hopi prophecy to the white world in 1948. Only Banyacya remains.

6. See chapter 7, p. 100.

7. There are several different versions of the Twenty-one Praises to Tara.

These praises are adapted from "A Short Tara Puja" (Kagyu Shenpen Kunchab, 751 Airport Road, Santa Fe, N.M. 87501), the text we used for the Tara *puja*.

8. George C. Berticevich, "Sera Monastery, Near Lhasa, Tibet," April 1985 (Sausalito, Calif.).

9. See Janusz S. Pasierb and Jan Samek, *The Shrine of the Black Madonna at Czestochowa*. Photographs by Janusz Rosikon, Chris Niedenthal, Jozef Jurkowski (Warsaw: Interpress Publishers, 1985), p. 5.

10. Nagarajuna, "Praise of Khadiravani Tara," in Martin Willson, *In Praise of Tara, Songs of the Saviouress* (London: Wisdom Publications, 1986), p. 284.

11. Erich Neumann, *The Great Mother*, translated by Ralph Manheim (Princeton, N.J.: Princeton University Press, 1974) p. 165.

12. Conversation with Marija Gimbutas; see also her book, *The Gods and Goddesses of Old Europe* (Berkeley: University of California Press, 1982).

13. Emile Saillens, *Nos vierges noires, leurs origines* (Paris: Les éditions Universelles, 1945), as cited by Moss and Cappannari in James J. Preston, ed., *Mother Worship*, (Chapel Hill, N.C.: University of North Carolina Press, 1982), p. 68.

14. Conversation with Ean Begg. For a discussion of Black Virgins and a valuable gazeteer of locations of Black Madonnas around the world, see his *The Cult of the Black Virgin* (Boston: Arkana, 1985).

15. *A Memory of Fire 1: Genesis*, translated by Cedric Belfrage (New York: Pantheon Books, 1985), p. 277.

16. Ugyen Chudon translated the tape.

17. Also known as Yum Kusho, Kunsang Dechen related a handful of stories of Tibetan women masters, the two most important being Yeshe Tsogyel, eighth century, and Machig Labdron, the eleventh-century master. Machig had thousands of disciples, some of whom came from India to Tibet to hear her teach. She was married, had children, one of whom, a son, achieved enlightenment as her student. Machig is considered the source of *Chöd* practice in Tibet, the special form of meditation practice of which Kunsang Dechen is a teacher. Carol Savvas is translating Machig's biography and writing about the development

of *chod* practice under the guidance of Geshe Champa Lodro Rinpoche.

18. Maurine Stuart Roshi died February 26, 1990.

19. The history of the growing numbers of women teachers in Buddhism, both in the United States and around the world, is being documented by others. The handful I mention are in no way to be construed as being the only ones, the most important ones, the most significant ones. They are teachers with whom I have had some form of contact and know to be reliable. There are many other fine women teachers of whom I have heard but not yet had the opportunity to meet.

I refer the reader to the existing books on the subject in footnote 2, chapter 5. Also see the quarterly *Newsletter on International Buddhist Women's Activities, NIBWA,* (c/o Dr. Chatsumarn Kabilsingh, Faculty of Liberal Arts, Thammasat University, Bangkok 10200, Thailand), a small but important publication documenting the rapidly changing role of women in Buddhism around the world.

20. Jetsun Kushola is a Tibetan, the sister of Sakya Trizin, head of one of the four major lineages of Tibetan Buddhism. Trained alongside her brother, Jetsun Kushola has been teaching since she was eleven years old.

21. Jane Tromge, *Tara, Instructions for the Short Red Tara Practice According to the Teachings of Chagdud Tulku Rinpoche* (Box 387, Junction City, CA 96048).

22. Professor Robert Thurman's translation of the stages of the enlightenment experience. There are four stages that the mind can go through at death in ordinary experience, well-mapped in the Tibetan system, or during the experience of enlightenment. These stages and the colors associated with them are translated variously.

White is the first color encountered in the layers of the subtle mind, according to Thurman. This is the stage of *luminescence,* described by the Tibetans as moonlight. Then comes red, *radiance,* described as sunlight. Next comes black, which he translates as *imminence,* described as the starless midnight before enlightenment. Enlightenment is referred to as the "clear light," translated as *translucence* or *transparency,* which comes just before dawn and is beyond color, beyond dark and light.

23. By Angelos, sixteenth century, from the art exhibit and book *Holy*

Image, Holy Space, Icons and Frescoes from Greece (Greek Ministry of Culture, Byzantine Museum of Athens, 1988), #44, p. 125.

Chapter 18. On the Mountain

1. Namkhai Norbu, *The Crystal and the Way of Light, Sutra, Tantra and Dzogchen,* compiled and edited by John Shane (London: Routledge Kegan Paul, 1986), p. 135.

2. Documented reports to Amnesty International revealed the widespread use of torture. Tibetan nuns raped with electric cattle prods by Chinese soldiers, monks hung upside down and beaten with nail-studded wooden paddles, the list of abuses and human-rights violations is extensive.

   Amnesty International is an important source of information for human-rights abuses in Tibet. More comprehensive information on Tibet comes from such sources as the U.S. Tibet Committee in New York, the International Campaign for Tibet and *Tibet Watch* in Washington, D.C., Humanitas International in Menlo Park, and *News Tibet* published by the Office of Tibet, 107 East 31st Street, New York, New York 10016. The *Snow Lion* newsletter and catalog (P.O. Box 6483, Ithaca, New York 14851) is a helpful source of information on the situation in Tibet, Tibetan Buddhism and the Tibetan community-in-exile.

3. See note 3, chapter 17, Five Point Peace Plan.

Selected Bibliography

Allione, Tsultrim. *Women of Wisdom*. Boston: Routledge & Kegan Paul, 1984.

Anonymous. *Pass It On*. New York: World Services, 1984.

Aradi, Zsolt. *Shrines to Our Lady Around the World*. New York: Farrar, Straus and Young, 1954.

Ashe, Geoffrey. *The Virgin*. London: Routledge & Kegan Paul, 1976.

—————. *Miracles*. London: Routledge & Kegan Paul, 1978.

Atisa. *A Lamp for the Path and Commentary*. Translated and annotated by Richard Sherburne, S.J. Boston: George Allen & Unwin Ltd., 1983.

Avalon, Arthur and Ellen. *Hymns to the Goddess: Translated from the Sanskrit*. 2d rev. ed. Madras: Ganesh and Co., 1952.

Avalon, Arthur. *Hymn to Kali (Karpuradi-Stotra)*. Madras: Ganesh & Co., 1965.

Begg, Ean. *The Cult of the Black Virgin*. Boston: Arkana, 1985.

Berger, Pamela. *The Goddess Obscured: Transformation of the Grain Protectress from Goddess to Saint*. Boston: Beacon Press, 1985.

Bernal, Martin. *Black Athena: The Afroasiatic Roots of Classical Civilization*. Vol. 1, *The Fabrication of Ancient Greece, 1785–1985*. New Brunswick, N.J.: Rutgers University Press, 1987.

Bernbaum, Edwin, Ph.D. *The Way to Shambala: A Search for the Mythical Kingdom Beyond the Himalayas*. Los Angeles: Jeremy P. Tarcher, Inc., 1980.

Berry, Thomas. *The Dream of the Earth*. San Francisco: Sierra Club Books, 1988.

Beyer, Stephan. *The Cult of Tara: Magic and Ritual in Tibet.* Berkeley: University of California Press, 1978.

Blofeld, John. *Bodhisattva of Compassion: The Mystical Tradition of Kuan Yin.* Boston: Shambhala Publications, 1988.

——————. *The Tantric Mysticism of Tibet.* Boston: Shambhala, 1987.

Bly, Robert. *A Little Book on the Human Shadow.* San Francisco: Harper and Row, 1988.

Boucher, Sandy. *Turning the Wheel: American Women Creating the New Buddhism.* San Francisco: Harper and Row, 1988.

Chattopadhyaya, Alaka. *Atisa and Tibet: Life and Works of Dipamkara Srijnana in Relation to the History and Religion of Tibet, With Tibetan Sources.* Calcutta: Alaka Chattopadhyaya, 1967.

Chatwin, Bruce. *The Songlines.* New York: Viking, 1987.

Cleary, Thomas, trans. *Entry Into the Realm of Reality, The Text, The Gandavyuha, The Final Book of The Avatamsaka Sutra.* Boston: Shambhala, 1989.

Clebert, Jean-Paul. *The Gypsies.* Translated by Charles Duff. Harmondsworth, England: Penguin, 1967.

Craig, Mary. *Spark from Heaven: The Mystery of the Madonna of Medjugorje.* Notre Dame, Ind.: Ave Maria Press, 1988.

Craighead, Meinrad. *The Mother's Songs, Images of God the Mother.* New York: Paulist Press, 1986.

David-Neel, Alexandra. *Buddhism: Its Doctrines and Methods.* New York: St. Martin's Press, 1978.

Doboom Tulku and Glen H. Mullin, comp. and trans. *Atisha and Buddhism in Tibet.* New Delhi: Tibet House, 1983.

Dowman, Keith. *A Buddhist Guide to the Power Places of the Kathmandu Valley.* Kathmandu: Diamonds Sow, 1984.

——————. *Sky Dancer: The Secret Life and Songs of the Lady Yeshe Tsogyel.* Routledge & Kegan Paul, 1984.

Downs, Hugh R. *Rhythms of a Himalayan Village.* San Francisco: Harper & Row, 1980.

Eckhardt, Meister. *Breakthrough: Meister Eckhardt's Creation Spirituality in New Translation.* Introduction and Commentaries by Matthew Fox. Garden City, N.Y.: Doubleday & Co., 1980.

Ekelof, Gunnar. *Selected Poems.* Translated by W.H. Auden and Leif Sjoberg. New York: Pantheon Books, 1971.

Fausto-Sterling, Anne. "Science Writes Biology/Biology Constructs Gender." *Daedalus* 116, Fall 1987, 61–76.

Fields, Rick. *How the Swans Came to the Lake: A Narrative History of Buddhism in America.* Boulder: Shambhala, 1981.

Fleming, David, S.J. *Modern Spiritual Exercises: A Contemporary Reading of the Spiritual Exercises of St. Ignatius.* Garden City, N.Y.: Image Books, 1983.

Friedman, Lenore. *Meetings with Remarkable Women: Buddhist Teachers in America.* Boston: Shambhala Publications, 1987.

Galeano, Eduardo. *Memory of Fire.* Vol. 1, *Genesis.* Translated by Cedric Belfrage. New York: Pantheon, 1985.

Ghosh, Mallar. *Development of Buddhist Iconography in Eastern India: A Study of Tara, Prajnas of Five Tagathas and Bhrikuti.* New Delhi: Munshiram Manoharlal, 1980.

Gimbutas, Marija. *The Goddesses and Gods of Old Europe 6500–3500 B.C.: Myths and Cult Images.* rev. ed. Berkeley: University of California Press, 1982.

Golden, Renny, and Michael McConnell. *Sanctuary: The New Underground Railroad.* New York: Orbis Books, 1986.

Govinda, Lama Anagarika. *Foundations of Tibetan Mysticism.* New York: Samuel Weiser, 1969.

Gross, Rita M. "Hindu Female Deities as a Resource for Contemporary Rediscovery of the Goddess." *Journal of the American Academy of Religion* 56:269–291.

Gyatso, Geshe Kelsang. *Meaningful to Behold: A Commentary to Shantideva's "Guide to the Bodhisattva's Way of Life".* London: Tharpa Publications, 1986.

Gyatso, Tenzin, Dalai Lama 14. *Kindness, Clarity, and Insight.* Translated and edited by Jeffery Hopkins. Co-edited by Elizabeth Napper. Ithaca, N.Y.: Snow Lion Publications, 1985.

H.H. the Dalai Lama, Tsong-ka-pa and Jeffery Hopkins. *Deity Yoga: In Action and Performance Tantra.* Ithaca, N.Y.: Snow Lion Publications, 1981.

Harding, M. Esther. *Woman's Mysteries: Ancient and Modern.* San Francisco: Harper & Row, 1976.

Hawley, John Stratton and Donna Marie Wulff, eds. *The Divine Consort: Radha and the Goddesses of India.* Boston: Beacon Press, 1986.

Heyob, Sharon Kelly. *The Cult of Isis Among Women in the Graeco-Roman World.* Leiden, Netherlands: E. J. Brill, 1975.

Hopkinson, Deborah, Michelle Hill, and Eileen Kiera, eds. *Not Mixing Up Buddhism: Essays on Women and Buddhist Practice.* Fredonia, N.Y.: White Pine Press, 1986.

Ironbiter, Suzanne. *Devi.* Stamford, Conn.: Yuganta Press, 1987.

Jackson, Carl T. *The Oriental Religions and American Thought: Nineteenth-Century Explorations.* Westport, Connecticut: Greenwood Press, 1981.

Kinsley, David. *Hindu Goddesses: Visions of the Divine Feminine in the Hindu Religious Tradition.* Berkeley: University of California Press, 1986.

Klein, Anne Carolyn. "Nondualism and the Great Bliss Queen." *Journal of Feminist Studies in Religion,* Vol. 1, 1: 73–98. Also available through Stanford University: Institute for Research on Women and Gender.

——————————. "Finding a Self: Buddhist and Feminist Perspectives." *Shaping New Vision: Gender and Values in American Culture,* Harvard Women's Studies in Religion Series. Ann Arbor: UMI Research Press, 1987, 192–218. Reprint, Stanford University, Institute for Research on Women and Gender.

——————————. "The Birthless Birthgiver: Reflections on the Liturgy of Yeshe Tsogyel, the Great Bliss Queen," *The Tibet Journal,* Dharamsala, India, Winter 1987, 19–37. Also available as Working Paper #61, Stanford University, Institute for Research on Women and Gender.

Kurtz, Ernest. *Not God.* Center City, Minnesota: Hazelden, 1979.

Lao-tzu. *Tao Te Ching.* Translated by Stephen Mitchell. San Francisco: Harper & Row, 1988.

Lernoux, Penny. *Cry of the People: The Struggle for Human Rights in Latin America—The Catholic Church in Conflict with U.S. Policy.* New York: Penguin Books, 1982.

——————————. *People of God: The Struggle for World Catholicism.* New York: Viking, 1989.

Levi, Primo. *The Drowned and the Saved.* Translated by Raymond Rosenthal. New York: Summit Books, 1988.

Life of Sri Ramakrishna. Compiled from various sources. Calcutta, India: Advaita Ashrama, 1983.

Lopez, Barry. *Arctic Dreams: Imagination and Desire in a Northern Landscape.* New York: Charles Scribner's Sons. 1986.

Lopez, Donald S., Jr., and Steven C. Rockefeller, eds. *The Christ and the Bodhisattva.* Albany, N.Y.: State University of New York Press, 1987.

Machado, Antonio. *Times Alone: Selected Poems of Antonio Machado.* Translated by Robert Bly. Middletown, Conn.: Wesleyan University Press, 1983.

Matt, Daniel Chanan. Translation and Introduction to the *Zohar,* The Book of Enlightenment, The Classics of Western Spirituality. New York: Paulist Press, 1983.

Matthiessen, Peter. *Indian Country.* New York: Viking, 1984.

Merton, Thomas. *New Seeds of Contemplation.* New York: New Directions, 1972.

Milosz, Czeslaw. *The Collected Poems: 1931–1987.* New York: Ecco Press, 1988.

Moacanin, Radmila. *Jung's Psychology and Tibetan Buddhism: Western and Eastern Paths to the Heart.* London: Wisdom Publications, 1986.

Mookerjee, Ajit. *Kali: The Feminine Force.* New York: Destiny Books, 1988.

Mullin, Glenn H., comp., ed., and trans. *Selected Works of the Dalai Lama I: Bridging the Sutras and Tantras.* Ithaca, N.Y.: Snow Lion Publications, 1985.

_____, ed., comp., and trans. *Selected Works of the Dalai Lama II: The Tantric Yogas of Sister Niguma.* Ithaca, N.Y.: Snow Lion Publications, 1985.

_____, with Doboom Tulku and Chomdze Tashi Wangyal, trans. (Pl.) *Six Texts Related to the Tara Tantra.* Dharamsala: Tushita Books, 1980.

Munro, Eleanor. *On Glory Roads: A Pilgrim's Book about Pilgrimage.* New York: Thames and Hudson, 1987.

Nelson, Richard K. *Make Prayers to the Raven: A Koyukon View of the Northern Forest.* Chicago: University of Chicago Press, 1983.

Neumann, Erich. *The Great Mother: An Analysis of the Archetype.* Translated by Ralph Manheim. Princeton, N.J.: Princeton University Press, 1974.

Nhat Hanh, Thich. *Being Peace.* Berkeley: Parallax Press, 1987.

_____. *Interbeing: Commentaries on the Tiep Hien Precepts.* Berkeley: Parallax Press, 1987.

_____. *The Heart of Understanding: Commentaries on the Prajna-paramita Heart Sutra.* Berkeley: Parallax Press, 1988.

Norbu, Namkhai. *The Crystal and the Way of Light: Sutra, Tantra, and Dzogchen.* Compiled and edited by John Shane. New York: Routledge and Kegan Paul, 1987.

Olson, Charles. *The Collected Poems,* excluding the Maximus poems, edited by George F. Butterick. Berkeley: University of California Press, 1979.

Pagels, Elaine. *The Gnostic Gospels.* New York: Vintage Books, 1981.

Pasierb, Janus S., and Jan Samek. *The Shrine of the Black Madonna at Czestochowa.* Warsaw: Interpress Publishers, 1985.

Paul, Diana Y. *Women in Buddhism: Images of the Feminine in the Mahayana Tradition.* 2nd. ed. Berkeley: University of California Press, 1985.

Preston, James J., ed. *Mother Worship: Theme and Variations.* Chapel Hill: The University of North Carolina Press, 1982.

Quispel, Gilles. *The Secret Book of Revelations: The Last Book of the Bible.* San Francisco: McGraw-Hill, 1979.

Ramprasad Sen. *Grace and Mercy in Her Wild Hair: Selected Poems to the Mother Goddess.* Translated by Leonard Nathan and Clinton Seely. Boulder: Great Eastern, 1982.

Ross, Nancy Wilson. *Buddhism: A Way of Life and Thought.* New York: Alfred A. Knopf, 1980.

Rumi, Jelaluddin. *This Longing, Poetry, Teaching Stories and Letters.* Translated by Coleman Barks and John Moyne. Putney, Vt: Threshold Books, 1988.

Savvas, Carol Diane. "The God Practice of Machig Labdron: Spiritual Exercises of a Tibetan Woman Saint." Paper presented at Carleton College, Northfield, Minnesota, January, 1987.

Savvas, Carol, and Lodro Tulku. *Transformation into the Exalted State: Spiritual Exercises of the Tibetan Tantric Tradition.* Rikon-Zurich: Tibet-Institute, 1987.

Shantideva. *A Guide to the Bodhisattva's Way of Life.* Translated by Stephen Batchelor. Dharamsala: Library of Tibetan Works and Archives, 1987.

Shikibu, Izumi and Ono no Komachi, *The Ink Dark Moon,* Love Poems, Women of the Ancient Court of Japan. Translated by Jane Hirshfield with Mariko Aratani. New York: Charles Scribner's Sons, 1988.

Sidor, Ellen S., ed. *A Gathering of Spirit: Women Teaching in American Buddhism.* Cumberland, R.I.: Primary Point Press, 1987.

Smith, Catherine F., "Jane Lead: Mysticism and the Woman Clothed with the Sun," in Sandra M. Gilbert and Susan Grubar, eds., *Shakespeare's Sisters: Feminist Essays on Women Poets.* Bloomington: Indiana University Press, 1979.

Snellgrove, David L. *Indo-Tibetan Buddhism: Indian Buddhists and Their Tibetan Successors.* London: Serindia Publications, 1987.

Steingesser, Martin, ed. *Hauling Up Morning: The 1990 Peace Calendar.* Philadelphia: New Society Publishers, 1990.

Stutley, Margaret and James. *Harper's Dictionary of Hinduism: Its Mythology, Folklore, Philosophy, Literature, and History.* San Francisco: Harper & Row, 1984.

Taranatha, Jo-Nan. *The Origin of the Tara Tantra.* Translated and edited by David Templeman. Dharamsala: Library of Tibetan Works and Archives. 1981.

Titchenell, Elsa-Brita. *The Masks of Odin: Wisdom of the Ancient Norse.* Pasadena, California: Theosophical University Press, 1985.

Trefil, James. *The Dark Side of the Universe: A Scientist Explores the Mysteries of the Cosmos*. New York: Anchor Books, 1988.

Tsomo, Karma Lekshe, ed. *Sakyadhita: Daughters of the Buddha*. Ithaca, N.Y.: Snow Lion Publications, 1988.

Turner, Victor and Edith. *Image and Pilgrimage in Christian Culture: Anthropological Perspectives*. New York: Columbia University Press, 1978.

Tworkov, Helen. *Zen in America*. Berkeley, Calif.: North Point Press, 1989.

U.S. Helsinki Watch Committee. *Detained, Denied, Deported: Asylum Seekers in the United States*. Helsinki Watch, 1989.

Unitarian Universalist Service Committee. *A Journey to Understanding*. Boston: Unitarian Universalist Service Committee, 1988.

Van Sertima, Ivan, ed. *Black Women in Antiquity*. New Brunswick: Transaction Books, 1988.

Waddell, L. Austine. *Tibetan Buddhism: With Its Mystic Cults, Symbolism and Mythology, and in Its Relation to Indian Buddhism*. New York: Dover Publications, 1972.

Warner, Marina. *Alone of All Her Sex: The Myth and Cult of the Virgin Mary*. New York: Alfred A. Knopf, 1976.

Willis, Janice, ed. *Feminine Ground: Essays on Women and Tibet*. Ithaca, N.Y.: Snow Lion Publications, 1989.

Willson, Martin. *In Praise of Tara: Songs to the Saviouress*. London: Wisdom Publications, 1986.

Wolkstein, Diane, and Samuel Noah Kramer. *Inanna: Queen of Heaven and Earth*. San Francisco: Harper and Row, 1983.

Young, Marjorie B. *Journeys to Glory: A Celebration of the Human Spirit*. Photographs by Adam Bujak. San Francisco: Harper & Row, 1976.

Index

Page numbers in *italics* refer to illustrations.

FOR THE BEST IN PAPERBACKS, LOOK FOR THE 🐧

In every corner of the world, on every subject under the sun, Penguin represents quality and variety—the very best in publishing today.

For complete information about books available from Penguin—including Puffins, Penguin Classics, and Arkana—and how to order them, write to us at the appropriate address below. Please note that for copyright reasons the selection of books varies from country to country.

In the United Kingdom: Please write to *Dept. EP, Penguin Books Ltd, Bath Road, Harmondsworth, West Drayton, Middlesex UB7 0DA.*

In the United States: Please write to *Penguin Putnam Inc., P.O. Box 12289 Dept. B, Newark, New Jersey 07101-5289* or call 1-800-788-6262.

In Canada: Please write to *Penguin Books Canada Ltd, 10 Alcorn Avenue, Suite 300, Toronto, Ontario M4V 3B2.*

In Australia: Please write to *Penguin Books Australia Ltd, P.O. Box 257, Ringwood, Victoria 3134.*

In New Zealand: Please write to *Penguin Books (NZ) Ltd, Private Bag 102902, North Shore Mail Centre, Auckland 10.*

In India: Please write to *Penguin Books India Pvt Ltd, 11 Panchsheel Shopping Centre, Panchsheel Park, New Delhi 110 017.*

In the Netherlands: Please write to *Penguin Books Netherlands bv, Postbus 3507, NL-1001 AH Amsterdam.*

In Germany: Please write to *Penguin Books Deutschland GmbH, Metzlerstrasse 26, 60594 Frankfurt am Main.*

In Spain: Please write to *Penguin Books S. A., Bravo Murillo 19, 1° B, 28015 Madrid.*

In Italy: Please write to *Penguin Italia s.r.l., Via Benedetto Croce 2, 20094 Corsico, Milano.*

In France: Please write to *Penguin France, Le Carré Wilson, 62 rue Benjamin Baillaud, 31500 Toulouse.*

In Japan: Please write to *Penguin Books Japan Ltd, Kaneko Building, 2-3-25 Koraku, Bunkyo-Ku, Tokyo 112.*

In South Africa: Please write to *Penguin Books South Africa (Pty) Ltd, Private Bag X14, Parkview, 2122 Johannesburg.*